Are you aware that over 100 missionaries of color were sent by the General Conference of Seventh-day Adventist Church to carry the gospel to countries outside of the United States? Although only representing about one-tenth of the total number of missionaries sent by the Church, these stories clearly indicate that missionaries of color have made a significant contribution.

Noteworthy:
- The first woman of color was sent to India in 1901 and the first couple of color was sent to South Africa!
- People of color were sent to Africa as "testers" to see if they could succeed!

It is our hope as you learn about the history of missionaries of color that these stories will impact your spiritual development with Christ.

We are thankful to Dr. Sharon Johnson, DC, for proofreading the book and for giving us the hope needed to dare dream that these stories will be an inspiration to all who read them.

Editing the book while she was preparing for surgery, Dr. Johnson states that "she was not leaning into God as she should have been." As she read these wonderful stories of missionaries waiting their "call," she realized she hadn't been listening closely for her own call. "I had many new conversations with Him totally prompted because of this task." She has no doubt that many, many people will think they are going "to read a little history here only to discover the special impact this book will have over and over in their lives."

Dr. Johnson further commentated, "How great to have this history of missionaries of color gathered together in one book—even if the individuals have their own books, this will be a great historical addition. I would like to express the pride I feel knowing that these sweet and precious fellow Christian Americans overcame their own trials and tribulations and "chose to persevere" and still make the personal sacrifices needed to keep their spiritual hearts open to the Lord in order to serve as missionaries. Our society will be enriched by having these stories available."

The authors of these stories have agreed that the proceeds from the sale of the book will be used for scholarships primarily but not limited to students who have elected to follow their example.

Precious Memories
of
Missionaries
of Color

A COMPILATION OF STORIES AND EXPERIENCES
OF AMBASSADORS FOR GOD!

Carol Hammond Ph.D.

TEACH Services, Inc.
PUBLISHING
www.TEACHServices.com • (800) 367-1844

World rights reserved. This book or any portion thereof may not be copied or reproduced in any form or manner whatever, except as provided by law, without the written permission of the publisher, except by a reviewer who may quote brief passages in a review.

The author assumes full responsibility for the accuracy of all facts and quotations as cited in this book. The opinions expressed in this book are the author's personal views and interpretations, and do not necessarily reflect those of the publisher.

This book is provided with the understanding that the publisher is not engaged in giving spiritual, legal, medical, or other professional advice. If authoritative advice is needed, the reader should seek the counsel of a competent professional.

Unless otherwise noted, all Scriptures are taken from the Holy Bible, New International Version®, NIV®. Copyright © 1973, 1978, 1984 by the International Bible Society. Used by permission of Zondervan. All rights reserved.

Scripture references marked KJV are taken from the King James Version of the Bible.

Scripture references marked NASB are taken from the New American Standard Bible, © 1960, 1963, 1968, 1971, 1972, 1973, 1975, 1977 by The Lockman Foundation. Used by permission.

Copyright © 2019 by Carol Hammond, Ph.D.
Copyright © 2019 TEACH Services, Inc.
ISBN-13: 978-1-4796-0947-5 (Paperback)
Library of Congress Control Number: 2019937672

www.TEACHServices.com • (800) 367-1844

Table of Contents

Acknowledgments			ix
Introduction			xi
James E. Patterson	Jamaica	1892	15
Miss Hannah Moore	Liberia & Sierra Leone	1896	16
Miss Anna Knight	India	1901-1907	17
Thomas Branch	Malawi Union Mission	1902	22
Elder & Mrs. J. M. Hyatt	Sierra Leone	1905	23
Elder Benjamin & Celia Abney	Cape Town, S.A.	1931-1938	24
Elder & Mrs. G. N. Banks	Liberia	1945-1952	29
Elder Dunbar & Lorraine Henri	Liberia, Kenya, Ghana	1945-1973	30
Elder Philip and Violet Giddings	Liberia & Ivory Coast	1945-1954; 1964-1971; 1971-1979	41
Elder David & Eunice Hughes	West Africa & South England Conference	1953-1967; 1979-1982	48

Dr. Ruth Faye Davis	Ghana	1954-1957	54
Elder Maurice & Esther Battle	Liberia & Ghana	1956-1979	59
Dr. Johnny & Ida Johnson	Liberia, Ghana, & Nigeria	1957-1985	68
Elder Alvin & Lucy Goulbourne	Bermuda	1959-1965; 1977-1986	89
Elder Leland and Lottie Mitchell-Harris	Liberia	1959-1963	100
Dr. Samuel & Bernice DeShay	Nigeria & Sierra Leone	1961-1973	121
Drs. James & Carol Hammond	Ghana & Sierra Leone	1961-1974	124
Carol Ann Jones	Ethiopia	1962-1966	140
Elder Samuel & Elita Gooden	Nigeria	1963-1967	142
Miss Eula Gunther Evans	Ghana	1964-1967	144
Elder Owen & Ann Troy	Sierra Leone, Ghana, & Trinidad	1964-1966; 1972-1977	145
Miss Lois Raymond	Sierra Leone	1966-1978	149
Elder James & Geraldine Edgecombe	Trinidad	1967-1970	153
Dr. DeWitt & Margaret Williams	Congo, Rwanda, Burundi	1967-1972; 1979-1982	178
Elder Dennis & Dorothy Keith	Sierra Leone & Korea	1967-1975	195
Elder Theodore (Ted) & Esther Jones	Indonesia & Uganda	1968-1971; 1974-1975	204
Elder Walton & Leola Whaley	Sierra Leone, Ghana, & Ivory Coast	1968-1998	214
Sister Ruby Graves	Nigeria & Sierra Leone	1968-1970	230
Dr. Harold & Barbara Lee	Trinidad	1968-1975	237
John & Sara Pitts	Sierra Leone	1971-1977	240
Clarence Lemuel Thomas, III & Carol Barron	Brazil	1971-1983	263
Elder Robert & Rose Carter	Uganda	1971-1972	264

Samuel & Sarah Jackson	Jamaica, Lebanon, & Kenya	1973-1985	278
Elder Harry & Beverly Cartwright	Sierra Leone & Gambia	1974-1979; 1981-1986	283
Elder Jason & Carolyn Mccracken	Brazil, S.A.	1975-1976; 1979-1986	288
Dr. Ruth Naomi Rhone	Rwanda	1976-1986	291
Elder Kenneth & Elizabeth Bushnell	Kenya & Uganda	1977-1987	297
Elder Edward & Dorothy Dorsey	Liberia	1979-1981	304
Elder Louis & Dr. Janice Preston	England & Zimbabwe	1979-1991	315
Elder Lloyd & Etta Antonio	Ghana	1979-1984	329
Elder Robert & Barbara Patterson	Burundi	1980-1984	347
Elder Jerome & Yvonne Pondexter	Ethiopia	1981-1988	356
Elder Pierre & Jocelyne Deshommes	Ethiopia and Cameroon	1982-1986; 1994-1998	361
Dr. Carmelita Troy	Lebanon	1989-1992; 1992-1994; 1994-1996	371
Ronald & Marilyn Lindsey	Zimbabwe	1985-1990	374
Raymond & Carol Cantu	Kenya	1987-1994	396
Anita S. (Moreland) James	Palau, Koror	1992-1997	409
Elder Benjamin & Dr. Janice Browne	Ethiopia	2001-2005	424
Elder Victor & Candice Harewood	Dubai	2002-present	428

Black Seventh-day Adventist Mission Service Honor Roll	433
Letter from Elder Battle's Mom	437
Dolly Dot And Me—Our Call To Florida	443
References	458

Acknowledgments

What an opportunity and pleasure it was to compile these stories of the many God-fearing missionaries who made the ultimate sacrifice to leave family and friends to go to an unfamiliar place on a continent unknown to them. We literally placed our lives in God's hands and went to serve, but were served!

A debt of gratitude is owed to all of the missionaries who willingly shared their stories. Special thanks to Elder Maurice and Esther Battle, Dr. Sam and Bernice DeShay, Elder Owen and Ann Troy, Elder Ted and Esther Jones, Dr. DeWitt and Margaret Williams, and my husband, Dr. James M. Hammond for the time spent once a month in meetings in preparation of this book. They have provided their resources, input, and encouragement to the project.

Many thanks to God and family for the energy and time needed to complete this project. My grandson, Darius, has been extremely helpful with his technological intelligence in assisting with the scanning of the pictures and my computer literacy. My son-in-law, Vincent Smith, Sr., has also been a tremendous asset in sharing his knowledge and expertise in the printing of this book. Thanks also to Attorney Renee Brooks and Dr. DeWitt Williams for taking their time to read and edit this book.

—Carol H. Hammond, Ph.D.

INTRODUCTION

Many thanks to God for providing the inspiration and motivation needed to compile and publish these stories. For missionaries of color, this historical journey began in 1892 some 18 years after the first missionary was sent by the Seventh-day Adventist Church to work outside of North America. James Patterson, the first missionary of color was sent by the Seventh-day Adventist Church to Jamaica to assist in the work there.

The first missionary to be sent outside of the United States was John Nevin Andrews, who was commissioned to go to Switzerland in 1874. Two years before he left for Europe with his children, his wife died. He was sent to minister to the converts and to do personal work with interested persons. Because of poor health, Andrews died after being in Europe for nine years at the age of 54. To-date, the Seventh-day Adventist Church has sent out a total of nine hundred and seventy-nine (979) missionaries around the world to help in spreading the gospel via our schools, colleges, universities and medical institutions.

The purpose of this book is to high light the many contributions made by missionaries of color. This book began about two years ago in the summer of 2006, when the inspiration for writing the book was shared with close fellow missionaries living in the Washington/Metropolitan area. They became my consultants and helped in getting the information out to missionaries of color around the world. The idea to have stories of people of color published was presented and received with great enthusiasm. Letters were drafted and from a list provided by Elder M. T. Battle, letters were sent requesting that stories and pictures of interest be sent. The response was great!

Precious Memories of Missionaries of Color

Anna Knight was considered by many as the first missionary of color. Anna Knight returned from India in 1907 and from this time till 1931, there were no missionaries of color (to our knowledge) serving the Seventh-day Adventist Church. In 1931, the Abneys were asked to go to Cape Town, South Africa.

Records indicate that for a period of seven years, no missionaries of color were sent to serve the Seventh-day Adventist Church. During this time, the Henris expressed their desire to serve as missionaries, but were never called. The door that was closed was opened again when three missionaries of color, the Banks, Henris, and Giddings, were sent to Liberia, West Africa. It has been said that these missionaries felt that they were "testers" to see if missionaries of color could stand the test of time! They passed with flying colors, opening the door for those missionaries that would follow.

The Hughes, Battles, and Johnsons, followed in the footsteps of the three pioneers to Liberia and once again proved that missionaries of color had the faith, courage, and stamina necessary to be successful.

For many years, the majority of missionaries that would follow were asked to go to the continent of Africa. Whether they were in Nigeria, Ghana, Sierra Leone, Kenya, Ethiopia, or in the Congo, they served the "Mother Country" with distinction. God be praised! In recent years, missionaries of color have served in South America, England, Middle East. South Pacific, Iran and Dubai—to name a few.

In terms of longevity, the Whaleys spent the longest time period as missionaries overseas in Africa for a period of thirty years from 1968-1998. The Henris and Johnsons each spent twenty-eight years, and the Battles spent a total of twenty-three years. To God be the Glory!

Volunteers who served the Adventist Church for a short period of time and student missionaries should not be forgotten. They have blessed others with their talents and resources and indeed have made a difference. Records indicate that the first student missionary sent from Oakwood College to Peru in 1968 was Chaplain of the U. S. Senate, Rear Admiral Barry Black. Two students responded who served as student missionaries while they were at Oakwood College: Dollene Smith (1976-77) taught at the Lowry Memorial High School in India; Walter W. Fordham III (nicknamed Skoog) went to Pusan, South Korea, and served as Institute Coordinator and English Teacher at Yong Ju Dong Seventh-day Adventist Language Institute. Walter wrote that he had the privilege of seeing many of his students baptized—one was of particular satisfaction because of his previous staunch beliefs in Buddhism. This experience Walter says, served as a pivotal point in his life so much so that he eventually became a development and relief worker. Presently, Walter works for CARE

Introduction

International, one of the largest international development and relief agencies in the world. He is also starting a non-profit organization which will assist Blacks in taking educational trips overseas. Walter attributes his mission experience to the direction his life has taken.

Dr. Craig Newborn and family were serving in the country of Iran when the government was toppled. As President of the mission in Iran, he and family were evacuated leaving their personal belongings behind. Before going to Iran, Dr. Newborn served as Bible Teacher at the Kamagambo High School. Presently, Dr. Newborn serves at Oakwood College as the Director of the E. G. White Estates. In a telephone interview with Dr. Newborn, he stated that he enjoyed the interaction with the people. This was indeed the greatest joy that we as missionaries of color experienced which were the lasting relationships that were developed with the people. As missionaries of color, we were and are still blessed by the opportunity to be warriors for God!

Many missionaries are presently in lands that are foreign to them and representing Missionaries of Color. WE SALUTE YOU!

It has been exciting and encouraging to discover the large number of missionaries of color who have served the Seventh-day Adventist Church. Consequently, this project is only the beginning and hopefully there will be a second edition which will continue to highlight the contributions of missionaries of color. It is the hope of missionaries that have contributed their stories that the next generation will be inspired to answer the call to serve where God leads.

1

James E. Patterson 1892

Probably very few people have heard of James Patterson. However, he was sent to Jamaica by the Seventh-day Adventist Church as the first missionary of color.

Miss Hannah Moore 1896

M iss Hannah Moore was a lay woman who went to Liberia and Sierra Leone as a member of another church. She later became a Seventh-day Adventist and continued to make a difference winning many converts to the Seventh-day Adventist Church.

3

Miss Anna Knight 1901–1907

Reflecting upon our collective experiences, as missionaries of color many of our journeys' inspirations began with Anna Knight, the Dean of Missionaries. She went to Calcutta, India in 1901 as a nurse. Anna left Battle Creek, Michigan accompanied by Elder J. I. Shaw and his wife, Elder G.K. Owen, Mrs. Shaw's father, and Miss Donna Humphrey. Another missionary joined them later in France as he chose to visit some interesting places in London and France. They arrived in Calcutta in June of 1901 and were met by Elder Elery Robinson, Dr. R. S. Ingersoll, and Miss Samantha Whiteis. Miss Knight spent her first year working in a sanitarium in Calcutta and one in Karmatar. Later she and Miss Donna Humphrey were sent out to distribute medical and religious literature. In addition, they conducted seminars introducing healthy foods.

During their first six weeks in Alahabad, Miss Knight and Miss Humphrey went from house to house with literature and conducted seminars in health. They also carried with them the list of subscribers to the *Oriental Watchman* and made every effort to get a renewal which they were usually successful in doing. They were advised to go to Simla during the summer because of the extreme heat in Alahabad. In Simla, they spent the summer doing house to house visitations, giving treatments, selling books, and taking subscriptions for the magazines. They also conducted seminars in Simla dealing with health issues.

Miss Humphrey spent all of her time talking to the aristocracy. Anna spent most of her time with the more humble folks selling books, magazines, and giving Bible readings when time permitted. Miss Humphrey was able to give massages which brought in enough money to pay their expenses, and she was even able to send some cash back to the mission in Calcutta. As she traveled from place to place, she discovered that she was covering the same area that W. C. James had previously traveled selling literature. Knight and Humphrey indeed sowed the seed for others who would come later. Dr. H. C. Menkle later established a sanitarium in Simla.

At the close of the summer in 1902, Knight and Humphery went to Delhi in the North West Province of India. This was the winter headquarters of the Lieutenant Governor of Punjab. Miss Humphrey became the private nurse of Lady Rivaz, the wife of the Lieutenant Governor. Two months later Miss Humphrey was asked to resume her work as a nurse at the sanitarium in Calcutta. Anna was advised to go back to Calcutta as well, as opposed to remaining in Delhi alone. In Calcutta, Anna continued to carry on the literature and Bible work the rest of the winter.

In 1903, Anna's co-worker, Donna, died and she was left alone to continue the field work. She got permission to go back to Simla so that she could continue the work she started there. Later Anna was joined by Miss A. Helen Wilcox who carried on the medical work being done by Miss Humphrey.

Anna recounted an experience which occurred at Dhola, a junction where she had to wait a whole day for a train to take her out of that state. At noon a train going the other way stopped and four men got off and came to where she was on the platform and greeted her in English. One asked her if she was a missionary. She said, "Yes." "From America?" "Yes." "Do you know Sahibs Lenker and Stroup?" "Yes." (Anna had met them in Mount Vernon, Ohio, on their return to the States while she was attending school in Ohio.) Then they told her that years ago these men had sold them a wonderful book, *Man the Masterpiece*. They asked if she had any books. Thank God, she did and proceeded to sell each of them a copy of *Heralds of the Morning*. They were happy to have her renew their subscription to the *Oriental Watchman* and to get a copy of the book. She was happy that she had gone down into that state. In addition to meeting the four men, she was able to meet two lonely women who had not seen any expatriates except their own immediate family since the Robinsons had passed through.

During Anna Knight's colporteur work, she sold scores of books and took hundreds of subscriptions for the *Oriental Watchman* and the *London Good Health* magazines. In addition, she gave hundreds of Bible readings when the time was right. She returned to the United States in 1907 to reopen a school she had founded in Mississippi, which closed because she was unable to get any other teachers to teach at the school.

Miss Anna Knight 1901–1907

The story of Anna Knight's life can be read in <u>Mississippi Girl</u>, a biography detailing her life. She was born in Mississippi in 1874 and died in 1972, living to the ripe old age of 98 years. She founded the National Colored Teacher's Association of Seventh-day Adventists in the 1920s, and until her death she remained the president of this organization. The elementary school at Oakwood College, Huntsville, Alabama has been named in her honor. The Anna Knight Educational Building has seen many outstanding Oakwood College graduates. Recently we were told that the orphanage in India (the Karmatar) will be named in her honor.

Anna Knight was a woman who demanded respect. Anna was a creature of habit and would occupy the same seat in church. For those of us who knew Anna Knight, she is remembered for wearing a long, black two piece suit, white shirt and pink tie, a standard for all occasions. We thank her for being one of the "trail blazers" who paved the way for the mission experiences that would follow.

Ms. Anna Knight (on the right)

Precious Memories of Missionaries of Color

Anna Knight–North East India–Conference
About 1902

Miss Anna Knight 1901–1907

Karmatar Mission School, Orphanage and Dispensary
Anna Knight was bookkeeper and nurse

Thomas Branch 1902

Just one year after Anna Knight left for India, Thomas Branch, along with Joseph Booth, became the first missionaries to Nyasaland or Malawi as it is presently called. In 1902, the General Conference bought the 2000 acres Plainfield Mission from Joseph Booth, a former Seventh-day Baptist. When Booth became a Seventh-day Adventist, he was sent back to the mission along with Elder Thomas Branch and family. Thomas Branch, an American Negro, the term used at that time, established an elementary school, and his daughter became the first teacher in Nyasaland. Thomas Branch gave much attention to manual labor as part of the activities of the school. The first baptism took place in 1905 when seven young men joined the church. One of Branch's notable converts was Morrison Malinky, an African who had served as his translator. Malinky went back to his home in Monekera where he opened several schools that supported themselves. Later these schools were taken over by the mission. Branch gave a lifetime of service to the church as a minister and a teacher. The Plainfield Mission was later called Malamulo, a word in the Cinyanja language meaning "commandments" or "laws" as the people's attention was drawn to the mission because of the Ten Commandments. Today, the Malamulo Secondary School is operated by the Malawi Union Mission.

Elder Branch's grandson, W. C. Webb is a retired minister of the Central California Conference and the Branch family is from Colorado.

Elder & Mrs. J. M. Hyatt 1905

Elder and Mrs. Hyatt were the first known Seventh-day Adventists to preach in Sierra Leone. Elder Hyatt was a layman who came to Freetown from the Gold Coast—now known as Ghana. He started out his work in Freetown, Sierra Leone, by holding prayer meetings in his home and by passing out literature.

Sierra Leone, a member of the Commonwealth of Nations, received its independence on April 27, 1961. At the time of this writing, there were 52 churches in Sierra Leone with a membership of 13,545.

6

Elder Benjamin & Celia Abney
1931-1938

Elder & Mrs. Benjamin William Arnett Abney received a call to go to the Southern African Union in Cape Town, South Africa, in 1931. They sailed from New York on the S. S. Olympic on July 16 dedicating their lives for a period of seven years to work among "colored people." Many churches were erected and many souls were won to the truth. Many have become ordained ministers and even conference presidents. Elder and Mrs. Abney were accompanied to South Africa by their two children—a son, Benjamin Abney, Jr. who was employed by the General Conference which was then located in Washington, D. C. and a daughter, Celia Abney Cleveland, (now deceased) the wife of Dr. E. E. Cleveland, an outstanding evangelist now residing at Oakwood College.

Elder Abney gives an interesting account of three obstacles that stood in the way of his going to South Africa. The first obstacle was passing the physical exam which he was afraid that his wife wouldn't pass. Then the report came back saying there was no physical reason why they should not be able to go. The second obstacle dealt with getting a permit from the South African government to enter the country. Would they allow an American Negro a permit to work in their country? Imagine the joy when the second obstacle was removed and the South African government allowed them to come into their country. The third obstacle was leaving behind an ailing mother—a grave concern. How would his siblings feel about his leaving the sole responsibility of their mother to them? To show how God works in mysterious ways, the third obstacle was

Elder Benjamin & Celia Abney 1931–1938

removed by the death of his mother in January, 1931. The Abneys sailed for South Africa in July, 1931.

The Abneys were disturbed by the discrimination and apartheid that they found in South Africa but were determined that they would learn to adjust. Adjust they did. They were well liked by those with whom they came in contact with during their seven-year stay.

Benjamin and Celia attended public schools and learned to speak Afrikaans, the language of the Dutch descendants of South Africa. Despite the fact he was designated to work with the colored people (descendants of the native Black and Whites), he also had opportunity to work with other groups in South Africa, specifically the Blacks.

In one of Elder Abney's experiences, he recounts the day he baptized a young man and his wife. When this gentleman was a boy, he dreamed while sleeping on the doorstep of his home that God spoke to his mother instructing her to tell him about the seven signs. He never thought anymore about the dream until he received the advertisement concerning a meeting where the seven signs would be presented. He concluded that this was the end of his dream.

Elder Abney was instrumental in establishing several churches in South Africa. One of the churches in Kensington is one of the strongest churches in Cape Town. Many of his converts became teachers, preachers, literature evangelists, conference presidents, and Bible instructors. One of his converts promised him that he was going to take his place as a worker. True to his word, he became the first president of the colored conference in South Africa.

When one of his converts from Catholicism joined the church, three of her sisters came for a visit with new clothing for her children. They wanted her to give up her new faith and return to Catholicism. She refused the clothing and said her soul was not for sale. She is still a faithful member of the Seventh-day Adventist Church today.

It is important to cite that Mrs. Abney (the former Celia Hart) worked alongside of her husband, visiting members and non members and working as a Bible instructor.

When their daughter Celia and her husband, Elder Cleveland, visited South Africa some years later, they found a convert of Elder Abney's still in the church. According to Elder Abney, the greatest goal one can attain is to win a soul for the Lord. It is no doubt that Elder Abney's willingness to leave his home, friends, and family to go to a place unfamiliar to him to preach the gospel opened the way for those of us who followed. Elder and Mrs. Abney lived to be ninety-six years old. They attributed their long life to having been vegetarians for sixty-six years and to eating only two meals a day.

Precious Memories of Missionaries of Color

The Abneys returned from South Africa in 1938. It would be seven more years before another missionary of color would go to the mission field. In 1945, the General Conference extended a call to three missionaries of color to go to Liberia, West Africa. Elder and Mrs. G. N. Banks were sent to direct the Seventh-day Adventist mission in Monrovia, the capital of Liberia. Elder and Mrs. P. E. Giddings accepted the call to be the educational director, and Elder and Mrs. C. D. Henri served as mission president and principal of Konola Academy.

The Abney Family–Elder Earl & Celia Cleveland and Elder Benjamin Abney, Jr. with family

Elder Benjamin & Celia Abney 1931-1938

The Abney Family--Elder Earl & Celia Cleveland and Elder Benjamin Abney, Jr. with family

Precious Memories of Missionaries of Color

ELDER BENJAMIN W. AND CELIA ABNEY

Elder Benjamin W. and Celia Abney, first missionaries to South Africa representing the General Conference Regional Department of the Seventh-day Adventist Church.

7

Elder & Mrs. G. N. Banks
1945–1952

Elder Banks did such an outstanding job in Liberia that the President of Liberia took notice. On several occasions, the President invited the Bankses to dinner at his presidential palace. Because of this camaraderie, when the country made a ruling that all teachers and students were required to attend classes on Saturday and arrested all who refused to attend classes, the president, upon hearing of the ruling, made a proclamation that all members of the church who observed the Bible Sabbath did not have to attend classes on Saturday. To God be praised for His mercies endure forever.

To further indicate God's leading and mercies with our pioneer missionaries, when the government built a large pavilion to be used for government events only, Elders Banks and Henri approached the president about the possibility of dedicating the building to God. The president agreed and they prepared a 30-day religious celebration in Liberia. The Bankses spent seven fruitful years making a difference in the lives of the people of Liberia.

G. N. Banks

Elder Dunbar & Lorraine Henri 1945–1973

    Elder Dunbar and Lorraine Henri were instrumental in helping many make the decision to become missionaries. When they were on furlough, they visited many churches sharing their love for the people of Africa. They wore the national dress and showed the many different types of artifacts made by the people. What an eye opener for many of us who only heard stories of people who were heathens and ran around naked. The people of Africa were characterized in such negative ways that African Americans felt ashamed to be associated with Africa instead of having a sense of pride. It was good to get a more positive perspective of the people from Africa. As a young girl of twelve, this writer had the privilege to witness one of the Henri's presentations and was inspired to the point of making a decision to become a missionary.

    As pioneer missionaries, the Henris, Giddings, and the Bankses had the burden and challenge that they had to succeed. Failure was not an option since their success hinged on whether others would be asked to go. Elder Henri's interest in becoming a missionary began while he was a student at South Lancaster, MA. He observed that many were being sent overseas; however, none who were being sent were people of color. In spite of this, he remained hopeful and prayed that God would make a way if this was His will. The call came many years later. He read many books about Africa and even enjoyed *Tarzan of the Apes*. The Henris were real trail blazers in that they lived in a house that resembled a tent with no windows, bathroom, or running water. Dry wells were built and tanks were placed on top of the house to collect running water. The water had to be boiled before it could be used for drinking and cooking.

Elder Dunbar & Lorraine Henri 1945–1973

It was not only important to the Henris to preach the gospel to the people of Liberia, but also to educate them in healthful ways of living and eating. Mrs. Henri conducted cooking classes utilizing the vegetarian diet. She also played for and conducted choirs.

From 1948 to 1951, Elder Henri served as mission president and as principal of the Konola Academy. His work with the people of Liberia was so outstanding that it came to the attention of William V. S. Tubman, President of Liberia. Elder Henri was asked to be one of the ministers who officiated at President Tubman's wedding. To show his gratitude for all that he was doing for the people of Liberia, President Tubman knighted Elder Henri as the Knight Commander of the Liberian Order of Humane Redemption, on September 16, 1948. This was a special honor given by the government to individuals who performed humanitarian service to Liberia. Elder Henri believes that he was the first Black American to be knighted. What a tremendous honor and to God be the glory!

The Henris left the United States as a family of two. However, when they returned they were a family of five. Added to this beautiful family were two daughters, Burdetta Leona and Patricia Elaine, and one son, Coleridge Dunbar, Jr.

It would appear that the Henris' motto was, "where you want me to go, I will go!" Their mission experiences after Liberia would include some time in Ghana where he served at the Union. Later in the 70s, they were asked to go to Nairobi, Kenya, East Africa, to be the President of the East African Union.

After serving in Africa, for twenty-one and one half years, the Henris returned to the United States where he continued to serve his church as the General Vice President of the General Conference of Seventh-day Adventists from 1973-1980. Upon his retirement, he and Lorraine moved to Atlanta, Georgia, where he continued to serve as needed as Pastor, interim Pastor, and counselor until his death in January, 2002. Thank God for men and women like Elder and Mrs. Henri who gave their lives to teach others at home and abroad.

Precious Memories of Missionaries of Color

The Henris say good-bye to their children as they flew to Beirut, Lebanon, for school

Elder Dunbar & Lorraine Henri 1945–1973

Dr. Mutuka Mutinga and Elder Dunbar–Nairobi, Kenya, East Africa

Precious Memories of Missionaries of Color

Elder and Mrs. C. D. Henri, and family Burdetta, Patricia and Dunbar

Elder Dunbar & Lorraine Henri 1945–1973

Dr. Mutuka Mutinga and Elder Dunbar–Nairobi, Kenya, East Africa

Precious Memories of Missionaries of Color

Elder and Mrs. C. D. Henri, and family Burdetta, Patricia and Dunbar

Elder Dunbar & Lorraine Henri 1945–1973

Nigeria, West Africa–Workers and Ministers of the Evangelistic Team
C.D. Henri in the middle dressed in African garb

Pastor Henri conducted marriage ceremony in Kenya, East Africa

Precious Memories of Missionaries of Color

Sophia & Christine with Mrs. Henri.
Sophia was an excellent seamstress and very helpful with Mrs. Henri's girls.

Elder Henri baptizing in Ghana

The Henris in Sweden

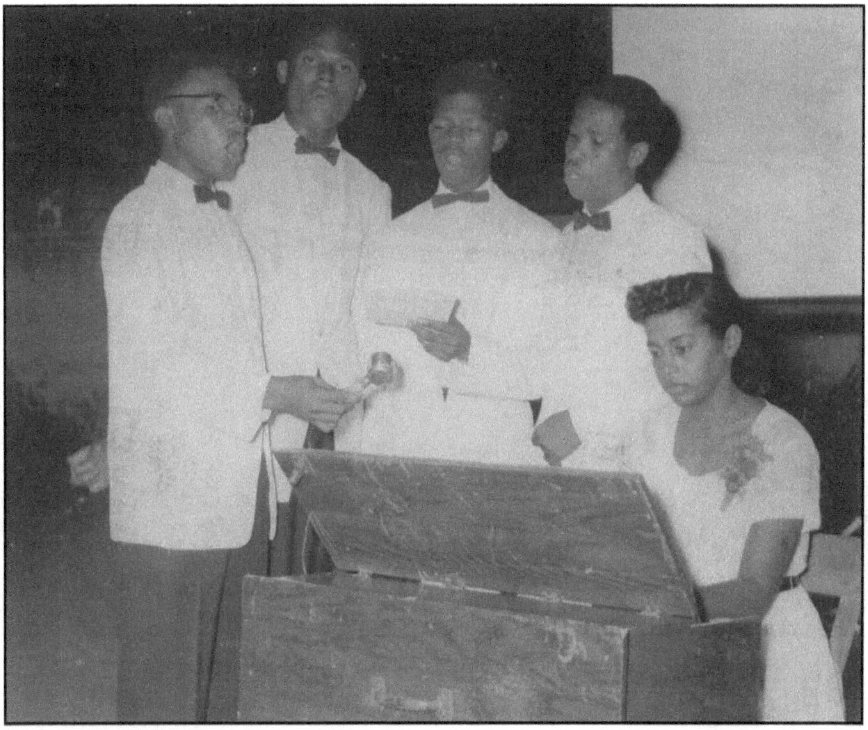

Elder Dunbar & Lorraine Henri 1945–1973

"20 Century Quartelle" sang at the Henri's farewell program in Nigeria

The family sang for meetings in Sweden, 1961

Precious Memories of Missionaries of Color

The Henris with wives of former missionaries

Elder Henri received Honorary Doctorate from Gulf Coast Seminary

Elder Dunbar & Lorraine Henri 1945–1973

Brother Gibson, a Liberian Ambassador to the Hague, was baptized by Elder Henri

Precious Memories of Missionaries of Color

Workers in the West African Union
Accra, Ghana
January, 1964

Leland Mitchell (deceased)
C. Dunbar Henri (deceased)
Maurice Battle
David Hughes
Samuel DeShay
Theodore Cantrell
Lucius Daniels

9

Elder Philip & Violet Giddings 1945–1954; 1964–1971; 1971–1979

The third pioneer missionaries to go to Liberia were Elder Philip E. Giddings, Jr., and his wife Violet Blevins Giddings. The two made quite a team—he as the director of education and she as teacher and organizer of the school choir. Violet spent many hours in rehearsal resulting in the choir being known as the best choir in Liberia. Her choir had the honor of performing before many dignitaries, notably of these was President Tubman. The president gave the directress $200.00 after one song received an encore three times. The newspaper reported that the group "Sings like Angels."

Elder Giddings was born in Rosseau Dominica, British West Indies, of parents who were also missionaries, Louise Peters and Philip Giddings. What a joy for parents when children follow in their footsteps! Elder Giddings, Jr. was a graduate of Atlantic Union College and Pacific Union College where he received a B.A. and M.A. degrees. He also had a doctor's degree of optics from Philadelphia Optical College. His training prepared him well to be able to minister to the people of Liberia. While he was Principal of Shiloh Academy in Chicago, he met and married his wife, Violet Blevins, in 1943.

For ten years they endured hardship as did many of our missionaries, such as only one dirt road from Monrovia to the hinterlands sixty miles away to where they lived. Sometimes the wooden bridges would wash away during the heavy rains making travel to the schools and missions very difficult. Sometimes they had to wait days, weeks, and even months for the bridges to be repaired.

One of Elder Giddings' most important contributions was the building of the girls' dormitory at Konola so that many more students could attend the

Precious Memories of Missionaries of Color

Adventist School. The story is told that the dormitory that existed before this one was not fit for human living and before the powers that be would agree to build another, the old one had to be destroyed. A small match directed in the right position did the job! They had the task of making the bricks which required that they dig for sand from the riverbed several miles away. In spite of this hardship, Elder Giddings succeeded in erecting the dormitory to the Glory of God! Many of those students have become evangelists, teachers, and workers for the mission.

After nine years in Liberia, the Giddings returned to the United States in 1954 after discovering that Philip had high blood pressure. He was voted permanent return and was asked to teach at Oakwood College. It was there that many students, including this writer, got to sit at his feet and learn French. Many were further inspired by him to get on the band wagon and become missionaries. He spent four years at Oakwood before getting another call to be principal of Los Angeles Union SDA School in California.

The Lord was not quite ready to retire him from the mission service just yet, and in 1964, Elder Giddings received another call to go to Rouake Ecole Adventiste on the Ivory Coast in West Africa. Realizing the tremendous asset he could be in a French speaking country such as the Ivory Coast, and because he was able to control the high blood pressure, the permanent return status was immediately changed.

At the Rouake Ecole Adventiste, over 900 students were present for registration on the first day. Some of these students had been standing in line before the break of dawn. The people were starving for an education, so much so, that two schools were started—one school for the young and one for the old. The Ecole Regulaire was the school for the adults and the Ecole Regularie was for the regular age students. At registration, the students were required to bring a birth certificate so that they could determine which school each student should attend. The Giddings recall a man seated with the first graders with whiskers carrying a birth certificate that stated that he was eight years old. He had borrowed the birth certificate from his cousin. The story illustrates just how eager the people were to get an education.

Because the Giddings worked so hard during their stay in the Ivory Coast, they received recognition from the Northern European Division for the expert and efficient way they handled the school's finances. Mrs. Giddings once again shared her talents and directed the school choir. Elder Giddings translated many of the English songs into French, despite the fact that the students sang very well in English. Once again under her direction, the choir received notoriety and won first-place in a city-wide competition in which they sang the only

Elder Philip & Violet Giddings 1945-1979

religious song on the program. Many students enrolled in the school because of the reputation of the choir. To God be the glory for the wives of missionaries who willingly shared their talents which sometimes went unnoticed.

The Giddings spent six years in the Ivory Coast and returned to the states for one year where he served as Vice Principal of Lynwood Academy in Los Angeles, California. One year at Lynwood was enough to convince them that their place in the Lord's work was in Africa. The Giddings received another call in 1971 to go to Kenya, Africa. For seven years, Elder Giddings served as director of education for the East African Union located in Nairobi, Kenya. He willingly gave up this position when Dr. M. Mutinga a native of Kenya returned with his Doctorate in Education. The goal of all missionaries was to work themselves out of a job while preparing the people who were indigenous to the country to take over. He was planning to return to the states when he received the honor of being elected the Chaplain for all East African University students in Kenya, Uganda, and Tanzania. During this time, he also served as the pastor of the Nairobi Central church. The attendance was so outstanding that he instituted two services. The only problem was that those attending the first service also stayed for the second service to be sure they didn't miss anything.

In addition to serving as the director of the choir, Mrs. Giddings worked as a secretary in the departments of Youth, Education, Voice of Prophecy, and Personal Ministries. Among their memories of Kenya are the beautiful terrain and the friendly receptive people. Not only did our pioneer missionaries pave the way for us, they gave of their lives and spent many years working for the people of Africa. The Giddings spent nearly twenty-five years of dedicated missionary service which set the stage for those of us who followed. Elder Giddings, in every sense of the word, gave his life for the people he loved so dearly, and when the trumpet shall sound and the dead in Christ shall arise, he will come forth from his dearly beloved Africa with the people he loved and worked for. Elder Giddings died of a heart attack in 1979 and is buried in Nairobi, Kenya. During Mrs. Gidding's time of distress, she experienced the love and support of the Kenyan people. They came in droves giving their love and monetary gifts.

The Giddings have three children: Cynthia and Philip III were born in Liberia and Don in California. Cynthia (Burns) and husband were also missionaries in Burundi, Rwanda, and Ethiopia. Philip III teaches in the Junior High at Andrews University at the Ruth Murdoch Elementary School. Don is a Deputy Sheriff in Cassopolis, Michigan, and works for Andrews University Campus Safety. Cynthia teaches elementary school at Loma Linda Academy. As was their Father's wish, all of the children speak fluent French. Presently, Mrs. Giddings is married to Mr. Wilbur Matthews and resides in Berrien Springs,

Michigan. Mrs. Giddings stated that she counts it a privilege to have had the opportunity to share in spreading the gospel in East and West Africa.

Just recently, we have received word that Mrs. Giddings has passed away. We look forward to the day when we shall all be reunited.

1. Builiding girls dorm - Ivory Coast

2. Girls Dorm finished - Ivory Coast

Elder Philip & Violet Giddings 1945–1979

Philip Giddings III

Cynthia Giddings

Don Giddings

Precious Memories of Missionaries of Color

Elder Giddings baptizing in Bouake - Ivory Coast

Elder Philip E. Giddings Jr.

Violet Giddings Matthews

Elder Philip & Violet Giddings 1945–1979

Bouake teaching staff. Mrs. Giddings seated third from right
Elder Giddings standing third from right-Ivory Coast.

Bouake choir with Mrs. Giddings holding the first prize cup
won in city-wide contest. Ivory Coast.

10

Elder David & Eunice Hughes
1953–1967; 1979–1982

Like other missionaries that preceded them, the Hugheses dedicated an incredible number of years in service on the continent of Africa. It appears that Liberia was the training ground for missionaries of color during this time. The Hughes were asked to serve the Liberian Mission as District Leader, evangelist and teacher for six years. In those days especially, one needed to be prepared to wear many hats. The Hugheses were well prepared to do just that. God used them mightily, and they left a tremendous impact upon the people they served.

The missionaries who went to Africa during this period were such stalwart, honest, and God-fearing people that they were noted by the people of Liberia. They could not fail as they were the trailblazers for those of us who would follow. Like his predecessor Elder Dunbar Henri, Elder Hughes was honored by being knighted into the order of African Redemption by President V. S. Tubman in 1958. This was ten years after Elder Henri was knighted in 1948. These "men of God" had to be about their Father's business to be so duly recognized.

In 1959, Elder Hughes was asked to join the West African Union Mission as Director of the TV and VOP Ministries in the following countries: Liberia, Sierra Leone, Ghana, Ivory Coast, Nigeria, Togo-Benin, Upper Volta, and Gambia. What a tremendous territory he had to cover! Hats off to all of their wives who stayed at home and kept the home fires burning! Elder Hughes served in this capacity for four years. (1959-1963)

In 1963, the Hugheses responded to the call to go to the North Nigerian Mission as President. Again David was responsible for a large territory. This job

ELDER DAVID & EUNICE HUGHES 1953-1982

required that they minister to the needs of eight countries: Baushi, Gongola, Kano, Plateau, Barno, Kaduna, Niger, and Sokoto. After four years as President of the Mission in Nigeria, Elder Hughes and his family returned to the United States where he served as a pastor in the Southern California Conference.

In 1979, the Hugheses (Dave and Eunice) had another opportunity to serve as missionaries. Elder Maurice Battle requested that they go to Ethiopia—which they accepted. After receiving their training at Andrews and three days before they were supposed to leave for Ethiopia, they were informed that their work visas were not accepted. The call then came to serve outside of the continent of Africa in the South England Conference, in London, England. Pastor Hughes shepherded three district churches. (Lewisham, Peckham, and Deptford). These churches consisted primarily of adult members who were native to the West Indies and of young people who were either born or raised in the UK. The Hugheses were informed before they left the United States for England that the greatest concern of the church in England was that they were losing their young people from the church at a rate of seven out of every ten. What a challenge they faced, for a church without young people is a dying church! At that time, there were no local Christian Seventh-day Adventist schools at the primary or secondary level for the young people to attend. Consequently, many attended the very secular schools in the areas in which they lived. This was of grave concern to David and Eunice, also. They determined that their primary focus would be to inform and teach the members of the importance of Seventh-day Adventist Christian education.

When the Southern England Conference held its Convocation, Doctor Calvin Rock, the current President of Oakwood College, consented to be the speaker. The Hugheses believed that this was ordained by God. Before Elder Rock spoke, he took time to tell the audience about Oakwood College and the value of a Christian education. He informed them that he was leaving applications with the Hugheses for anyone who was interested in attending the college. The response was overwhelming! This was the opportunity that many of these young people had dreamed of.

The Hugheses met with many young people in their homes to talk further about Oakwood College. An organization called the Black-British Oakwood Student Society (B.O.S.S.) was started. These students were so excited and determined that they could work toward their goals to get a Christian education. They prayed, planned, and worked until their goal was reached. There were seven students in the first group who left England to get an education in the United States—more specifically at Oakwood College. These students became some of Oakwood's most outstanding students. Christian education made an impact on their lives. Notably, one of these students, Dr. Audley Chambers, Ph.D., was appointed in 2004 as chair of the department of music at Oakwood College. He also received the Oakwood College Distinguished Teaching Excellence Award in 2003. Dr. Chambers is also a graduate of Ohio State University and Northwestern University where he completed his doctorate in 1997.

Dr. Hyveth Williams, noted author and lecturer, currently serving as senior Pastor of the Campus Hill Seventh-day Adventist Church, was baptized by Pastor Hughes. She holds the distinction of being the first female to become the Senior Pastor of a Seventh-day Adventist Church. She is a graduate of Columbia Union College, Andrews University, and Boston University School of Theology where she received her D.Min degree. Dr. Williams received a Fellowship from the Episcopal College for Preachers, National Cathedral, in Washington, D.C. She is the first non-Episcopalian to receive this prestigious award.

As the years went by, the Hughes were able to take credit for recruiting a large number of students who left England for the United States in search of a Christian education. To God be the glory! There will no doubt be many stars in their crowns for equipping the church with so many outstanding workers for God.

The Hugheses observed that the churches were segmented and not working cohesively. To alleviate this problem, they came up with a novel idea to start a monthly newsletter called the "District News" to bring the churches together. Each church was assigned a reporter whose job was to provide news about what their church was doing. The Hugheses saw their district come together and despite the fact that they admitted that the project took a lot of work, they also feel that it was worth it!

The evangelistic spirit was kept alive, and Elder Hughes was kept in the baptismal pool. All three churches were among the top ten churches in reporting Bible Studies in the Southern England Conference. During their three year stay, God used Elder David and Eunice Hughes mightily to make a difference in this part of God's vineyard.

Elder David & Eunice Hughes 1953-1982

Pastor D. Hughes and Master Guides

Sister McGregor organized a program to raise money for the church and received 1,263.95 pounds.

Eunice Hughes, Associate Editor of District News

Precious Memories of Missionaries of Color

Michael Hamilton

(Left to Right) Glendora, Dr. R. L. McKenzie (Assoc. Prof., School of Education, LLU), and Pat in front of the McKenzie's home.

Elder David & Eunice Hughes 1953–1982

Elder David Hughes

Elder and Mrs. David Hughes

11

Dr. Ruth Faye Davis 1954–1957

During Dr. Davis' senior year at Emmanuel Missionary College (now Andrews University), Mrs. Alice Marsh, her nutrition professor, required that she take a food seminar on vegetarian food preparation. She sent photographs and a description of the seminar to the General Conference of Seventh-day Adventists. Immediately, a call was sent for Dr. Davis to accept a position teaching home economics at the Bekwai Training College in Ghana, West Africa.

Ruth told her mother and the young man who was her special friend about the call from the General Conference for mission service; however, her mother and her special friend did not want her to accept the call. Her special friend said he wouldn't wait for her for the two and a half years she would be away because he wanted to get married before that time. This caused much distress; however, she presented this matter before her heavenly Father.

After graduating from Emmanuel Missionary College with a B.S. degree in home economics and a minor in biology, she went home to Greensboro, North Carolina, and prayed earnestly that God would guide her in her decision to work in His vineyard. Like Gideon, she wanted a sign. She asked God to change her mother's heart if it was His will that she should go to Africa. Almost overnight, it seemed, she said, "You know Faye, I think it is a good idea for you to go to Africa." This helped Faye to finally decide to accept the call to Africa. Upon hearing Faye's decision, her special friend was very upset. He again said, "If you go to Africa, I will not wait for you." The Lord gave me

Dr. Ruth Faye Davis 1954–1957

the strength to say to him, "God will provide a Christian husband for me if you do not wait for me."

During that summer, Faye was busy preparing for the trip to Africa. She purchased a twin size mattress and box spring from the General Conference Supply House known then as ESDA. Summer clothing was purchased and sewn. Bedding, towels, and other household articles were packed for the trip. In the fall of 1954, she left New York City on the SS Queen Elizabeth and sailed for South Hampton, England. From England, she flew to Accra, West Africa. No one met her there because the cable had not gone through to inform the mission employees about her arrival. After consulting with the airport officials, she was encouraged to take a plane to Kumasi, West Africa, where the Conference office was located. After arriving in Kumasi on Sabbath morning, she took a taxi and asked the driver to take her to the Seventh-day Adventist Mission. He did not seem to know where the Mission was located. She told him to keep driving, and they were blessed to see a group of people worshipping in a pavilion on the side of the road. She asked him to stop and ask those people. They gave him the right directions, and they arrived at the conference office and were greeted by Mrs. Welch, the wife of the president of the conference. After a good meal, Elder and Mrs. Welch took her to the Bekwai Training College where she spent two years and three months teaching at the Bekwai Secondary School.

Ruth's duties included teaching home economics, Bible, English, and history. She was also in charge of the young women who lived in the dormitory. Her one bedroom home was located across from the girls' dormitory. She was blessed to have running water in her home. It was pumped from her back porch which purified the water. The kerosene stove had wicks that needed cleaning frequently. The refrigerator was also operated by kerosene. The electric lights which went out each evening at 9:00 P.M. were operated by a private generator. She used a flashlight and kerosene lamp after the lights went out.

On weekends it was her privilege to attend services at the campus church when she was not visiting in Accra at the Adventist Union Offices. Fridays before sunset, they had room inspection for the dormitory rooms. The students had to have everything ready for the Sabbath. The dormitory rooms and clothing were inspected for the young men and women. The students all stood in front of their dormitories during this inspection. On Sabbath afternoons, Ruth and the students went into the villages with the picture rolls to tell the story of Jesus to the children and adults in the villages. They also sang songs for them and gave them religious literature.

During Ruth's stay in Ghana, she conducted a Women's Seminar on improving the home. Food demonstrations, sewing classes, home management classes, and parenting classes were conducted during the seminar to help the ladies improve the quality of their lives in their homes. They made a field trip to the market to learn to choose nutritious food and home articles wisely. They utilized a large clay oven to bake bread. The ladies learned how to prepare many new dishes for their families. They also had worship each day as a part of the Seminar to encourage the ladies to establish an altar each morning and evening with their spouses and children.

One night Ruth awakened suddenly and went into her living room. There she saw a long snake weaving its way into her house through the window. Without thinking, she put on her house coat and ran across a dark field to get the watchman who slept on the front porch of a big house near her house. He wore a long robe and a pillbox hat. She awakened him with her screams and asked him to come quickly to her house to kill the snake. He came running with his bag of sticks to kill the snake. The snake was in the house when they returned, and he was blessed to catch and kill it. This let her know that the angel of the Lord encamps around about them that fear Him. Traveling ants and lizards came into her home frequently; however, she eventually learned not to be afraid of them.

Ruth's time was occupied with her students, class preparation, community activities, and church work. She had a monkey whom she named Oscar, a dog named Troubles, and her rabbit—these comprised her pets during her stay in Ghana. Her dog followed her to school each day and sat under her desk. Even though individuals broke into other homes on the compound, God spared her from this experience. The people in the area were afraid of dogs. Ruth would hear individuals walking outside around her home; however, her dog's barks frightened them away. Troubles slept under her bed and always barked when she heard someone outside of the house. Also, the watchman was paid by the school to protect the homes in the area.

The young ladies in her sewing class made dresses from Simplicity patterns which they bought at the market in town. They used treadle sewing machines which did not require electricity or sewing machines that were operated by a handle. The completed garments were modeled on a Saturday night for the student body's social event.

Many of the graduates from the Bekwai Training College and the Secondary School became teachers and pursued higher education in Africa and in the United States. They were blessed to have their school expenses paid by the government and their parents. The General Conference also assisted some of the students to attain higher education.

After spending two years and three months in Ghana, West Africa, Ruth was called to replace Dr. Douglas Tate who became ill and had to be accompanied

Dr. Ruth Faye Davis 1954–1957

by a doctor on a plane back to the United States. This gave Ruth the wonderful opportunity to work with students and faculty in Liberia, West Africa. There Professor and Mrs. Ted Cantrell directed the secondary school where she taught home economics, English, Bible, and history classes. Mrs. Cantrell, a registered nurse, operated a dispensary for the people in the village. They went to the villages on Sabbath afternoons to share their faith with the people and encouraged them to bring their children to their dispensary for medical help. They went to Monrovia once a month to purchase food and other household articles. Elder and Mrs. Maurice Battle directed the mission work in Liberia at that time. Several African teachers and students from the Adventist school were privileged to pursue higher education in the United States and England. (Some of the African workers have also sent their children to Oakwood College and other Adventist colleges in the United States.)

After spending two years and nine months in the West African Union, Ruth returned to the United States to pursue graduate studies at Michigan State University and the University of North Carolina in Greensboro. God blessed her with a wonderful Christian husband, Oliver James Davis. After their wedding in Greensboro, North Carolina, they went to Merced, California, where they spent four wonderful years in church and public school teaching. Oakwood College called them to join the faculty in 1964. They have given their services to this institution for over 41 years.

God blessed them with three children who are now adults: Rose Davis Phillips, Olivia Angela Davis Turner, and Oliver James Davis, Jr. All of them are married to Christian spouses. Ruth and Oliver have five granddaughters: Constance, Roscille, Alexandria, Starr, and Erica.

Truly God has been good and His promises are sure. He stated that He would provide for all of our needs, and He has fulfilled all of His promises. What a wonderful God we serve!

Precious Memories of Missionaries of Color

Dr. Ruth Faye Davis

12

ELDER MAURICE & ESTHER BATTLE 1956–1979

Africa, that great continent! Who would have thought the Battles would end up spending a good portion of their adult working years living and working on that continent? They had a very interesting and exciting service during their many years in Africa. Going to Liberia was a big decision. They were going to a Republic rich in a great tradition. They would not find all the comforts that one experienced in the United States. Roughing it, operating makeshift, or doing without had its challenges. They were leaving their family, kinfolk, and friends. It was very difficult to say farewell.

Maurice was born in Oberlin, Ohio, and at an early age his parents moved to a small town in central Alabama. His mother felt it an obligation to care for her aging father. Because there was not a Seventh-day Adventist church in the area, his dad started a church in their home. The family came together each Sabbath for Sabbath School and church. Maurice's dad would speak unless there was a visiting minister. During his early life, he was always thrilled when he heard mission stories about the trials and joys of those experiences beyond the sea in the countries of Africa and Asia. After graduating from high school, Maurice went to Oakwood College to study for the ministry. While attending college and after graduation, it was still exciting to him to see color slides and motion pictures brought back by missionaries from those mysterious countries where wild animals still lived on the fringes of civilization and where many thousands of people were without God.

Maurice met and married Esther Coleman from Oberlin, Ohio. Maurice felt somewhat shocked when they were asked to consider traveling to the land

Precious Memories of Missionaries of Color

of Africa, where such brave men from Europe as David Livingstone, Albert Schweitzer, and many others had spent their lives. Now it was a decision that Maurice and Esther had to make. They decided to serve humanity in West Africa. Why did they decide to make this their life work? It stems from a belief still held in common with many people today—that time for the job of preaching is limited. For reasons not fully understood, the opportunities to preach the gospel in many lands are greatly limited. The feelings of nationalism are stronger now, and the tendency to reject the gospel under the mistaken feeling that it is a tool of politics is more widespread. Moreover, the Bible has much to say in reference to Christ's second coming and the end of the world and the warning of this end which is to be preached to every part of the globe before Christ returns and the end occurs. The gospel of the kingdom, God's Word assures us, "shall be preached in all of the world, for a witness unto all nations, and then shall the end come" (Matthew 24:14). This job must be done, and it demanded dedication to achieve the goal of reaching every nation, kindred, tongue, and people.

The official call to mission service came in April of 1956, while Maurice and Esther were working in the South Atlantic Conference as a departmental secretary. A letter from the Secretariat of the General Conference extended an invitation to become the President of the Liberian mission in West Africa. While in college, the Battles started preparing for mission service by starting a missionary club. However, now it was the real thing. Getting ready for mission service was now in earnest. Maurice and Esther had to sell their home, dispose of their furniture, bid farewell to the South Atlantic workers and visit their parents. Carla, their toddler daughter, had to say good-bye to her grandparents. In addition, as a part of their preparation, they had to pack everything that they would need while in Africa. These possessions were shipped in advance of their leaving the United States. It took approximately 2-3 months for their possessions to arrive in Liberia. The types of things that were sent ahead were clothes, household goods like linens, pots and pans, dishes, and food. American food was not readily available to them.

The trip to Liberia was an eight thousand mile journey. First, they took a train from Philadelphia to Montreal, Canada. Second, they took an eight-day ocean voyage from Montreal to Liverpool, England. Third, they took an old-style propeller DC-6 airplane from London to Roberts Field Monrovia, Liberia. They stopped in every country along the African coast including Casablanca, Morocco and Dakar, Senegal, taking approximately two days to arrive in Liberia.

They arrived in Liberia, West Africa, on August 6, 1956, the day before Maurice's birthday. They arrived during the rainy season. Liberia has six

Elder Maurice & Esther Battle 1956-1979

months of rain and six months dry season. It was hot and humid when they landed. They were met at Roberts Field by the mission's secretary-treasurer. Everything was different! They traveled in a 2 ½ ton truck with only their suitcases. They crossed streams and rivers, all without bridges. They traveled on dirt paths, muddy paths, roads, and bush. As you can imagine, because of the rainy season, the truck would get stuck in places. This was the first time they had experienced anything like that. It was at times very frightening wondering if the truck would turn over and drown them—but exciting at the same time. They traveled in this truck a distance of about 70 miles, taking four hours to arrive at their new home. West Africa would become their home for the next eleven years. While living in Liberia, Maurice Jr. was born in Monrovia.

Some of Maurice's most challenging experiences during his stay in Liberia were his travels to the hinterland. His very first experience occurred one week after arriving in Liberia. He traveled with one of the local pastors by taking a Cessna three passenger plane from Monrovia to Lower Buchana, a distance of approximately 200 miles.

Because of the conditions, they landed on a dirt runway between palm trees. Upon arrival, they were met by the mission station director, David Hughes, also an American missionary. After driving about 40 miles over dirt roads, they spent the night at the mission station where they were to get ready for the long bush trek. On their trek, they were accompanied by 25 local young men who assisted them during their trek by carrying boiled water, a "chop box" used to hold food, cots, and mosquito nets. The boiled water was a necessity because drinking the local water could make them extremely sick.

The water was boiled not only to kill germs, bacteria, and various amoebas, but it had to be strained to get rid of all of the dirt and mud in it. The mosquito nets were used to ward off malaria-carrying mosquitoes because being bitten by mosquitoes would mean sickness and possible death. They traveled part of the night due to the extreme heat during the day. The temperature was in the 90's all year round with 100 percent humidity. This type of temperature and constant humidity is very hard on the body, and takes its toll on one's health.

Traveling during part of the night had its own brand of danger. Protecting oneself from the mosquito and predatory animals are just two small examples of the dangers of traveling at night. Men carrying lanterns to ward off those animals would travel at the front and at the back of the large party. They were also placed in the middle of the two young men at night in order to protect them from dangerous animals. When they stopped campfires were used to keep other predatory animals away. Their long trek through Lower Buchana was approximately 100 miles on foot—traveling through lion, boar, wild cow,

Precious Memories of Missionaries of Color

and elephant country. When they crossed rivers, they had to wade through sometimes chest high water with alligators and poisonous snakes in the water. Snakes residing in the trees and other wildlife indigenous to Liberia and the jungles reminded them that they were as far away from the United States as one could possibly get.

Their first destination was Palmberg in order to deliver a paycheck to the local pastor. He was paid in cash every three to six months because there were no banks. Payday was every three to six months because during the rainy season travel was impossible and there was no mail service to the hinterland. During this trek, they had meetings with members and workers of the church, baptized new members, held communion, mediated disputes among the people, and a host of other duties. Maurice's first trek took ten days!

Surface mail from the United States always took between six weeks to two months to arrive in Liberia. Maurice received a letter dated September 6, 1956 from his mother who lived in Philadelphia with his father. It had taken approximately 2-3 weeks to reach them. This was his first letter bringing news from home, and it seemed so far away and so foreign. It seemed a lifetime away. This letter is found in the appendix.

Meanwhile, looking at Africa through the eyes of Esther, she could not imagine anything like this! She grew up in Oberlin, Ohio, an extremely progressive place, surrounded by three sisters, three brothers, a hardworking father, an uncle and other relatives. Esther relates that when they first arrived in Liberia, she cried for one month. Sabbaths were the hardest to adjust to because the differences were the most glaring. Although she had spent time before leaving to Africa with returning missionary families, she was not prepared for what awaited her even though they had painted a realistic picture. Things that were the most apparent were the differences in the food supply. In West Africa, there was no fresh milk—it was all powdered milk. Because of the climate, six months of rain made it difficult to grow a variety of foods. The soil was not good for growing things. Vegetables consisted of cucumbers, tomatoes, and collard greens leaving them to desire foods such as corn, green beans, spinach, carrots, and broccoli.

The simplest tasks took hours. For example, bread had to be made daily from scratch. You could not just pour the flour and other ingredients into a bowl to mix. First one had to sift the flour and other ingredients to get rid of the bugs. All water had to be boiled and then filtered after the boiling process. However, the thing that permeated every facet of their life was the constant smell of latex in the air which came from the rubber factories.

Elder Maurice & Esther Battle 1956-1979

After living in Liberia for two months, Esther met an American woman who changed her entire outlook. The woman's husband was the director of the YMCA. She had lived in Liberia for many years and her attitude and spirit were extremely upbeat. This, Esther says, really helped to point her head in the right direction.

In 1959, the Battles were elected to go to the West African Union to serve as Departmental Director. During the next seven years, they lived in Accra, Ghana, the capital. The West African Union covered territory from Gambia to Eastern Nigeria. During their time in Accra, their second daughter and son were born—Renee and Michael.

Their duties while at the Union included travel to nine countries which included Gambia, Sierra Leone, Liberia, Togo, Dahomey, Ivory Coast, and Nigeria. These travels were usually overland, by car, and sometimes by commercial air.

One event worthy of note was the coup which deposed President Kwame Nkruma. Esther relates the event. Because all borders were closed by air, sea, and land, Maurice could not return. Esther was all alone in Ghana with their four children. Maurice being very worried about the safety of his family, contacted the American Embassy in Accra. They assured him that his family would be safe. He was not able to return to Accra for another 10 days. Esther tells of gunfire beginning at four o'clock in the morning, armed men running through the streets, and a neighbor being taken away at gunpoint by a group of soldiers. Because of the time of year, all of the missionary men were traveling when the coup occurred—leaving only women and children at home on the mission compound.

In 1956, at the General Conference session in Detroit, Michigan, the Battles were transferred from Accra, Ghana, to serve as Director of Lay Activities and the Communications Departments in St, Albans, England, at the Northern European Division.

In 1970 the General Conference was held in Atlantic City, New Jersey. During that session, we were transferred from St. Albans, England to Takoma Park, Maryland to serve as Director of Lay Activities for the General Conference,

In 1975, the General Conference session was held in Vienna, Austria. During that session the Battles were transferred from Takoma Park, Maryland, to Beirut, Lebanon, to serve as the Secretary of the Afro-Mideast Division. In 1979, they were asked to return to the General Conference of Seventh-day Adventists to serve as Associate Secretary of the General Conference. Elder Battle held this position until his retirement in February of 2001.

Precious Memories of Missionaries of Color

On the HMS Queen Elizabeth enroute to Liberia, West Africa.
Carla, Esther, Maurice Jr. and Maurice Sr.

Maurice Battle, Naomi Daniels, and Esther Battle

Mission House in Liberia, West Africa

Elder Maurice & Esther Battle 1956–1979

Mission Office in Liberia, West Africa

Liberian Mission Workers (1956)
Back row (Left to right): Douglas Tate, Maurice Battle, Ted Cantrell, David Hughes Front Row: Richard Simons

Precious Memories of Missionaries of Color

Back Row (Left to right): Samuel DeShay, Maurice Battle, Owen Troy, David Hughes, Lindsay Thomas
Front Row: Ann Troy, Ted Cantrell, Esther Battle, C. E. Moseley, (visitor) Eula Gunther, and Phillip Giddings

Monrovia Seventh-day Adventist Church

Elder Maurice & Esther Battle 1956-1979

Dunbar Henri, Esther and Renee Battle (child)

67

13

DR. JOHNNY & IDA JOHNSON
1957–1985

Dr. Johnson likes to talk about the time that he was a "fighter for men" and how he became a "fighter for God!" Dr. Johnson was literally on a career path to becoming a great Middleweight champion having won numerous titles during his boxing career. God had other plans for this stalwart giant of a man! In an evangelistic meeting conducted by Elder H. W. Kibble, Dr. Johnson accepted the Advent Message. Dr. Johnson thanks God that instead of training to use his God given strength to physically destroy bodies, God called him through the preaching of the gospel to save lives. To God be the glory!

Dr. Johnson and his dear wife, Ida, were both members of the Methodist church; however, after hearing their pastor admit that the Seventh-day is the Sabbath, they were both baptized into the Seventh-day Adventist Church.

The Johnson's love affair with Africa also began in Liberia at Konola Academy. They continued the work that was begun by pastors Phil Gidding, Dunbar Henri, and the Cantrells. When they arrived at Konola, the Cantrells (Ted and Frankie) became their mentors. Elder Cantrell was serving as the principal and his wife, Frankie, was in charge of the Mission Dispensary. After the Cantrells left, the Johnsons continued the building program started by the Cantrells. The chapel was completed and hosted the first graduation program. The school's main classroom building was completed and dedicated, and shortly thereafter the school received full accreditation from the Liberian Department of Education. The first four-year graduation class during the summer of 1960 was the highlight of the Konola administration. Ida organized the first Konola School Choir that sang on the national radio ELWA.

Dr. Johnny & Ida Johnson 1957–1985

It was apparent that some of the students coming to school from some of the remote villages needed something more than a secondary education. As a result, a two-year trade course in carpentry was started. The school was fortunate to have a skilled teacher in carpentry, Mr. S. T. Kilby. His class provided the classrooms with much needed desks and chairs. Unfortunately, the program had to be discontinued when Mr. Kilby was fatally struck by an automobile in Monrovia.

The classrooms were refurbished in other respects as well, such as colorful Bible and science wall charts, a modest science laboratory, and a library which provided a place of study. The science lab for the first time provided a place where lab demonstrations in chemistry and biology could be held. The addition of the school's first science lab and library marked the school's transition into a senior secondary school.

White limed buildings and stones on both sides of the main campus driveway gave a luster to the grounds. In addition, a Home Economics course was added to the curriculum and taught by Mrs. Johnson and Miss Lois Raymond. In 1960-62, the first official Konola School Bulletin was printed and circulated. An iron overhead gate sign was erected over the road entrance to the school, as well as a large concrete block sign that was implanted on a hillside overlooking the school site. Both were inscribed "Konola Academy" and gave the school a much needed face lift. In addition, the manicured grass kept so immaculate by the gift of a riding mower provided by the Shiloh Church of Chicago added to the transformation of the school.

When the Johnsons left Liberia in 1963, Konola Academy was the preferred secondary school of choice for many elite families because of its high Christian and academic standards. The Johnsons thank God for the opportunity to share their lives with the students and people of Liberia. Above all, the Johnsons pray that because of their example and the lives that they lived, many students were inspired to transform their lives and have a personal relationship with Jesus Christ.

Ghana holds a special place in the hearts of the Johnsons. It was here after twenty-three years of a childless marriage, that God blessed them with a daughter, Afriyie. Today, Afriyie is a Certified Nurse Practitioner on the teaching staff of the Graduate School of Nursing at the University of South Florida in Tampa.

Bekwai Secondary School and Teacher Training College provided the Johnsons with another privilege of working with other mission families from America and other nations. The experience gave them a sense of the universality we will experience in the heavenly kingdom of God when the redeemed sons and daughters from all of the nations meet around the throne of God. It was here that they first met the Hammond family who lived just a short distance from their residence.

The Johnsons both worked as teachers while at Bekwai. Ida taught children of missionaries and Johnny taught Bible and was the pastor of the institution's church. At that time there was tension between Western colonialism and the post war African Independence Movement. The Christian Mission was challenged to offer more than "future eternal salvation," and was forced to deal with the needs of the "here and now." The function of the missionary was changing in all parts of the world. The focus changed to being fraternal brothers and workers sent to help indigenous people build brighter, stronger, healthful, and productive communities to live in. Christ is concerned with man's total well being—mental, physical, and spiritual. The dedicated missionary ministers to all three.

Teachers and students at Bekwai Teacher Training College and Secondary School visited several villages in the surrounding area. Among these were Kwamang, Dompoase, Sanfo-Aduam, Assanso, Feyiase, and a few other villages in the area. All benefited from the school's Christian commitment to uplift humanity, body, soul, and spirit in every way possible.

Overseas missionaries and students joined together in leading out–to take charge of, in the Sabbath services and at the same time gave their attention to the physical conditions of their places of worship—especially in the villages. Together they addressed the problems that were within their ability to remedy.

Most of the churches were constructed of bare mud blocks badly deteriorated from the lack of cement. The church furniture, window shutters, leaking roofs, and doors were badly in need of repair or replacement. In light of such conditions, Pastor Johnson thought it would be spiritually uplifting to the village members and a wake-up call for the secondary students to include community service as a part of their curriculum. Pastor Johnson felt that it was important for the students to treat community development as an urgent Christian concern of the gospel task to help indigenous people build strong, healthy, and productive communities in which to live. This is the humanitarian dimension of the gospel task reflecting the fullness of God.

In order to encourage and train those under his influence, Pastor Johnson was impressed to select five upper class secondary students to form the core of a "Rural Gospel Ministry." They would minister to the villages with the emphasis in church development and evangelism. Pastor Johnson involved them in his village church planting projects which he had begun in five churches already. Other interested students joined them from time to time out of casual interest.

Dr. Johnny & Ida Johnson 1957–1985

Three churches, Kwamang, Dompoase, and Assano, suffering from a lack of trained leadership and funds, were typical "bare bones" undeveloped churches. These poorly constructed, uncompleted, and unpainted churches were impressionably restored by the dedicated manual labor of the "gospel five" with village and student help. Evangelistic follow-up meetings were conducted with an undetermined number of souls joining the church. The Sanfo-Aduam church was in such deteriorating condition that it had to be demolished and a more attractive church was built on the former site of a Palm Wine booth on the village property.

The fifth church, Feyiase, had a different origin from the others. When Pastor Johnson and his wife Ida were conducting a branch Sabbath School in Feyiase, a village located about a mile or more in the forest area behind Bekwai, they were approached by one of the villagers requesting that they build them a school. The Johnsons thought and prayed about it before agreeing to take on such a task.

The village population at that time was not more than one hundred villagers—including children on any regular week day. Domestic farming was the main livelihood of the people; however, a few of the men were palm wine tappers. Aside from selling farm products, baking bread, and the earnings of the tappers, there was no other means of livelihood. Their original meeting place was an open veranda on one side of a large compound house in the village. One of the Bekwai secondary students who assisted Ida as an interpreter while she taught the children's Sabbath School class was a young man named Matthew Bediako. (Matthew is presently the Executive Secretary of the General Conference.)

With the aid of the villagers, men, women, their children, and the student trainees, the chapel-classroom was completed in several months. They had agreed to construct a school room so long as a section of it would be only for Sabbath church services. In compliance, a part of the school facility was sectioned off by a folding partition. On Sabbath, it folded back to allow use of the full room for services. During the school week, the partition was pulled out across the room separating the pulpit area from the classroom section for classes 1-3.

Contributions from the Shiloh Church in Chicago and other contributors paid for the simple but durable classroom furniture. The government Educational Supervisor was highly impressed by the facilities, desks and chairs, large blackboard, teacher's supply cupboard, and the partial concrete block structure of the school. It was an honor and a blessing to receive certification from the Department of Education in Ghana to operate such a small forest-surrounded school with an enrollment of twenty-five students. Before their departure from

Precious Memories of Missionaries of Color

Ghana, the school attracted wide attention in the area. The desire to attend the school far exceeded the space provided by the church-classroom facility. Because the Johnsons were about to leave, it was expedient that the local Ghana Conference incorporate this school into the educational system of our church. This was done in an official ceremony before they left. To meet the increasing need for classroom space and school enrollment, a crash building program was undertaken to construct a separate church building just before the Johnsons went on furlough. With the help of the Feyiase supporters (students and relatives of Feyiase villagers from Bekwai town) a sizable and attractive concrete block church was constructed before the Johnsons departed. It was painted and supplied with well-constructed benches and pulpit furniture. The church was dedicated by the local Ghana (Kumasi) Conference president before their departure from Bekwai. This school and church established forty-two years ago are still functioning by God's providence. Both have demonstrated their permanency and will to survive.

Before the Johnsons departed from Feyiase, they also constructed a large and badly needed village public latrine facility. It was approved by the local government Sanitation Officer who was very impressed by their concern for village sanitation. It should be mentioned that Mrs. Johnson had been given permission to employ a young man with some teacher training education to take over after their departure. He was also an expert gardener and did an exceptional job of beautifying the school and church grounds with the most attractive flowers and plants. It was a privilege for the Johnsons to work hand in hand with the villagers in labor and supervision of the original one room school and church block. Mrs. Johnson had the privilege of being the first teacher in the school. (This brief history would not be complete without mentioning the faithful leadership of Mrs. B. S. Aning who has been a faithful and tireless worker on behalf of Feyiase's spiritual and community development for over forty years. May she be fully rewarded in the kingdom of heaven.)

By addressing some of Feyiase's major community development needs as an inclusive part of the gospel, the full measure of the spiritual and temporal impact made on the village and others will not be fully known until the heavenly records are made known to the redeemed. Presently, the villagers know—as has been said—that something "wonderful" has happened in their village and may they know that it was born of God and not of man.

The next sixteen years took the Johnsons to Nigeria—which is the longest period of time they have ministered in any one of the three West African countries they were assigned to. For the first six years of service, they were asked to serve at our largest hospital and nursing school located in Ile Ife, West Nigeria. Dr. Johnson was asked to be the hospital chaplain, Bible teacher, and

Dr. Johnny & Ida Johnson 1957-1985

church pastor of the main hospital-institutional church. Mrs. Johnson was the principal and teacher in the overseas workers elementary school. In addition to all of his assigned tasks—Bible teacher, chaplain, and pastor—Dr. Johnson managed to find time to train a core of lay evangelists to meet the growing need for more Bible workers. He states that he counts it all a privilege!

Nigeria being the largest populated country in West Africa warranted a larger workforce to meet the needs of millions—a need which demanded a larger evangelistic outreach program. So, Dr. Johnson organized a group of men into a lay pastoral training program. An appreciable number were added to the membership at the Ife church because of the number of Lay evangelistic "Bible Speaks" outdoor meetings. Two young men (one directly and one indirectly) related to the training program have continued on to becoming ordained church pastors. Pastor Hezekiah Oyeleke, currently pastoring in the West Nigerian Union, and Pastor Lawrence Oladini, presently completing a doctoral dissertation at Andrews University Seminary, were a part of that "Training Program." The most important contribution that any mission worker can accomplish in their field of labor is to permit God to use them as a channel of motivation. In the course of time, some three hundred and forty souls were added to the Ife church as a result of the combined effort of the pastor-student team work.

The young men in the "Training program" were significant instruments in the completion of the construction of the five new churches in the Ife district. Mr. Ed Moon, an expatriate nursing instructor, provided significant financial assistance needed to purchase building materials. The Johnsons envision that when the roll is called up in heaven, hopefully all of the young men in the Lay Minister's Training Program will hear their names called.

Just after completing the five new churches, the hospital church faced a crisis. The government was in the process of taking over the hospital and the property. In order to save the church, immediate action needed to be taken. The suggestion was made by the Ife church brothers that legal authority should be obtained from local traditional chiefs to separate the church land from the hospital land. Following the suggestion of the church brothers, quick action was taken to legally separate the church from the hospital land. As pastor of the church, Dr. Johnson rallied the Training Program lay pastors, Conference office, and church members to lead out in a plan to build a wall separating the church grounds from newly acquired government property. Pastor Johnson called upon the members for monetary donations as well as for their labor. In record time a six foot concrete block wall was constructed separating the church from newly acquired government property. The Ife church membership records the "wall event" as a blessed event to be remembered in the annals of their church's physical and spiritual journey giving God the glory that all things worked out well.

The "Creeks" is a mission field within a mission field in Nigeria. It is an area that embraces the Niger River tributaries into the Gulf of Guinea off the Atlantic Ocean. It is an area that has a number of water-surrounded Adventist churches—seemingly floating churches. To bring the gospel to this area and provide medical supplies to sick, malaria-laden villages required an all day canoe trip. The only medical attention and supplies that these people received came from the Ile Ife Hospital. The normal transportation provided was slow-moving, public river boats picking up and dispatching goods and passengers all along the river. This means of transportation could take just as long as the ride in the canoe and might not go to the village desired. What the hospital needed was its own river boat! This feat was accomplished by a major contribution that indigenous District Pastor J. O. Eregare and Pastor Johnson initiated with funds from a forgotten source. Constructed by a local boat builder, Pastors Eregare and Johnson painted the boat and later officiated at its launching. It was a small, enclosed outboard motor boat for six to eight passengers. It was christened "The Adventist Dawn" and the blessings it brought to the Creeks will not be fully known until we all get to heaven. The Adventist Dawn had opened the Creeks to a new dawn of accessibility and service. It provided more time on the trip to preach the gospel and more efficient medical service to a sick, isolated, and suffering people who need healing of soul as well as of body.

During the last years that the Johnsons served in Nigeria and in Africa, in general, was in the Muslim north. They were sent there to set up a local mission headquarters in a Muslim controlled city. By law Christian churches could not own land there—only rent it. The present rented site where the local national pastor lived was notably a large vacant lot area, which was a combination goat pasture, foot path, and community dump. With the assistance of that pastor, Dr. Johnson was able to hire a local tractor grader to clear the lot of the rubbish and level the land. The previous General Conference President Neal Wilson viewed the site and was pleased with their efforts. After the construction of a high concrete block fence, leveled ground and trash removed, the site looked habitable and the surrounding Muslim community showed delight with the improvement. Union funds had been appropriated for a modest but attractive residence to be built for overseas workers which the Johnsons would be the first to occupy. In order to win the hearts of the dominant Muslims and few Christian neighbors, they organized some of the church youth to clean up the street where their headquarters were located. This also helped them gain congratulations and community acceptance.

Dr. Johnny & Ida Johnson 1957–1985

It was their main purpose to establish a permanent Kaduna Mission headquarters by winning the respect and support of educated Muslims. To this end they hastily renovated the local pastor's dwelling, constructed a medium size worship Chapel and Children's Care Center with a Director's Office and two teaching classrooms. In addition, a separate office was provided for the Mission Director. A newly constructed Chapel building—as they could not get a permit to construct a Christian church at that time—served their purpose. A well designed and painted building, its recreation area had swings and a sliding board provided for the children. Daily chapel services were conducted each day for grades one to three. Two teachers, members of the Kaduna Church, along with Mrs. Johnson composed the teaching staff. Upon their arrival, the completion of the Kaduna Church was one of Pastor Johnson's first assignments. The church was incomplete and unusable for service, but after some months of supervising and working with those eager to have their own church, it was completed and dedicated along with the Care Center by the Nigerian Union officers. Pastor Johnson labored in evangelistic efforts as far North as Kano as well as other sections of the North. God blessed the Johnsons mightily and only heaven knows the rich rewards of souls that will be found in the kingdom because of their dedicated service.

For the last twenty years since the Johnsons retired, they have been living on a five acre piece of land in Idlewild, Michigan. They enjoy their home surrounded by forest abounding with deer, wild turkeys, rabbits, and not so desired snakes. In their retirement, the Johnsons taught for many years in the local public schools in Baldwin, Michigan. Mrs. Johnson accepted the challenge to be the Youth Director with the Michigan Extension Youth Camp program and later became involved in the RCI (Rural Community Initiative)—an adult education program. Pastor Johnson enjoys writing and is fascinated with the study of flying saucers or UFO phenomena. His study is titled *Signs of the Saucers*—a phenomenon in the final spiritual crisis between Christ and Satan and the coming New World Order. The mystery has serious prophetic implications that will in time impact the entire world. He also has a mail-out Literature Ministry, "What Every Christian Should Know." It focuses on the Sabbath question in the context of salvation, history, and spiritual renewal. Pastor and Mrs. Johnson are both involved in their local church activities.

The Johnsons have been married for sixty-three years. She is a former principal of the Shiloh Elementary School and Academy of Chicago and he is a former Bible, science, and math teacher. They are both graduates of Andrews University which was Emmanuel Missionary College at the time Mrs. Johnson graduated. Pastor Johnson earned the Master of Divinity and the D. Min. (Doctor of Ministry) in 1977. According to Pastor Johnson, he was the

Precious Memories of Missionaries of Color

first Afro-American to receive the D.Min. from the Seminary. Previously he received a M.A. in teaching Social Studies from the University of Illinois at the Champaign-Urbana campus. Pastor Johnson states that the social studies prepared him for more than "preaching the gospel," it prepared him to be able to apply the gospel of Jesus Christ through improving living conditions to meet the needs of fellow men in the nations they served.

Dr. Johnny and Ida Johnson

Dr. Johnny & Ida Johnson 1957–1985

Members of Konola Academy Faculty–Pastor & Mrs. Johnson in the Center

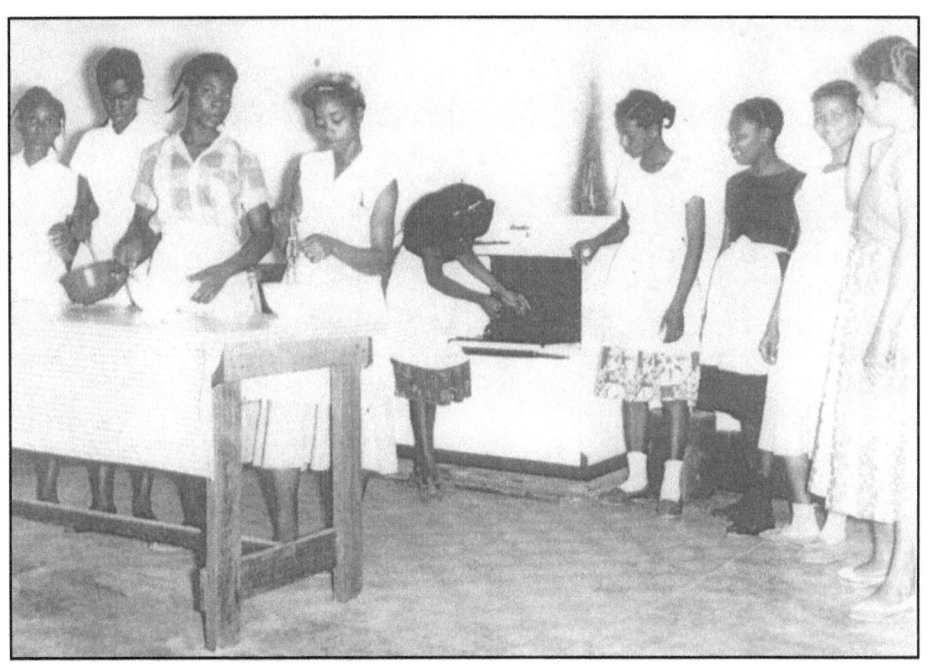

Mrs. Johnson's Home Economics and Cooking Class

Precious Memories of Missionaries of Color

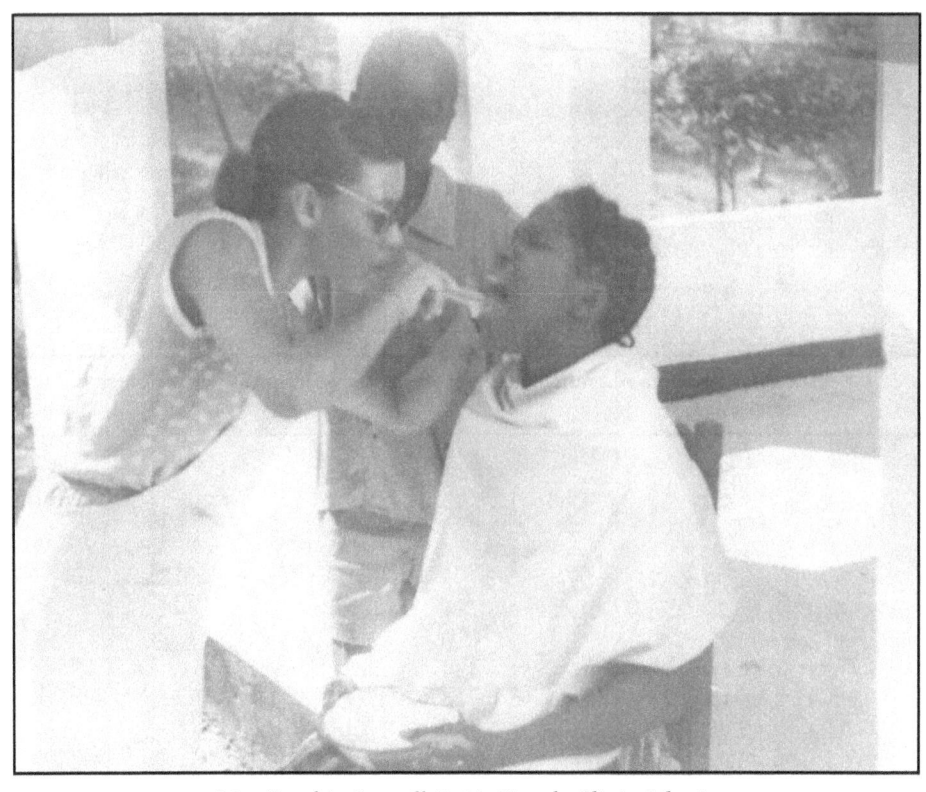

Mrs. Frankie Cantrell, R. N.–Konola Clinic–Liberia

Dr. Johnny & Ida Johnson 1957–1985

Mr. Mensah's Chemistry Class

Pastor Johnson's Bible Class–Konola Academy-Liberia

Precious Memories of Missionaries of Color

School Library at Konola Academy–Liberia

Dr. Johnny & Ida Johnson 1957–1985

One of the churches built in Ashanti, Ghana

Precious Memories of Missionaries of Color

Training for the Gospel Ministry

Teacher James Boateng (does excellent work) and students at Peyiase.

Dr. Johnny & Ida Johnson 1957–1985

Child received a new brace; Inside the classroom (center) Mr. Higley donated money for an oven so the lady could bake and sell bread instead of palm wine

Precious Memories of Missionaries of Color

Top: First Fruits for Baptism at Feyiase–Ghana
Bottom: Leadership Training Class for Secondary Students

Dr. Johnny & Ida Johnson 1957–1985

The Old Church had to be torn down, and the new one was built in its place

Dr. Johnny & Ida Johnson 1957–1985

The Bible Speaks
Pastoral Training Project

Baptisms (Pastor/Laymen/Church Involvement).

14

Elder Alvin & Lucy Goulbourne 1959-1965; 1977-1986

These days Bermuda is hardly thought of as a mission field. Things were surely different in 1959 when Alvin was called to go to Bermuda as a missionary. He had only heard of Bermuda and had no idea where it was. The call was for a pastor who knew something about building. Alvin had just built a church in Mount Vernon, New York making him a good candidate. Alvin and his wife, Lucy, had two children—Alvin Jr. who was three years old and Apryl Joy who was one year old. They also took Jewel Peck (Jewel Kibble) with them, and she spent one year in school there.

The Goulbournes traveled to Bermuda by ship on the Queen of Bermuda. They shall always remember the great send off they received from everyone who came down to the docks. This was a big thing!

In 1915, Bermuda became a part of the Atlantic Union Conference. Before this time, the work on the islands was directed by the General Conference as one of their miscellaneous missions. The Bermuda mission was fully organized in 1959. Young pastors usually were sent to the mission for only one year at a time; however, the Goulbournes were sent to Bermuda for two years and ended up staying for six years. Alvin was the first Black Adventist pastor to be sent to Bermuda where he pastored the Southampton Church and built a new church building. The membership increased making it the largest SDA church on the island. The church was paid for during the six years that they resided in Bermuda. They were fortunate to be able to come home on furlough to the states every year for three weeks.

Precious Memories of Missionaries of Color

Things were so different then and now. Earlier on, very few Bermudians traveled outside of their island. However, just recently, parents started sending their children away to school, mostly high school, since education at the high school level was not free in Bermuda. Most young men worked as an apprentice and learned a trade. When a house was being built, many men would rally around and give a free day's work to help build the house and the women would cook and serve a good meal. Many of the families owned a piece of land.

There were not too many cars on the island; consequently, you might see a bride dressed in her wedding gown on a motor bike on her way to the church. The island at one time was covered with beautiful cedar trees, until blight killed almost every cedar tree. People didn't realize the value of the trees—many of which were cut down and burned. When the Goulbournes arrived, it was hard to find any cedar trees, dead or alive. When Alvin saw the beautiful furniture made from Bermuda cedar, he made up his mind that their church would have Bermuda Cedar furniture. He was told that there was not enough cedar on the island for that project. But, the Lord provided the trees! Whenever Alvin saw a dead cedar tree in a yard, he would ask that it be donated to the church for pews. Alvin and Leroy Darrell would go and cut the trees down and take them to the saw mill. Not only did they find enough cedar for the pews, they found enough for the doors too. To God be the glory! Alvin visited Jamaica and found the pattern for the pews. Elder James Pearman who drew up the plans for the church also built the furniture for the church.

There were only three Adventist churches on the island—Southampton, Hamilton, and St. George. A church was built in Warwick to serve the Caucasian brothers. This caused a great deal of concern. Land was also purchased to build a church in Midland Heights.

The school was in one building housing six grades with five teachers. They were Mrs. Barnes, Mrs. Vanlowe, Edward and Marjorie Richardson and Mrs. Lightbourne with Edward Richardson as the principal. Later, two more classrooms were added, thus housing eight grades. Many of the students attended Pine Forge Academy in Pottstown, Pennsylvania, or Jamaica BWI when they graduated from the eight grades.

The Goulbournes lived in a house rented from George and Darlene Ray on Horseshoe Road. The church needed a parsonage, and when Elder Reese Jenkins shared the plans for a new house with Lucy, she observed that it did not contain a pastor's study. Realizing the importance of the inclusion of a study, they offered to stay in the house where they were staying until such could be included. The Goulbourne family participated in cleaning off the lot where the new house was eventually built just behind the Southampton Church.

Elder Alvin & Lucy Goulbourne 1959–1986

There were two things that made Alvin's work successful. He loved the young people and they knew it. He believed in visiting his members. When he went back as President and didn't have time to visit, the people still expected him to visit as he had when he was the pastor.

The Goulbournes left Bermuda not realizing that God was not finished with them as yet in Bermuda. They returned to the United States with a new addition to the family, one year old, David Michael.

God moves in strange ways. Alvin was asked to pastor the regional Springfield, MA, church in the Northeastern Conference. They were just getting to know the people and feeling welcomed when the President, Elder Hudson asked him to be the new manager of the Book and Bible House which were experiencing trouble. Alvin said, "No" that he was happy in Springfield and had plans for the church. He was told to pray about it and to put the fleece out. Alvin put the fleece out and the Lord said "Go." They were not happy about it, but it was the Lord's will. There were times when they questioned as to whether it was really the Lord's will. God blessed Alvin's efforts as manager of the Book and Bible house which after three years were out of debt. From there, he pastored the Mount Olive Church in Brooklyn.

In 1976, while they were still wondering what place the Book and Bible House would have in their lives, Alvin was called back to be President of the Bermuda Mission of Seventh-day Adventists. At that time the President held all of the offices of the conference; Treasurer, Education superintendent, Youth Director, Chairman of the School Board, and Book and Bible House Manager. Alvin found the Book and Bible House was in a hole and had never run in the black. Now they understood that the Lord was preparing him for this work. Using what he learned at the Northeastern Book and Bible House, he was able to get the Bermuda B&BH out of debt. It has never been in the red again, and they learned never to doubt the Lord.

They went back to Bermuda with two different children this time, David Michael who was twelve, and Julie who was nine years old. The older two, Alvin and Apryl, were at Oakwood College. Returning to Bermuda after a twelve years absence, they found many changes everywhere. The first thing they noticed was how the economy had changed. Many exempt companies had come to Bermuda. People had better jobs and larger and better homes. They had better education and more people owned cars.

There was and had been a lot of building going on both on the island and in the Mission. A new Conference office now existed with housing for the Book and Bible House with two guest rooms and some offices. There was also a large auditorium in the back of the Hamilton Church—one of the largest meeting places on the island. Two more rooms had been added to the school

Precious Memories of Missionaries of Color

in Southampton, and a duplex house had been built behind the Southampton parsonage. The President of the Conference and the Principal of the school lived there. That was great for them because the children could walk to school. There was a lovely house in the city of Hamilton overlooking the harbor where the white presidents lived. That house had been given to the conference years ago with the stipulation that no black people were to live in it. Alvin and Lucy could have moved in it but chose instead to live close to the school. (Elder Edward Richardson, the President after them, was the first black man to live in the Hamilton house with his family.)

The next generation of young men who went off to school no longer acquired the skills necessary for building. Young people held jobs that had never been held by blacks before. There had never been a Bermudian pastor! Now many young men were taking the ministry. Elder Mack Wilson was the first national minister to be hired.

One of the first things Alvin did as the new President of the Bermuda Mission was to organize the Conference with an executive committee so that one person would not make all of the decisions for the conference. As the work grew many meetings needed to be attended away from the island. Alvin found that these meetings were keeping him away from the island too much. He began to assign the different departments to the ministers. That gave them a chance to leave the island and to get some experience as well.

Two of Alvin's goals were to evangelize the island and buy as much property as he could for the growth of the work. With land at a premium, he knew in time that they would need to build more churches and there would be no more land. The churches also needed to have parsonages for their pastors.

Once a year Alvin tried to bring in some evangelists from the States because he found that foreign speakers were a better drawing card. Some of these speakers included Raymond Sanders, Breath of Life, Oscar Lane, Doc Smith, Ronal Center, and Joseph Meloshenako. The efforts were very successful and many souls were added to the church. The local pastors took part in the tent efforts which were also good training. Any pastor who wanted to have an effort in the summer was encouraged to do so. Some of the local pastors holding tent efforts were Elder Mack Wilson, Elder Carlyle Simmons, Elder Sidney Gibbons, Elder Patrick O'Mara, and Elder Hector Mouzon.

The government of Bermuda would only allow the Adventist Church to have one school, but that school was supported by all of the churches. The house between the church and school was purchased and classes were held there. The first floor was used to prepare lunches. The Bermuda Institute started in 1943 with one room at the old Southampton church and one teacher and approximately twenty-three students. The school grew at a rapid rate. When

Elder Alvin & Lucy Goulbourne 1959-1986

Elder Goulbourne was there, in November of 1981, they had a ground breaking ceremony to build a new elementary school and administrative offices. That building had 14 classrooms, a library for the elementary students, and administrative offices. It now has about 30 classrooms, a multipurpose auditorium, and approximately 50 faculty and staff members.

In light of the fact that a Community Service building was needed, the house by the road between the school and church was purchased. Elder Correia, who was ready to retire, was put in charge of running the Community Service building. He and many volunteers did a wonderful job.

In 1971, the Somerset Church was started. The ground breaking took place in August, 1977. They began using the downstairs in 1981 and began using the sanctuary on May 23, 1983.

It is important to mention Brother James Pearman. He was the general contractor for the school and most of the buildings built by the church. Brother Pearman was a gifted craftsman and builder. Under the leadership of Elder Goulbourne, three churches were built; Somerset, Devonshire, and St. George. His goal was to have a parsonage for each church. Three homes were bought, one in St. George and two in Devonshire.

The church was growing fast and many changes were needed. It was time for the Bermuda Mission to become the Bermuda Conference and that took a lot of work and planning. The Bermuda Mission became the Bermuda Conference under the leadership of Elder Goulbourne.

In 1986, Alvin was called to be the Executive Secretary of the Atlantic Union Conference; Elder Aaron Brogden had just retired and was moving to Greensboro, North Carolina.

It was in December 1928 that Alvin was born in New Rochelle, New York to David and Hilda Goulbourne. He was third of four sons—Eric, Donald, Alvin, Sidney, and then the long awaited girl, Etoy, 10 years later. The three older boys were sent to Jamaica until they were around age 10 where they lived with their grandmother. Alvin finished high school in New Rochelle and went to Oakwood College in Huntsville, Alabama. When Alvin was a teenager, he was in charge of showing the slides for Elder Norman McCloud who also baptized him. During that time he began to feel the call and to think of going into the ministry.

At Oakwood, Alvin studied the ministerial course and a minor in elementary education. For two years after graduation, he taught church school in Louisville, Kentucky. In July 1953, he married the love of his life and Oakwood College friend, Lucy Cummings of Florence, South Carolina. Lucy taught school for two years in New Haven, Connecticut. They moved to New York City and both taught at the Manhattan Elementary school for two years when Elder Singleton called Alvin to pastor the Mount Vernon, New York church. Alvin completed the building of the Mount Vernon church. Because of his building experience, he was called to Bermuda.

In 1995, Alvin retired and he and Lucy moved to Huntsville where it all started. The children are all grown. The two girls, Apryl Joy and Julie are nurses. Alvin is a CPA and works for the Bermuda government. David and his wife Joan moved to New Hampshire after teaching in Bermuda for over 10 years. They have five grandchildren: Alvin's two—Alvin Roy the third and his sister Illiana; Julie and Michael Brown have three—Mikey, Alyssa, and Logan where they live in Laurel, MD.

In retirement, Elder Goulbourne has been a Real Estate agent and for the past four years was in charge of the Community Service Center, started by Mrs. Chester Harris. He worked with a number of volunteers who gave out bags of food to the needy four days a week. Every Wednesday over 100 hot meals were served.

Elder Alvin & Lucy Goulbourne 1959–1986

Goulbourne Family in Bermuda, Southampton Church, and the Bermuda Institute

Precious Memories of Missionaries of Color

The Bermuda Institute-Class of 1985

Elder Alvin & Lucy Goulbourne 1959–1986

Ladies and Men's Group at the Southampton Church

Precious Memories of Missionaries of Color

Pathfinders from the Warwick Church

Elder Alvin & Lucy Goulbourne 1959–1986

The New Southampton Church. In the far left corner is the school
with its first new addition in the back.

15

Elder Leland And Lottie Mitchell-Harris 1959–1963

It was 1957 and Elder C. E. Mosley of the General Conference of Seventh-day Adventist was leaving the Central States Camp meeting. As he started down the hill, he turned and asked, "Brother Mitch, have you ever thought about going to Africa?" Without waiting for an answer, he added, "You and your wife pray about it and write to me." They looked at each other in astonishment. There had never been any hesitation before as to whether they would say "yes" or "no" when they received a call from God to go to a different field. However, Africa was a field that was far away. These thoughts ran through the mind of a woman who had married a preacher four years before in 1953, who was on a rare pastor/colporteur internship with the phenomenal salary of $50.00 dollars a month. The rest of the living expenses were to be made by selling religious books. Nevertheless, they prayed that if it were God's will that they should go that the General Conference would extend the call through the executive committee of the Central States Conference.

Leland and Lottie had recently moved from Wichita, Kansas to the St. Joseph, Missouri, Leavenworth, Kansas district and were adjusting to that move. Early in 1958, they wrote to Elder Moseley, stating that they were willing if it was God's will. Because they had not received any word from the General Conference, Leland began focusing on plans for a tent effort in Atchison, Kansas, that the conference president wanted him to conduct in 1959. Meanwhile, family and friends were telling them that they had heard through the grapevine that they were going to Africa despite the fact that they had not received an official notice. Near the end of 1958, they finally received the official letter.

Elder Leland And Lottie Mitchell-Harris 1959-1963

They later found out that the president of the Central States Conference knew about the call, but was determined that the tent effort in Atchison would be conducted by Elder Mitchell during the summer of 1959. Under pressure from the Union Conference president, the call was passed on to them. Early 1959 found the family preparing for a fall departure to Africa where Leland would serve as Superintendent of the Seventh-day Adventist Mission in Grand Bassa County, Liberia, and as pastor of the church in Lower Buchanan, the county seat. Furniture had to be sold; numerous shots had to be taken, etc. It is hard to remember all of the details that such a move requires.

By September of 1959, Leland and Lottie found themselves bidding farewell to the congregations in St. Joseph and Leavenworth. They then took time to visit Leland's Aunt Dorothy and three of Lottie's sisters in Chicago. After traveling to Michigan to visit with Lottie's father and mother, a sister and two brothers, they spent time with another sister and some cousins in New York before leaving America. On October 8, 1959, they set sail for England on the Il de Franc with Aunt Dorothy accompanying them. The voyage was not like going on a cruise ship. When taking a trip today, if you are a vegetarian, you can order a special menu. It seems all that they could offer them for dinner was spaghetti and dry Parmesan cheese, and a vegetable similar to celery but not as good as celery. It sounded like the waiter said salsify, but they couldn't find the name in the food dictionary. Anyway, Lottie has no more desire to eat this dish ever again. After a cold seven-day voyage, Leland and Lottie arrived in Le Havre, France, and took the train to London, England.

The General Conference provided a week's stay in London for sightseeing. It was a wonderful experience. This was the first of three visits to London. History came alive! While there, they visited the newly opened New Gallery Center for church services on Sabbath. It was amazing that there were very few black faces in the congregation. Two and one half years later on their trip home for a six months furlough, there were very few white faces in the congregation.

One very humorous experience concerning Leland was the day he asked the concierge at the hotel about a barbershop. Leland is very particular about shaving and having his hair cut. (Keep in mind that they had seen only a few black faces in the neighborhood). Lottie suggested that maybe he should wait until they arrived in Monrovia, but he was determined. The concierge directed him to a barbershop. When he came back to the hotel, Leland had the funniest looking haircut. They had to laugh. He said the barber kept saying in his very British accent, "I can't get your hair up on the comb. It was a blessing that they had a week's stay in London, so his hair could grow out some and he could arrive at his post of duty with some semblance of dignity.

Precious Memories of Missionaries of Color

After a wonderful week's stay in London, they bade Aunt Dorothy goodbye and she returned to the States. They then took a small jet to Paris where they boarded a regular plane to Liberia. It was a night flight. Lottie was very uneasy, because as she looked out of the window she could see sparks coming out of the engine and the sound was very loud. The whole trip to Roberts Field, Liberia, took about twelve and one half hours, with a one and a half hour layover in Dakar, Senegal. They were finally in Liberia! They arrived on a day that was considered a typical day during the dry season—meaning there was no rain—but the humidity was around 80 percent. The heavy clothing that they were wearing when they left England was not appropriate.

When they landed at Roberts Field Airport, there was no one to meet them. Not knowing what to do and no telephone to call anyone at that time, they engaged a taxi to take them to Monrovia which was about one hour away. They were on their way when Lottie recognized Ted Cantrell, treasurer of the Liberian Mission speeding toward Roberts Field in his little Volkswagen. They had the taxi driver turn around, but Ted was going too fast, so they didn't catch up with him until he got to the airport.

Once they arrived in Monrovia, the capital of Liberia, they were met at the mission headquarters on Camp Johnson Road by Lucius Daniels, the president of the mission and Ted's wife, Frankie Cantrell. The Cantrells lived above the mission office because their house was not yet completed.

Leland and Lottie spent the next two weeks in a whirlwind of activities in preparation for their trip and stay at the mission station in Bassa. There were so many legal things to be done such as checking in with the American Embassy, getting a separate passport for Lottie, which later proved to be providential.

During the time they spent in Monrovia, they became acquainted with many people. They made two trips to a place called Bomi Hills where iron ore was being mined. There they met a family named Flossmans. The husband was an engineer from Germany and his wife was a Seventh-Day Adventist. Lottie was very impressed by their home because they had their own power plant which provided them with electricity and running water. When they visited them the second time, they were able to get a hot bath. Oh, yes, the mission houses did not have electricity at that time. They quickly learned how to take cold showers. The Flossmans had a monkey and five cats for pets. They also visited Konola Academy. Lottie was very impressed with her first view of the academy. There were palm trees that lined the entrance drive and each was uniformly white washed about 3 feet from the ground up. Everything was so neat and orderly. They met Johnny and Ida Johnson and their nephew Bill Burns and Henry and Marilyn Reesberg, missionaries from the United States.

Elder Leland And Lottie Mitchell-Harris 1959–1963

Johnny Johnson was principal of Konola and Ida Johnson and the Reesebergs were teachers. They ended up staying the night because Lucius had a flat tire. Communication with loved ones back home was better than it was for the earlier missionaries; however, today, it is hard to imagine not having instant communication by telephone. While in Monrovia, they were able to talk to Lottie's parents and Leland's aunt over Ted Cantrell's ham radio. In order to catch them at a decent hour, they had to talk in the middle of the night, Liberian time. Ted would contact someone in the States with a phone patch who lived in a state near their people and the dispatcher would call collect to their folks. Lottie's mother could never get used to the fact that the cost was on her phone and that it was not costing them anything but a little sleep. It was wonderful to hear their voices.

There were some necessities that we had to shop for in Monrovia. Firestone Rubber Company had a rubber plantation between the airport and the city of Monrovia. They had a store for their employees with American products, so Lottie and Leland went there to get some supplies to take to Bassa. The night before leaving for Bassa, there was a dinner at a Doctor Little's house that was given by the Minister's wives union. The wives served a mixture of American food and African food, potato salad, fried plantain, carrot sticks, rice, olives, chicken and ham.

At last on Friday, November 6, 1959, they left to the place that was to be their home for the next two and one half years. They boarded a small plane loaded with as many of the things they had purchased in Monrovia as they could carry. There were four of them on the plane—the pilot of course, and Leland, Lottie, and Elder Daniels. The pilot took off toward the ocean and headed down the coast. To say the least, they were very nervous in such a small plane, but the pilot was so at ease, that they calmed down. Lottie was relieved when they landed on a dirt field in Upper Buchanan. Teacher Nolan was waiting to escort the group to the mission station in Lower Buchanan. A wonderful welcome awaited them. The school children were in the yard singing, "Thank you Pastor Daniels for bringing Pastor Mitchell here." Then they sang, "How do you do Pastor Mitchell, how do you do! Is there anything that we can do for you?"

Lottie's first impression of the house that was to be their home was one of pleasant surprise. Because of the stories she had heard all of her life, she was prepared to live with three rooms and a path, but praise the Lord, they had five rooms and a bath! Lottie was thankful for the prior missionaries who had paved the way. The Dunbar Henris were the first Americans to live in Bassa when the living conditions were somewhat primitive. The David Hughes family were the ones responsible for making the living conditions better by having the home built. Having grown up in rural Michigan, Lottie was acquainted with outdoor plumbing in her early years and thought that this was the kind of situation she was going into. Someone with an engineering mind had planned a system where they could have running water and toilets that flushed—even without electricity or a water system in the area. There was a well in the yard, and a pipe ran to a hand pump that was attached to another pipe that ran to a large concrete tank above roof level. Daily a young man from the school would spend an hour or so pumping water to fill the tank. Gravitation would then send the water into the plumbing and they had running water. An amusing incident occurred at the end of their first two and one half years. Ruby, Lottie's sister, came to visit and decided to take a shower. Once in the shower, they heard an exclamation of surprise, and she called out, "Where is the hot water?" They have laughed about this over the years.

The Mitchell's goods had not arrived from the states as yet, and their kerosene stove and refrigerator had not arrived from Monrovia. They had no way of preparing food or keeping it. One of the sisters in the church, Sister Janie Brownell, a registered dietician trained in the United States, sent them two hot meals a day. She was the main dietician at the government hospital in Lower Buchanan. She was so kind and became a good friend. Even after Leland and Lottie moved to Monrovia, and Leland had to travel, Lottie would drive to Lower Buchanan and stay with Sister Janie.

The Monday after their arrival in Bassa, the school gave a reception for them. There was singing and welcome speeches by some government officials, judges, and members of the House of Representatives, ministers, and leaders in the community. Lottie remembers well the warmth with which the people received them. Before they left the States, a farewell was given for them in Chicago and Elder Russell Bates sang, "In times like these you need a Savior." This night at the reception in Lower Buchanan one sister rose and sang the same song. It let them know that the God they serve is everywhere and that they need Him on both sides of the ocean. And, as the song says, "Our anchor holds and grips the solid rock, and that Rock is Jesus." It was amazing that the days and nights were almost evenly divided into twelve-hour periods with little variation. There is very little twilight. It was as if a large shade was slowly pulled down, and it was night. Consequently, the people would go to bed early and get up early. There were no electric lights so the daylight was advantageous. It was not unusual for someone to drop by the mission house to visit them at seven o'clock in the morning just to talk. The nights were very dark when there was no moon. But on moonlit nights, you could almost read

Elder Leland And Lottie Mitchell-Harris 1959-1963

by the moonlight. Lottie had to get used to hearing the drums. You see their arrival coincided with the Christmas season, and some of the people would celebrate on into the night—singing, dancing, and beating the drums. The sound carried for miles and it seemed eerie in the darkness of the night, but she soon got used to it.

A week after arriving in Bassa, their goods came from America. They were happy to have some things that were familiar to them. Their things had been shipped before they left St. Joseph and had gone to the Adventist headquarters by truck and then to West Africa by ship—arriving at their station almost two months later. They were surprised to find only one dish and one glass were broken. Later on Leland broke more than that chasing a bat out of the house with a broom.

Life settled into a busy routine. Leland was in charge of the Grand Bassa Station with several pastors in the interior coming to report once a month. Some of them had to walk for days to bring their offerings and reports of baptisms and deaths. Others were nearby where they could catch a truck with less walking. Sometimes their offerings were in the form of eggs or other produce. Because their house served as the headquarters for the mission, Lottie was anxious to get everything finished. The mission allotted them the money to get tile for the floors which they did themselves. Then their furniture finally arrived. Being a Home Economics major in college, Lottie put her knowledge and skills to work to make the place more homey and presentable by making curtains and cushion covers for the furniture. There were two bedrooms, a living room/dining room combination, an office and a kitchen with a small open-air back porch. There was also a full porch across the front of the house. God blessed so that they were able to screen it in with louvered windows to keep the mosquitoes and other flying insects out. Lottie was finally ready to receive guests. When the pastors came from the interior, she'd serve them a cool drink and cake or cookies. They were always so polite and pleased for anything. On the other hand, they would bring oranges and mangoes in season, and always bananas.

Their home was located on the mission compound along with the church and the school. Lottie was surprised when they attended church the first Sabbath to see the people seated to the left wearing the traditional colorful African garb, and to the right there were people dressed in European or American garb. It seemed strange and like segregation at first, but she soon realized that it was because of the Sabbath School classes and the interpretation of the sermon and also the singing which separated them. You see, the congregation was part English with an interpreter speaking Bassa. There were the traditional hymns

Precious Memories of Missionaries of Color

in English by the folk in European garb and the call and response chant type of singing by the people in the African dress. There was a mingling of the singing when some of the hymns were done in Bassa; such as "O Lord have mercy," and "Come to Jesus."

Because of the heat, there was a temptation to be less than formal in one's dress when going to church, but Lottie kept the same standard that she had grown up with. She had been taught that she should wear her best to worship the Lord, so she dressed up every week.

As has been stated before, electricity had not come to Bassa in 1959 and the humidity was around 80 percent so it was difficult to own a piano. The keys on the piano will stick and not play in high humidity. The church had an organ that you had to pump with your feet. Lottie had taken a few music lessons in college and in St. Joseph, Missouri, so she was able to make a little music on the organ. She admits that it was a challenge to make music while pumping with her feet to get the sound out while finding the right keys with her fingers. She only played when the regular organist, Sister Dunn, was not there.

Early in 1960, they were invited to Monrovia to the Inaugural Ceremonies of President W.V.S. Tubman. It was quite an event. They attended many of the parties that surrounded the event. All of the heads of the Missions were extended official invitations. Lottie especially remembers the state dinner at the presidential palace. As they arrived, they were assigned a seat partner who was not their spouse. The table setting was elegant! There were gold chargers, fine china etched in gold with the insignia of the president, gold plated flatware and fine crystal. During this time they were also invited to the American Embassy to meet the American delegation attending the inauguration. Lottie was thrilled to shake hands with such legendary leaders as Thurgood Marshall, Ralph Bunche, Andrew Young, and William O. Douglas. It was amazing how far people went to impress others with their wealth and status. One movie star attending the occasion had a fur stole rapped around her neck. Mind you the climate is mostly warm and humid, so most likely the sister was quite uncomfortable.

At the time they lived in Liberia, the heads of the religious community were welcomed and treated with much respect. They were privileged to attend many of the state affairs that were held at the executive mansion when dignitaries from other countries visited Liberia. The visit of the Queen of England was significant with all of the pomp and circumstance surrounding her visit. There was a parade for all of the people, and then Elders and their families were invited to a reception at the executive mansion. Lottie was surprised that the Queen was not as tall as she imagined. When she entered the ballroom, the

Elder Leland And Lottie Mitchell-Harris 1959–1963

guests lined up on two sides and the Queen walked between the two groups with the president at her side and Prince Philip and Mrs. Tubman walking behind. Prince Philip is a tall impressive man and one would wonder how he felt trailing behind her! Some of the women curtsied, but they were told in advance that it was not necessary if they were not used to it. Since Lottie was not accustomed to it, she opted to just smile and nod. She did not want to make international headlines by falling flat on her face. Another time, Lottie went to Monrovia to stay with Naomi Daniels, while their husbands were away at a Union meeting in Ghana. They had invitations to a reception at the executive mansion for Haile Selasse, the Emperor of Ethiopia. Lottie had heard of this man all of her life and really wanted to go to the reception. There was a dilemma, she had brought nothing to wear to such an occasion, and the reception was the next evening. She told Naomi that she was going to make a dress. They hurried downtown to the waterfront and bought some material, and came back to the house and started creating a dress. Lottie finished it about an hour before time to go to the reception. Naomi had been standing over Lottie wringing her hands and telling her that she wasn't going to be ready; however, she was and had to admit that she was looking good, and with the help of some safety pins, she was off to see the Emperor. Lottie felt like she was viewing history. Haile Selasse was not tall in stature; however, he was very impressive.

There were various methods of travel that they used to go from one point to another. The government was building a road to Grand Bassa County that was not yet complete, so everything had to go by air or surfboat. In lower Buchanan, since they did not have a car, their first method of travel was by foot. The road to Monrovia was soon completed, and they purchased a Buick Opel Station Wagon that served them well. Traveling back and forth to Monrovia at the most took about two hours, but they were sometimes on the road many hours during the rainy season. The good Lord and the Opel took them through, although they would get stuck in the mud over and over again. The road was clay and when wet it was slippery. It was not unusual to be bogged down clear to the cab of the car. Sometimes they had to go through standing water. God always sent some strong men to help push them out of the mud. One concern they always had when returning from Monrovia was to reach the St. John River before the ferry closed for the night. They were careful to leave Monrovia early enough, because there was no place to stay overnight at the river. They usually did not travel much in the rainy season, but for some reason it was necessary to make a trip to Monrovia. On the way home a terrible storm came and they were slipping and sliding in the wet clay. They heard later that two people were killed and eight were injured in the storm. It was raining so heavily…They

Precious Memories of Missionaries of Color

truly felt God's protecting hand over them. They were more careful after that about traveling on clay roads during the rainy season.

There were times when Leland had to visit the mission stations in the interior. Always some of the workers accompanied him. They would take a truck as far as possible and then would walk for hours. Sometimes he'd be gone for three or four days. He would take some provisions with him, but the people would also provide food for him. Being the adventuresome person that Lottie is, she wanted to visit and meet some of the people in the interior. So Leland made arrangements for her to go on one of the treks that was not too far away. They left early one Friday morning traveling by car for about an hour. They left the car in the care of one of the members at the nearest Mission station. They then started their walk through the jungle. Some would ask if they encountered any dangerous creatures. They did, but they were not the large kind. Actually they were ants. As they walked, they would come upon droves of driver ants crossing the road. These ants were very dangerous as they moved through the jungle killing and eating everything in their path. They were warned to be very careful, as they had to sometimes jump over colonies almost three feet wide. The people told them of having driver ants coming through their huts. They said the only thing to do was to move out and let them go through. They said after they passed through every other insect or rodent was gone. With the driver ants being the only danger that they encountered, they arrived in the village on Friday evening. The members were so glad to see her. They were so gracious and happy that the pastor had brought the "Missus" to meet and worship with them. That night they slept in a mud hut with a thatched roof. A nice clean bed of straw covered with a sheet was made for them. Lottie didn't sleep well that night, because she heard every rustle of the breeze in the roof and kept thinking about those driver ants.

Early Sabbath morning, with the sun barely up, Lottie heard a sound, the blowing of a horn. There was a brother high up in a tree, blowing the horn, telling the people in the surrounding villages that it was time to get up and to get ready to come to church. Lottie was fascinated by the horn; they gave it to her before she left. Before the time for Sabbath School to start, people were coming from all directions in their Sabbath best. This was a place where the pastor had been a Methodist minister and had studied the Bible and was convinced that Saturday was the true day of worship. He then taught his congregation and they all became members of the Seventh-day Adventist Church. They spent a wonderful day with them, having communion and baptismal services.

When one of the young pastors heard that Lottie had gone on the trek, he was very surprised. Lottie had made a pair of peddle pushers to wear because she knew that they would go through places where a dress was not good. When

Elder Leland and Lottie Mitchell-Harris 1959-1963

this young pastor heard that she had worn pants, he looked at her and said very seriously, "Pastors wives don't wear pants." She thought it was very funny, but he was so serious that she could not laugh. She always wanted to be very sure not to insult anyone because they had different ideas.

In 1961, Leland was asked by the West African Union to go to Nigeria to hold an evangelistic meeting. It was decided that they would go overland. They knew that some of the roads over which they travel in some countries were not developed and would be little more than cow paths. Nevertheless they were willing to try it. A West African constituency meeting was being held in Ghana. Elder Daniels, Leland and Sister Janie Brownell were going as delegates. The Daniels traveled in their Renault Dauphine and Leland and Lottie traveled in their Buick Opel.

Leaving early in the morning, they headed north toward Guinea. They only touched the southeast part of Guinea, before coming to Cote'd'Ivoire (The Ivory Coast). In the Ivory Coast they slept in a government house. Back in the days of colonization European countries claimed portions of Africa. The European countries that governed before independence had officials who traveled throughout the African countries they had colonized, so that they would have a suitable place to stay, they built government houses that were equipped with beds and other provisions. Missionaries were able to take advantage of these houses, too. When they arrived in Abidjan, they stopped at the Mission station and visited in the home of Pastor & Mrs. Henri Kempf from France. They stayed overnight in Abidjan and left the next morning for Ghana.

Driving was interesting! In some countries, they were driving on the left side of the road and in others on the right side. As they came to the borders of each country, they had to show their passports and state the reason they were visiting the country. They arrived in Accra, Ghana, in time for the delegates to attend their meeting. While the meetings were going on, Lottie visited with some of the missionaries' wives and did some sightseeing. After the meetings, the Daniels and Sister Brownell returned to Liberia and Leland and Lottie continued on their journey to Nigeria. The rest of the trip seemed kind of lonely after traveling with five other people. Actually from the Ivory Coast through Ghana, Togo, Benin, and Nigeria, the roads were all developed and mostly paved. Arriving in Nigeria, they passed through the city of Lagos to Ibaden where the headquarters of the West Nigerian Mission of Seventh-day Adventists was located. They met Pastor and Mrs. David Hughes who were the first ones to live in the house back in Lower Buchanan. They stayed with them for a few days while Leland took care of some business in preparation for the evangelistic meeting. After that they traveled to Ile Ife where the meetings were

Precious Memories of Missionaries of Color

to be held. Ile Ife is the home of an Adventist hospital. At that time doctors, nurses and technicians from the U.S., Finland, and England staffed it. While there they met some interesting people. One dear older nurse they became acquainted with had served with her husband in the South Sea Islands. It seems that he became ill and died suddenly. Because there were cannibals among the natives, she, along with some faithful members, had to secretly dig the grave at night and bury him. She was quite aged when Leland and Lottie met her, but she was still working for the Lord as a nurse. Lottie became friends with a young nurse from Finland who had lived in Liberia when her parents were missionaries there. She wanted to see Liberia again, so when they returned to Lower Buchanan, she came to visit them.

The evangelistic meeting was held outdoors. They built long rows of wooden benches with no backs to accommodate hundreds. There was a high platform in front with a large screen for Leland to show slides. The West African Union had engaged Sister Rosalie Jones, a Bible worker from the Northern Conference, to come and help in the effort. She was a delightful person with a wonderful sense of humor. Several Nigerian pastors were assigned to help also. They had pleasant living quarters and often took time to go swimming with some of the hospital staff.

Sister Jones was fearless. She was warned to be careful about going out alone to pass out handbills and not to let crowds of people surround her. This was said, because sometimes in their eagerness to get the literature she might get trampled. She let it be known that she was used to crowds in New York. Well, one day she failed to heed the warning and went out alone to pass out handbills. A group surrounded her pushing and grabbing for the bills and getting crushingly close to her. She panicked and threw the bills up in the air and ran. Needless to say, she never went out alone after that.

At the end of the campaign, Sister Jones organized a musical program a grand finale of the evangelistic meetings. The main number on the program was sung by the mass choir. One of the young ministers had a beautiful bass speaking voice. Sister Joes felt that she could groom him for the solo part in the hymn, "How Great Thou Art." She practiced diligently with him to keep him on key. When it was time for him to perform the night of the program, he was nowhere on pitch, but she took it in stride. When he couldn't get it right, she merely pointed to Leland and he took over the solo part without hesitation. The Lord blessed with many baptisms. The converts were baptized in the beautiful Ile Ife church that Dr. Nagle was responsible for building. During the baptismal service there was a particular tall young man to be baptized. The pool was not very long so Leland instructed him to bend his knees when the

Elder Leland And Lottie Mitchell-Harris 1959–1963

time came to put him under the water, so that he would not bump his head. He must have misunderstood, because while Leland was raising his hand and saying, "I now baptize you in the name of the Father, Son, and Holy Ghost," the young man had bent his knees and gone backward into the water by himself. Lottie noticed Leland feeling around in the water to bring the brother up. He had completely lost his grip on him. Sister Jones was standing by the pool trying to maintain her dignity. They all had a good laugh later on about the man that Leland almost lost in the baptismal pool. These were just some of the delightful times they experienced with this dedicated Bible worker.

God blessed them on that trip and Lottie has many wonderful memories of the people who treated them so graciously. While in Nigeria, they were privileged to spend some time at the newly formed Adventist College of West Africa. They returned to Liberia before the rainy season began. It did not seem that the return trip was as arduous as it had been three months earlier. For one thing, they had become a little more accustomed to driving on the left side of the road in some countries.

Upon returning to Liberia, Lottie became involved in the school, teaching art until the school year ended. That was a slow time for Leland because of the rainy season which made traveling into the interior risky.

In Flint, Michigan, God blessed them to purchase a 1953 Chevrolet in good condition. The General Conference would reimburse them for their travel that summer. They were to visit churches and camp meetings that summer and talk about the mission field. Lottie recalled attending camp meetings in Grand Ledge and Cassopolis, Michigan, as a child and how exciting it had been to see the missionaries and hear their stories of how God was spreading the gospel throughout the world, and here she was a partner in the great work.

They traveled many miles across the United States between June and September. They criss-crossed the country attending camp meetings. They started with South Central, at Oakwood College in Alabama, to Southwest Region in Texas, to Central States in Kansas, to South Atlantic in Florida, to Allegheny at Pine Forge, Pennsylvania, and to Lake Region, in Cassopolis, Michigan. After visiting with Lottie's parents for a few days, they headed for Chicago to visit Aunt Dorothy. There they met up with Teacher Nolan who was flying in from Lower Buchanan, Liberia. He would travel with them to San Francisco to the 48th General Conference Session, to which they were all delegates. Teacher Nolan was so excited to be in the United States. While they were in Liberia he had often talked of America, and how much he would like to visit. The trip in the car gave him an opportunity to see more of the land. He was so impressed when they stopped at the Grand Canyon in Arizona—and so was Lottie! At one lookout point he would not get too close to the railing. He stayed an arm's length away from the rail and said over and over, "Its wonderful It's awesome!" They stopped in Los Angeles and spent a day or two visiting some friends from college, and even went to Disneyland. While there they attended the University SDA church on Sabbath.

They left Los Angeles and drove up the coast to San Francisco. They were there for the pre-session, and all of the ten days of the conference. Teacher Nolan was very pleased with his visit and participation in the session. He carried the Liberian flag for the thrilling parade of nations in which they also took part wearing the colorful African dress. What a wonderful experience it was for the three of them to represent God's work in the Liberian Mission. They left Teacher Nolan in San Francisco for his return to Liberia, and they continued up the coast to Seattle to the World's Fair.

Lottie's oldest sister, Helen Friend, had joined them at the General Conference session and traveled back to Michigan with them. Their journey took them through Oregon where the Bing cherries were in season. They ate cherries all the way through Oregon. They spent Sabbath in Denver, Colorado, enjoying again the beautiful scenery.

They arrived in Michigan in time to help with the preparation of a double wedding in the family. Lottie's sister and brother were wed to their spouses on their father's birthday, with Leland conducting the ceremony. They spent the month of September visiting with family and preparing for their return trip to the mission field.

October found them on their way back to Liberia. This time it was arranged for them to travel by freighter to Liberia. It was just what they needed, after all of the travel across America while they were on furlough. They had actually driven through 30 of the 49 contiguous states—some more than once. The 13-day trip back to Africa began in New York. Leland's cousin, Joyce Davis and her two children, Janice and Louise, Sister Rosalie Jones, Lottie's sister, Ruby Jones, and Aunt Dorothy came to the ship to bid them bon voyage and Godspeed. The weather was quite cool crossing the Atlantic but once they got to the west coast of Africa it was warm and pleasant. Lottie concluded that in two and a half years she had become accustomed to hot weather. There were only eight passengers on the ship and they ate with the captain each evening. The food was much better than that of the Ile de France two years earlier, and the company of the other passengers was pleasant.

The members in Bassa welcomed them back and they were united with Teacher Nolan who was still on a high about his trip to America and the General Conference Session. David Whea, one of the students and the young

Elder Leland And Lottie Mitchell-Harris 1959–1963

man who helped out at the mission was still there. He had looked out for the house while they were gone, along with Barnee, the watchman, who was still on the porch with his lantern every night and sleeping. When they were on furlough, they asked Barnee what he wanted them to bring him. He told them through an interpreter that he wanted them to bring him a uniform, so they bought him some khaki pants and a shirt and Leland also gave him a pair of flannel pajamas. They kept waiting for him to wear the uniform,; instead he would come out in the pajamas. Finally David told them that some of the older people would put some of their nicer things in a trunk or a box and when they died, people will look at what they had and say that he was not a poor man. Maybe Barnee preferred the flannel pajamas because they kept him warm as he sat in the wicker chair to do his watching as he slept all night. They knew that he was sleeping, instead of walking around, but his presence there kept predators away.

Barnee was a very pleasant man who was very amused when Lottie tried to speak the Bassa language. Through an interpreter he related to them how he came to be a Seventh-day Adventist Christian. He had gone hunting with some relatives and they had wounded a bush cow. He said that the bush cow is very smart. After wounding the animal they started tracking it, but the bush cow had backed up into the bush in its own tracks and when they got near, it attacked. Barnee showed them the scars where the bush cow gored him with its horns down his side and leg. He was taken to a clinic that was run by Christian nurses, and they were so kind to him showing him the love of Christ, that when he got better, he decided to become a Christian, too. Later when he learned about the Sabbath truth, he joined the Seventh-day Adventist Church.

The people in Lower Buchanan were concerned that Leland and Lottie had no children. Barnee and his wife brought their granddaughter to them. She was a pretty child around six years old. Their hearts went out to her, but upon questioning the grandparents they found out that they were only to raise her and school her, that she would never be theirs to legally adopt, which was their desire. Lottie knew in her heart that when they would eventually leave the mission field, it would be difficult to leave the child. They had long thought about adopting a child, but other things came into play at that time.

Early in 1963 Leland was appointed president of the Liberian Mission and also pastor of the Monrovia church, so they packed, again, and moved to Monrovia. In reality they moved into one of the two mission houses in Sincor, right outside of Monrovia. The Daniels who preceded them had move to Nigeria. Brother Lee, the mission treasurer lived in the other house with his wife. They were from England and previously served in Sierra Leone. The setting was

Precious Memories of Missionaries of Color

beautiful. The house had three bedrooms, two baths (with cold water), living room, dining room, kitchen, and an attached garage. Pastor Maurice Battle, a former president of the Liberian mission, was responsible for building these homes. They were near the Atlantic Ocean and at night they could hear the waves crashing on the shore, especially during the rainy season. They had no watchman there, but there were bars set in concrete in the windows. They only had one incident of a break in. On returning from church one Sabbath, they found that someone had bent the bars in the dining room windows at an angle wide enough to break the window and enter and had stolen something like a radio, not much, but they assumed that they had been looking for money.

Leland settled into his duties as president of the Liberian Mission, which involved quite a bit of traveling. Lottie was in charge of the Bible Correspondence School in the office on a part time basis. Whenever the brethren came to visit from the General Conference Office in Washington, DC, the Northern European Division, or the West African Union headquarters in Ghana, they entertained them in their home. So they were kept quite busy. Lottie enjoyed entertaining these gentlemen who brought news from the worldwide work of the church and sometimes news from home.

The Mitchell's thoughts again turned to children and they actively began searching for a child to adopt. They visited many orphanages, thinking that this would be the logical place to start. To our surprise, they found out that because they were run by various religious organizations, they did not want to give the children up to be raised in the home of people of another religious persuasion. They searched many avenues. Then, one day, a nurse in their church told them about twin boys who had been brought to the Baptist hospital in Monrovia. The mother had died in childbirth and the father had walked from Careysberg, a distance of several miles, to bring the twins to the hospital. They went to see them when they were three weeks old, and started proceedings to adopt. They ended up with one of the boys and nurse who worked in the hospital adopted the other boy. They named their son Leon Barrett Mitchell. It was ever in Lottie's heart that these two boys would meet again. It did happen, but that is another story by itself, to be told in a later writing.

Lottie's duties increased as of August 18, 1963 when they brought Leon home at six weeks of age. He was a scrawny little boy weighing about six pounds, but with love and good care he rapidly grew. The people in the church took such delight in his growth. The Liberian people had a way of saying, "feed the baby until his belly shines," and they did. Elder Maurice Battle, who was an official in the West African Union, was visiting Liberia, and they asked him to conduct the dedication service for Leon in the Monrovia church on

Elder Leland and Lottie Mitchell-Harris 1959–1963

September 13, 1963. Thirty-five years later on March 21, 1998, Elder Battle dedicated Leon's son Leland Kouami Mitchell to the Lord on this side of the Atlantic Ocean at Dupont Park Church in Maryland.

The latter part of the year of 1963 was a busy one. Leland held an evangelistic meeting in the Monrovia church in November. Upon arriving at the church one night, the Deputy Chief of Protocol, who was a member of their church, met them at the steps telling them that they had his sympathy. Lottie thought that he was teasing because she was bringing the baby out each night, but he said, "Haven't you heard that your president John F. Kennedy has been shot?" When you are miles away from home it seems as if some things hit you harder. They were in shock!

Leon became officially theirs when they met with his birth father with a lawyer and signed the adoption papers on February 13, 1964. This was a joyous occasion. It seems that sometimes when good things happen in one's life, tragedy follows. In April of 1964, Lottie received word by cable that her sister, Pauline Jones Taylor, had finished preparing for the Sabbath one Thursday night and went to sleep that night and did not wake up. She left behind her husband and three young children. Lottie was devastated and wanted to go home for the funeral, but they did not have the resources and the General Conference would not have paid her way in that day. Lottie cried her heart out in the yard. Leland kept telling her that she was only going to make herself sick. She felt such a separation from her family at that time, but she did not know that God was preparing her for a greater separation. With God's help, Lottie consoled herself with the fact that all of her siblings had lived to adulthood, and they were still blessed. As president of the Liberian Mission, Leland was frequently called to different parts of West Africa for committee meetings. He was also away from home visiting other areas in Liberia. In June, the officers of the West African Union asked him to conduct a Week of Prayer at Bekwai School in Ghana. Upon returning home he showed Lottie a lump on the left side of his face. He had suffered through the years with ingrown hairs that formed bumps when he shaved. They thought that this was the case, but as they explored it, this was not so. Leland went to a doctor who had trained at Meharry School of Medicine in Tennessee. The doctor performed a biopsy and they anxiously awaited the result. The report came back that the lump was malignant. It was the only time throughout his illness that Leland broke down. Truly, their faith in God was being tested. They cried and prayed for God's healing. There was still so much superstition among some of the people in Liberia. They felt that Leland should have returned to the United States for the biopsy. The doctor advised that he should return home for treatment.

Precious Memories of Missionaries of Color

While this was going on in their lives, they celebrated Leon's first birthday. Then another bombshell hit them. Leland received a cable from a play aunt (not a biological aunt) in Chicago stating that his deceased mother's sister, Dorothy Smith, a Bible Worker, who had been his mentor was dying of cancer. She encouraged him to come home to see to her affairs. Dr. Cooper had wanted him to go to New York to the Cancer Research Center, but in light of his aunt's illness, he opted to go to Hinsdale Seventh-day Adventist Hospital in Illinois, where his aunt was being treated.

Leland returned to Chicago in the latter part of July, 1963 and began therapy at Hinsdale. When the doctors told him that the cancer had spread, the General Conference advised that they should come home on medical leave. When informed of this decision, Lottie faced a monumental task. All of their household goods except furniture (which belonged to the mission) were to be packed in barrels, boxes, and trunks. Whenever a family is on furlough they have to pack as if they are not returning, so that no one else has to do this in case the trip becomes permanent. Having adopted Leon for not quite a year, Lottie had to obtain a passport for him, because he was still a Liberian citizen. Thank God that Leland and she had gotten separate passports earlier when he had to travel so much and leave her at home. In obtaining a passport for Leon, he had to go through a series of painful shots because he was coming to the United States for the first time and he was a native Liberian. Lottie felt so sorry for him. The car had to be sold. There were so many things to wind up, but she found out again, that no matter the circumstances, God is in control.

He sent an angel to help Lottie. A lady from California had sold her nursing home and came to Liberia desiring to open a nursing home there. She gave no advance warning; she just showed up and said she was a Seventh-day Adventist. Lottie took the lady home with her without hesitation. She was a seamstress, and helped her to make some clothes to travel in; she helped her pack along with the Brysons, a teaching couple at Konola Academy. The lady bought the car because she needed transportation, and she stayed in the house after Lottie left to finish packing and disposing of some items when they found out that they were not returning to Liberia.

Leon and Lottie finally left Liberia in August on KLM Royal Dutch Airlines. They had an overnight stop in Amsterdam. Leon cried most of the way to Amsterdam, except when he was sucking on his bottle. The flight attendant said that his ears where probably bothering him. On the second day of the trip, Lottie was so looking forward to seeing Leland again. She told Leon, "I'm going to put you in your daddy's arms when we get to Chicago." How disappointed she was when they arrived at O'Hare and there was no one there to meet them.

Elder Leland And Lottie Mitchell-Harris 1959-1963

She called the home of the pastor of Shiloh Church, and he said that Leland was out getting flowers for Aunt Dorothy's funeral. She had died while they were on their way. Leland finally arrived and Lottie was able to keep her promise to Leon and put him in his daddy's arms. Actually that went for both of them. The next two days were a blur, spent in preparation for the funeral. Lottie had no appropriate clothes, so she had to go shopping for a dress and help make arrangements for housing for the family that was coming from out of town.

They didn't have much time to discuss Leland's illness during those few days because they were so busy. After everything was over they turned their attention to their own problems. In consultation with the doctors at Hinsdale Sanitarium and Hospital, they found out that Leland had an aggressive form of cancer of the lymphatic system, which was to eventually affect many parts of his body. During the time that he had been home, he had developed a nodule over his left eye and the doctors had started radiation treatments. They did not give them much hope for a full recovery unless God would perform a miracle. They prayed to that end, all of the time not letting go of the hope that they would return to the mission field. They still had hope, but the Brethren at the General Conference recommended that they should apply for permanent return to the States.

They stayed in Aunt Dorothy's apartment for the next few months. Leland was able to travel back and forth to the hospital for outpatient treatment. On weekends, they visited various churches in the area with Leland preaching and singing solos. One of his favorite songs was JESUS IS ALWAYS THERE. In spite of the circumstance, they knew those words to be true.

On a Sunday near the last of January, Leland went to the bathroom and Lottie heard this loud "thud." His legs had given out and he had fallen and could not use his legs to get up. With the help of God and her adrenalin, she was able to get him up and into bed. He was taken back to Hinsdale Hospital. The doctors assessed that the cancer had traveled into his spine, thus taking away his ability to use his legs. They then accepted the fact that it was not God's will for them to return to Liberia. He had other plans for their future.

Lottie began staying at her sister Gwendolyn Smith's home. They invited her to stay there so that her brother-in-law, who worked in the evenings, could watch Leon while she visited Leland in the hospital, which was several miles away. About 3:00 a.m. one Monday morning, Lottie was wide awake. It seemed as if she had clearly heard Leland call her name. Elder Myers, pastor of the Shiloh Church called and told her that the hospital had been trying to reach her to let her know that Leland had begun hemorrhaging from the brain about 3:33 a.m. and was in a coma. She went to the hospital and stayed with him until

Precious Memories of Missionaries of Color

Thursday night. The bleeding seemed to have stopped, and he seemed to be resting peacefully. Lottie was getting dressed to go back to the hospital Friday morning when her friend Jackie who was working at the hospital called her and told her that Leland had quietly slipped away. She was devastated that she had not been there. But the words of this song that Leland sang are always true:

> Sometimes our skies are cloudy and dreary
> Sometimes our hearts are burdened with care
> Whether the days may be cloudy or dreary
> Jesus is always there
>
> Never a burden that He does not carry
> Never a sorrow that He does not share
> Whether the days may be sunny or dreary
> Jesus is always there.

Africa? Almost fifty years later, it is still exciting to think about it and Lottie thanks God for the experience and the privilege of serving Him. It has broadened her culturally and most of all spiritually. It has given her a larger family than her blood family, because she has kept in touch with friends made

Elder Leland And Lottie Mitchell-Harris 1959–1963

while serving the Lord there. Her son Leon is ever a reminder of the country of Liberia and she thanks God for him, he is a good son. Lottie can still remember attending camp meetings in Grand Ledge, Michigan, and Cassopolis and listening to the missionaries who served the Lord in foreign lands. She never knew then that she would grow up and marry a minister and that they would also be called to serve Him in another country. Africa? It was a privilege to go there in the name of the Lord.

Precious Memories of Missionaries of Color

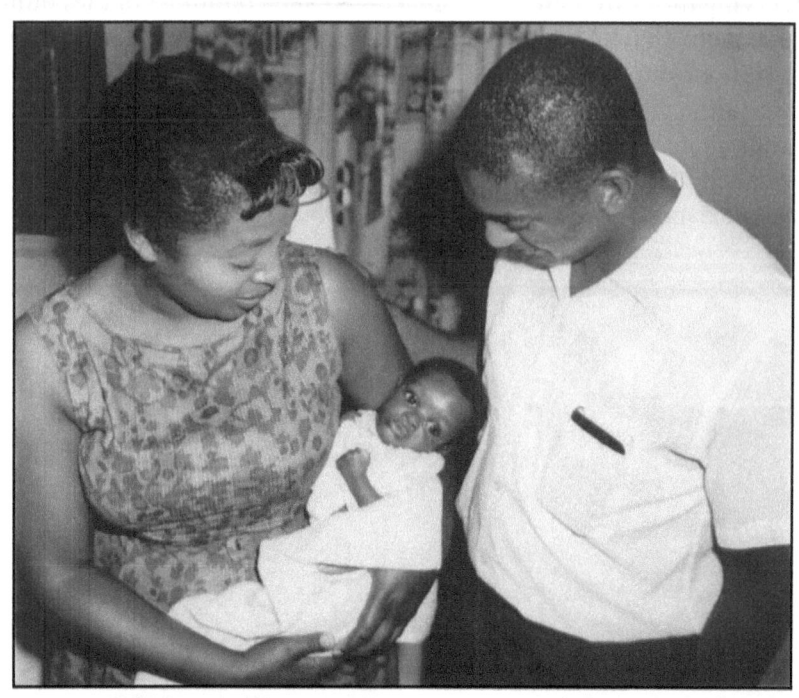

Top: The Mitchells with baby Leon
Elder Ted Cantrell, the Mitchells & Elder Lucius Daniels
The Mitchells in Nigeria

16

Dr. Samuel & Bernice DeShay
1961–1973

The DeShays were originally scheduled to go to Ghana when they left New York on the Queen Elizabeth, Cunard Lines in 1961. When they reached England, five days later the assignment had changed. They were being sent to Nigeria on Air France through Tunis. From there they flew to Kano, Nigeria, and on to Lagos, where they were met by other long term missionaries from Ife, Nigeria. They worked in West Africa from September 1961 to May, 1973. This was during the period of the Biafran conflict within the country of Nigeria which took many lives during the civil war that took place there.

The fighting during the war took place less than 80 miles away from their hospital at Ahoada in Rivers State in Nigeria. Dr. and Mrs. Cyril Hartman and Mrs. DeShay traveled out to Aba, Nigeria, to purchase supplies for the hospital. There had been some unrest because many of the people from the north were living in the area near the hospital. This represented conflict due to the rising animosity between the peoples from the two regions. Dr. DeShay was alone at the hospital in terms of overseas professional staff.

A lorry pulled up to the hospital filled with wounded persons attacked that day by bands of self-styled soldiers who decided to get even with those in the area who represented the factions from the north of the country. They were badly injured and bruised. They needed bones set, lacerations repaired, and intravenous fluids given, and much more.

When the word got out that these northern peoples were being treated at the Adventist Hospital at Ahoada, a band of armed men, about fifty in number started for the hospital to attack these injured men again, and ensure that they would not get away alive. The Chaplain's wife ran up to Dr. DeShay crying bitterly to do something because these armed men were almost at the hospital gate, and that they must not be allowed to enter the hospital. Later, one of the nurses became very agitated and she too insisted that they must do something immediately because the armed men were approaching the hospital—they needed to do something to protect themselves and the patients. One of the nurses suggested that they lock the hospital with all the patients inside, and see if that would deter the armed mob who was determined to enter the institution. So, they locked the doors and windows and waited.

Finally the mob arrived at the gate of the hospital. Dr. DeShay and the hospital staff had to make an effort to meet with them to see what they wanted. DeShay finally decided to go out and meet with the mob to see just what they were demanding. He decided to speak roughly to them to let them know they were not afraid.

"We understand that you are treating the wounded enemies brought to you by the police vehicles today. We do not want them to be treated. We have come to kill them right here and now." Dr. DeShay responded, "this is a Seventh-day Adventist Hospital, and that hospitals are neutral ground in war. This is not the place for battle, and this Christian hospital is here to offer help to the wounded of any country or persuasion. We are not here to kill or allow anyone to be killed while in our care. You cannot enter this hospital under any circumstances."

They replied that they would enter, and that they would be killing these people today. One of the Senior Chiefs then came and stood by Dr. DeShay's side and pleaded with them to calm down and stop this activity. Without restraint they lunged forward as if to force themselves into the hospital building.

Dr. DeShay looked into the mob and saw a young man who had been in need some time before, and had come to him to ask for help. Dr. DeShay had given him money and help at the time and had forgotten the occasion. When he saw this man in the mob, he immediately walked into the mob, placed his hand on the shoulder of this young man, and spoke sternly to him. "Young man, you should be ashamed of yourself out here with this group of murderers. God forbid that you should do this. I am so disappointed with you today."

Dr. DeShay then said to the mob, "Since you are determined, I shall stand in front of the doorway to the hospital." No one moved! Some made a feeble gesture to lunge forward, but then backed away. After a time they gradually began to fade away. After retreating a short distance, they turned and made a threat, "Dr. DeShay, we are going away now, but we will be back during the night, and we will finish this job!"

Dr. Samuel & Bernice DeShay 1961-1973

They turned and left at that point. Dr. DeShay collapsed at that time, and then got into his car and drove as fast as he could to the police station to relay the message that the mob had left. The Chief of Police immediately dispatched a large number of police to guard the hospital at gun point every eight hours around the clock for nearly a month until the animosity had settled down.

No one could believe that Dr. DeShay had done this. The Baptist missionaries came to see him because they were afraid. When their fellow Adventist missionaries returned to the hospital and found it surrounded by police and all of the excitement and activity that had incurred, they, too, were surprised.

About two weeks later, the young man whom Dr. DeShay had helped came to the doctor's house and sat in the garage early in the morning waiting for the doctor to come out. When Dr. DeShay alighted from the doorway, the young man met him and exclaimed, "I have sinned greatly, and I am sorry. I have done wrong, I want you to pray for me that God will forgive me for the things I have done and the people I have injured. Please, Dr. pray for me now." After prayer he said, "I want you to know that I am genuine. No one will feed these people. They have to be fed by only you or the people will kill them. Even though my life will be in danger, I want you to allow me to feed them from henceforth. This is to show you that I am repenting of what I have done."

For the next three weeks that young man came daily, and fed those people even though many considered this a bad thing to do. They thanked God and praised Him for what He had done! This was a bright spot in the war!

Dr. Samuel & Bernice DeShay with Joy

17

Drs. James & Carol Hammond
1961–1974

When Carol was ten years old, Elder and Mrs. C. D. Henri visited her church in Knoxville, Tennessee. They shared their experiences as missionaries in the faraway continent of Africa. They wore the indigenous national costumes for Ghana. Elder Henri wore the beautiful kente cloth, which was a symbol of royalty in Ghana. The cloth was hand-woven with many different colors. The concepts of Africa that Carol had were thatched roof houses, elephants, and lions running around and people with less than nothing on. At the close of Elder and Mrs. Henri's presentation, her concept of Africa changed drastically. She learned that elephants and lions for the most part were in zoos very much like in the United States. She was impressed at how much the Henris loved the country and the people of Africa. They planted the desire in the hearts of those who listened to become a missionary some day. It was on this day that the commitment to be used by God in Africa or wherever He chose to send her was made.

At the age of 10, how this dream would be realized was nowhere in sight; however, Carol trusted God to work it out. It was easy to trust God and allow Him to work out His plan for her life at this age. God kept her through the teenage years, by keeping ever before her the commitment she made as a child. Even in college, Carol took French as one of her major concentrations so that she would be prepared to go to a French speaking country should God desire. Now she can understand more each day why God expects us to have and exemplify a child-like faith. It was this constant and persistent faith that in later years helped her to realize her dream of someday going to Africa to be a missionary.

Drs. James & Carol Hammond 1961–1974

Thirteen years later, Carol met James M. Hammond, the man who would later become her husband. He, like Carol, had this burning desire to serve in Africa as a missionary. After a year and a half, they were married, and a year later they received a call to go to Bekwai, Ghana, in 1961. Many thanks to Elder Maurice Battle, the call was sent to the General Conference with their names on it. This was the glorious opportunity they had been praying for. To God be the glory!

Several months later, they found out that they were expecting their first child. After checking with several persons as to the feasibility of having a baby in Ghana, they felt comfortable with God's leading. Carol's parents, however, felt somewhat uneasy about her traveling, but put their trust and faith in God.

The next thing they knew, they were on the Queen Elizabeth sailing for England. After five days of eating, sleeping, and enjoying the activities provided on the ship, they arrived in London. While in London, they went to Buckingham Palace to see the changing of the guard, and crossed the London Bridge, a childhood dream. From London, they took Ghana Airways to Accra. They will always remember disembarking from the plane, which felt as though they were entering a sauna. It didn't take long for them to adjust to the warm, humid air that surrounded them.

Accra was an interesting place with people wearing colorful dresses, robes, as well as European and western dress. The streets and sidewalks were filled with people from all walks of life walking to and from the shops, banks, supermarkets, post offices, and government buildings. Cars and lorries (small trucks) driving on the left side of the street initially gave them a fright. There were no grass huts, dirt roads, or elephants roaming the streets! Wow! How different from Carol's previous concept of Africa!

Once in Accra, they headed for the West African Union Mission. The homes, office buildings, and grounds at the Union office were well kept. There were flowers and fruit trees (bananas, mangoes, papaya, etc.) that dressed the gardens. After seeing the well-kept and immaculate homes, they were really curious as to how their home would look. The missionaries residing in Accra treated them royally. Three delicious meals every day at different homes were the order of the day. Before leaving for their place of abode, they were given a tour of the city which included the American Embassy. The embassy is a good place to be aware of when you are so far away from home. They were also taken to the supermarkets, which were at that time filled with exports from Europe and America.

After being in Accra for several days, they traveled to Bekwai. Bekwai is a small town and the name for the compound for the secondary school and teacher training college for the Seventh-day Adventist churches in the area. Upon their arrival at Bekwai, they were taken to the home of Dick and Jean Jordan. Dick

Precious Memories of Missionaries of Color

was the Principal of the Teacher Training College and Jean taught in the secondary school. They received a repeat performance and for the next three or four days, they were fed three meals a day at the home of each missionary. At that time there were at least six or seven expatriate missionaries on the compound. James was called to be the Science teacher at the training college.

The home that they so anxiously awaited to see exceeded their expectations. They had three bedrooms, a large dining and living room area and a full bath. There was just one small problem; they had deep pink walls, red furniture and burgundy cement floors. The problem was easily corrected with some cream paint. Little did they know at the time that this would be their home for the next seven years! Later, James and Carol put tile on the cement floors after a quick lesson from a fellow missionary named Hartley Berlin.

Their first daughter was born in Kumasi, which was twenty-three miles from Bekwai, and the second largest city in Ghana. Carol's doctor was a Ghanaian who was trained in America. His clinic, called Allen Clinic, was standard for Africa. He provided her with a private room, which had screens and a toilet, which was somewhat an upgrade to other parts of the clinic. They praise God that all went well with the delivery. Their daughter, who they named Endea, was beautiful and healthy weighing seven and one-half pounds. As with most parents, she was the prettiest, most perfect child to be found on earth. They truly believe that children are a gift from God.

When they arrived at Bekwai, they learned that the college church needed an organist and a choir director. One of the highlights of Carol's experiences was as director of the college choir. When Endea was born, the choir marched to their home and serenaded her with songs and gifts of chickens, eggs, and other items from their gardens. They shall always remember and appreciate the choir's hospitality. This was a tradition that they came to appreciate.

During the hours that Endea slept, Carol taught English at the Bekwai secondary school. It was here that Carol had the privilege of teaching Elder Matthew Bediako who presently serves as Executive Secretary of the Adventist World Headquarters of the Seventh-day Adventist Church in Silver Spring, MD. He is also the first African to hold this position.

When Carol discovered that she was pregnant with their second child, they felt comfortable having the same doctor deliver the baby. Unfortunately, there were complications and the baby died after ten hours. They owe a bit of gratitude to Dr. Jan and Kari Paulsen who helped them get through this experience. Jan conducted the funeral for the baby and Kari became the sister away from home. They look forward to being reunited with this baby one day.

In time, they sought to have a playmate for Endea. In consultation with the doctor, Dr. John Bilson, they elected to have this child in the states. Melleri

Drs. James & Carol Hammond 1961-1974

Renata was born at the Hinsdale Sanitarium in Hinsdale, Illinois. Their doctor, a female Seventh-day Adventist by the name of Dr. Semincova, who had served as a missionary, gave them her services free of charge. We give God the praise!

One of the days to be remembered during their stay at Bekwai, Ghana was the day that Dr. Kwame Nkrumah was ousted from leadership as President of Ghana. In many ways, it was frightening in that they were afraid to leave their homes. Rumors were spreading that the rebels had spies even among their students. News on the radio was scanty and very solemn music took the place of the lively music they were accustomed to hearing. They heard that the statue of Kyame Nkrumah had been broken into pieces and the military walked the streets with guns. This went on for several days, and then they experienced the calm before the storm.

Prior to the coup, students were required to participate in activities (similar to our Pathfinders) where students were to pay homage to Mr. Nkrumah. Students sang songs such as "I will make you fishers of men, if you follow me." This song as we know it, pays homage to God, however, Nkrumah referred to himself. Children marched through the streets in uniforms similar to the pictures they have seen of the Nazis. These children were indoctrinated to seek first the political kingdom of Nkrumah. Spies were placed in their schools and even in our churches.

Eventually they began to see less of certain foods (imported ones) in the stores. When they first arrived in Ghana, they enjoyed imported foods from different places in Europe and a few things from other countries. In order to survive, they learned to substitute and enjoy many of the local foods. They also saw an increase in the number of beggars on the street. This was a difficult time not only for the missionaries but for the indigenous people as well. They thank God for his protection and care for them during this difficult period.

While James was chair of the Science Department at the Teacher's College at Bekwai, Ashanti, Ghana, he decided on an adventure of evangelism and building churches. In a certain village, everything about the church was completed except for putting on the roof. The members promised to raise the money on the weekend if he advanced the cash. So that the church could be completed, he ventured to spend the food money for the month. At the appointed time the membership was not able to repay the money he advanced for the iron sheets. As a result, he had to go to the next town to obtain money from friends in order to keep the family afloat. In this instance, as he let God guide him through this experience, it taught him how to understand God's purpose for his life and the life of the people with whom he was working. Today, this is a thriving well-kept church that has its own bank account for maintenance and repairs. With the help of donations from friends and God sustaining them, James was able to build five churches during their stay in Ghana.

In the village of Ankasi in Ghana, James had the privilege of building a church. He traveled to the village at 5:00 A.M. to get the work started and returned to Bekwai Teachers College to start teaching at 8:00 A.M. On one of his trips to the village, James met a young man who attended church occasionally and had been invited to join the baptismal class. He indicated that he would. In the afternoon, James visited some of his Amoaful members at the hospital in Bekwai. While walking on the ward, he passed the bed of the same young man he had invited to join the baptismal class in the morning in Ankasi. He had climbed a coconut tree during the day to collect coconuts and had fallen from the tree crashing his chest. He never regained consciousness. He later died and James did the eulogy after obtaining permission from the family. It pays to do what the Lord requires of us today. Tomorrow is not promised to any of us. We cannot tell what a day will bring. As in the case just cited, it is important to do what the Lord requires of us today.

In one of the churches that James built, they were asked to conduct the first Vacation Bible School held in the area. Carol teamed up with one of the teacher's wives at Bekwai named Mrs. Dadzie and they had a very successful Vacation Bible School. The church was packed day after day for one week with smiling and grateful children wanting to learn of God's love for them. The magnitude of its influence on the children who attended can only be known by God! They were grateful for the opportunity to share the love of Jesus with the children.

A person born on Saturday in Ghana is usually named Kwame. Kwamendada is God's day; Kwasiada is the Sun's day. Long before the Europeans came to Christianize the Gold Coast, (now Ghana) the people of this nation worshiped on Saturday. It was the European who tried to convert the Sabbath keepers to Sunday keepers.

In the 1960's James was asked to go to the University of Science and Technology to intercede on behalf of two Seventh-day Adventist students who chose to serve God rather than man. They requested permission to take their final examination for their bachelor's degree on a day other than Saturday. The invigilators or examiners refused to give them permission to do so. James appealed to the authorities on their behalf. James suggested that they be locked up in the University jail all day Saturday night or Sunday under the supervision of a European Seventh-day Adventist professor on one of the faculties at the University or under armed guards. Unfortunately, his plea fell on deaf ears; however, the students decided to obey God and observe the Holy Sabbath rather than to obey and serve man.

Drs. James & Carol Hammond 1961-1974

After seven years at Bekwai, James received a call to be the President of the Sierra Leone mission. Elder Dennis and Dorothy Keith were already in Bo to welcome them. Dennis served as Secretary-Treasurer of the mission and the Hammonds received a warm welcome from them. When they arrived in Bo, Carol was pregnant with their fourth child, Rona Miata. When they learned that Dr. Samuel and Bernice Deshay were at the Masanga Leprosarium, eight miles away, they felt comfortable having their daughter being born in Sierra Leone. The roads to Masanga were not super highways; consequently, they traveled several weeks before the due date to avoid any mishaps. For reasons that were not immediately apparent to them, Rona didn't want to come and Carol went beyond the due date. Dr. DeShay tried inducing Carol to no avail. After some time, it was decided that she should have a Cesarean in the theater (operating room) in the Leprosy hospital. It was then discovered that she had two placentas and that one was blocking the baby's entrance into the world. Dr. and Mrs. DeShay nursed Carol back to health for which they will be eternally grateful. Whenever, they needed a refuge, the Masanga Leprosarium was the place.

While serving as superintendent of the Sierra Leone Mission, James had under his care nineteen primary schools. During one of his usual rounds, James came upon a school that had boards at the doorway to keep the chickens and pigs out. There were holes in the walls for windows or shutters, but no windows existed. Realizing it was an awkward situation for learning or for an increase in knowledge to take place, he ordered their carpenter and mason to go to the school at once to put in doors and windows. He did not know any of the students by name, but he knew that they were there to learn. It was his hope that some increased their knowledge to live in fellowship with Him, for the more we learn, the more we honor Him.

Shortly after taking the leadership of the Mission in Sierra Leone, James discovered that three churches needed to be completed. But, the mission was not financially healthy to complete them. A workers retreat was held at Masanga Hospital at the behest of the DeShays. There was spiritual refreshing, good food, volleyball, and fellowship with all of the fraternal workers (missionaries) in the country. On a voluntary basis, they appealed to the overseas workers to give one week's salary and the national workers to give 2 1/2 day's salary to complete the churches. They all gave and the churches were completed. To God be the glory. As of this writing, some of the expatriate and national workers who made that sacrifice now rest until Christ returns.

The Hammond's fifth child was born after they left Sierra Leone, and James was asked to serve as President of the mission in Tamale, North Ghana. Fortunately the baby was born while James was on study leave to complete his doctorate at Southern Illinois University. James received both his Doctor of Philosophy degree and a son, James Jr. in 1972. With his birth, they fully agreed that this would complete their family structure. Their long-awaited son James Jr. was born in Marion, Illinois, and was delivered by Dr. Bullock.

Recently while going through some materials for a Bible study, James discovered a flyer he had used in an evangelistic campaign in Bogatanga. They prayed for a good harvest of souls. Things appeared to be moving slowly towards their goal. On a Sunday night, the subject was Adam's mother's birthday. Seventy-seven persons made decisions for Christ. Monday night under the topic, "Do fortune tellers know the future?" forty-two persons made decisions for Christ. The Lord heard their prayers. The campaign ended with a large baptism—in fact, one of the largest in our ministry. The church became the second largest church in the North Ghana Mission. Evangelist C. A. Lombart and E. K. Asante were in prayer during these meetings and witnessed the power of prayer.

After two years of service, the Hammonds completed their tour of duty in Tamale, North Ghana. As did many wives of missionaries, Carol had as one of her jobs the daily teaching of her children through Home Study International. Being a professional teacher helped tremendously with this task. When they returned home in 1974, Endea was in the seventh grade, Renata was in the fourth, Rona was in a half-day kindergarten and James Jr. was two years old.

A dear friend of Carol's, Kay G. Carter provided care for their two younger ones while Carol worked. Her first job upon their return was at Columbia Union College as the loan supervisor. During this time, Carol completed her elementary certification and later accepted a job to teach at Sligo Adventist School in grade five. Carol held this position for twenty-two years retiring only to complete her dissertation for her Ph.D. in 1998.

Presently, their eldest, Endea Thibodeaux-Artis is married to Anthony Artis and is the mother of three children: Darius, Aron and Aliyah (twins). Renata is married to Julian Craig, M.D. and they have two children: Hayley Dawn, and Julian, Jr. Rona is married to Vincent Smith and they have three children: Vincent, Jr., Miata and Sierra. Their youngest, James M. Hammond, Jr. is married to Anita Harewood Hammond and they have two children: Jada and Sydnie. The Hammonds praise God for their children and grandchildren!

They thank God for the gift of children and for keeping them safe and well during those years. They were fortunate that they were really never seriously sick with malaria during their stay in Africa despite the fact that when they had a blood test, malaria showed up. They thank God for giving them the privilege to serve as missionaries in Africa!

Drs. James & Carol Hammond 1961–1974

One of five churches built by Pastor Hammond with the help of
donations from friends in America

Precious Memories of Missionaries of Color

Liala Paulsen and Endea. Dresses made by Mrs. Paulsen

Some Ghanaian beauties! (Standing in front of church in Accra)

Drs. James & Carol Hammond 1961–1974

Renata's first birthday party. Faculty members' children on the compound at Bekwai Teacher Training and Secondary School.

Bekwai S.D.A. Secondary School

Precious Memories of Missionaries of Color

Dedication of church in Ghana

Massanga Leprosy Hospital: Pastor Hammond praying dedicatory prayer while Elder Dennis Keith and Dr. Samuel DeShay and others bow in prayer.

Drs. James & Carol Hammond 1961–1974

Dr. & Mrs. J. D. Johnson and Drs. James & Carol Hammond
Afriyie, Endea and Renata in Bekwai, Ghana

Endea's first birthday. Laila Paulsen with brother.

Precious Memories of Missionaries of Color

Front row: Pastor Mabena, Mrs. Bediako, Mrs. Ann Troy. (Second row) Pastor Owen Troy. Pastor Bediako, Dr. James Hammond in the rear.

Principal O. Gjertsen handing over the keys to the new Principal E. K. Boateng at Bekwai, Ghana

Drs. James & Carol Hammond 1961-1974

West African Union Constituency Meeting

Pastors (Sierra Leone) and Administrators of the West African Union of S.D.A.

Precious Memories of Missionaries of Color

Children's Choir in Tamale, North Ghana

Drs. James & Carol Hammond 1961-1974

James & Anita Hammond ; Jada & Sydnie

Back row left: Dawn Craig, (Julian's sister), Renata, Julian, Jr. (in front of Renata) and Julian, Sr., Darius, Anthony and Endea. Carol, Aron, James Sr. Hayley and Aliyah.

Vincent & Rona Smith
Vincent, Jr., Sierra & Miata

18

CAROL ANN JONES 1962-1966

Carol served at the Ethiopian Adventist College as clinic nurse for the mission compound, the community, and as dean of girls. She served at the Taferi Makonnen Hospital as Matron (Director of Nursing). This facility increased from 20 beds to 100 beds overnight when Ethiopia changed from driving on the left side of the road, as they do in England, to the right side, as we do in the United States.

The hospital was located in Dessie in the Wallo Province which is located at the top of a mountain. Apparently, a large truck collided with a highway department truck which was transporting workers and their families to another location when the collision occurred. They admitted over 50 severely injured women, children, and men.

Two nights later another accident occurred between a large truck and a bus. Again they admitted far over their capacity until they were able to transfer some of the injured to the other hospital in town the next day.

Dessie is located at the zenith of the mountain. The scenery surrounding the mission compound is breathtaking. They could look to the east of our compound and see Monkey Mountain where several nationals and Carol would hike on Sabbath afternoons. It was always enjoyable and most relaxing to sit there and watch the monkeys play around them.

Once a month the physician assigned to the compound, Carol, and several of their Dressers (vocational nurses) would hold clinic in the Danakil desert. These trips were always exciting and interesting. The variety of maladies they treated was staggering—one never knew what would walk in the door. The

Precious Memories of Missionaries of Color

clinic sessions were conducted after the sun went down because the desert was unbearably hot in the day and it was impossible to do any work during the daylight. They would try to sleep so that they could work all night. However, very little sleep was accomplished. The nationals who traveled with them would keep the floor wet to cool the house so that they could sleep. The one redeeming factor was that they knew night would come and it would be extremely cold. They found it easier to cope with the cold than they could with the heat. It was always amazing to look out over the dessert at sundown and see people coming from kilometers around over the white sand. Traveling to the clinic they would drive for kilometers and not see a house and maybe only one or two people with their camels traveling along. Night would come and the desert literally would come alive. The blessing of those weekend trips to the desert couldn't be measured. These were times of hard work but spiritually the most rewarding. The people who came to the clinic not only received physical help, but the clinicians were able to deliver words for their eternal salvation. Of all of the many experiences she had in Ethiopia, Carol deems the experience in the Danakil Desert as the most rewarding.

They were blessed to be able to start a Dresser school at Dessie. The need for the increased Dresser staff was because of the sudden influx of patients after the road accidents. They were blessed to be able to enroll eight students in their first class and doubly blessed to graduate all eight of those students.

In brief, Carol Ann Jones now lives in Huntsville, Alabama. She is a graduate of the following schools:

School of Nursing: The Brooklyn Hospital School of Nursing
Brooklyn, New York

The College of White Plains–Pace University–B. S.
White Plains, New York

Alabama A & M University–MBA
Normal, Alabama

She served overseas at the Ethiopian Adventist College in Kuyera, Ethiopia from 1962-1963. From 1963-1966, Carol served at the Taferi Makonnen Hospital in Dessie, Ethiopia.

19

ELDER SAMUEL & ELITA GOODEN
1963–1967

Samuel and Elita were both born in Jamaica, West Indies. Samuel came to the United States in 1944 as a student and worked his way through Union College in Lincoln, Nebraska. While Elita was visiting her sister in New York, she met her future husband and they were married in 1951.

He began his denominational service in the Northeastern Conference as an elementary teacher, science and Bible teacher, and as principal. He earned his Masters degree from Columbia University in Biology and Chemistry.

In 1963, the General Conference of Seventh-day Adventists requested that they serve in Nigeria, West Africa. He was asked to serve as the science and religion teacher in the high school. Later he was asked to be the principal of the school. The Goodens also served in Nbawsi in East Nigeria where Samuel was the President of Nigeria Training College and principal-manager for the Mission Station at Ihie. During his administration, he upgraded the staff (as the student body grew) from twelve teachers with two graduates including him to nineteen teachers with nine university graduates.

Among his many accomplishments were the building of a three-classroom complex with an auditorium, a baptismal pool next to the church, and a housing development for graduate teachers. Before he left, five homes had been completed and occupied. He later learned that the area bears his name—Gooden.

The Goodens returned to the states in 1967 when they received a call to the South Atlantic Conference of Seventh-day Adventists to serve as Director of Education.

Precious Memories of Missionaries of Color

Some of the highlights of Samuel's accomplishments while in South Atlantic Conference include:

1. He started the Senior Youth Camp in 1969 on Labor Day weekend.
2. He started a number of new Pathfinder Clubs.
3. He upgraded the teachers salaries from being the lowest in the Southern Union to the top of the salary scale set by the General Conference.
4. He upgraded the school teacher's Academic preparation from a low status to 100% college graduates and up to 96% certification.
5. He organized the Education Promotion Committee (EPC) which was responsible for providing thousands of dollars to needy parents to help them keep their children in church school.

The Goodens have two daughters, Rose and Sharon.
The Goodens are both resting from their labors awaiting the call of God!

Elder Samuel and Elita Gooden

Miss Eula Gunther Evans
1964–1967

Miss Gunther was among those who went as a unit to serve as a missionary for the Ghana Mission where she taught science at the Asakore Teacher Training College in Koforidua, Ghana. We owe a debt of gratitude to those who were single and gave their lives to serve as missionaries in far away lands.

21

ELDER OWEN & ANN TROY
1964-1966; 1972-1977

How shocking it was to hear Pastor Warner say that they were being considered for Africa! As a child, Owen had always wanted to travel and become a foreign missionary. While at Pacific Union College, he placed his name on a list to become one of these exciting missionaries and he waited to hear if the power leaders at the General Conference had made the selection so that he could join the group of God's soul winners. Many of his classmates received letters inviting them to join the ranks of the missionaries. At Alumni weekend at Pacific Union College a Mission Map was put on display where a bulb was lit for each missionary in the field from PUC. There were so many missionaries from PUC that there were not enough bulbs to represent them all.

While attending a General Conference Session, the Troys learned that Nathaniel Banks, Dunbar Henri, and Phillip Giddings represented the New "Colored" International Missionaries. These three men were sent to Liberia to replace a group of German Missionaries during World War II. During this time period, practically all of the "Colored" Missionaries were appointed to Africa.

Owen and Ann waited for some time before being informed that the GC was inviting them to become missionaries in Sierra Leone. They accepted God's call and in January, 1964, made their way to Africa. Like most missionaries, they had to prepare for physical tests. Their daughter Carmelita was two years old and took the first shot without any complaint. However, after that, she was conditioned so much so that when she saw the doctor's office, she squealed terribly. She even cried when she was only one block away from the doctor's office. Today, we are greatly blessed with much thinner needles.

Packing was a chore! The Troys had to decide whether to take or sell their belongings or send some of their things to their mother's place. They had to sell their home, travel to say good-byes to parents, and finally get to the ship. When they arrived at the ship, they found that the Bridgeport Church members had made arrangements to have a bus load of people to send them on their way. It was wonderful! They also gave them some of the most beautiful fruit.

Their room on the ship was very comfortable. They met another missionary traveling on the ship with them and so they spent the Sabbath together. Their ship took them to London. From there they flew to Paris, Geneva, Marseille, Barcelona, Madrid, Lisbon, Rabat, and Conakry before arriving in Freetown. In Paris they had the unfortunate experience of having a taxi driver double the cost of their trip and having their watch stolen. On Sabbath, they found a church, and while they were in Sabbath School Ann left Carmelita with Owen while she went to the rest room. In the meantime, Carmelita relieved her breakfast on the pew. Owen didn't have a cloth to clean up around him so he sat there hoping someone would come to the rescue. The Saints around him just looked at him. When he tried to ask for a towel, no one had any. From the other side of the church, one young lady from Martinique came over to help. She let him know that she was a nurse. He was most grateful for her help.

While in Geneva, they visited Collonges. Several students gave them a tour of the campus and the church. They next went to Nice, and although nearly every hotel was filled, they finally found a room on the fourth floor of a hotel with no elevators. So Owen had the privilege of climbing more than a hundred steps with luggage.

The first African country in which they stayed overnight was Guinea. Ann says that she was already to walk across the Sahara Desert and return home. They finally arrived in Freetown, Sierra Leone, where Borge Schants took them to the Mission house. Once they arrived, Ann had made up her mind that she could make a home in a tent. Imgard and Johann Thorvaldsson were gracious to them. To her surprise, their home in Bo was a lovely cottage on the Sierra Leone Mission Compound. They quickly made friends with all of the workers and visited their homes and ate their food.

One evening they attended a service along with Borge, Iris, and their boys. As was the custom at that time for missionaries, they sat in the front rows of the church. This caused Owen much concern because this practice set them apart from the national workers. Once when Owen attended services alone, he sat in seats that were not the customarily used seats by missionaries. When

Elder Owen & Ann Troy 1964-1966; 1972-1977

the service began, not one local person moved near the row that he sat on and also no one sat in front or behind him. One of his friends told him that the new Mission Secretary and Treasurer was a subject of discussion at a meeting held at one of the widows of a former church pastor. The next time he attended a meeting at the church, he found that Brother Boamah arrived there before he came, so he moved to sit with him. The meetings stopped and it appears that he was able to break down a barrier that should not have existed in the first place.

Some days when there was no mail, Ann would cry and think that their families had forgotten them, but they had not, the mail was SLOW! They were expecting their second child and their local British doctor suggested that they return home for the birth because of complications, but they decided to contact Lynn and Alyce Hartzler in Monrovia, Liberia. They were told to come there and Dr. Cooper delivered the baby in his private clinic. Once again, friends came to their aid. The Lord was with them all the way.

While they were in Kumasi, Ghana, Mrs. Margaret Owusu and Ann conducted a vegetarian cooking class for the ladies in the church. They used only the traditional cooking utensils and stove (3 stones with fire wood). Their first recipe was "Garden Egg Patties" (Eggplant). Samples of the dish were passed around, and one lady put it in one side of her mouth and out it went on the other side, and she said in Twi, "It tasted very good." Margaret and Ann had to smile—if it tasted so good, why did she spit it out!

Since Owen volunteered to be a pastor, he was assigned to the Amakom Kumasi Church. The Deaconess would come to their home each quarter to prepare the communion bread. At first, one member of the office staff would come to the house to translate. After the second time, they all understood each other. Prayer was offered before preparing the bread, everything was cleaned; and then the bread making went as scheduled. The recipe was taken from the Minister's manuel. This was a great occasion to get to know the deaconess.

The Children's Sabbath School was another interest that Ann had. Some of their friends sent children Sabbath School teaching aids and Kumasi Church used all of them. One Easter, the children came to their home for an Easter egg hunt and refreshments. They colored the boiled eggs and a couple of the boys went out in the yard and hid them. There was lots of laughter and fun finding the treasures. The children with the most eggs were given a token.

On another occasion, the Central Ghana Conference office staff wanted a party. They were told "if you want a party, you'll have to prepare the food." A few brethren assisted with baking cakes and decorating them. There were cakes all over the dining room, and all of them had an enjoyable baking experience. At the end of the party, not one crumb remained.

Precious Memories of Missionaries of Color

They were asked to house a blind worker. He was shown the bathroom, and where to find his tooth brush, and which ones were theirs. It was a pleasure to have this man of God as a guest in their home and a privilege to be asked to use their home for a Ghanaian brother.

The Western Union Mission's year-end meetings were being held in Accra, and Owen had to attend. Calling from Maurice and Esther Battles' home, Owen told Ann to take a taxi and come to Accra. From Accra, Ann called and paid for the three back seats in the taxi for her, their three year old daughter, Carmelita, and baby, Owen II. She thought that she would have a comfortable ride. To her surprise a very, very large lady slid in the back seat taking up most of the space. They were jammed together those 180 miles or so to Accra. But it was worth it because they were able to visit with so many of the other workers. The Battles and Hammonds were their support and fellow workers.

Johnny and Ida Johnson, who taught at Bekwai with the Hammonds, were good friends. They would go out of their way to visit when they came to shop. Ida was expecting a baby, and because they lived near the Okomfo Anokye Hospital, she stayed with them the last few weeks of her pregnancy. This was a long waited for child, and the Johnsons had literally given up hope of having a child. Every night, Owen parked the little VW bug by the door. They did not want anything to happen to this special baby, and believe it or not, Ida had an easy time with her delivery.

Elizabeth Mensah, the daughter of the president, was a close friend. Ann would go over to her home and eat there. One time, some of the youth from church made some fufu for them to eat. They watched the women trying to eat it with a spoon and chewing. They really had fun laughing at them. One is supposed to use ones fingers to pull a piece of the fufu off the lump, dip it in the stew and swallow it whole. Elizabeth would stay with Ann at night when Owen traveled. Before Elizabeth left for England, she left some of her national dresses which Ann wore on many occasions and in the villages. The saints would clap when they saw that she was wearing their national attire.

In 1972, the Troys went to the Inter-American Division to serve in the South Caribbean Conference in Trinidad. At the Cleveland Temple Church, Ann was the Sabbath School leader for the cradle roll and kindergarten classes and the Vacation Bible School Coordinator. The members all worked well to make these programs successful. Special guests for VBS included an officer from the police force, the band, someone from the fire department, and the Pathfinders. Ann volunteered with Freida Jensen and others. The years they spent in Trinidad were rewarding!

22

Miss Lois Raymond 1966–1978

The town of Yele in central Sierra Leone, West Africa, sits in the middle of the 28,000 square mile country. Sandwiched between the long, winding Tyre River with its glistening sand banks, lustrous mahogany trees, and blue hills, the town is punctuated with delicious mango, orange, guava, and banana trees. Inhabited by the Temnes, one of the largest ethnic groups in Sierra Leone, Yele is a farming town. With rice as its staple food, the people of Yele farm the land first by clearing the trees, burning them, and later planting the rice after digging the land with hoes. The men would cut the trees, burn them down, clear the remaining sticks to prepare the land for digging. Once the digging was done and the rice was planted, it was the women's turn to weed the farm and prepare the crop for a bountiful harvest. Here, like many other parts of Sierra Leone, many of the men have two or three wives to help them with farm work and to raise children. During the time that Jacob, the writer of this story, was growing up in the late sixties and seventies, education was mostly reserved for boys who were trained as teachers and administrators. Many girls got married early and started having children.

Life for girls in Yele, and the entire area, changed for good in the 1970s when Lois Raymond, a feisty, yet gentle and loving missionary from Natchitoches, Louisiana, in the United States arrived at the Yele Seventh-day Adventist Secondary School to become Dean of Girls. From the moment she arrived, Miss Raymond made it clear that she was going to change the dynamic of the school by making girls first class students. Her first major task was to oversee the building of a modern facility for girls with glistening ceramic toilet seats, comfortable bunk beds, and tiles to match. With help from her family and friends in the United States, she sponsored many of the poor girls to help with their school fees, uniforms, and books. She taught the girls English, Literature, writing, home economics and how to cook, sew, and clean. She also protected her girls from the boys.

Each Wednesday night, Friday night, and on Sabbath, the girls dressed in crisp white uniforms marched single file from their dormitory to the school chapel. They would sit on the right hand side of the pews, while the boys sat on the left side. The girls fondly called her "Mommy." Her protection of the girls from the boys and fighting for their rights earned her a lot of respect not only from her students, but also from their parents and other community leaders.

Nearly two decades after Lois Raymond left Yele and ultimately passed away here in the United States, her legacy still lives on. Several of her girls have gone on to college or excelled in other professions. Among the Raymond girls here in the United States are Musu Kamara, a nurse who lives with her family in Pasadena, California. Others include Mary Bangura, Kadiatu Kanu, Marie Thoronka in Virginia, Hannah Sandy in Colorago, Elizabeth Turay in Massachusetts, Mary Kanu in Maryland, and scores of women scattered all over the world who owe their education to Lois Raymond. While Miss Raymond focused on girls, she also helped several boys like Samuel Koroma in Rhode Island, and many others. But her ultimate contribution was to change the perception of the people of Yele and to make them believe that girls are able to get an education and get good jobs, not just to help with farm work, cooking and having children.

Lois was born into a large family. Because she was the oldest, she helped shoulder the responsibility of caring and nurturing of the others. She seemed to have a natural talent for leadership and was always a very caring and giving person. She was like a mother to her sisters, Gustavia and Pearl, "training" in every sense of the word many years before she went to Africa.

She was born in Louisiana and received a teaching certificate from Louisiana State Normal College at Grambling—now known as Louisiana State University/Grambling. She taught school in Louisiana for several years before going to California where she became a Seventh-day Adventist and a member of the Wadsworth Adventist Church whose pastor at that time was Elder F. L. Peterson who was not just a pastor. He was even then an educator who saw in Lois someone who had stamina, strength of character, fortitude, courage, intellect and not least, a genuine, caring Christian young woman. He recognized that she needed to further her education in order to be able to take on greater responsibilities. Through his encouragement and the benefit of a

Miss Lois Raymond 1966-1978

scholarship that Elder Peterson sponsored, Lois went to La Sierra and received her bachelor's degree. Some years later, between tours from the mission field, she received her Masters of Arts degree from Andrews University in Berrien Springs, Michigan.

Lois loved people and especially the people on the continent of Africa in the countries of Liberia, Sierra Leone and Ghana, where she served many years. Even after her diagnosis, even though she knew she was very sick, Lois wanted to return to Africa for one last visit with the people she loved so much.

As indicated earlier, throughout this country and in many parts of the world, there are students who credit her with giving them a start to a better life here on earth and opening their eyes to the "Great Beyond."

Musu Kamara was one of the young ladies that Lois took into her home. Musu came from a Muslim family that treated her like a servant. She literally walked ten miles to reach the school where Lois took her in and provided for her as her own child. It was evident from the marks on her body that she had been abused. When Lois transferred to Ghana, Musu followed her. Musu was determined to be a real daughter and eventually came to the U.S. Of course, Lois helped her secure a visa and fare to California where Musu later married an American Muslim man who fathered four children. She has since divorced and now resides in Pasadena with her four beautiful children. She is a Member of the Altadena Adventist Church and she and her children are "members" of the Raymond's extended family. They helped her to go to school and get training to become a nurse—she is considered a very good worker.

Another young lady, Mary Bangura, was literally picked up off the street by Lois and was taken to her home to live. She must have been quite young because Lois took care of her as though she were her own. Mary went to Russia to study and currently resides in Virginia. An article appeared in the *Washington Post* some time ago in which Mary Bangura quoted that "This donation is in honor of a wonderful lady who came from a very far away land to my country of Sierra Leone and befriended me when I was just a girl. She literally took me off the street and put me in her home and cared for me just as though I was her very own child. I want to give back so some child who is in need may be helped because of the love and kindness of this dear missionary woman." It was evident to Gustavia that the wonderful woman to whom she referred was her sister, Lois.

Gustavia visited Lois in Sierra Leone, and she was welcomed with open arms. People came from far away villages to meet the sister of Miss Raymond bringing presents because of the love and respect they had for her. Gustavia actually saw one of the little churches that Lois and her students had built. As

Precious Memories of Missionaries of Color

a matter of fact, Gustavia got to put one or two mud bricks in place. They also worshiped one Sabbath in another church Lois helped to build.

Gustavia was told when Lois died that people literally formed relays from village to village to spread the news of her passing. People cried, pulling off their clothes in the streets when told of her death, saying, "God has taken a real saint from among us."

On a number of occasions she used some of her shipping allowance for her students. When she came home on leave, she was constantly shopping to fill some of the many needs and requests of the children in the school who had pleaded with her to bring back things for them. When she returned, it was like Christmas. Grown men and women came from adjoining villages to see if Ms. Raymond had brought back something for them from America. She kept items such as shoes, belts, hats, perfume, and toiletries which she shared generously.

For those of us who knew this dear "saint of a lady" know that her labors have not been in vain! She has touched the lives of many and great will be her reward in heaven! The first account of this story was written by Jacob Conteh, a Sierra Leonean, whose life was touched by Ms. Raymond. The last parts of the story were memories of her life written by her sister Gustavia Smith.

23

ELDER JAMES & GERALDINE EDGECOMBE 1967–1970

This book highlights for our learning and instruction the activities of successive apostles—pastors, evangelists, and other great men and women of faith—who have embraced the gospel mission after Paul was forced to lay it down. Apostles have continued in each succeeding generation to do wonderful exploits for God, ever since, as similarly recorded in Acts of the Apostles.

Down through the centuries its writing has continued as spiritual hero after spiritual hero, faithful martyr after faithful martyr, faithful adventurer after faithful adventurer, humble volunteer after humble volunteer, for no other reasons than love and loyalty to their God, have embraced this noble work, joined this distinguished band, and added their contributions and testimonies to its writing,

This is the extraordinary story of one such contributor in the mid-twentieth century, Elder James A. Edgecombe—the Apollos of the Trinidad Triumph orchestrated by God through Elder E. E. Cleveland. Elder Edgecombe became the first pastor of the Cleveland Temple Church in Port of Spain, Trinidad in the West Indies.

In order to appreciate Elder Edgecombe's contribution in the years following 1967 when he arrived to take up his pastoral responsibilities, one must go backward in time several years earlier to a General Conference encounter between Earl E. Cleveland, then a Secretary in the Ministerial Department of the General Conference, and Samuel L. Gadsby, then President of the South Caribbean Conference.

Precious Memories of Missionaries of Color

The 1960s were a period of considerable political turmoil in Trinidad and Tobago. A crown colony of Great Britain for over one hundred and sixty years, the fires of nationalism were now burning brightly and the move for political independence was on its way. Led by the young nation's founding father, Dr. Eric Eustace Williams, the independence movement quickly gained ground and independence was achieved in 1962. The young nation was on the move. Urged on by state policy, nationals were busily preparing themselves to take over what was regarded as "the commanding heights of the economy" from English expatriates. The object in view was that the destiny of the country should be in native hands.

It was inevitable that the church would in some way become affected by the spirit of the times. A movement for full conference status, which had anticipated national independence for years, now took on new meaning and culminated in a demand for native workers to replace foreign workers in leading the Trinidad and Tobago Churches.

The movement has as its champions two very able sons of the soil–Charles Manoram from the East Indian Community and Samuel Gadsby of African decent. In 1965, national fervor brought Elder Gadsby to the presidency after which the local church entered a period of unprecedented growth.

It was the new president's determination to set the church on a new evangelistic course that resulted in an historic meeting between him and Elder Cleveland. Gadsby readily proposed and Cleveland readily accepted to undertake a massive crusade in Trinidad and Tobago with the objective of revitalizing evangelism in the local conference.

What started as a South Caribbean initiative quickly picked up momentum and became, first a Union, and then a Division-wide offensive. Trinidad would be the venue, but the core evangelistic effort would be incorporated into a larger Division-wide field-training school in public evangelism. Pastors, would-be evangelists, interns and Bible workers with a capacity for speaking English would be identified from across the Division and sent to Trinidad to learn the skills of public evangelism and to be part of this gigantic, eye-opening experience. It was hoped that this would give evangelism across the Division a fillip in the years ahead. The Inter-America Division became a world church leader in baptisms.

A massive mobilization was mounted for this Trinidad Crusade. The field was prepared by thousands of lay workers in churches all across the country, taking Voice of Prophecy lessons to friends, relatives, and interested people, visiting and building an interest in the Word of God, and sparking interest in them to plan to attend the Crusade to learn more. Health and Welfare initiatives

Elder James & Geraldine Edgecombe 1967–1970

sensitized people to the more caring and humanitarian aspects of the Advent message. Prayer vigils were organized, revival series conducted, and public announcements made.

A strategic location was identified and secured—the spacious grounds of a famous Port of Spain landmark—the Princess Building, named to honor a visit by British royalty in colonial times. The site commanded a view of the sprawling Queen's Park Savannah, the recreational center of Port of Spain, and of the majestic mountains of the northern range. Mass transportation was arranged in order to make attending the crusade convenient for people coming into Port of Spain from all across the country; and a number of hotels and guest houses were booked for the accommodation of the workers coming in from across the Division.

The crusade and field-training camp was a signal success. Night after night Elder Cleveland's powerful voice echoed across Port of Spain bringing messages of life and light into the hearts of many; and during the day the team learned both through theory and practice how to cultivate the massive interest that was developing and bring them to the point of decision. The crusade quickly became the number one attraction in the city. Going to the crusade became the thing to do in the evening. During the crucial stages of the meeting Elder Cleveland approached Elder Gadsby with a special request. He would like to bring in a singing group that had worked with him in several crusades in the United States. He felt that they would greatly enhance the meetings.

This initiative resulted in the arrival of the Cathedral Quartet on the beautiful Island of Trinidad which had a population of more than 80,000—the place where a modern-day miracle was being birthed. Although they had been team members in previous efforts, they were overjoyed to be standing on holy ground once more with their spiritual father, singing to the glory of God. Their voices thrilled and completely captured the hearts of the listeners. Their message in song brought encouragement to the doubters, and inspiration to the weak. Weeks of musical ministry followed, during which lasting friendships were made as the quartet members endeared themselves to the locals.

One of the members of the quartet was Elder James A. Edgecombe. Eight hundred and fourteen precious souls gave their hearts to God and were baptized in the beautiful blue waters of Careenage Bay in successive baptisms, as the quartet sang "Take Me to the Water to Be Baptized." The gigantic triple tent crusade had indeed become the "Trinidad Triumph." God's Word was vindicated. It had not returned unto Him void.

When the dust eventually settled as the crusade wound down and the massive crusade team returned home taking with them their new found enthusiasm and their newly-acquired skills in public evangelism, church leaders were left behind to carry on the work and follow up the interest, headed by Elder Gadsby, began to appreciate in all its fullness the challenge that caring for such a large influx of new members would bring. Makeshift arrangements were hastily made as they tried to find suitable accommodation for the large influx. Queens Hall, the City's main center for the performing arts was booked for Sabbath use. Elder Westphal visited and ministered for a month, and an annex was added to the Stanmore Avenue Church (the main city church) to accommodate some of the overflow. Churches all along the east-west corridor between Port of Spain and Arima were encouraged to expand their facilities to accommodate the influx. The entire arrangement, however, was, to say the least, unsatisfactory.

In addition to this problem, there was a large interest list left over from the Cleveland Crusade. Challenged by this twin problem, the creative minds in the Conference came up after much prayer with the bright idea of organizing a second crusade to follow Elder Cleveland's. George H. Rainey was the man selected for the job and a site on the sea-front to the south of the city was identified. This had the effect of providing temporary accommodation for the unchurched hundreds while buying time for the Conference to come up with a solution to the larger problem. This second crusade initiative was equally successful, and four hundred-odd accepted the Advent message as a result. The difference this time around was the large tent complex would remain after the crusade was over as the temporary home of a new church, and that the new influx would be cared for there until better could be done.

Caught unprepared the first time, the Conference was determined not to be caught again. They had consequently prepared for the challenge ahead, and were diligently at work building a church on a strategic city hilltop in Belmont to house the influx. But now that these arrangements were in place, they faced yet another massive challenge–that of finding a suitable pastor to take charge of the new church and of building it into a living vital organism.

As they had done previously, they turned once again to Elder Cleveland. Could he handpick a man who possessed the requisite skills for the job? Elder Cleveland's nominee was James A. Edgecombe, and plans were put into action to acquire this pastor for the new church.

It was the morning after the camp meeting. Unaware of the erosion that was about to take place in their lives, the Edgecombes rose early and began to plan their day. They packed the car and cleaned the cabin. They were anxious to get home but didn't have the heart to wake the children. So, they took a walk. The air was clean and crisp, birds were singing, small animals scampering here and

Elder James & Geraldine Edgecombe 1967-1970

there, and butterflies were gracefully floating from flower to flower. Halfway down the trail, the sun began to rise. It was so beautiful; Geri felt panicked that she couldn't save it. They watched the sun burst into a billion watts of light and tried to appreciate it even though they couldn't keep it.

By the time they returned to the cabin, they were no longer in a rush to leave. They took the children to breakfast, chatted with co-workers, and said their goodbyes and headed for home. The drive was 200 miles from Hyde Park to West Hempstead, New York. They had been away for fifteen days and were wondering how high the grass had grown and how big the pile of mail was inside their front door.

They were simply delighted when their car turned the corner and into their driveway. They thanked God for a safe return and gleefully jumped out of the car and headed for the door.

They had no idea what was waiting for them inside. When they opened the door, they were met with a stench so strong that it cut their breath. They backed out, closed the door, got towels from the car and used them as masks, and re-entered without the children. Part of the source of the stench was found on the first level. All six of their beautiful white angel fish were floating in a mass of decay in the fish tank. The pump had stopped working and the rest was history. Everyone was very sad. The fish were their babies and they loved talking to them.

They went to the second level. The freezer door was open and all the food had spoiled. The house smelled like a city dump. It took all the courage and strength in them, and then some, to get things back to normal. They didn't let the children enter the house the second time for any reason. When they were finished they joined them on the steps of the front porch. They sat there numb all over, wondering what happened to their beautiful morning.

Edgecombe suggested they buy some Lysol and sanitize the house, close the doors, and find a motel. Geri nodded in agreement but could not move. The children volunteered to go with him. They were gone for a very long time, or so it seemed. That was a good thing. She needed some time to herself. It allowed her to shed a few tears, sort the mail, catch her second wind and take in a sunset as it soaked into caldera.

The hunters finally returned with 12 cans of Lysol and a big smile across each face. They had found a suite at a reasonable rate. Everything was saturated with the spray. Then, off they went to their new found palace. They should have been hungry by that time, but they couldn't eat for days.

Everyone showered and got ready for a long deserved rest. Before hopping in bed, they decided to read the mail. At the top of the pile was a letter marked

Precious Memories of Missionaries of Color

General Conference. That one caught her husband's attention. He opened it first, read it and without saying a word, he handed it to his wife. She read it and was not silent. It was a letter of invitation accompanied with an application form inviting him to work as pastor of the newly-formed Cleveland Temple Church in Port of Spain, Trinidad. Geri asked if he had applied while in the mission field. He said that he had not. "What are the procedures for applying?" she asked. He informed her that one applies directly to the General Conference. The General Conference reviews it and if they have an opening, they will pass the call to the Conference president. The president can block the call or pass it on to the applicant. "Then, how did they get your name?" she asked. They were bewildered and perplexed by the method used to send the call to them. They were very fond of their president. He had been very kind and generous to them. He was their friend, and they had nothing but respect for him. Then, they began to play mind games. Maybe the president was in on it and wanted them out. Nothing made sense, because they had recently been moved to a new location with a large congregation, less than two years ago. They had bought a new five-bedroom house and a new car. Their children were in excellent schools and they were employed by one of the best regional conferences that existed. Why would they think of leaving!

The General Conference and Inter-American Division were in a dilemma. They had a newly formed church in Trinidad with 800 new members but no shepherd. They wanted an answer immediately. The Edgecombes were unable to give an answer that fast but began to pray and fast for divine direction. They had cast lots on three different occasions in the past. Each time the answer was "Go."

They only wanted to be in the will of God. So they accepted the call. There were many unknowns. What would their salary be? What was the status of housing? Did they have Americanized schools for U. S. children? These were just a few of the questions. They continued to ask questions as they packed. But, they received no answers to any of their questions.

They were given a packet of information on General Conference and government policies and some Bible texts and quotes, like Deuteronomy 8:18 (God gives wealth), Matthew 7:11 (God is our source), and Matthew 6:32 (Our Father knows our needs). They supposed that their answers were to be found in the texts. They began to feel guilty. Maybe they were too materialistic or just didn't have enough faith. So, with blindfolds on, they continued to prepare for departure.

During the process, her husband became very ill and was hospitalized. Many tests were done, but they couldn't find the origin of the problem. Then,

Elder James & Geraldine Edgecombe 1967–1970

their son became ill just two weeks before leaving the U.S. He was hospitalized. They couldn't find the cause of his illness. But then, the pain just ceased.

Realizing the challenge to every Christian who takes the discipleship of Christ seriously, no matter what the circumstances are, they have to follow the outline in Christ's first sermon (Luke 4:18, 19):

> The spirit of the Lord is upon me. He has appointed me to preach the good news to the poor. He has sent me to heal the broken-hearted and release the captive.

Once they reconciled to the fact that God was leading, nothing else mattered; a tent or a cottage. They sold their house, cars and packed what was suggested they would need and gave the rest to family members. On September 24th, they boarded a jet and landed on the beautiful Island of Trinidad. They were met by eight officials of the Caribbean Conference. As they descended from the plane, they felt the incredible sense of God's approval.

They spent the first few days adjusting to negotiating the young nation's narrow streets in English right-hand driven cars, getting acquainted with employees of the Union, the Conference staff and learning the layout of the island.

The children and Geri had never been on an island before. So, they were fascinated with the beauty; the tall palm trees, the brightly colored birds with loud distinct sounds, orchards of oranges and other fruit, fields of feathery sugar cane, deep blue sea, gay butterflies with three to four-inch spans flittering among gardens, and sea weeds waving fans of mauve, purple, yellow and electric blue. Geri was lost for words to describe their beauty.

In the middle of their first week, Elder Edgecombe experienced his first honest-to-goodness Conference Committee meeting, after which, he understood clearly the reason for the unorthodox method of the call and the unanswered questions. They explained how the system works. The Union owned houses, but only union employees/missionaries could occupy them. The Caribbean Union College also had houses available, but they were not affiliated with them. So, they could not stay there.

Edgecombe was informed that he was a pastor and he would work under the direction of the local Conference president. Housing was not provided for Pastors. He was responsible for finding his own place of residence. He was told that he would be paid in TT dollars. At that time three TT dollars equaled one American dollar. This information had been withheld from them until they took their post. This would pose a problem in trying to rent a house, pay tuition, life insurance, education funds and mutual funds in America, and other living expenses.

Precious Memories of Missionaries of Color

Although life seemed bleak, they knew beneath every disaster, every disappointment, beneath all perverse things that come to wreck God's plan, there was a divine purpose and a benevolent hand guiding and there was no place for discouragement or despondency in their lives. In faith they prayed intensely, believed, waited, and listened for God to show them the house he had for them.

In their search for housing they ran into a very wonderful, fine, wealthy Catholic gentleman. He, at one time, owned most of Maracas Valley. He sold the college their land and was very much acquainted with Seventh-day Adventist missionaries through the years. He said that he had heard about the Edgecombes' plight and was going to make sure they had the best house possible. He did just that. He rented a beautiful glass house to them for whatever they could afford to pay. They were thankful to God and the gentleman.

Their hotel stay was much longer than they anticipated and they were very anxious to get settled in their new home. Pastor Edgecombe dived into his pastoral assignment with foot and toe. Geri was left with unpacking boxes, making draperies for a glass house, helping the children adjust, and transporting them to different schools. Their daughter attended a rural school. Drinking water was provided in a bucket of water and a dipper sitting near the front door of the school. The restroom situation was that of a rural setting. Their daughter would go all day without drinking water or using the restroom. She never once complained. When Geri had the car, she would pick her up, bring her home to refresh herself, and would then take her back to school.

In an effort to accommodate everyone's needs and make things run smoothly, Geri overlooked her own needs. As time passed, she started having difficulty swallowing. At first, she thought it would go away, but it didn't. It only got worse. It had become impossible to swallow water. She became concerned and thought she had a growth. They sought out the best doctor on the island. He gave her a prescription for an anti-depressant. When she read it, she was appalled. She began to cry. "So you think I am imagining this painful block in my throat, huh?" she asked. "No", the doctor said in empathy. "I believe you should just take the pills for three days and call me", he said. Reluctantly, she agreed to try the pills if she could get them down. She didn't see how she could. He decided to give three shots instead. At the end of the three days, she was able to eat and drink with no difficulty at all. The doctor also arranged for her to attend counseling sessions while she was completing her acclimation to island life.

Normally, all missionaries receive transitional classes at Andrews University before departing the U.S. But, that was not so with them. They went from the

Elder James & Geraldine Edgecombe 1967–1970

pulpit in Brooklyn to the pulpit in Trinidad. Lack of knowledge caused them to make some very unwise decisions. Some of which were seriously harmful to their health. Nonetheless, God winked at their ignorance and kept them alive.

The speed at which they changed lifestyles made it difficult. One day they were surrounded by family, friends, co-workers and all the amenities of life in the U.S. The next day they were in another country trying to communicate with people with such heavy accents Geri had no idea what they were saying. No T.V., no telephone, no malls to shop when you are bored. It was hard at first, but God helped them to cope.

She recalls one occasion when her husband was out of the country and she was at home juggling chores along with a six-week-old baby boy. Two of the boys from the church came to play with their oldest son, who was eleven at the time. They asked to go swimming in the lake. She said yes. All went well, she thought. A few days later, she left the children with the maid and started to walk down the hill to hail a cab. Mike, their oldest, yelled "Mom, let me go with you." She stopped, turned to tell him no. When she heard a voice say "let him go, let him go." She said, "If you can catch up with me." She looked back to see how close he was. He was trying to run, but his legs were wobbling. She walked back to meet him. "What's wrong?" she asked. "I don't know. My legs won't go where I want them to." She put her arms around him and told him to lean on her.

Together they walked slowly down the hill, hailed a cab and went straight to the Caribbean S.D.A. Hospital. The doctors were baffled and didn't know what was wrong. So, they gave her some baby aspirin and sent them home. It was a rough night between the baby and him. His fever rose higher and higher.

When morning came, she knocked on her neighbor's door and said that if someone didn't help her, Mike was going to die. She could see her neighbor was frightened. She was cooking at the time. She quickly turned off the fires, washed her hands and said "Come with me." They piled all the children into her car and off they went, not giving much attention to the potholes which were more like mini-ditches, and the curves were so steep. She began to be concerned not only for Mike, but for the safety of all of them. It wasn't a new car and she was not sure if the trouble was in the wheels or the steering column. She had to fight to keep the car on the road. Her high speed wasn't making it any easier either. However, they arrived safely at her doctor's office.

The doctor was expecting her, so he saw Mike right away. It took a long time it seemed. But, he finally came out with a diagnosis. He told her that the boy had gone swimming in a lake where sewage was being dumped and he had an infection that there was no cure for. He said people do not live more than four days with it and he offered to keep him at his clinic. Because she had a small baby, the doctor felt she should not be left alone with the sick child. She was not led to do that and she told him no. She asked the doctor to tell her what he would do and she would do it herself. He said to give him plenty of raw juice and to pray. She did as he suggested. She prayed and spoon fed him continuously. As soon as he would swallow, it would pop back out of his throat.

During the night his temperature continued to rise. He became delirious and tore her clothes off, tore the bed covers up. The fever rose to 107 and he dipped into a coma. She stopped all efforts to help him and fell on her knees and began to pray. She is not sure how long she prayed. But, at some point, she felt two large blocks of ice roll off her shoulders, down her back. It startled her. She opened her eyes and saw her son sitting up in bed. He ask what she was doing down there. "You were sick and Mom was praying for you" she answered. "Who was the man standing over you?" he asked. "No one," she said. "Mom, there was a man standing over you in a white suit with blue eyes. And, when you opened your eyes, he turned and walked out of the room." It was then she knew they had a visitor and God had heard her cry.

They witnessed many manifestations of the Lord's care and keeping during their mission in Trinidad. The enemy was not pleased with their decision to be there. They came across many attacks, some severe, some not so serious. But, there was nothing too hard for God to handle. Despite the many obstacles, blessings prevailed—because God was truly in control.

Cleveland Temple welcomed the Edgecombes with open arms and open hearts. With Edgecombe's being a member of the Cathedral Quartet and a person they had met earlier at the great Crusade only added to their enthusiasm. If there were any lingering doubts in anyone's mind, his first sermons at the Temple put them eternally at rest. Cleveland Temple now belonged to James Edgecombe and James Edgecombe belonged to Cleveland Temple. It was a love relationship from the very first that was to last for the entire three years that he spent at Cleveland Temple. To the older members he was and will always be their adored pastor, and to the young people he was simply 'Uncle James.'

James Edgecombe arrived at Cleveland Temple one sunny Wednesday morning shortly after taking up his responsibility in time to see a huge truck carting away scores of tent benches which had up to that time been used as congregational seats. All that was left behind was the pastor's desk, the chairs on the rostrum, and about ten regular church pews. He discovered that the conference was moving the benches to a crusade that Elder Rainey was about to have in San Fernando in the Trinidad Southland.

Elder James & Geraldine Edgecombe 1967-1970

Bewildered by actions so incomprehensible, but not undaunted, he called an emergency church board meeting that evening to deal with the situation. The board was enthusiastic in its support. Whatever money the young church had, it was agreed that it would be used to (a) provide temporary rented seating for the Sabbath and weekly evening services, and (b) permanent seating for the church. An order was therefore immediately issued for the purchase of one hundred pews, which were delivered in batches of twenty at a time over the following three to four weeks. It is by such decisive action that the crisis was diverted and Elder Edgecombe announced his arrival at Cleveland Temple.

Situated on the level summit, a hill overlooking sections of the city of Port of Spain, Cleveland Temple was a church built to seat approximately five to six hundred members (large by Trinidadian standards). It was, as we have noted, a church made up primarily of new converts; but older Adventists, recruited from surrounding churches, had been used to make up its officer core. Jules Calendar, an Elder from the major city church had been appointed its First Elder. Melvin Gadsby, the president's son, was the MV Leader.

Edgecombe's first task was, like David's, to transform this diverse and motley group of people brought together by providence into a Christian brotherhood—he went at it with a will. He held private sessions with each of his officers, first listening to their plans, then sharing his larger vision for the work with them. They could be assured, he told them, that they could depend at all times on his fullest support. Inevitably he won their unstinting loyalty.

James overwhelmed the membership by his sermons—messages of faith and hope—and, in tandem with his Bible worker, by his numerous visits to their homes. "No hill," he told them, "was too high"—and there were many hills—"no road too difficult." Nothing would prevent him from coming and having a word of prayer with them. And he kept his word. He did not only preach Jesus; he also lived like his Savior lived. In response, there was an unstoppable out-flowing of genuine love and loyalty from his members.

Cleveland Temple became, literally speaking, the members' second home—a home away from Home—since so much of their time was spent there. The fellowship was really sweet. Something was always taking place at the Temple—choir practice, maintenance work organized by the deacons and deaconesses, welfare, pathfinder meetings and progressive classes for master guides, youth social and cultural activities, prayer meeting, Bible study classes, teachers' meeting, early Sabbath morning prayer circles, etc. One sister who lived up the road from the church was known to leave her home every morning, walk down to the church, climb the hill, look at the church, say "Thank God" and then return home blessed (her testimony).

Precious Memories of Missionaries of Color

Elder Edgecombe gave a strong spiritual mold to the young church and his family. He taught them to have faith and trust in God even in the face of adversity. He encouraged Bible study and a deeper understanding of "Righteousness by Faith." He made the prophecies clear and easy for all to understand; and built a strong sense of expectation of the Second Coming. His quarterly communion services were deeply moving experiences and solemn occasions. A phrase that became associated with him was "a high day in Israel." It was remarkable that after services were over, instead of filing out to go home, people lingered to talk and fellowship. It was as though separating from each other was too painful.

His work among his Elders, Deacons, and Deaconesses was particularly effective. It was his aim to teach them to be efficient and thorough in everything they did and to set the example for the rest of the church. But if he devoted much of his time to training his lay leaders, it was not at the expense of working with his young people, with whom he had an extra special relationship. His youth leader, Melvin Gadsby, always knew he had the ear of the pastor and consequently led the society into an activity program built on FEDS principles—fellowship, education, devotion, and share your faith. Gadsby also had Edgecombe's support which led to great MV programs, camps and outdoor activity, Voice of Youth crusades, missionary work, prayer circles, MV Hour of Power programs, Week of Prayer—made up of our youth. But of one thing they were always assured—their pastor was with them.

Ingathering at the Cleveland Temple was a delightful event. Cans and literature were given out after church at the beginning of the campaign. The victory would be announced at the time. They were reminded of the date one week before. The next Sabbath, no one was without his or her goal. Even the lame and blind came with a full goal. The little children's goal was the same as the adults. Some adults came with two or three goals, but for sure no one was without a goal. The new believers had learned rapidly the realization and the responsibility of each to do their part to finish the Work.

The Saints of God at Cleveland Temple were different from any church the Edgecombes had pastored. They had a passion for God. They honored Him with their gifts of time, talents and treasures. Their love and commitment took the ministry to a higher level. The excellent structured programs helped even the youngest to recognize God's presence. They had passion. They sensed their value and were eager to serve in any capacity, no matter how humble. They spent many hours, morning and evening, searching, studying and memorizing the Word of God. They recognized and accepted the challenges to share their newly found faith. Sharing was not new to them, but sharing the gospel was not so familiar.

Elder James & Geraldine Edgecombe 1967–1970

However, love and worship were something they did well, both to God and their fellow men. Their deep concern and loving spirit were contagious, even the small children and teens exhibited a sweet, sweet spirit.

No matter what we say or how we sermonize, the place of value that God has in our lives will be communicated through memories of our church members, friends, our children and even strangers–by the lives we live, not by words. Others will know what we treasure without our saying anything. Our value system shows, and we can be sure others are watching. Our esteem for God will come out of our passion—not our preaching. The more we value the Scripture, the more easily we will treat His Word as the solid rock. And our lives will be built on that certain foundation, no matter what part of the world we live in.

The fellowship at Cleveland Temple was truly great, and this blessing extended to include St. Marks, their much smaller sister church in the Belmont Hills, which along with Cleveland Temple made up Pastor Edgecombe's district. Indeed, so encompassing was the fellowship that on any ordinary Sunday afternoon, the time was set aside for Pathfinder and Master Guide meetings. Non-Adventist youth were attracted by what was taking place as a normal practice on Sabbath. Everyone came prepared to spend the entire day in worship and fellowship.

The same spirit was shown during the tent efforts. The members would never think of coming to a meeting without bringing a guest. Handbills and advertisements were not necessary. Climbing hills to tell someone about Christ was a pleasure for them. Many were great walkers. Although they had taxis and city bus transportation, many chose to walk with parcels on their heads, shoulders and backs without giving it a second thought. They were earnest in reaching the nationals.

Trinidad was populated with East Indians and the Hindu religion, but there was no fear of entering their world with the Gospel. The Saints worked with boldness to bring their Indian neighbors to the meetings.

Many natives practiced spiritualism. The Edgecombes had some hairy experiences during their stay. One man that comes to mind was a Voodoo Priest. His wife started attending the meetings. He told her not to get baptized. One Sabbath morning, she came with her bundle and was baptized along with 350 others. Everyone was praying for the lady's protection.

After baptism, she and the other Bible workers returned to the tent and continued to pray until vespers was over. Feeling tired and weary, she went home, lay across the bed and continued to meditate. Darkness fell, but she did not get up to turn the lights on. All was still—her husband had not returned home. Suddenly, something came through the window as though it had wings and landed on the floor with a loud thud. She quickly reached out and turned the bedside light on.

There on the floor, a large cobra was next to her bed, body raised, head aimed at her face, ready to strike. She recognized the snake. It belonged to her husband. He had full control over the snake. He could set it on one side of the city and command the snake to go anywhere he directed it and kill people, and it would obey. She had seen it happen many times. She was trusting God to give the command this time. She commanded the snake to go in "the name of Jesus" and the snake left with a greater force than it had come. She began to praise God with loud alleluias and thanks, saying, "You are Christ the King whose love shall never end."

Elder Edgecombe led out in two crusades during his sojourn in Trinidad. The first was held in Barararia, in answer to a Conference request: the second held up the road from Cleveland Temple to gather in tremendous interest in the area. Both were enormously successful. Between them, they brought three hundred-odd new members into the church. It was during the second of these crusades that a young deacon, trained and ordained by Elder Edgecombe, who had been asked to serve as caretaker at the tent, got himself into trouble and broke the seventh commandment.

Genuinely pained by this but more for the brother's sake than for the church's, Elder Edgecombe handled the situation with such care and skill, such concern and sensitivity, that when the matter eventually came to the church during a business meeting, both the brother and the entire church were in tears. It was a wonderful experience of forgiveness and rebirth. Within three months both the brother and sister were married, re-baptized, and back in church fellowship. He is still today a pillar in God's church. The memory of how this was handled has been used as a model by the members ever since in their handling of people in similar situations. It recalls so much the methods of the Master of whom it was said, "A bruised reed shall not break, and the smoking flax shall he not quench: He shall bring forth the judgment unto truth."

One of the problems, that several members at Cleveland shared, grew out of the fact that, being non-Adventists at the time of their marriages, their union had been transacted legally without the blessings of God and of His church. Now, though many years had passed, they desired to correct that situation. To meet this need, Elder Edgecombe organized a Renewal of Vows ceremony. It was easily one of the most beautiful occasions ever witnessed at Cleveland. More than twenty couples, ranging from very old to very young, dressed in wedding garments and participated in the processional down the aisle. The renewal of vows was done in a solemn ceremony. A delightful reception

Elder James & Geraldine Edgecombe 1967–1970

followed in the church's annex that was associated with Elder Edgecombe's stay at Cleveland. He understood people's need and found a way of supplying and satisfying them.

There are many other treasured memories still talked about among old-timers when the conversation recalls the Edgecombe years. They recalled the time his English Vauxhall car stalled on the Belmont hills and how people rallied to solve the problem to get him home. He was totally embarrassed and vexed that his brand new Vauxhall had cost so much, but had such little power that the members had to push it up a small hill. They recalled the monthly baptisms incorporated into the Divine service, resulting from his policy of opening the church at every service to the many non-Adventist visitors who continued to attend church. Young people, also, still remember his visit to their camp on Galera Airstrip in faraway Toco, when, to the amusement of all, he ate his lunch from a coconut shell. And, at his return to Cleveland that evening for Sunday evening service, he held up the coconut shell and told the church, "This is what your young people served me my lunch in today" to the amusement of everyone. They remember finding him working at the crusade tent in the mud, and how they had to instruct him to sit down and relax himself and prepare his sermon instead, while they took over the work themselves.

Great memories are these! And yet, nothing, however, can eclipse the memory of the massive send-off that Elder Edgecombe received from the church when it eventually came time for him to return permanently to the United States. Cleveland Temple went into a celebration mode. An entire week of activities were organized, beginning with a fellowship activity on the first Sabbath in which he preached a consecration sermon and concluding with his farewell sermon on the second Sabbath, a gigantic farewell program on Saturday evening and a motorcade to the airport on the Sunday of his departure; each day of the week having had its own additional unique activity.

It is generally accepted, certainly by the first generation of Clevelandites, that Elder Edgecombe was the best pastor to have labored at Cleveland Temple. Though he performed equally well in both fields, however, he was more pastor than evangelist. That was very obvious, even in an age when the demands of the time, following Cleveland and Rainey, downplayed the pastoral in favor of the evangelistic ministry. His interest in and genuine concern for people—people in all walks of life, with or without pedigree—was extraordinary. He was a very simple man who gave of himself to all without reservation, allowing people to see into his heart. As a result people genuinely trusted him and clung to his every word.

Precious Memories of Missionaries of Color

He certainly blessed those he came into contact with. And as a result of his work at Cleveland Temple, scores of men and women who have gone on to become giants for God in their work for the church and for humanity. They said thanks in no small measure to this little man with the big voice—Elder James A. Edgecombe.

Days pass, seasons change, months mold into years, and we stand looking back into our lives' memories—exciting memories, crises and turning points. In January we think of new beginnings. In February we think of Valentines. May brings thoughts of Mother's Day. June brings thoughts of anniversaries and Father's Day. Summer evokes memories of family trips. Then there is November and December; they bring to mind family traditions and celebrations.

Like ivy on the garden trellis, their lives are especially intertwined with seasons and months of the year. But, none can compare with the reflections of the birth and growth of their children. The heart of a mother draws closer and closer to her child as she shares the experiences of a lifetime.

> The future is a field to sow,
> A child the grain it yields.

Geri decided to see her doctor for no other reason than that she had no energy. He informed her that she was four months pregnant, had an ovarian cyst, and needed an operation immediately. She was told that she would miscarry within a few hours after the procedure.

They asked her husband to arrange for an anointing service with an elderly retired minister by the name of Elder Carrington. They met with her on the morning of the operation. They sang one song; read a scripture and Elder Carrington began to pray audibly as they prayed silently. There was an interruption before he was finished. She felt a rush or a flush of something go through her from the top of her head through to the bottom of her feet. She opened her eyes. Elder Carrington opened his eyes. He smiled. "You are going to be all right daughter," he said. "Yes, I know," she replied. Still smiling, he said "yes, I know, you know."

They gave praise, got up and went to the hospital. She had the operation. The doctor ordered a private duty nurse to stay with her because it was going to be a messy ordeal. She sat in her room for six hours, nothing happened. The doctor returned about six-thirty that evening. "How did things go?" he asked. "Nothing happened," she replied. He could not believe it. "Take all the gauze packs out," he instructed. She took seven out, all of them were dry, not one drop of blood on any of them. The doctor was bewildered, "that cannot

Elder James & Geraldine Edgecombe 1967-1970

be, there must be one more," he said. The nurse tried, but there were no more. They had prayed, given their fears to the wind and put their hopes in God. Once more God had girded them. Praise His holy name.

On March 10, 1970, Michael, his oldest child, became ill and had to return to the U.S. for treatment. Because of the seriousness of the condition, Michael was not allowed to return to Trinidad. So, Pastor Edgecombe ended his work there and returned to America on April 5, 1970 but returned as guest speaker for each anniversary celebration.

He was privileged to have accompanied Elder E. E. Cleveland to Port of Spain, Trinidad and to return as the "First" African American Missionary to the Island. Following that, he was blessed to serve as pastor of City Temple in Dallas, Texas; Park Hill S.D.A. Church in Denver, Colorado; and Bethany S.D.A. Church in Miami, Florida. It was during his service in Miami that Elder Edgecombe experienced another "First" in his ministerial career. In 1981 he was asked to serve as the inaugural president of the newly organized Southeastern Conference. His leadership skills were proven effective as membership doubled during his administration.

The last churches to benefit from his ministry were Beacon Light and South Mountain S.D.A. churches in Phoenix, Arizona. This led to one last "First" in his distinguished career: first African American Departmental Director for Community Services, Inner City Ministries, Prison Ministries and Stewardship for the Arizona Conference of Seventh-day Adventists. He remained active as Conference Director until his death.

Over the years, Elder Edgecombe's ministry resulted in seeing many churches built, purchased, and renovated. Many precious souls added to the army of God and many workers brought to full potential.

One day a storm entered his atmosphere. The wind was strong and he was very weak. Even so he tried to stand firm. The wind continued to increase in strength. When he could no longer stand, he sat down. The wind grew ever stronger and when he could no longer sit, on March 26, 2004, he lay down and the wind blew his candle out. Now he waits for Christ to come to light it again.

Precious Memories of Missionaries of Color

Elder James Edgecombe

The Cathedral Quartet–Elder E. Shepherd, Dr. Benjamin Reaves, Elder William Scales and Elder James Edgecombe

Elder James & Geraldine Edgecombe 1967–1970

Their oldest son's marriage to Lois Kum from Trinidad

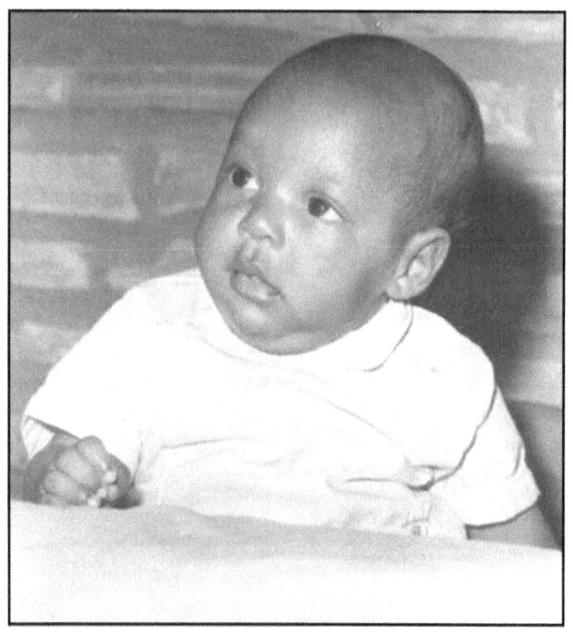

Their second son, David, born in Trinidad

Elder James & Geraldine Edgecombe 1967–1970

Baptism

Precious Memories of Missionaries of Color

Elder James and Geraldine (Geri) Edgecombe

Elder James & Geraldine Edgecombe 1967–1970

Elder E. E. Cleveland and Edgecombe, Anniversary Speaker

The Church Treasurer, one of Elder Edgecombe's favorite people

Precious Memories of Missionaries of Color

Tent meeting in Trinidad

Elder James & Geraldine Edgecombe 1967–1970

Bible Workers for Tent Efforts

24

Dr. Dewitt & Margaret Williams 1967-1972; 1979-1982

Dr. Williams had always wanted to be a Seventh-day Adventist missionary. He grew up in the Philadelphia Ebenezer church which boasted its own missionary. Ebenezer kept its eye on Elder Maurice T. Battle, its "missionary son" who had gone to Africa. His heart beat faster every time Elder Battle returned to gave a real live mission story. At camp meetings he heard stories about medical missionary, Dr. Samuel DeShay. Consequently, DeWitt had his mind set on going someplace overseas.

He remembers signing up for mission service during a special mission emphasis week at Oakwood College. Before he graduated, he filled out a more in-depth form that gave his personal history and let the General Conference secretariat know that he was still interested in overseas service.

Having married Margaret Norman, the newly-wed Williams family went from Oakwood to Pine Forge Academy for one year and then on to Andrews University Seminary. DeWitt can remember the ecstatic feeling he had when he first knew in the seminary that he would be sponsored by Southwest Region Conference. He had written a letter to all of the conference presidents trying to get them to adopt the new program which helped ministerial students get through the seminary.

Regional students were spending most of their non-class time working trying to raise funds to stay in school while their white counterparts were spending their time in the library studying and turning out good grades. Williams thought this was very unfair and discussed it with everyone he met. He

Dr. DeWitt & Margaret Williams 1967-1982

decided to take the matter into his own hands and wrote letters explaining the situation and asking for help to all of the nine Black presidents. About half of them answered! Some empathized with his plight. DeWitt was impressed with the letter he received from Elder V. L. Roberts, president of Southwest Region Conference. He not only empathized with him but asked a poignant question. "Do you want to work in Southwest Region Conference? You didn't mention whether you wanted to work in our conference." DeWitt hastily got on the phone and let him know that he definitely wanted to work in the Southwest Region since he was married there and his wife came from there, along with many other reasons. DeWitt had another moment of elation when he got another letter a few weeks later stating that they would sponsor him and his wife retroactively starting at the moment they went to the seminary that past June. It was now in February, 1964. What a wonderful surprise and blessing! They not only had some money to tide them through their seminary days but a job!

Pastor Williams was pastoring in Oklahoma City when he got his first call. Elder H. D. Singleton, from the General Conference called to ask if he was still interested in mission service. He was (any place in a French speaking country), but he was in the middle of an evangelism meeting. He had pitched a tent on 19th and Eastern Avenue and the Lord was blessing Pastor Williams and his small congregation. Thirty precious souls were the first fruits of his efforts and in his second baptism, the Lord blessed with 36 more souls. Mission service was forgotten in the responsibilities of the moment. Preaching every night and visiting prospective members was taking all of his time and attention. Pastor Williams had one more baptism and then began making plans for building a new church to house the growing flock.

Their first daughter was born in Oklahoma City in 1966. Pastor Williams had arranged to study French at Oklahoma University at the first class in the morning at 7:00 A.M. He returned before his members were up and calling him on the phone. He took beginning, intermediate and advanced French and a reading course. He had a gift for language and made excellent progress. At the end of the four courses, he had a very good reading knowledge of French.

When the 10th Street Adventist Church burned down, some years before, the small congregation had been pilgrims and wanderers. The orphaned group met in the Methodist Church for many years and then purchased land and struggled to build a little school building which had become their official meeting place. It was small and had crude, second-hand pews and a big-potbellied stove in the back of the church. On very cold days the seats would be arranged around the stove instead of facing the front and the make-shift pulpit.

Precious Memories of Missionaries of Color

The new edifice was a beautiful brick building with green carpeting and a gorgeous skylight and stained glass windows.

When the roof was going on the new church, Pastor Williams let the General Conference know that they would soon be ready to go wherever the conference would send them.

There were a lot of preparations. They had to sell their house, car, furniture, and personal belongings. They were given a weight allowance from the General Conference transportation department and couldn't take very much. The lovely church was just being finished and Elder C. E. Moseley was coming down to do the dedication service. All that week they were celebrating the new edifice with other denominations. A wedding, a few meetings, and a couple of sermons were all they would enjoy in this beautiful building.

They would have loved to stay in this new edifice for a little longer but Africa was calling. They sent a letter to Elder Singleton and asked how many Black missionaries had been to the Trans Africa Division and how many had been to the Congo. He wrote back and said that as far as his records indicated only one other, Elder William Robinson had been to that division and no other Negro Adventist had served in the Congo. They would be the first.

They had a little time to visit the Williams family in New Jersey and the Norman family in Texas. They would first go to Switzerland to study French. The former Belgium Congo was going through a revolution. Patrice Lumumba had been assassinated and the rebels had ransacked and damaged the Congo Union office. Many of their friends were advising them not to go since it all seemed so turbulent. They prayed about it and decided it was God's will and they would look at it again very closely after they finished their French study.

The little Williams family landed in the beautiful village of Neuchatel in September of 1967 and got settled into their little apartment. Eurocentre was the school that would be their life for the next five months. Their teachers informed them that everything would be spoken in French and if they spoke their mother tongue in class they would have to cough up a franc for a dinner at the end of the class. After taking Deitrice, their baby girl to the church where she was incorporated into a wonderful Italian family during the day, they hopped on a bus and went to Eurocentre. They talked and read French, went to labs and did French exercises all day long. At first, Pastor Williams understood very little.

Everybody spoke so fast. After about a month, he noticed that he understood more. After about three months there, he noticed in class that he really understood what his teachers were saying! He couldn't believe it. He understood!

Dr. Dewitt & Margaret Williams 1967–1982

They were instructed to purchase a car and use it in Switzerland so they wouldn't have to pay taxes on a brand new car. They were proud of that Peugeot break (station wagon). Church on Sabbath proved to be a wonderful learning experience, also. Studying the Sabbath School lesson and looking up all the new words was a chore but soon it began to pay off. Every shopping experience was a learning experience. They made so many mistakes but the Swiss were kind and helpful and soon they were able to make themselves understood on most subjects. They did a bit of studying at the library to find out something about the place they were destined to go. Here is a little of what they learned.

King Leopold II was a man filled with as much greed, cunning, duplicity, and charm as any of the more complex villains of Shakespeare. Leopold personally owned the Congo and accumulated a vast personal fortune from ivory and rubber through Congolese slave labor. 10 million people were estimated to have died from forced labor, starvation, and outright extermination during Leopold's colonial rule. His brutal exploitation of the Congo eventually became an international cause célèbre, prompting Belgium to take over administration of the Congo, which remained a colony until agitation for independence forced Brussels to grant freedom on June 30, 1960. Belgium sent paratroopers to quell the civil war, and the United Nations flew in a peacekeeping force.

Patrice Lumumba became prime minister of the new Republic of the Congo in 1960. He was educated in mission schools and later worked as a postal clerk. When the Republic of the Congo came into existence, Lumumba appealed for aid to the United Nations but was killed by a strange coalition of CIA agents and Belgian mercenaries. Riots of protest took place in many parts of the world. Here are some other facts they learned about the Congo:

Population	54,000,000 (2.5 times Australia)
Population density	51 per sq. mile
Geographical area	905,446 sq. miles (¼ size of U.S.)
Arable land area	3% (20% in U.S.)
Major river	Congo River 2,718 mi. long (Mississippi 2,340 mi.)
Principal languages	Chiluba, French (official), Kikongo, Kiswahili, Lingala
Religions	70% Christians, 10% Muslim
Literacy	72% (U.S. 97%)
Life expectancy	51 years (U.S. 75)

Precious Memories of Missionaries of Color

The country that won its independence on June 30, 1960 was renamed the Federal Republic of Congo. The Federal Republic of Congo was shortly after renamed the Democratic Republic of the Congo (DRC). In 1965, after years of rebellion, Mr. Mobutu seized power. His rule lasted 32 years. He implemented a massive program of education and created a solid sense of national unity. But the country also went through a succession of economic crises caused by mismanagement and widespread corruption.

Mobutu Sese Seko was born Joseph Désiré Mobutu. He returned from study in Brussels to the then Belgian Congo, joining the nationalist movement in 1956. Mobutu soon became the army chief of staff. In a second coup (1965), he assumed the office of prime minister (1966), then established (1967) a presidential form of government headed by him; the constitution did not come into force until 1970. As part of his program of "national authenticity," Mobutu changed the Congo's name to Zaire (1971) and his own name to Mobutu Sese Seko (1972). Citizens were required to drop their Christian names; place names were Africanized. Power was concentrated in Mobutu, who, backed by Western intelligence agencies, established a one-party state and a cult of personality. He suppressed tribal conflicts and encouraged a sense of nationhood. By 1991 economic deterioration and unrest led him to agree to share power with opposition leaders, but he used the army to thwart change until May, 1997. Mobutu died in Morocco.

The Williams finally said good bye to all of the friends they had made in Neuchatel and drove their car down to the coast of France to be shipped to the Congo. They booked an airplane to Lubumbashi, the former Elizabethville. Pastor Williams was to be the Union Sabbath School, Lay Activities, and Youth Director. He enjoyed his work and traveled all over enthusiastically promoting and preaching. What a country! He loved the people and his job. Some of his trips took him away from home for up to six weeks. They lived in a compound with a fence around it and all of the missionaries' houses and the Union office were enclosed within this fenced-in area. He felt that his wife and daughter were quite safe when he was gone. Margaret had a large garden and grew all kinds of vegetables. Mangoes, guavas, bananas, avocadoes, and other fruit grew right in their yard and around the house. Their second daughter was born on New Year's Eve 1969 right after midnight. They had to get the Belgium doctor from a party to deliver Darnella. They often kid her about being the first baby born in the Congo in 1969.

Mr. Saraya Mangukira agreed to teach them Swahili and every evening after work they met in the conference room and struggled with another language. Pastor Williams' Swahili was getting good but his French was not progressing too much. There were too many English speaking missionaries on the

Dr. DeWitt & Margaret Williams 1967-1982

compound and they all tended to talk in English. After they were there for a year and a half, they were informed that Pastor Williams had been appointed president of the West Congo Field. They readily accepted this new challenge and packed up their belongings and flew to their new home all the way on the other side of the country. Kinshasa was the capital of the Congo and they would be the only Adventist missionary in the new territory. Their home was not in a compound and their neighbors were merchants and businessmen from various countries. They soon made the acquaintance of many other missionaries from other churches and all of them met and prayed and fellowshipped together each Sunday evening.

Williams' territory was vast. He had such a small group of pastors and literature evangelists. The largest work force was the teachers. How often they prayed for more workers and more members. They were in Kinshasa the nation's capital and they didn't have a single medical facility. The West Zaire Field had several primitive clinics in the bush hundreds of miles away. One area that they prayed about often was the Katanga province. There was so much potential and so few workers and churches there. The field had a clinic there called Lullengele but Pastor Williams' heart felt pained every time he visited it because it had closed down. It was equipped with beds, tables and surgical instruments but had no missionary doctors or nurses there and no trained nationals who could be sent there to open this potentially wonderful facility. He often prayed for a miracle and put in several requests for workers, but the Zaire Union had no funds or budgets to call a doctor to this isolated area.

By now President Mobutu had decided that he didn't like what he saw among the Christian churches. There were too many churches in Zaire. Families could declare that they were a church and avoid paying taxes. One day after visiting the Katanga province, President Mobutu Sese Seko decided that he was going to Africanize his country. He changed his name from Joseph Desire to Sese Seko, and required all the citizens to change their Christian names to African names. The tall statue on the Congo River of Charles Stanley who had come searching after Dr. Livingstone was hurled down. The country would no longer be called Congo but Zaire. Hospital Queen Elizabeth was renamed after Mobutu's mother, Hospital Mama Yemo. Our pastors were forced to change their names. Pastor Williams would get letters from pastors and he really didn't know who they were sometimes. It was a turbulent period. Mobutu set up stringent criteria for the leaders of all the churches who wished to remain in Zaire.

What were the requirements?

Precious Memories of Missionaries of Color

1. Doctrines codified and written out
2. Leaders with theological degrees
3. $250,000 in Banque du Zaire

"What are we going to do?" Williams inquired. "Will we be able to meet these requirements?" Williams felt proud to be a Seventh-day Adventist and he admired the organization of his Church. You may not give too much thought to the world wide Adventist organizational structure, but God has given us a wonderful organization! All Williams had to do was contact his Union president who contacted the Division president who contacted the General Conference President and help was on the way. President Williams got counsel and help.

He felt happy to be an Adventist because Adventist doctrines were all codified and written out. Adventists didn't have to guess what they believed. They just had to Xerox a few pages from their church manual and doctrinal books and they were able to meet that requirement. Many churches and especially the national churches did not have their doctrines written out and they were unable to meet the time deadlines on getting them written out.

The second requirement mandated that the leaders had to have theological degrees. Again, Pastor Williams was happy to be an Adventist. The Adventist church does not just send out anybody. It sends out those who are qualified and qualifies those they send. All of our leaders had theological degrees, both missionaries and nationals. It was good to belong to a church that had high standards for its workers and leaders. Sharp axes cut more wood. We just had to compile the list of our leaders and attach the certificates, and degrees. Many churches, especially the national churches had great difficulty here. Their leaders may have been naturally endowed with eloquence and leadership ability but they had not received formal training to sharpen their skills. Many of their churches had to close down.

The last requirement was the hardest to reach. To remain in Zaire the church had to prove that they had $250,000 in the Bank of Zaire. What a challenge for some churches! Even some of the churches that had missionaries had to struggle to meet this challenge. Some missionary stations were run by two or three local churches in America. They were committed to missions but they did all they could just to pay the salaries and expenses of their missionaries. To have $250,000 as well (this was a lot of money in the seventies) in the Bank of Zaire was impossible.

Of the thousands of churches in Zaire at the time (1971) only a handful were able to meet the strict requirements demanded by President Mobutu Sese Seko in the time he had allowed. Again, we say what a great privilege to belong to a church that has such a wonderful organization and such high standards.

Dr. Dewitt & Margaret Williams 1967–1982

The Adventist Church was well able to meet the requirements in the time limits imposed by the government. Our completed report was taken in to the Minister of Justice and when a list of the 49 churches that had made the requirements was published the name of the Adventist Church was on that list.

Pastor Williams was sitting in his office one morning, feeling somewhat depressed. Nothing was going as fast as he wanted. At the year-end meeting he learned that because of the recent events the field would not get as large an allocation as requested. Some of the missionaries that he thought would be coming had been sent elsewhere. Their mission field hospital in Lulengele was still closed. He was somewhat depressed.

There was a knock on his door. His secretary told him that someone from L'Eglise du Saint Esprit (Church of the Holy Spirit) was there to see him. He was not in a very positive mood. He really didn't want to see him.

The representative came in quickly and shook Pastor Williams' hand. "Je suis le representant de L"Eglise du Saint Esprit,' he volunteered. ("I am the legal representative of the Church of the Holy Spirit") "We have 117,000 members. We were unable to meet the requirements imposed on us by President Mobutu Sese Seko. We went to see the Minister of the Justice and asked him what we would do with all of our members and all of our churches and schools. He gave me the list of 49 churches that had met the requirements and told me to study them and join the one that most closely resembled ours. "We have studied them and your church is very similar to ours. You see, our leader went to a Seventh-day Adventist Church school when he was a young boy. He went from grade one to grade five. He never had a chance to go to get any more schooling but he remembered what he was taught. We keep the Sabbath." (They ate pork and other unclean foods). Here was a group of Sabbath keepers in the province where we had just about no members who wanted to become a part of the Seventh-day Adventist Church. He wanted to give us their members, their churches and their schools. Everything! Williams could hardly believe it. He got all the information from him and got ready to make a call to the Union to let Elder Lemon know what had happened. While still contemplating this miracle, his secretary knocked on his door again. "There is another man to see you." In walked another stranger. He spoke in French.

"I am the legal representative of the Church of Light. We have 27,000 members. We were unable to meet the requirements imposed on us by President Mobutu Sese Seko. We went to see the Minister of the Justice and asked him what we should do with all of our members and all of our churches and schools. He gave me the list of churches that had met the requirements and told me to study them and join the one that most closely resembled ours. You see", he said, "our leader was given a copy of the book *Great Controversy* many years ago and he read it through many times. When he preached he often quoted from that book. We keep the Sabbath." They believed in infant baptisms but here were 27,000 Sabbath keepers down in the Katanga Province that we didn't even know existed. Pastor Williams was getting a little excited by now.

Before the week was over, several more strangers entered his office and each one started out with the words..."I am the legal representation of my church. We were unable to meet the requirements imposed on us by President Mobutu Sese Seko. We went to see the Minister of the Justice and asked him what we should do with all of our members and all of our churches and schools. He gave me the list of churches that had met the requirements and told me to study them and join the one that most closely resembled ours. Your church is like our church. We are Sabbath keepers." There were thousands and thousands of Christian Sabbath keepers! There were some problems. Some did not believe in Mrs. White or had never heard of her. Mrs. White, along with her husband, was a founder of the Adventist Church as we know it today. Her vision guided the early church in establishing many of our fundamental principles and doctrines. She also encouraged missionaries to go all over the world. Some kept the Sabbath from 6:00 am to 6:00 P.M. on Saturday. But each had had an experience to bring them into the knowledge of the truth. They were down in the province where we didn't have any work. And they were requesting to join our church. Dr. Williams couldn't believe his ears. Here was a restriction imposed by the president of the country that we thought of as very severe at first but which in the long run blessed us beyond belief.

Sure, we couldn't accept members in groups like this. We had to set up training programs to train the leaders who would in turn train their members. Some would never accept our doctrines exactly as we taught them. Many would never be baptized. The Williams family came away from this experience with the strong belief that God is in charge of His work and that He was leading. They thought of the quotation below:

> In the annals of human history the growth of nations, the rise and fall of empires, appear as dependent on the will and prowess of man. The shaping of events seems, to a great degree, to be determined by his power, ambition, or caprice. But in the word of God the curtain is drawn aside, and we behold, behind, above, and through all the play and counter play of human interests and power and passions, the agencies of the all-merciful One, silently, patiently working out the counsels of His own will. *Education,* p.173

Dr. DeWitt & Margaret Williams 1967–1982

The secretary and Global Mission Coordinator of the Northern Pacific Union Elder Duane McKey did his doctoral dissertation on this challenging and exciting experience. His dissertation is in the Andrews University library.

The Williams do believe that God holds this world in His hands and when He gets ready to pour out His Holy Spirit on the world, many who have read a book or a tract, or attended our schools or attended a Stop Smoking clinic will hear God's voice and join our church. God is pouring out His Spirit and if He can't make up His number in America, He will find the honest of heart and the sincere in Africa and Asia, in undeveloped countries and in places all over the world. May God help us to keep working as His Spirit keeps reaping.

Zaire became the Democratic Republic of Congo again in May, 1997.

The Williams family returned to Africa in 1979 where Elder Williams served as president of the Central African Union, the countries of Rwanda, and Burundi. They lived in Bujumbura, Burundi.

Dr. DeWitt S. Williams, Director Health Ministries Department, North American Division

Scientists say that eating right and exercising regularly can actually increase our life span. That may not seem important now, but decades from now, most of us will welcome the extra energy and the years. Our health is important and thanks to health ministries workers like Dr. Williams, we can obtain guidance in leading a healthy life.

DeWitt Stanton Williams was born in Philadelphia, PA. He is a graduate of Oakwood College and Andrews University (M.A. in Theology), and was ordained a Seventh-day Adventist minister, in Oklahoma City, in 1967. He earned his Doctor of Education degree from Indiana University in 1975 and his Master of Public Health from Loma Linda University in 1985.

Elder Williams joined the General Conference Health/Temperance Department in 1983. He lectures, writes articles about the importance of good health, and talks to young people about the dangers of drugs. He has spoken in over 100 countries.

Before his appointment with the Health/Temperance Department, Pastor Williams held positions such as pastor in the Southwest Region Conference; departmental secretary for the Congo Union, Africa, and assistant and associate director of the General Conference Department of Communications.

Precious Memories of Missionaries of Color

From 1979-82, he served as president of the Central African Union, Bujumbura, (pronounced Boo jum bóo ra); Burundi, (pronounced Boo roón´dee) Africa where he learned to speak French and Swahili.

His book, *She Fulfilled the Impossible Dream*, tells the story of Dr. Eva B. Dykes, a teacher for whom he once worked. She was the first Black woman in the United States to earn a Ph.D. degree. He has co-authored several books: among them *Profiles of Service* with Dr. Delbert Baker, *For His Honor* with Kay Rizzo and *Energized!*, the 1998 health devotional, with Jan and Kay Kuzma.

Despite his busy work schedule, Dr. Williams still finds time to stay fit. He is an avid exerciser and has run in several marathons.

Dr. Williams is married to the former Margaret Norman of Dallas, Texas, a retired English teacher, and has two daughters: Deitrice Chapman, a family practice physician in Dayton, Ohio, and Darnella Williams, an elementary school teacher in Washington, D.C.

Dr. Dewitt & Margaret Williams 1967-1982

Pastor Williams with General Conference Treasurer Elder Lance Butler and General Conference President Elder Neal Wilson and three of the national presidents

Adventist Missionaries evacuating the Congo waiting at the border trying to get into Zambia

Precious Memories of Missionaries of Color

A worker tries to clean up some of the trash made by the soldiers who invaded the Congo Union office

Deitrice (on left) with Darnella and Patches, the dog, in their home at Kinshasa, Zaire, where Pastor Williams was president of the West Zaire Field

Dr. Dewitt & Margaret Williams 1967-1982

The Williams' car dwarfed by a giant anthill. The block of their motor was cracked by one of these anthills while Dr. Williams was traveling on a dirt road that had hundreds of these smaller anthills hidden in the grass.

Darnella was born in Lubumbashi, Congo, January 1, 1969. She reigns in her highchair.

Precious Memories of Missionaries of Color

Darnella (on left), Margaret, Deitrice Williams in front of their apartment in Belgium where they were sent to study French before going to Burundi

Dr. DeWitt & Margaret Williams 1967-1982

Pastor and Mrs. D.S. Williams with baby daughter, Deitrice in 1967. They left for the Congo from Oklahoma City, OK, where Pastor Williams was pastoring three churches. This was the picture that appeared in the Union paper announcing their departure.

Precious Memories of Missionaries of Color

Hole in the Congo Union office produced by shell fire by the invading rebels

Hole in the Congo Union office produced by shell fire by the invading rebels

25

ELDER DENNIS & DOROTHY KEITH 1967-1975

As the *Tema*, a Norwegian freighter, weaved its way across the Atlantic Ocean in approximately eighteen days to Sierra Leone, a small country on Africa's western "bulge," north of the equator, it carried a young family by the name of Dennis Keith, Sr. his wife, Dorothy, and two small children—Dennis, Jr. and Denise. Added to the family later was a third child named Dwan. The Keith family looked forward with great anticipation to serve as missionaries in Sierra Leone, West Africa.

The Keiths arrived in Sierra Leone in March of 1967. Sierra Leone at that time, was slightly larger than the state of West Virginia and had about as many people as the state of Iowa. The thrill of an unforeseen future only known to God was an exciting venture for the young missionary family.

Sierra Leone, a country with one of the world's most valuable treasures—diamonds—ranked as the world's third largest producer of gem stones and the sixth largest producer of industrial diamonds was an interesting place to live.

Freetown, the capital of Sierra Leone, stands on the tip of a rocky peninsula on the Atlantic Coast of Africa founded by freed slaves in 1787. Its robust life style boasted various industries such as fish processing, soap factories, and ship-repair yards. The rich soil of this great country produced chromites, ginger, gold, kola nuts, palm oil, kernels, and platinum. What an exciting country to live in and serve as missionaries for the Seventh-day Adventist Church!

The Sierra Leone Mission of Seventh-day Adventist was located in Bo, the second largest town in 1967. It was the home of the Keith family for nine years.

Precious Memories of Missionaries of Color

Dennis was the secretary-treasurer of the mission and his wife, Dorothy, taught their children with the aid of the church's international school called Home Study Institute. She also assisted her husband doing various assignments in his office.

December 31, 1967, the membership of the Seventh-day Adventist Church in Sierra Leone was 3,160 with 19 churches, 21 elementary schools, two secondary schools, and one hospital. What a privilege it was to work with a total active workforce of 165 dedicated workers; it was a family. The mission finances and membership grew over the nine years the Keith family served as missionaries and many souls joined the Seventh-day Adventist Church as a result of their labor.

There were many experiences the Keiths encountered during their service in Sierra Leone. It is impossible to live in a foreign country, which is not your original home, and not be enriched with relationships which would last for a life time. Life as a missionary is rewarding because God has a plan for every worker who gives service to His Church and is willing to be used as a vessel in His vineyard.

The Keiths were able to save enough money to purchase a Polaroid camera when they went home on furlough. Now, for those of you who were born in the digital Camera era and want to know what a Polaroid Land camera was; it was a camera that developed its own pictures—a finished, dry, and positive print 10 seconds after the picture was taken. (The Polaroid camera has no tanks or liquids. Instead, it uses a special double roll of film that consists of a roll of negative material and a roll of self-processing positive paper. Small sealed pods containing special chemicals develop itself in one minute.)

"What a joy it was to take pictures of remote villages and people we came in contact with, schools, churches, and our Sierra Leonean friends. Numerous pictures were taken and in ten seconds the picture could be seen and given to friends as a gift or placed in a photo album. On many occasions when pictures were taken and in ten seconds the print could be seen immediately, it was interesting to witness the puzzled, shocked, and inquisitive expressions on the face of village friends who perhaps had never seen a camera and then to see a print of them was like magic."

It was a delight to take pictures and immediately see the print; however, one day the inevitable happened. The Keith family was visiting a missionary family in Freetown for the weekend. They had in their possession the camera to which they had become so attached. Taking pictures with their Polaroid camera was a daily routine. There was no place they would go without taking their camera.

Elder Dennis & Dorothy Keith 1967–1975

It is not unusual for one to go through life with a prized personal possession, and all of a sudden you are not sure if you misplaced the object or if it was lost. One day they were unable to find the camera. The first thought came to their minds was did they misplace the camera? As normal human beings would do, they searched, searched and searched for the camera. Then they started asking the questions, who had the camera last? Where was the camera placed? Who took the last picture and where? Was the camera left somewhere by mistake? You can imagine the unsatisfied emotions which swelled in their hearts and minds.

How could a camera disappear and no one knew anything? Every inch of the house where they were staying was searched. Every piece of furniture was removed and every room in the house was searched with penetrating eyes. The camera could not be found.

The next logical step was to go outside and look around the house and in the car. Soon they were doing the inappropriate inspection. Do you know what is meant by "inappropriate inspection?" When one starts looking in places where you know it is impossible for a camera to be—such as under the body of the car, behind trees and bushes, around the next door neighbor's house, and up and down the outside driveway. Their search became so ridiculous that they decided to just stop looking for a camera that just disappeared.

They knelt down and prayed, "Lord, you know where the camera is. Please help us find it and forgive us for not seeking your guidance when we discovered it had disappeared, Amen." With confidence and assurance they knew God would assist them to find their camera. They did not stop looking; however, there was one room located in the half-basement of the house which was not searched.

Also, unaware that a young male Sierra Leonean was watching their every move, they failed to ask him if he had seen their camera. When they asked if he knew where their camera was, the reply was "No." Again, they raised the question whether he had seen their camera and the response was again, "No." After questioning the young man several times, they proceeded to the room which was located in the half-basement of the house. The young man followed them to the basement and to their surprise they saw parts of the camera broken in pieces lying on the basement floor.

Questioning the young man as to how the camera pieces became strewn over the basement floor they discovered he was the missionary's "house boy." They became suspicious and felt he had knowledge about the camera. After a further series of questions, they noticed that the young man was frightened and confused in his response to their inquiries. It was apparent he knew something about the camera, but he would not admit what took place. They went to the police station and it was explained what had happened. The policemen questioned the young man and again it appeared he knew something about the missing camera—but he did not want to talk.

If a person was caught stealing in Sierra Leone, they would be beaten by the people who caught them as well as the police. They did not want the young man to be beaten; all they wanted was an admission to why or how the camera had disappeared. This was on Friday evening prior to sunset. The policemen were confident the young man knew something about the camera, so they said he should spend the night in a cell and perhaps tomorrow, Saturday, he would talk. The young man was left in the custody of the police. However, they emphasized not to beat the young man.

After attending church on Sabbath afternoon, they went to the police station to visit the young man. On their way into the police station's office, a middle age Sierra Leone man, under the influence of alcohol, bumped into Dennis and asked if he was an American and why was he dressed in a suit on Saturday? He mentioned to him, "Yes, I am an American and a Seventh-day Adventist returning from church; however, there is a young man locked in a cell and I want to visit him." He said to me with the smell of alcohol on his breath, "my wife is an American. Would you like to meet her?" I said, "Yes, as soon as I visit the young man in the cell." He followed Elder Dennis inside the police office and waited in a small room until he returned.

To their surprise, when they reached the police officer's office, they were informed the young man had indicated to the police that he had stolen the camera and broke it in pieces because he wanted to see what was inside the camera. The young man said he had never seen a camera develop a print immediately. He mentioned he was very sorry for causing them the trouble they had experienced. The policemen asked what they wanted to do with the young man. Their response was, "Please release him and do not charge him for stealing our camera." Immediately, the young man was released after saying he was sorry several times.

The man who was drunk then followed them out of the police station and asked them to follow him. They were concerned about following a person who was drunk; however, Dorothy, who was in the car waiting, also wanted to meet his wife. When Dennis shared the story with Dorothy about what took place in the police station with the young man, they thanked God for helping them to know what happened to their camera.

As they followed the man who was drunk and driving his car very slow, a total stranger to them, questions came to their minds if they were doing the right

Elder Dennis & Dorothy Keith 1967–1975

thing by following someone who claimed his wife to be an American; however, they placed their trust in God's care on this Sabbath afternoon. All of a sudden they noticed two large gate posts and a driveway as the drunken driver in the car in front of them made a left turn into the driveway. To their surprise, the man drove straight into the left gate with a loud bang! They could not believe their eyes. Now they have witnessed a terrible accident. The man was drunk, the car damaged, and the man was leaning over the steering wheel. Their immediate thoughts were, *Is he dead?* There was total silence and no movement from the man behind the steering wheel. They could not believe what they had witnessed! They whispered a silent prayer. "Lord please, do not let him die." Then they noticed movement in the car. Thank God, the man got out of the car and asked them to follow him up some stairs which led to his house. As he stumbled up the stairs with them behind him, they were very concerned as to what would happen next. They entered the house and the man in an incoherent manner asked them to have a seat in the living room while he went into the bedroom to get his wife. They sat and waited for five minutes, ten minutes, twenty minutes, a half an hour and no one came out of the bedroom. They looked at each other with astonishment and uncertainty wondering what to do now. Should they leave, should they knock on the bedroom door, or should they stay longer? Suddenly, they heard some crying from the room. It was a woman's cry which was getting louder, louder, and louder. Then they heard the man's voice. They could not understand what was going on or what was being said. So they sat and waited to see what was happening. Yes, they were whispering prayers for God to help in this strange situation. Then the man came out of the bedroom and asked Dorothy to go in the bedroom. Dennis stood up with uncertainty in his heart as his wife proceeded to the bedroom.

The man sat in the living room with Dennis while Dorothy was talking to his wife. After several moments passed, which seemed like hours, Dorothy came out of the room after having prayer with the woman. They had prayer with the man and departed from their house and went back to the mission house where they were staying. On their way back home, Dorothy mentioned that the woman was going to commit suicide because she was a prisoner in their own home. Also, the woman expressed how happy she was to meet Dorothy and to share her personal feelings and concerns as to what she should do under the circumstances she was facing. Dorothy informed the lady after prayer and counsel about the Seventh-day Adventist Church in Freetown. She stated she would like to become her friend and introduce her to Pastor Harry Cartwright and his wife Beverly, who also were Seventh-day Adventist American missionaries. Pastor Cartwright was the pastor of the Freetown Seventh-day Adventist

Precious Memories of Missionaries of Color

Church and Sierra Leone mission evangelist at that time. They stayed in contact with the young lady and her husband. Several months later their contact with the husband and wife grew into a friendly spiritual relationship. Pastor Harry Cartwright baptized the woman and she became a member of the Seventh-day Adventist Church in Freetown, Sierra Leone.

To their knowledge, the husband did not join the Seventh-day Adventist Church; however, he did not oppose his wife attending the church as a member. Their relationship grew as the months passed by and we thanked God for giving them an opportunity to meet this couple. Now, as they look back on this beautiful experience their understanding is much clearer as to how God used them to meet this lady and her husband—a simple Polaroid camera had disappeared, but a soul was found.

Elder Dennis & Dorothy Keith 1967–1975

Dorothy, Dennis, Denise and Dennis Jr. at Massanga

Precious Memories of Missionaries of Color

Our home in Bo, Sierra Leone, W. Africa

The Tema ship we sailed to Africa on

Elder Dennis & Dorothy Keith 1967–1975

Dennis & Denise one Sabbath afternoon

26

ELDER THEODORE (TED) & ESTHER JONES 1968-1971; 1974-1975

For many years, after becoming a member of the Great Adventist Movement, Ted had a deep yearning to become one of those fearless persons who represented Jesus Christ in far away places on planet earth. It did not matter where the Lord would send him, because he knew deep down in his heart that the word of the song was true, "Anywhere with Jesus I can safely go!" It was not in his spirit to be an ordinary worker in God's cause. He wanted to be a successful missionary—preaching the gospel and helping people to live healthy and productive lives.

While studying at the Seminary in Takoma Park, Maryland, he met two men who were missionaries in India—the Jensen brothers. They loaned him books about India and frequently told him that he could be a success with his preaching and trumpet playing. He also treasured the stories from African American men who were home on furlough from lands afar, he had heard while studying at Oakwood College. They were thrilling to his young heart and he hoped to someday join their honored ranks. He even learned to do sidewalk evangelistic preaching from Elder Bobby Roberts, a white missionary who served in Columbia, South America. Ted joined Bobby and Wendell Lacy for many weeks doing sidewalk preaching on the corner of 7th and S Street in downtown Washington, D.C. Yes, the Lord was fanning the flame in the direction of becoming a missionary and Ted was feeling the heat.

Before graduating from the Seminary in the late summer of 1958, Ted had the great privilege of working with Elder E. E. Cleveland in a major evangelistic campaign in Washington, D.C. More than 270 souls were baptized and another

Elder Theodore (Ted) & Esther Jones 1968–1975

dimension was added to his growing satchel of soul-winning tools. Cleveland employed him as his minister of music for the three month series of meetings. He also had his own Cathedral Quartet—Joyce Bryant, Charles Lee Brooks and T. Marshall Kelly. It was enriching!

Someone from the General Conference office, located around the corner from the Seminary, came to the Seminary and offered application forms for those who wanted to apply for foreign mission service. Naturally, Ted took one and he distinctly recalls a section of the long form which asked him to list in the order of preference the areas of the world where he would like to serve. After a few minutes of contemplation, he wrote the following: Far East, India, and Africa. South America was added later. Even after being in pastoral-evangelistic work for nearly ten years, he received no calls to work overseas. He discovered that God was in control of His work and when the fullness of time comes, no man or group can prevent His will from being manifested.

One Sabbath morning, while teaching his Sabbath School class in the front center section of the Bakersfield Southside Church in central California, he noticed a thin Caucasian man and a young lady enter the sanctuary and sit on the last pew of a class on the right side. This class was being taught by a deacon named Robert Jackson. The visitor kept scanning the six classes busily engaged in discussion as if he was trying to find someone. When the class period ended, the man asked Robert where the pastor was and Robert immediately pointed to Ted. The visitor then whispered something to Robert that made his eyes stretch and a smile swept across his face. Robert came hurriedly down the aisle and told Ted that the visitor was a member of the committee in the Far Eastern Division and that they had just voted to give him a call as a missionary to India or something that sounded like that. He asked Robert to get the man and to bring him to his office. What a great way to get ready to start a church service! That visitor was Dr. Neil Thrasher, a surgeon in the big Seventh-day Adventist Hospital in Bandung, Kava, in the great nation of Indonesia. Yes, it was true! Ted's name had just been checked out and approved to become the first African American to be called as a missionary to the Far Eastern Division. The job description was to serve the West Indonesia Union Mission as the Evangelistic Center, located on Jakarta's biggest six lane boulevard, Jalan Thamrin. Ted and his wife, Esther, took Dr. Thrasher and his daughter home with them and learned as much as they could about this revelation of their future. This was truly a time of great excitement for them!

It must be mentioned that two of the church's greatest preachers had already been to Indonesia and no doubt had helped to influence the brethren that someone of color could go there as a missionary and be accepted. Those

Precious Memories of Missionaries of Color

men were Elder E. E. Cleveland and Elder C. E. Moseley, Jr. Indonesia has several island areas where the people are Negroid and many of its over 200 million people are racially mixed. The people in Indonesia were found to be open hearted, generous, athletic, loving, and anxious to learn.

After the usual intense months of preparation, the Jones were finally ready to take their journey into foreign mission life. They studied the Indonesian language for several months with a single, young Indonesian man who also taught his native language at a United States military establishment on the west coast in California. After bidding farewell to family and friends, they flew from San Francisco to Hawaii and then took a flight which seemed to last forever from Honolulu to Tokyo. Arriving in Tokyo with a full blown case of jet lag, and after the Japan Union treasurer took them sightseeing, he asked what they would like to eat and the response was pizza of all things. This man knew his way around in the city and took them to a very nice restaurant where they ordered pizza. Half way through the huge pizza, their four children dropped off into a deep sleep and the three surviving adults were left with food to spare.

They had touring tickets arranged by the General Conference, going through Hong Kong, Manila, and Singapore before finally arriving in Jakarta. Japan was simply their first stop in the Far Eastern Division. By the time the family arrived in Manila on a very hot Friday afternoon, they were all very, very tired. They were to have been met at the airport by someone from the North Philippine Union Mission, but that did not happen. After waiting at the curb with thirteen pieces of luggage and surrounded by at least a dozen men, many of whom had pistols in their belts, Ted was instructed to call the Union office and tell them that they had arrived and needed help in the worst way. They discovered that someone had been there to get them but he did not know that we were people of color and passed by them without realizing who they were. The nationals in the Philippines rejoiced to meet them and after two or three days, someone sent a telegram to the Division office telling the brethren there that they liked what they saw and wanted them to stay in Manila. In exchange, they would send their ministerial man to Jakarta. The Division office responded quickly and ordered that they should fly down to Singapore so that they could get ready to work in a city wide meeting to be conducted by Don Jacobsen, their newly-appointed ministerial director and evangelist.

In Singapore, Ted and Esther were part of a large evangelistic team directed by Elder Jacobsen. Each night, they supplied a trumpet solo and daily worked with a Chinese pastor visiting homes and apartment buildings, seeking those who were attending the meetings. This campaign formed the basis of understanding the Asian mind and culture which proved to be very helpful

Elder Theodore (Ted) & Esther Jones 1968-1975

for his future work. Esther's skills on the organ were greatly appreciated by everyone.

Finally, arriving in Jakarta, Indonesia, they were met at the airport by a delegation of workers who greeted them enthusiastically and drove them to the Evangelistic Center for a grand reception. This was a foretaste of great things to come. When they finally arrived at the American Adventist compound, they found a lovely home and friendly neighbors awaiting them. When their shipment of personal effects finally arrived, they were delighted. Their children enjoyed the freedom of a nice large yard, plenty of fruit trees, and beautiful plants and flowers. The oversea school was next door and other families had children who were classmates and playmates for the four Jones children.

There were more invitations to preach than he could accept. So many wanted to see the first African American family to live in Indonesia. Ted's first assignment to conduct an evangelistic meeting came later in 1968. It was to be conducted in Surabaya, East Java. The president of the Mission was a handsome man who spoke at least four languages fluently, Janz B. Th. Umiboh. When Ted preached his first sermon in the large church in Surabaya, the sound of the voice translating his message suddenly stopped. Turning to see what had happened, he discovered that his interpreter was leaning on the pulpit, weeping. As he approached him to ask what the matter was, he said, "You are making the scene too real!" His sermon that day was, "Were You There When They Crucified My Lord?"

At the end of that six week campaign, the Lord gave them 157 baptisms, which was the highest number of baptisms in the history of that Mission. The Division leaders and workers were very happy that the Lord was blessing them with such good success. The team of men and women who worked with them did an excellent job with home visitations. They had a quartet that sang Negro spirituals and hymns to add more flavor to the nightly meetings—in addition to the trumpet solos he rendered. The children who attended the meetings gave Ted a nickname, "Ohm Trompet" which is Uncle Trumpet.

There were other large evangelistic series conducted in cities like Medan, North Sumatra, where many unusual things happened—including a trap laid for Ted in a question submitted during Question and Answer section of the nightly meetings. Someone asked, "I have been attending these meetings for three weeks now. All I hear you talk about is the Bible, this man Jesus Christ, and some place called Heaven. Tonight, I want you to compare Christianity with Islam and then state which of the two is the true religion." Ted's poor translator, Urbanus Aritonangm became very agitated as he recognized this question to be a religio-political bomb. He refused to read the question to the

Precious Memories of Missionaries of Color

audience of some 1,600 people but the Holy Spirit impressed Ted to proceed with a reading of the question and then to answer the request. When he finished, taking about seven minutes to respond, the audience applauded for several minutes. Many in the audience were university students. When this campaign ended after six long weeks of preaching and teaching, they rejoiced in the Lord for 139 baptisms, many of whom were medical school upper classmen, nurses, and other professionals.

It was later that year when Ted was riding a train to Central Java that another strange experience occurred. Things were going smoothly when suddenly he noticed people passing the door in the compartment where he was sitting. They were crying and pointing to me. He was amazed and felt like asking someone what was wrong when a man walked over to where he sat and offered his condolences in English, spoken for his benefit, he announced, "What a pity, what a pity, someone in America has killed a good man, Dr. Martin Luther King, Jr. He is your tribesman, sir! A great American is now dead!" The people of Indonesia knew of the struggles of African Americans and felt a kinship to us! They had suffered under the colonial rule of the Dutch for so many years and could empathize with our people who had continued to suffer under racism and prejudice. Ted knew that he was among friends.

The Lord gave the Joneses so many rich experiences during their sojourn in Indonesia that they must someday write a book. There were two occasions when Ted was asked to teach in their colleges—one located in Java and the other situated in the North Celebes. There were many invitations to conduct Weeks of Prayer, and the Holy Spirit was always there to bless the preaching of the Word. One Sabbath stands out for a very special reason. As his translator, William Hutapea, stood to Ted's left as he preached, a lady sitting on the last row of seats in the chapel, suddenly stood and pointed at the platform where they were standing. We didn't know what was going on but we did observe her husband encouraging her to sit down. After the service had ended 23 students came forward making decisions for baptism. Then, the husband of the lady took us aside and explained what was happening during our sermon. He said, "My wife embarrassed me by her actions. While you men were preaching, she said that she saw an Angel standing beside Pastor Jones." Her husband looked and saw nothing and told her to be seated. A few minutes later she said that the Angel appeared again. Then, as the students began to go forward, they knew that the Holy Spirit was truly in this place.

Ted felt that his goal as a missionary was to train Indonesians to be better pastors, better evangelists, better leaders, and stronger Christians. He thanked God for opening the door for him and family to go to the former Far Eastern

Elder Theodore (Ted) & Esther Jones 1968-1975

Division to serve and represent Him. From Sumatra to Java to Kalimaritan to the Timor Islands to the North Celebes to West Irian to Sarawak, we shall one day see many souls in the eternal kingdom.

In 1974, the Joneses went out again as a missionary family, this time to the former Afro-Mideast Division where Ted was called to serve as the Chairman of the Department of Theology and Biblical Languages. Elder C. D. Henri arranged this call to service. This was during the time when the infamous Idi Amin Dada was the President of Uganda and the college where Ted was to work was Bugema Adventist College. Located some 24 miles northeast of the city of Kampala, Bugema was the only college operated by the Adventist Church in Uganda. Ted taught upper level classes, oversaw the operations of the campus clinic, and for a short while was the pastor of the campus church. Heaven came down to earth on Friday nights during vespers. The singing in the chapel was powerfully harmonious and on Sabbath mornings it was very heart warming! During the Week of Prayer that same year, Dr. Earl Richards, who served as a dentist in our medical clinic in the city of Nairobi, Kenya, opened a new avenue of music to the students and campus family. Before he preached each night, he taught a Negro spiritual to the congregation. One song still stands out in Ted's mind: "I'm Gonna Sit at the Welcome Table." The next day you could hear the students singing that song as they walked between classes from building to building. Life in Uganda became bearable as human spirits were lifted through the words and music of spirituals. What a great blessing Dr. Earl Richards was to Bugema Adventist College. Many decisions were made for baptism.

In spite of the presence of many deadly, poisonous snakes on the campus like the black and the green mamba, cobras, and Gaboon Vipers, they managed to stay alive and do the Lord's work. Ted killed a 7 foot, angry black mamba one eventful afternoon in the garage of an uninhabited house just up the road from where they lived. One day after they had arrived at their house, their daughter was playing with the child of their Filipino neighbor, Daniel Poblete, when a cobra was discovered very close to where they were standing. Before Ted could blink twice, the father rushed out of their house, grabbed a stick and killed the snake. Naturally, this incident struck fear in Esther's heart and she began praying hard for all of us who lived in such a snake-infested area of the campus. God heard her prayers because very soon a group of mongooses came to live in their yard and suddenly there were no more cobras around to scare them. They did have monkeys who shared the fruit of our yard boy's labors and occasionally a leopard would come to our end of the campus, causing the dogs to scratch on the doors, pleading for entrance before the big cat would devour them. Uganda also had its share of huge birds and a great variety of wild life.

Precious Memories of Missionaries of Color

Times were so difficult in Uganda during their stay, that the post office clerks would beg the Joneses to bring them some eggs from their chicken farm on the campus. They also begged for body soap and when he was able to bring them the desired items, they would let him send books to the college without paying the usual high fees from the customs department. President Idi Amin learned that the United States Department of State had worked out an arrangement with Ted to bring into Uganda a hugh ship load of machines, vehicles, clothing, school supplies, road paving materials and machines, institutional water pumps, foods, shoes, buses, cars, ambulances, furniture, cooking oil and other necessities. President Amin personally talked with Ted as he sat in his VW bus grading papers about the program called Operation Recovery for Uganda or ORFU. Unfortunately, Ted's endorsement letters from the General Conference and the Ugandan Embassy in Washington, D.C. and the special letter of commitment from the State Department were confiscated by two non-governmental persons, thus blocking the project. That was his worst heartbreaking experience because it would have brought help to hundreds of thousands of people—and especially to the college. At the same time Esther continued teaching the children of missionaries who worked on the college campus plus the two children of Bugema's first Ugandan President Pastor Yoswa Gwalamubisi. These times were full of daily difficulties but God was with them, overshadowing all kinds of conflicts and problems.

After serving in Uganda for one and a half years, Ted became seriously ill with a parasite called bilharzias. Finding no help in Uganda, he received permission from the chairman of the board of their college who resided in Nairobi, to go there for treatment. He was having total body pain and great weight loss. Dr. Obie Alozie, a Nigerian, who worked in the large hospital in Nairobi finally came up with an accurate diagnosis which saved his life. The medicine was very strong and had to be in order to kill this parasite. Ted's energy level went down to 10 on a 1 to 100 scale. After the cure was pronounced, he got the disease again even though he had not been swimming in Lake Victoria where the parasite was commonly known to reside. Dr. Alozie ordered him to leave Africa immediately or face death within six months. With heavy hearts his family departed from Africa and headed to North America for care and treatment. While temporarily residing in Loma Linda, California, with the family of Dr. Samuel L. DeShay, he received word from Elder W. W. Fordham that the General Conference wanted him to move to Nashville and become the Editor of the *Message* magazine.

God continued to lead in their lives and after retiring from the position of Associate Secretary of the General Conference, they shall be moving to the

Elder Theodore (Ted) & Esther Jones 1968–1975

Midwest where they hope to slow down a bit while still serving our Master. After 48 and one-half years of service, it is time for them to change their pace of living and continue to share the message of truth that "we hold dear to our hearts. God is faithful! God is good! God is love! He is coming soon! Maranatha!"

Wedding in Indonesia; Esther usually played the organ.

Precious Memories of Missionaries of Color

First Baptism in 1968 from a six week campaign in Surabaya,
East Java, resulting in 157 baptisms

The Evangelistic team in Medan, North Sumatra, where 139 souls were added to the church

Elder Theodore (Ted) & Esther Jones 1968-1975

Elder Ted Jones preaching

Elder Ted Jones playing the trumpet; he was accompanied by his wife, Esther, on the piano or organ.

27

Elder Walton & Leola Whaley
1968-1998

The Whaley family left the United States of America on the 8th of December, 1968, on the way to their first mission assignment, Freetown, Sierra Leone. By the grace of God, they sold their newly purchased house, car, furniture, myriads of belongings, and gave away their precious German shepherd, named Lady. They packed an astounding array of "will need" household goods, foodstuffs, books, and what have you; paid off all of their bills, took all of the immunization shots needed, and said good-by to church members, relatives, and friends within six months of receiving the call to mission service.

By way of introduction, Walton was born in Jersey (New Jersey), raised in Newark, and nurtured in the Trinity Temple Church and school on Bergen Street. He moved to New York, graduated from 8th grade in PS 3 in Brooklyn and from the 12th grade in Northeastern Academy. The Bethel Church in Brooklyn planted the seed in Walton's heart for mission service through the Sabbath School mission stories and visits from missionaries. He entered Oakwood College in January, 1954, dropping out twice, but finally graduated with the class of 1960.

Leola Johnson was born and raised in Baton Rouge, Louisiana. She was baptized into the Seventh-day Adventist Church by the late Elder Walter Fordham, and the still much alive, Elder Charles E. Bradford. The brethren did a very good work, and they are eternally grateful. Leola is a graduate of Oakwood College and Loma Linda School of Nursing. Her seed for mission service was planted firmly.

Elder Walton & Leola Whaley 1968–1998

Walton and Leola met on the steps of the old Wadsworth Seventh-day Adventist Church in Los Angeles during Walton's second drop-out from college. He noticed Leola on several occasions in her role as Sabbath School secretary, and the meeting on the church steps was a defining moment. They were married on December 14, 1958. Their first child, Susan Marie, was born while they were at Andrews University in 1961. Next, came Walton Jr. and Janice Faith, who were both born in California where the Whaleys spent their first seven years of ministry. They took the long journey from Pittsburg, California, to Freetown, Sierra Leone and celebrated their 10th wedding anniversary in their new mission home a few days after arriving. A little surprise, who they named Sharon Mariama Abioseh, joined their family five years later. They were now six. Full stop!

A fast forward on their children: 2004, finds Susan as an accomplished registered nurse and mother of Steven, her talented thirteen year old son; Walton, Jr. is a district manager at United Parcel Service married to Phoebe Mati. They have three sons: Aaron, Walton Sahil, and Daniel Sameer; Janice is a highly respected COO in a major organ transplant company in Texas. She has two very protective little Yorkies named Max and Minnie; Sharon, a teacher by profession, is married to Evangelist William Pergerson, and they have two children—William III, and Jaissa. If you've been counting, they have eight grandchildren! OK, six grandchildren and two grand dogs.

During their seven years as pastor/evangelist in Freetown, they conducted eleven major evangelistic meetings. In the very first campaign, it was their privilege to baptize Samuel Bangura, the Governor of the Bank of Sierra Leone. The Sunday morning Bible Studies in his executive residence were times of deep thought and searching questions. On the day of Samuel's baptism, his baptismal robe wasn't quite a good fit and it brought a giggle or two from his witnessing friends. But the joy of putting on Christ through baptism overshadowed the outward appearance as he came up out of the water, his face beaming with the peace of Jesus.

Their last evangelistic campaign before leaving Sierra Leone was conducted in Kissy, a village suburb of Freetown. The community center was packed nightly. The little children sang the theme song day and night around the village: "In the name of Jesus, in the name of Jesus, we have the victory!" More than thirty new believers were baptized and the Adventist Church was firmly established in Kissy. That congregation produced a then future mission president, Sahr Sandy. The Freetown district included Waterloo and Samueltown. Freetown and Waterloo each had a church. The Samueltown believers worshipped in a low mud hut with a thatched roof. The hut sat on the ground.

Precious Memories of Missionaries of Color

Kerosene lamps provided light for the study of the Sabbath school lesson and the preaching task. Spiders and other critters were at home in the thatch that rubbed against one's face if he didn't bow low enough. The hut began to lean downward as Pastor Whaley visited from time to time. It wasn't difficult to persuade the members to tear down their place of worship and build anew. They tore it down and worshipped in the chief's compound until a new church was erected to the glory of God. That was one of several times they emptied their savings during their Africa sojourn. They do remember with fondness the gift of several hundred dollars that came to them for this project by Sister Esther Simpson of Pittsburg, California. The Freetown church was boxed into a triangle piece of property on Circular Road, a main street traversing the city. A cemetery was on the left and a well traveled road was on the other side. The proud cornerstone said that the church was built in 1907 by D. C. Babcock, pioneer missionary to West Africa for the Adventist Church. Behind it was a three story frame apartment building. The tax assessor found cause to auction off the three story building. Their bid was accepted and the territory was enlarged. The rents aided the church for several years. But one day, the news came that the first church built in West Africa by the Seventh-day Adventist Church had burned to the ground. They learned that the house behind the church caught on fire and that sparks from there fell on the church roof setting it on fire. With the additional space afforded to the church by the purchase of the now destroyed apartment building, there now sits on that enlarged triangle, an imposing place of worship that can be seen from afar.

They were given the privilege of pioneering a junior college in Ghana. The college began with the name, "Adventist Missionary College." The name was later changed to "Valley View College," and then to "Valley View University." After only fifteen years of existence, it was chartered by the Government of Ghana to be a degree granting institution of higher learning. To have been associated with such a dramatic history giving rise of a humble junior college into a prominent Adventist educational institution is awesome. Their beginning was extremely difficult with a military government in power. Food was in short supply and petrol or gasoline was difficult to obtain. Tires for vehicles were nearly impossible to buy. They started the college without proper capital funding, with rented quarters for classrooms, library, offices, assembly room, and dormitories. Water for cooking and washing was a constant concern. But the pioneer students were magnificent! Instead of complaining, they made the best use of what was available. They organized themselves for the service-needs of the school. They prayed! They went out for missionary activities! They won souls! They studied hard! When the then GC Department of Education

Elder Walton & Leola Whaley 1968–1998

Director, George Akers, came to inspect and evaluate the school, he said, "In spite of the lack of adequate infrastructure, learning is taking place here." His interview with the students gave him great satisfaction and he led his committee to vote for 'limited accreditation.' They were instrumental in securing over two hundred acres of land for the permanent campus—a beautiful campus which is now a reality.

The eleven final years of their African service, were spent in Abidjan, Cote d'Ivoire, where Pastor Whaley served as Ministerial Secretary for the Africa-Indian Ocean Division. The soul-winning programs of the World Church ignited the African membership across the continent. "90 Days of Reaping," "Harvest 90," and "Global Mission" were the catalyst that gave impetus and direction to the evangelistic thrust that propelled the Division into the million member club, taking fourth place among the World Divisions. Coordinating evangelistic events throughout the 32 countries of the Division, budgeting funding for major campaigns, and personally conducting crusades along the way filled the Abidjan years with excitement and awe at what the Heavenly Father was doing to expand his church in Africa. Cooperating with Him, they saw great miracles of grace as souls, chained to superstition, tradition, and misapprehension of God, stretched their hands and hearts toward Jesus, the Light of the World. The chains were broken! Hearts were healed! Love was ignited! Souls were set free!

One season of evangelism stands out in Pastor Whaley's mind as something that should never be forgotten. Pastor Whaley's wife, Leola, was allowed to accompany him on a six week evangelistic tour. They conducted reaping meetings in Calabar, Nigeria, Lumbumbashi, Zaire (Congo), Freetown, Sierra Leone, Bolgatanga, North Ghana, and Berekum, Ghana.

Leola gave health lectures and family life tips each night. To their great joy, the result from that six weeks evangelistic safari was that over five hundred precious souls were baptized. Glory to God!

Support from America punctuated the evangelistic thrust. The Real Truth Evangelistic team, led by Pastor Whaley's friend, Elder Bill Scales made a tremendous contribution in Ghana and Zaire. Thousands responded to the preaching of the gospel and went down into the watery grave of baptism to unite their lives with Christ. Dr. Calvin Rock and his team stunned the city of Accra as he preached under the power of the Holy Spirit. The Quiet Hour teams, led by the late James Zachary, roamed Africa with the gospel. Ghana, Cameroon, Rwanda, and Burundi were just some of the hundreds of places touched by this prodigious worker for God. It was a great privilege to associate with these great men of God and coordinate their activities in their small part of the Lord's vineyard in the Africa-Indian Ocean Division.

Precious Memories of Missionaries of Color

Some very sad events scarred those eleven years in Abidjan. The outbreak of violence in Liberia, Sierra Leone, Rwanda, and Burundi caused them much pain and many prayers at the Division. Their people were on both sides of the complex struggles in each country. They loved them all. They were all our brothers and sisters in Christ. How could they not respond to their pleas for help in those wretched refugee camps? Why didn't they do more? Why didn't the gospel they preached temper the stark inhumanity of man to man displayed in those conflicts? What did they do wrong that such an outbreak of horrendous proportions should be unleashed on these countries on their watch? The only answer that stilled the disquietude in their souls was the realization that "an enemy hath done this!"

A final caveat of opportunity afforded to them in the mission field was to be the Division coordinator for the Global Mission Pioneer movement. Training humble youth to infiltrate areas where the Advent message had not reached was exciting and rewarding. Uniting with the Union and Conference/Mission leaders, they trained hundreds of pioneers. They went! They saw! They prayed! They worked! They conquered in Jesus' name! These undaunted pioneers established churches in unentered areas with startling rapidity. Their humble circumstances, pitiable stipends, and bouts with malaria and dysentery could not deter them from going into Moslem dominated cities and lifting up Jesus. They were calling for pastors to come and baptize their people after only six months of work in the field. Occasional inspection tours would find them glowing and growing and their people happy in Jesus. Someone once said, "What an army of youth, rightly trained, might furnish."

The Whaleys' twenty-nine and one-half years in the mission field gave them a deep love for the people they served. The contributions they were able to make were made possible by the grace and mercy of God. When God wants His people blessed, He will use whatever and whomever is available to send the blessing through. (He once used a donkey.) They praise God that He used them in Africa for nearly thirty years, and then gave them permission to return to the United States with sound minds and a reasonable portion of health and strength.

Elder Walton & Leola Whaley 1968–1998

Pastor & Mrs. Walton Whaley

Precious Memories of Missionaries of Color

In Gambia

Elder Walton & Leola Whaley 1968–1998

In Madagascar

Katrina at G.C. session in Toronto

Precious Memories of Missionaries of Color

Baptism at Tamale

Happy days in Abidjan

Elder Walton & Leola Whaley 1968-1998

Lubumbashi, Zaire

Evangelism in Cote d'Ivoire

Baptism of Paraplegic convert

Precious Memories of Missionaries of Color

Inspecting a church in Kinshasa

Evangelistic campaign in Katumba, East Congo

Elder Walton & Leola Whaley 1968–1998

Literature evangelist in Abidjan

Pastoral team in Ghana

Minister's wives in Congo

Minister's wives in Congo

Precious Memories of Missionaries of Color

Professor Gabrah in Kumasi

Colleagues at the Africa-Indian Ocean Division

Wedding reception in Abidjan

Elder Walton & Leola Whaley 1968–1998

Baptism in Ghana

Walton Whaley Jr. and family

Grandma & William

Precious Memories of Missionaries of Color

Sabbath at Konogo, Ghana

Sharon on her wedding day

Elder Walton & Leola Whaley 1968–1998

Mrs. Whaley & Friends at the New Town Church in Accra

AMC Quartet

Mrs. Whaley and AMC students

Oven where Mrs. Whaley baked bread

Baptism in Ghana

28

SISTER RUBY GRAVES 1968-1970

Ruby heard the voice of the Lord, saying, "Whom shall I send and who will go for us?" She responded, "Here am I; send me" (Isaiah 5:8). Like Isaiah, Ruby's promise to the Lord was finally becoming a reality since listening to the mission stories at the age of eight.

While en route from Kennedy International Airport to Lagos, Nigeria, West Africa, she toured several European countries. Among the most memorable were Lisbon, Portugal, where even in March it was cold, and Madrid, Spain, which had light snow flurries. Since Ruby was dressed in fall clothes, she looked forward to arriving in Africa were the sun's warmth would feel so good upon her body.

At the airport, two strangers from Ile-Ife School of Nursing (IISN) met and welcomed Ruby to the country. Her faith and trust in God remained strong as she traveled via car to the hospital's compound with these complete strangers during the Bi-African War who were the female Dean of Nurses and her male driver.

En route to the hospital's compound which was a four hour drive, they passed many interesting sites. One was a group of Muslims walking along the roadside as they were leaving their prayer ground. The men dressed in beautiful colorful national attire and walked in front of the women. Some of the ladies carried umbrellas to shelter themselves from the hot mid-day sun. However, many of the sites she missed seeing because of her dozing from being exhausted from jet lag. Nevertheless, once arriving at the compound, she immediately went to bed and was even too tired to respond to a small,

Sister Ruby Graves 1968–1970

fast-running creature that crossed the floor in front of her bed and hid in the open-door-closet. With her eye glasses lying on the bedside table, she could not see clearly; but she prayed to the Lord for His protection while sleeping. After awakening, she learned that the creature was a friendly house lizard that ate mosquitoes and bugs.

Ruby's compound apartment was nice—there were two bedrooms, a living room, bathroom, dining room and kitchen. However, the physical structure had three inconveniences which were that the dining room and kitchen were separated from the other four rooms. If the rooms had been joined, the temperature in the living quarters could get too hot when the outside temperature rose to 120 degrees Fahrenheit in the shade. So Ruby had to go out doors to get to the dining room and kitchen. All drinking water had to be boiled and filtered. Tap water was contaminated, and there was only cold water at the bathroom sink. However, over the bath tub was a hot water tank to heat water for bathing.

Concerning the food, Ruby had two favorite dishes: fried plantains and bean cakes. Plantains resemble large bananas which could be eaten ripe or baked when green. Bean cakes were made from black-eyed peas with hot spices. They were also fried. Both dishes were delicious! She says that she shouldn't have eaten those bean cakes because of the spices.

Domestic workers were essential. Elizabeth, Ruby's house girl was a student in the secondary school. She wanted to become a nurse and graduated several years later from IISN after Ruby returned to the United States.

Ile-Ife's hospital compound had five wards, clinic, diet kitchen, and surgery. Ruby was assigned as Head Nurse of the Pediatric Ward. There were many memorable moments. Although sad, she recalls a healthy three year old lad who had been admitted because his pregnant mother had suddenly died in the clinic before giving them any information. The frightened child was unable to tell his full name. Thus, the hospital placed notices in the local paper. It took several months before his father came. Most people had to work to save money for traveling expenses before walking many miles to the hospital. During the interim, Ruby brought the child Sabbath clothes and weekly took him to Sabbath School.

Then, there was the adventure of Ingathering in the rural areas (bush country). As she helped to collect the Lord's donations, Ruby encouraged each mother to bring her child or children into the clinic for free immunizations. One mother was so grateful for the information that she brought her children to be immunized and a fruit basket for Ruby. What a pleasant surprise!

Precious Memories of Missionaries of Color

Next, Ruby recalls the woman who had tetanus (lockjaw). A tracheotomy tube had been inserted into her trachea (windpipe) so that she could breathe. Ruby didn't know whether the illness or the "not so sterile suction technique" would kill her. But life was in God's hands, Amen? Ruby was told that the woman's husband had said one Saturday that if his wife lived, he would bring his entire family to worship services. Financially, he was in the upper class. He was also sincere. His wife survived and true to his word, one Sabbath, he, his wife and children walked into church thanking God for His blessing and thanking the hospital for his wife's care.

Ruby saw many miracles. It was rare however for a critically ill patient who had drunk cow's urine to survive. Cow's urine was given by the nature (witch) doctor as a last resort in hope of saving the patient's life. However, most of the patients that she saw who had ingested the substance usually died. But I recall one adult male patient who beat the odds (which was a miracle) and who walked out of the hospital praising God. We were praising God, too!

They also praised God that one hundred percent of the graduate nursing students passed their government examinations. Another one of Ruby's responsibilities was to teach surgical Nursing to the senior class. Prior to her arrival several students had done poorly—one female had failed twice. With God's help and that of the other faculty members, Ruby wanted each student to pass including those who had failed before.

It was her first experience in professional teaching and there were many very unhappy students; although, not all of them. Some were unhappy because Ruby required a comprehensive case study. Each student was required to choose an adult surgical patient with a disease of his or her choice. Next, he or she had to give that patient preoperative teaching, preoperative care, preoperative medicine, observe the patient's surgery, give immediate post operative care, and write a comprehensive care study. After the papers were graded and returned, each of the 25 to 30 students appreciated his or her semester assignment which was priceless.

Not far from Ile-Ife, annually, the Oshun Festival was held by the nationals. Ruby attended the festival to become knowledgeable and to be able to relate an accurate account of the happenings. What Ruby saw did not involve any animal or human sacrifices. However, earlier in the week animal sacrifices had occurred. According to the nationals there were never any human sacrifices. (Thank God that the most memorable human sacrifice was His Son's death on Calvary for our repented and forsaken sins.) The only sacrifices at the Oshun Festival were fruits and grains. The Nationals believed that they were thrown into the river as an offering to Oshun, the goddess of the river. They were gifts of thanksgiving for protection, health, long life, and a good harvest.

Sister Ruby Graves 1968-1970

Another memorable moment was attending a dinner at the Ambassador of Chad's residence. An Adventist girl friend invited Ruby to attend the dinner with her. The single Ambassador's apartment was very nice and the floor plan in Lagos was similar to the hospital compound's apartments. He lived in a two story building on the second floor at the end. On one side of the hallway were the living room, dining room, and kitchen. Across the hall were the bedroom and bathroom and both entrance doors had locks. Ruby's blessing in attending was the opportunity to sow gospel seeds during the meal.

Shortly after a year of service, Ruby left Nigeria to fill a need at the Masanga Leprosarium in Sierra Leone, West Africa. More memorable moments followed.

Masanga's compound had three wards, two settlements (for male and female for lepers not ill enough to be admitted into the wards), a surgery, clinic, and diet kitchen.

Often at Masanga, Ruby thanked God for experience from having worked at Glendale's Sanitarium Hospital Intensive Care Unit (California). Her training was utilized when Dr. DeShay and his wife, Bernice—a mid-wife—were away from the compound, she had to deliver babies, admit patients into the hospital, and suture emergency wounds. Once in the clinic, she recalls diagnosing and treating over thirty patients. On the female ward, she also recalls removing sutures from a patient with a cleft palate.

Numerous times, she thanked God for giving her guidance during each delivery especially with twins and breech births. One grateful Mom named her infant after Ruby. The child's first name is Temne, but her middle name is English. On the compound, they were known as "Bib" and "Little" Ruby. It was the Mom's sixth child and Ruby's first delivery with the Lord's help.

At Masanga, Ruby enjoyed participating with the Friday night singing bands on the wards. She was frightened by the terrible lightning storms, mice, snakes, bats, and ants. These ants were larger than normal and when they invaded a house, they came by the millions! It was in Masanga where she learned that the USA's mainland had leprosy hospitals. They all closed in the 1990's; however, there is still a leprosy colony in Hawaii.

After returning to the USA, Ruby, realizing the needs of both Masanga and IISN, solicited various denominations for items. Items such as artificial limbs for the leper patients who lost their legs to gangrene were donated. (One of the complications of leprosy is that the nerve tissue is destroyed. Thus one could cut his or her feet and never feel the pain. Infection would enter the wound and eventually the limb would have to be amputated to save the person's life if medicine had not been administered in time.) Leper bandages, commode

Precious Memories of Missionaries of Color

chairs, wheel chairs, and syringes were also needed. Thanks be to God, a ton of hospital supplies and equipment including school items were collected and shipped to West Africa by the General Conference.

During the 1970's, Ruby married in Ohio. She and her husband live in New York City with their three children. Elizabeth's husband, a Nigerian, is a pharmacist. She works as a Registered Nurse in the Emergency Room. Their three children are medical students. The oldest son is a resident. The middle daughter is an intern and the youngest son is in medical school.

The *Message* magazine published Ruby's first article concerning "The African Project." An inmate at the Colorado State Penitentiary read it and extended an invitation for Ruby to speak at the facility. Arrangements were made with the chaplain. Youth choir and church members helped her to conduct her first service in April, 1973.

In 1976, she attended the State University of New York at Buffalo School of Nursing. While attending school, she began volunteering in prisons in the western New York area. (For more information see www.alumni.buffalo.edu. Click on archives profile). Later, the one on one with inmates and letter writing grew into giving group Bible Studies, chapel services, collecting clothes and/or food for residents in a half-way house, Baptist soup kitchen, and to the homeless and needy. Then after the death of Ruby's husband, Harry Reed, in December, 1995, the Lord blessed her to become a full-time volunteer.

It was in 1997 that the radio ministry called Bible Truth Prison Ministry (BTPM) and Abundant Health (AH) began in August and December, respectively. The children's choir called "Jesus' Little Lambs" began in September 2000. The choir consists of female non-church members ages 8-13. They sing and sign in English, Spanish, Yoruba, Latin and French. The choir's most memorable presentations were on WIVB Channel 4 (CBS) in Buffalo; Baptist Church in Rochester; Adventist Buffalo Hispanic Church and on WUFO AM Radio in Buffalo/Amherst (every fifth Sunday). Both Channel 4 and WUFO transmitters beam from the Buffalo area to Rochester, New York, western Pennsylvania, and southern Canada (Toronto and Niagara Falls).

As a result of the AH broadcasts, BTPM members have conducted two Vegetarian Cooking Seminars. In 2003 and 2004, approximately 50 non-church members attended the seminars including an Italian physician who demonstrated the preparation of two Italian vegetarian soups—one had the option of using sheep cheese. Dr Frank Kelly also lectured and answered health questions.

The Lord heard and answered Ruby's childhood prayers and desires. As a result of keeping her promises to the Lord and serving as a missionary nurse

Sister Ruby Graves 1968-1970

for Him, He expanded her horizon. Now as funds are available, BTPM members send Bibles, medical and nursing textbooks and journals to IISN. In addition, other BTPM needs their funds to purchase Bibles for inmate use, funds for the radio ministry, a sponsor for Jesus' Little Lambs, literature and four ply yarn for a 90 year old blind member who crochets afghans for the needy. If you choose to help, please send your tax-deductible donation to: Bible Truth Prison Ministry, P. O. Box 364, Williamsville, New York 14231-0364. "For I was hungry and ye gave me meat...Naked. And ye clothed me: I was in prison, and ye came unto me." (Matthew 25 35, 36.)

Memorable Moments: Former Missionary Nurse

Sister Ruby Graves, R.N., M.S.
Late Husband: Harry Reed (December, 1995)
Parents: Mrs. and Mrs. Hugh Graves (7 children: 5 males & 2 females).

Education: Paradise Valley School of Nursing (R.N.), National City, California
Loretto Heights College (BSN) Denver, Colorado
State University of New York at Buffalo School of Nursing (MSN), Buffalo, New York.

Organization Positions: Bible Truth Prison Ministry, Leader
Eric County Alternative to Incarceration
Advisory Board Member
Adventist Prison Ministry Association (APMA), Ex-Board Member

Awards: Volunteer of the year, Women's Residential & Resource Center
Volunteer Award, Gethsemane Baptist Church
Religious Service Award, Martin Luther King, Jr.
Community Services, United States of America House of Representatives
Media Award–Women's Ministry
FBI Citizens Award
Appreciation Award, WUFO 1080 AM Radio

WUFO 1080 AM Radio:
Sunrise: Daily Minute Morning Watch Readings to start the Studio's broadcast day
Bi-Weekly: Minute Health Vignettes from *Vibrant Life*

magazine (Tuesday & Thursday)
Weekly: "Abundant Health" (co-host with Frank Kelly, M.D.) Sunday at 9:45 A.M.
"Bible Truth Prison Ministry" (every 3rd & 5th weeks). Bilingual in English and Spanish (Eva Perez, translator), Children's Program every 5th week) Sunday at 10 A.M.
Choir Directress: "Jesus' Little Lambs (females 8-13 years old, non-church Members)

Author: Message Magazine
American Journal of Nursing (co-written with Martha Markarian)
Nursing Research (co-written with Martha Markarian)
Gospel, Rhythm and News (WUFO's Newsletter) (Co-written with Frank Kelly, M.D.)

Ruby Graves in Nigerian Attire

29

DR. HAROLD & BARBARA LEE
1968-1975

Harold Lee's life has been a journey of choices. A former Glenville member, he is currently president of the Colombia Union Conference. His choices have led him to a closer relationship with God and a life of ministry and service.

Lee's journey began in the small town of Wellsburg, W.Va. (population 3,000). From an early age, this coal miner's son—a twin and one of nine children born to Robert and Lillian Lee—loved school and valued the learning process.

Upon graduation from high school, in Wheeling, W. Va., Lee moved to Cleveland, Ohio, where his older sister had taken up residence. There he joined the United States Air Force and was stationed in Atlanta, where he met his wife, Barbara. Shortly thereafter, he was transferred to Tokyo, Japan, where he served as a communications specialist during the Korean Conflict. In 1958, he left the military with the thought of taking over his in-laws' restaurant in Atlanta. "We chose not to enter the restaurant business and headed back to Cleveland where my sister Rosa lived. A short time later, she joined the Seventh-day Adventist Church," he explains.

Raised in a Christian home, Lee was eager to learn more about the Adventist lifestyle, beliefs, and values when Rosa invited him to an evangelism series at the Glenville Church. (She even won a free Bible for bringing the most guests one evening.) "The ambiance was overwhelming," says Lee. "The music, singing, praying, and powerful preaching of Pastor/Evangelist Walter M. Starks captured my attention. It made a deep impression on me and was a major turning point in my spiritual development," he recalls. "I was actually converted before the sermon began."

The following Sabbath, Lee gave his heart to Christ and joined others in distributing invitations to the evangelistic meetings. He was baptized into the Glenville Church in January, 1959, at the age of 22—along with 11 other family members.

After joining the Adventist Church, he moved to Huntsville, Alabama, where he studied to become a pastor at Oakwood College. Although married with two children, Lee still managed to complete a double major. He then graduated from Andrews University's Theological Seminary in Berrien Springs, Michigan.

Lee's first assignment, in the Allegheny Conference, was pastoring the churches in Akron and Canton, Ohio. "My parents were so proud of me and my decision to become a pastor," he says. More than that, they began sharing his newfound faith. In time, Lee had the privilege of baptizing his mother—the first Black Adventist in Weirton, West Virginia—along with some of his siblings.

In 1968, church leaders invited Lee and family to serve as a missionary in the Caribbean Union Conference. "At first I declined," he says. But sage counseling from Starks, a pastor, mentor, and then stewardship director at the Adventist Church World Headquarters, convinced him otherwise. Lee and his family spent the next six-and-a-half years in Port-of-Spain, Trinidad, serving in the Inter-American Division's Caribbean Union Conference. This territory includes the Windward and Leeward Islands and the northeastern section of South America—with Guyana and Surinam.

"I organized and served as director of the stewardship department," Lee states. He also worked as the Youth Ministries leader, Coordinator for the Spirit of Prophecy, and assistant pastor of the Cleveland Temple and Stanmore churches.

While teaching in the religion department at Caribbean Union College, Lee focused on presenting stewardship theology and methodology in an evangelism setting. "I encouraged everyone to double-tithe," he says. "The response was overwhelming!"

"This was another major turning point; it's where I learned about the scope and importance of the Church's worldwide missions," Lee says. "It's also where I was asked to serve on the Port-of-Spain Community hospital board, which was my first introduction to the health and healing ministries we espoused."

Following his ministry in the Caribbean, Lee and his family returned to Oakwood College where he served as vice president of development and public relations for four years. His ability to listen and lead has led to service in several of the Church's organizations in Pennsylvania, Texas, and New Jersey. Now president of the Columbia Union Conference, the Church's Mid-Atlantic Headquarters, Lee is still missionary-minded. He is involved with special missions in India, Africa, and McCormick Theological Seminary in Chicago.

These days, the father of three and grandfather of six divides his time between Dayton, Ohio, the Church's Mid-Atlantic headquarters outside Washington, D. C., and the eight Mid-Atlantic states where he lends administrative support to the Church's regional organizations, secondary schools, colleges, and hospitals.

Harold Lee's life has been a journey of choices, and it's evident that he has relied on his faith in God in making those choices. What has been the guiding force for this administrator and man of God through the many challenges and career changes? The Bible says, "Trust in the Lord with all your heart and lean not on your own understanding. In all your ways, acknowledge (God) and he will (guide) your paths." He quotes from Proverbs 3:5 and 6. "That's a promise I have counted on many a day." In fact, Lee's personal mission is, "To act justly, love mercy, and to walk humbly with God." Clearly, he's living out his mission.

30

JOHN & SARA PITTS 1971–1977

The Pitts family consists of John and Sara, father and mother, and two daughters, Angela, the elder and Johanna, the younger. John was born in Zanesville, Ohio; Sara in Delaware, Ohio, about 80 miles away from Zanesville. Angela was born at White Memorial Hospital in Los Angeles, California, and Johanna at Riverside Hospital in Nashville, Tennessee.

John and Sara saw each other for the first time at age ten, although they did not really become friends until two years later, when John became a Seventh-day Adventist in Columbus, Ohio, just 24 miles away from Delaware. Sara was already as pretty as a picture and immediately became an item of interest to John, who pursued her for many years, unsuccessfully. However, about the time that both were of college age, John was finally able to do whatever it took to capture her heart, and shortly after they both finished college, wedding bells were ringing in little Delaware, Ohio.

On their honeymoon, they went to Los Angeles and decided to stay a while to seek their fortunes. Among their close friends in Los Angeles were Samuel and Bernice DeShay. These two couples, along with others, and Dr. Warren Harrison as their sponsor, began an "Africa Club" to study and learn more about the continent in the hopes of someday going there.

The DeShays were the first ones to fulfill their dream, and in 1961 left a position at Riverside Hospital in Nashville, Tennessee, to go to Nigeria, West Africa, as a missionary doctor and nurse. They wrote letters often to the Pitts urging them to come into mission service. However, it took ten years before they actually did. One reason it took so long was that the Pitts felt that it was

John & Sara Pitts 1971-1977

not a good reason to go to mission service just to be with their good friends. And at that time if they had been asked where they would want to go, it would have been to Nigeria, to be with the DeShays. So they delayed making a decision and, instead, worked in the church here in America.

However, as the Lord would have it, one Friday evening in 1970 while living in Denver, Colorado, and working with Haskins & Sells CPA Firm, John was reading the *Review and Herald* and noticed an article emphasizing the need for accountants, nurses, and others in the mission fields. John was not happy being out of church work, anyhow, as he was an accountant and Sara was a nurse. So he asked Sara how she would feel applying for foreign mission work. It had always been in the back of their minds, but now it seemed appropriate to consider it. They discussed it and agreed that they would not go just to be near Sam and Bernice, but they would be willing to go where they were needed. By now they had two daughters, 8 and 5 years old.

The following Monday, when John was home during his lunch hour, he called the General Conference in Washington, D.C. and expressed an interest in their becoming a missionary family. The G.C. sent them an application which they promptly completed and returned. Several weeks passed before they heard anything, and when a response did come, it was very positive, expressing that the G.C. would welcome them as new missionaries. They talked with one of the leaders at the G.C. The first question he asked was if they had a preference of locations in the world field. Their immediate answer was that they would be willing to go wherever there was the greatest need. To their absolute and unbelievable surprise, his response was that the greatest need, at that point, was for a conference treasurer in Aba, East Nigeria, just a few miles from Dr. and Mrs. DeShay. (You see, God does have a sense of humor).

They began the long process of getting ready to go overseas for an extended stay: applying for passports, getting shots, selling the house, the cars, the furniture, getting rid of hundreds of books, and other attachments, etc., etc., etc.

Regarding books, they discovered that books could be shipped much less expensively than anything else. So they went through their huge library and selected only those books that had special meaning to them and boxed them up, sealed them in large, canvas post office bags, loaded them in the car and made several trips to the Post Office to send them to Aba, East Nigeria, West Africa, their intended destination. There were nineteen large bags of books.

Meanwhile, back at the house, other packing was underway. You see, only their most valuable possessions could be carried with them to West Africa. By this time the DeShays were aware that the Pitts family was finally coming to join them, after ten years of prodding. It just so happened that the DeShays

Precious Memories of Missionaries of Color

were home on furlough, and they were able to spend some time together. They counseled them what to bring to the mission field: since they were complete vegetarians, it would be necessary for them to bring enough meat substitutes and canned powdered soy milk to last for two years; plenty of dried beans, seasonings for two years; special treats to be enjoyed from time to time, such as Pringles potato chips, headache and any other over the counter needs; games; a record player and records; soft toilet tissue; (the toilet tissue in West Africa is unbelievable), a camera and film for two years; Christmas, birthday, and other special gifts for the girls for two years; and the list goes on and on. You see, none of these things would be available there. And they advised that one needed to do everything to make life as homey as possible, especially for the girls.

They also advised them to bring lots of extra clothes for give-away, because there are lots of poor, and there would be many opportunities to help if the clothes were available. They also advised that the best way to ship goods was in large 55 gallon metal drums that could be sealed and locked. Larger items that could not be put in drums would be crated for shipment at the G.C. warehouse in Long Island. In the final analysis, after shedding, and shaving and getting rid of, and selling and giving away, they finally reduced all their worldly possessions to fifty-five drums and eighteen large wooded crates. (Don't forget the nineteen bags of books sent earlier.) All of this took several months to process. If they had it all to do over again, I think that they would have shaved and shed a lot more than they did. You see, the G. C. will pay for a family to carry a certain limited amount with them, and any excess baggage over and above that amount is charged to the family and deducted monthly from their meager pay. The Pitts carried so much extra, that a sizable percentage of their pay went to pay their overweight bill for their first two years of service, a very expensive lesson.

By this time John was no longer with Haskins & Sells, expecting to ship out at any time. The house and cars (except for one) were sold, the goods had been shipped and they were prepared to utilize the month, the G.C. allows, visiting family and friends prior to departure. There was only one glitch. The Nigerian Embassy had not yet granted their work visas into the country, and these were long overdue. The Pitts left Denver in January, 1971 heading for Ohio to visit family and friends. It so happened that the DeShays were also in Ohio, Samuel's family home. Since Dr. DeShay was so well respected in Nigeria, the G.C. asked him to accompany John to the Nigerian Embassy in Washington to see if anything could be done to speed up the process. So they went to Washington together.

John & Sara Pitts 1971–1977

The Biafran civil war in Nigeria had just ended in 1970 and the Hausa, Northern Kingdom, had won the war. Unfortunately for us, the United States supported the rebel Igbo Southern Kingdom; therefore the current government of Nigeria was very anti-American. Even Dr. DeShay's influence was of no help, because his base of operations, and the Pitts destination was in the south and the powers-that-be were not anxious to do anything to help the south. As a result, they stamped the Pitts' passports with 90 day visitor's visas. This would not do, since they were planning to go for several years, so when the authorities were told that 90 day visas would do us no good, they cancelled the visas in the passports. This unfortunate act would one day come back to haunt the Pitts.

For some months the Pitts had been studying up on Nigeria attempting to become familiar with all their ways and customs. Now it was all for naught. By this time they were on the G.C. payroll and the G.C. sent them to the Lake Union Conference in Berrien Springs, Michigan, so that John could observe the conference accounting system. It so happened that their friend Frank Jones was the treasurer. They lived in a motel and the girls attended the elementary school at Andrews University. After a few weeks, it was obvious that this living arrangement was not acceptable, so the G.C. arranged for them to move back to Ohio where John could work with the Allegheny West Conference Office until their call came through. There they would at least stay with family.

God is so good! One church member in the Columbus, Ephesus church who possessed an empty house, saw their plight, and offered to let them occupy the house, free of charge. Others offered furniture, bedding, eating utensils, etc. until there was enough to make their lives livable. This continued for several months.

One Thursday afternoon John was in a Laundromat washing clothes. The phone rang and someone answered it, and asked, "Is there someone here named John Pitts?" He said, "yes," and went to answer the phone. It was the General Conference. (He never did discover how they located him there.) The voice informed him that a position had been found for him and his family at Masanga Leprosy Hospital in Sierra Leone, West Africa. Not only that, but travel arrangements had been made, and they would be leaving from John F. Kennedy Airport the following Wednesday afternoon.

John almost forgot his clothes that were washing and drying in his anxiety to get home and give his wife and daughters the news that they had five days to return all their borrowed possessions, find a buyer for their car, pack again for long distance, attempt to do some research on leprosy and Sierra Leone, say their goodbyes, and find someone who would be willing to take them and their baggage to New York in time to catch their plane for Sierra Leone on

Precious Memories of Missionaries of Color

Wednesday afternoon. This would take some doing. Nevertheless, they accomplished all that and made the flight.

The DeShays had said to be careful of what they ate or drank once they left the United States. The water, especially, is dangerous; however, bottled soft drinks are safe as long as they have not been tampered with. With this in mind, while in John F. Kennedy Airport, John picked up a number of candy bars and crackers and other snacks—just in case. Bottled water was not plentiful at that time, as it is now, or he would have picked up some of those too. They left these United States for the first time on June 10, 1971, around 5:00 in the afternoon.

They landed in Dakar, Senegal, about 5:00 AM the next day. It was their first introduction to West Africa. They had to wait a couple of hours for the Nigerian Airways plane that would take them to Freetown, Sierra Leone. Their first strong impression of West Africa was "hot and humid." At 5:00 in the morning it was about 100 degrees Fahrenheit and 100% humidity while they sat in the airport with no air conditioning.

The airplane finally came and, thankfully, it was fully air conditioned. They were struck also with a new experience—a commercial airplane with all Black personnel which was very interesting to behold. The flight from Dakar to Freetown took only a few hours and unlike planes in America, they were up and out of our seats once the plane was on the ground and before it came to a stop. The Pitts family was the first to disembark from the plane and was standing at the door as the plane taxied to a halt. As I mentioned earlier, the plane was air conditioned and it was probably in the low 70's inside the plane. When the stewardess opened the door and they stepped out of the plane, it felt as though they had stepped into a blast furnace. The temperature shot at once from 70 degrees to 110 degrees with 100% humidity. Imagine (if you can) what it would be like wearing a wool suit with a long sleeve dress shirt and tie under those conditions.

They walked from the plane to the terminal and immediately were subjected to the normal hassles of customs, and fighting off dozens of men, all of whom insisted on carrying their bags, to receive pay. At the terminal, after passing through customs and settling on two men to help with the bags, they boarded a bus which took them on a half-hour journey to the city center, where they disembarked at the Paramount Hotel, the finest in the town.

There was no one to meet or greet them, in spite of the fact that the General Conference had sent a cable informing of the time of their arrival. (They later discovered that the cable arrived two weeks after they did.) So they sat in the hotel lobby and waited, and waited, and waited. And while they waited

John & Sara Pitts 1971–1977

they called the one phone number that the G.C. had given them as a contact. They called about every 15 minutes. In fact, it reached the point that the hotel operator recognized their voices and knew what number to ring without their supplying it each time. The phone rang and rang each time without ever being answered. This went on for hours and hours, in fact from about 11:00 A.M. until about 6:00 P.M. They remembered what Sam had said about eating and drinking, so the supplies they purchased at JFK Airport became their only source of sustenance, even though they were boring and totally unhealthy. They also purchased bottled soft drinks, which were some help, but no water. (They later found out that the Paramount Hotel had totally safe, water, food and all, and in fact they went there many times during their stay in the country.)

About 6:00 P.M. a very kind lady, a hotel staff member, came up and spoke, saying that she had noticed the family sitting there all day and asked if there was something she could do to help. They told her their situation that they were first time Seventh-day Adventist missionaries going to the Masanga Leprosy Hospital. They had been given this number to reach a contact person after they arrived and they expected someone to meet them. She said that she knew the lady who plays the organ at the local Seventh-day Adventist Church, and would they like for her to call this lady. They said thank you, yes. So, she did. It turned out that the lady she called was the mother of the wife of the former ambassador to the United States, who was then the current ambassador to Liberia. The daughter, who was not an SDA, said for them to take a taxi and come right over to their home. She also told them just how much to pay the taxi driver. (If she had not told them, they very well might have paid five times too much, seeing that they were obviously new arrivals and ripe for picking.)

She fed them and gave them drink and made them comfortable for the night. Her mother, who was a member of the church, explained that the number they had been calling all day belonged to the Whaley family, a missionary family from the U.S. and that they had recently left Sierra Leone to return to the U.S. on furlough and would be gone for two months. The house was empty. They could have called for the next two months and would have received the same response—none.

She also told them that three hours away was another missionary family from the U.S.—Dennis and Dorothy Keith and their children. It so happened that these were old friends of theirs and they were able to contact them by phone. By then it was about 8:00 in the evening, nevertheless, Dennis offered to come right then and pick them up. If they had agreed, they would have arrived back at his house between 2:00 and 3:00 A.M. They explained that these lovely people had graciously offered to put them up for the night, but they would love to see him in the morning. And that is exactly what happened. Dennis came to pick them up and take them to Bo (the name of the city where they lived) and they spent that first very enjoyable weekend with them. The Keiths' children were about the same age as the Pitts' girls so it made a very good beginning for them. During the four years that the Keiths were in the country with them, they spent many happy weekends together.

They had their first "snake" experience (the first of many) on the way to church on that first Sabbath morning. The Keiths lived on the same compound where the church was; therefore, they walked to church. As they were walking, Sara looked down just in time, and had to jump over the snake to keep from stepping on it. The Keiths seemed to take it in stride and did not get very excited about it, so they continued on, but their hearts skipped a beat or two.

John was going to Masanga to be the business manager there. However, the missionaries who were in charge of the hospital were not aware that he was coming, because the cable informing of his arrival came two weeks after he did. On Sunday the Pitts traveled another three hours from Bo to the hospital, and when the new manager arrived, the staff was in conference discussing what could be done until a manager arrived. You can imagine just how happy they were to see any warm body coming in that capacity. Up to this time, the medical director had to serve as both medical director and business manager.

The leprosy hospital had been established about ten years before with the agreement that if the Sierra Leone government would finance the operation, the SDA Church would supply doctors and other overseas personnel to operate it. This relationship had been surviving for those years, but left much to be desired, even though improvements were being made all along. In fact, two years before the Pitts arrived; Dr. and Mrs. DeShay spent two years as medical director and manager while the Biafran War was raging in Nigeria. Under their leadership many innovations were begun and even two years later the local people were still lovingly talking about them as though they had just left.

Though the Pitts were on the continent for six years, and the DeShays were also there during the same time, they never saw one another. Once when the Pitts were prepared to go to Nigeria on holiday to visit the DeShays, they went to the Nigerian Embassy to get visas, and got them. Unfortunately, after stamping the visas in the passports, the official noticed that previous visitor's visas had been stamped in the passports and then cancelled. Because of this, without asking any questions as to the reason or explanation for the cancellation, he cancelled the current visas as well, assuming that if they had been cancelled once before, surely these people would again not be welcomed in the country. So, their passports were returned with two sets of cancelled visas in them and

John & Sara Pitts 1971-1977

no hope of ever getting into Nigeria, at least with those passports. Thus, they never saw the DeShays while they were in Africa together.

There were 300 beds at the hospital for leprosy patients who had special needs. Although there were thousands of people in the country who had leprosy, only the worse cases were brought to the hospital for treatment and rehabilitation. This hospital was the only hospital of its kind in the country and everyone knew about it, but most everyone was afraid of it. The Catholic Relief Services operated a small dispensary in another part of the country but it could only care for a dozen or so patients. Since both were involved with treatment of leprosy, however, they often worked closely with one another. In the six years while the Pitts were at Masanga, there were major changes in the way that leprosy was treated.

Leprosy is caused by *Microbacterium lepra* and affects the skin and nerve endings. The disease causes skin anesthesia in the extremities (hands, feet, ears, etc.) so that there is no feeling in these limbs. As a result, one could step on glass or a nail which might become buried in the foot, and the person would never know because there is no pain or feeling. Soon infection begins to destroy the tissue. Or one could pick up a very hot pot from the fire and seriously burn their hands, but never feel a thing. So at the hospital, they taught patients to examine their extremities regularly and get treatment if needed. They also manufactured shoes/sandals for them to wear to protect the feet, and thick gloves to protect the hands. They also performed surgery to repair some of the ravages of the disease. At the time medical science had not determined just how the disease was spread, though they believed that it was air-borne. Even though nearly everyone in Sierra Leone was deathly afraid of leprosy, probably due to the attitude toward it in the Bible, they learned that what they now call leprosy is not the same disease called leprosy in Biblical times. They lived on the compound and mingled with the patients every day but did not feel any danger as long as they took normal precautions and practiced good hygiene.

They saw many people whose hands and feet were very deformed. However, they learned that leprosy does not cause the fingers and toes to just drop off. What happens is that because there is no pain or feeling the bones in these extremities are constantly traumatized, and the trauma causes the bones to shorten, even to the point that they disappear almost completely.

The Pitts were stationed at Masanga for six years and since this is a very limited story they can only attempt to hit a few highlights of their time there. When they arrived, there was one large diesel generator and one small one which supplied electricity to the hospital and homes on the compound. The schedule for running the generator was two hours in the morning and again

Precious Memories of Missionaries of Color

from 7:00 to 10:00 in the evening. The reason for the limited time was that fuel was so expensive, more than $3.00 a gallon (At that time, it was well under a dollar in the U.S.) Shortly after his arrival, John discovered that half of that cost was due to duty, or taxes paid to the government. Recognizing that this was a government hospital, John wondered out loud why they were paying duty. So he went to Freetown and approached the government officials about this. After much discussion and persuasion, he was successful in getting all fuel delivered to Masanga duty free. This immediately cut their fuel bill in half. Over the course of time, they managed to procure two new, more efficient generators to replace the old ones, which further reduced their cost of electricity. Within a few years, they were able to enjoy electricity 24 hours 7 days a week (except during electrical storms) for little more than they were paying for part-time electricity when they first arrived.

Related to the problem of electricity was the type of refrigerators they found in the missionaries' homes when they arrived. Those refrigerators were operated by kerosene and were terribly cantankerous at times and were capable of causing great frustration. Although when they did work, they did the job well. Nevertheless, when they ran out of fuel, or the wick acted up, or any number of other problems that could occur, the smoke and soot could blacken an entire kitchen, requiring hours to clean up the mess. And this happened, more than once. Therefore, after they went on 24/7 electricity, they managed to eliminate all the kerosene refrigerators and replace them with electric ones—a major improvement.

The hospital consisted of a number of buildings or wards. Each ward housed about thirty patients. Besides the wards, there was a smaller building which housed the surgery theatre (or operating room—the only air conditioned spot on the compound), an administrative building with offices and a large general meeting room which also served as the church, a very large garage for storage and vehicle maintenance, and a number of other smaller buildings used for miscellaneous purposes. Some distance from the hospital area and across a small stream were several buildings housing the African staff members, and further yet, were several homes for the overseas or missionary families.

Most of the buildings comprising the hospital were constructed of mud mixed with cement. These buildings were well constructed and lasted for decades, however they had been originally painted some drab color many years before and by then were looking very somber. One of John's first initiatives as manager was to request paint from the government to paint all of the wards bright colors inside and out to make the place a lot more cheery. This went a long way toward improving the look of the hospital.

John & Sara Pitts 1971-1977

All of the homes had open windows and open doors that were without screens. To protect themselves from deadly mosquitoes, everyone slept under mosquito nets. To the Pitts, these were very depressing. So John went to the government officials and requested enough screening material to cover the compound and proceeded to put screens on all the windows and screen doors on all the doors, in an attempt to keep out mosquitoes, snakes, scorpions, and anything else that might otherwise choose to wander or fly in.

Next the Lord blessed them to be the recipient of a large capital grant from the government of Norway. With this money plus some additional from the church organization, they were able to construct sixteen new buildings during the six years they served there. These included a large physical therapy building, a large storage building, a large building to house their furniture factory and carpentry class, another building to house their tailoring class, several new homes for overseas families, and several new homes for African staff which included inside toilets and kitchens. Prior to this, there had been no inside plumbing for African staff.

The six hundred acre compound was bordered on one side by a fairly large river (yes, there were alligators in it.) A water distribution system was constructed when the hospital was established which delivered running water to the hospital, the overseas homes and the African staff area; however, the water came directly from the river without treatment of any kind and the color was medium brown and very dangerous. All drinking and other personal water had to be boiled and filtered. When we took a bath, we would run the tub full of honey colored water and add ¼ cup of "Detol" (a cousin of Lysol) to kill hopefully all of the dangerous microbes. At first it took a lot of bravery to climb into tub. But as time went by, the Pitts became used to it. It must have worked, because they survived it for several years until major improvements were made. After a few years, they received a grant to create a filtration and purification system for the entire compound. Before they left, one could safely drink the water from the tap.

John's job required him to go to Freetown at least once each week and sometimes several times. Often John stayed over for several days, because all food and supplies had to be purchased there and brought up country. Also, whenever anyone was coming to or leaving the country, they needed to be taken to or picked up from the airport (or the Paramount Hotel). Any shipments from overseas, whether personal goods of the missionaries or purchases for the hospital such as generators, automobiles or Lorries (trucks), had to be cleared from the quay (the docks). This sometimes took days. Before John's arrival, a company was paid to do all this for the hospital. But as manager, John chose to do this himself and save the hospital some money.

Precious Memories of Missionaries of Color

When the Pitts arrived in Sierra Leone it was a five hour drive to Freetown each way over very bad roads. During the rainy season you were subjected to mud and massive ruts in the roads. During the dry season you would be covered with red dust wherever you went on the roads. At that time, a typical trip to Freetown began by leaving the compound at 4:00 A.M. arriving in town at 9:00; taking care of whatever business you could by noon. At noon, everything closed down for two hours, and all you could do was get dinner and wait. At 2:00 you could resume your business activities until about 6:00, when most things again closed down for the night and you started your trek back up country, arriving at home around 11:00. Of course, during all that time there was no means of communication with your family. So if something prevented your leaving Freetown at the expected time, all the family could do was wait and pray for your safe arrival. Fortunately, while they lived there, the roads were improved and eventually this time was reduced to three hours each way.

Because John was in Freetown so often and involved in so many activities, he got to know most of the important people there. And because they were a government hospital he often had to meet with high government ministers and officials. John was even in the home or office of the President of the country, Siaka Stevens several times. Because they were making major improvements at the hospital and were very proud of the place, John freely invited business and government people he met to come to the hospital. Most people were very afraid of leprosy and would not even dream of coming there until he pressed and urged them and promised them that there was no danger to them. Most of the important ministers (e.g. the Minister of Health and the Minister of Finance), as well as key economic leaders of the country, spent at least one week-end at the Pitts' home while they were there. Of course, whenever anyone of that nature came, it was a big day on the compound and they would have special programs, etc. Twice, Siaka Stevens, the President, visited Masanga and ate dinner in their home. (They fed him vegetarian gluten steaks which he seemed to enjoy.) Of course those were very special days and people from all the villages for miles around came to take part in the celebration—especially the day the President came in his helicopter.

There were times when John's job required special determination and patience. For example, once the government was several months behind on the hospital's regular subsidy and they were running out of money. All appeals seemed to fall on deaf ears. So John announced to his family and staff that he was going to Freetown to see the Minister of Finance and would not return until he got the money. He arrived at the minister's office and explained that he was from Masanga and that they were out of money and asked his secretary

John & Sara Pitts 1971–1977

to allow John to see him. Of course she said that it was not possible because he was very busy. John thanked her and sat down to wait. He had armed himself with several books because he was pretty sure what would happen. He waited until lunch time, went out to eat and returned and waited and read until the office closed that evening. He spent the night in a hotel and when the secretary arrived the next morning, she found him waiting. John explained to her that there was no need for him to return to the hospital because they had no food, or medicine or supplies to run the hospital. So he waited all that day, and the next morning she found him at his regular spot, waiting and reading. He spent three full days in the same spot. On the morning of the fourth day, when they were convinced that he was not going to leave, he received the check that he had come for—although he never did see the Minister of Finance. When he got to the bank with the check to deposit it to their account, the banker, whom he knew said, "Wow, how did you get this? The government owes everyone in town, and no one is getting anything from them." John merely smiled, and said he had a special contact. Of course while he was waiting and reading, he was also praying for the Lord's intervention, and it came.

The people of Sierra Leone like to sing and do a lot of it at church. Traditionally the overseas people were not very active participants in the local music; however, being somewhat of a musician, John found it fairly easy to pick up the songs because there is lots of repetition and some of the songs had very simple words that were easy to reproduce phonetically. The first Sabbath John was at Masanga, he made something of a stir by joining in the singing. Of course, anyone who knows him, knows that his voice is not very soft or timid, so everyone who was within a mile (not really) heard him, and virtually everyone at church momentarily stopped singing to turn and look at him. He wondered if he had done something wrong, but realized that the locals were just completely flabbergasted that he could sing their songs with them at his first appearance. As time went by, his family all sang along with the local people also. Even some of the other missionaries began to sing with them as well.

Eventually John started a children's choir primarily of African staff children, but his own girls sang in it too, and often sang the lead or solo part of the songs. They sang in many of the towns nearby, and always the people could not believe that these overseas girls were singing in the local language. By the way, Dr. DeShay had started a choir when he was there two years before, and it was still operational, singing songs he had taught them.

Before they left America, John and Sara accumulated a dozen or so band instruments to carry with them, hoping to teach the Africans to play and start a band. Well, their dream never came to fruition. However, they did teach several of the missionaries to play and had a ten or twelve piece band among them. For a while one of their African staff joined them. Most of the time they played for their own amusement and pleasure on the long Sabbath afternoons, but on several occasions they were invited to play in the nearby town on national holidays.

When John arrived, one small corner of the garage was dedicated to the carpentry class where the goal was to teach men with leprosy to learn to be able to make a living for themselves. The teacher of the class was an excellent craftsman, and lumber of unusually beautiful quality was plentiful. John noticed that the exposed rafters of the meeting hall were made of mahogany wood, which would have been very valuable here in the U.S. Being somewhat of a "jack-leg" craftsman himself, John recognized the valuable commodity they had at their disposal. He often went out to surrounding villages to buy lumber, usually mahogany, and even watch the men cut down a tree and cut it up into lumber planks. (Once they found black walnut lumber, bought it all, and had some of the hospital furniture made from it. It was very beautiful.)

John procured additional high quality tools to be used in the class, and then he arranged for the class to provide certain furniture for the hospital and homes on the compound. Before long, all of the furniture needs for the hospital and the homes on the compound were being supplied by the carpentry class. When the Norway money became available, one of their first buildings was a new and larger facility for their "furniture factory." For they had become just that! Besides supplying all the needs of the hospital, they also took orders from outside customers and supplied furniture for surrounding areas, including pews for churches, a throne for the local Paramount Chief, and a gift bed for President Siaka Stevens.

Because they were missionaries, many people assume that John is a preacher or pastor. He goes to great lengths to assure them that he is not. He is an accountant and business manager and that was his major work while in the mission field. However, as a Christian, they have a responsibility to witness for Christ wherever they go and whatever they do. During their stay at Masanga, John taught Sabbath School virtually every Sabbath. This is his first love. He also served as a local elder and even preached a few times. He gave Bible studies regularly at Masanga and in surrounding villages. They started several branch Sabbath Schools and regularly went to visit nearby villages on Sabbath afternoon and sometimes on Sunday morning as well. Sarah prepared visual aids on many general health subjects at home and used them when they went to the villages. She would teach general health and hygiene lessons and then she would give a Bible study.

John & Sara Pitts 1971–1977

One village they visited often, required them to cross a small bridge about two feet wide, thirty feet high and about thirty feet long, with no side rails. The locals were used to it and walked across with no problem, but many of the foreigners had to get down on all fours to cross it safely. To get to the bridge, they had to walk through narrow, winding paths with grass ten feet tall on both sides of the path. The bridge was over a creek, but, to get to the village, they also had to cross a sizable river. When they reached the river, they had to call for someone in the village to come across the river and pick them up in a dugout canoe. Just crossing the river in the seemingly unstable canoe was enough of a harrowing experience, but add to that, the canoe leaked, and while one man at each end of the canoe paddled, the other eight or ten who were the passengers, used small buckets to bail out the water to keep the canoe from sinking. Nevertheless, they went regularly and taught and even formed a church there and built a church building with a pan (metal) roof. To build such a church cost about $500 and all of that was donated by the missionaries from Masanga Hospital. When they finished the church they painted it bright blue. When you consider that all the houses in the village were made of brown mud with palm leaf thatched roofs, this bright blue SDA church with a pan roof was the center of attention, the most outstanding, and the most important building in the village. While they were at Masanga, they built several churches in several villages, but the one mentioned above was the first and the one that is most outstanding in their memory.

John's wife is a registered nurse and most people assume that since they were at a hospital for six years, that she worked in the hospital. Well, this is not correct, at least most of the time. The hospital had regular overseas missionary nurses, as well as Sierra Leonean nurse's aids trained at the hospital.

Sara was kept very, very busy in many additional ways: her first duty was to their girls. Angela was starting the fourth grade, and Johanna, the first. Before they left the U.S. they enrolled them in the Home Study Institute, a correspondence school of excellent quality at the General Conference headquarters. It would have been a full time job for Sara just to administer two different grades, especially when that is not what you were trained to do. Some time after they arrived, another family came from Denmark who had adopted a Sierra Leonean girl near Angela's age and to accommodate them, so the father and mother could work, Sara taught their daughter, Katie, as well.

This responsibility involved not just academies, but also play time, creating games and diverse activities to keep the girls from getting bored and wanting to return to the U.S., teaching them to cook and sew, and generally being a 24/7 companion in lieu of other playmates. There were generally no other missionary children their ages on the compound, and the local girls lived far away or could not speak English or were kept busy caring for younger siblings or other work.

Now, add to this, the responsibilities of homemaking, preparing food for five, washing and ironing, cleaning, etc., you can see that her hands were full. Now it is true that in this area she had some help. She had a young man named Amadu whom she trained to help her with many household tasks. By the way, one had to have help, not only because of all the work, but because the locals expected the "rich" overseas families to supply work for a least one of them. If you did not, you were seriously criticized for being selfish.

Amadu came five days a week. He bathed everyday when he arrived and he was supplied with clean clothes for the day. He cleaned the floors (and it didn't matter how often you did it, the floor still needed to be swept because there were ants constantly bringing grains of sand/dirt onto the floor); he did the washing and ironing (everything had to be ironed including socks, underwear, bedding and any article of clothes that came into contact with your body.) There was a fly called a tumble fly that lays its eggs in clothes hanging out to dry. Ironing kills those eggs. If you wore an article of clothing that had eggs and had not been ironed, the heat of your body hatched the eggs and the microscopic larvae burrowed into your skin wherever they were, and would grow and grow, until one fine day you'd notice that you were developing a very sore boil, or several very sore boils, which developed to maturity. If you went to the doctor with it, out would come a very mature worn. There was not much you could do about it but wait for it to mature. They have seen people who had several of these "boils" growing simultaneously. So you understand why everyone ironed everything.

Amadu also baked the bread outside in a big black "missionary" pot with sand in the bottom and sitting on three stones with a fire under it. Sara taught him how to bake. He made 7 to 8 loaves at a time in large # 10 cans. When the bread was about done, he would heap red hot coals on the lid of the pot for several minutes, and this browned the tops of the bread in the cans. You could not go to the store and buy bread, or at least not bread that you would want to eat, so if you wanted bread, you had to make it. Oh, and by the way, one purchased flour in Freetown 199 pounds at a time and shared it. Naturally it lasted a long time. After a short while when you were ready to use it, you had to first sift out the bugs (that is, if you wished). But you would never think of throwing away the flour just because it had bugs. If you did, you would have no flour. There is a little anecdote that says you can always tell when it is time for a missionary to go home. When they first arrive, they pick all the bugs out

John & Sara Pitts 1971-1977

of everything, after they have been there a while, they do not bother to pick them out but just ignore them. When they start looking around for bugs to add to their food, it is a sign that they have been there too long.

Sara always did the cooking and preparing of the food (except for baking the bread). She never turned the rest over to Amadu (though many of the missionaries did have their workers prepare the food) but he washed the dishes and cleaned up after eating, while she taught the girls and did many of her other duties.

In addition, they often had lots of company. There were no hotels or restaurants other than in the city, and anytime any dignitary or visitor from the church or another church, or any place else, for that matter, showed up, the lady of the house had to be prepared to feed or even house them—and they came often. There were no phones or other means of communication, so there was no way to warn a wife when she was going to have company, they would just show up. The doctor and John were in charge of the hospital, so the more important the visitor, the more they felt that they should stay with the doctor or with John. Then because he was in Freetown so often, he would often spot an American or two (they were so easy to spot) and he'd automatically greet them and introduce himself and invite them to come to Masanga. Most tourists who came to the city never had an opportunity to go up country. There was a lot to see and it was very different from the city, so the doctor was always happy to give those he saw the opportunity. So, frequently he returned from Freetown with one or more persons without ever being able to let his wife know they were coming.

Because Masanga was a leprosy hospital, they would not and could not take care of non-leprosy patients. There was a government hospital just five miles away, but there were many problems there and people would prefer to come to Masanga than go to the government hospital, if possible.

They had a supermarket come to their back door every day in the person of ladies from surrounding villages coming with oranges, lemons, bananas, other fruit, rice, groundnuts (peanuts) and other things for sale in pans on their heads. Sometimes these ladies were also pregnant or carrying babies on their backs. In general they had walked several miles to get to them.

Sometimes when these ladies came, there would be an obvious medical problem of they would complain of some problem they were having. Since Sara is a nurse, she would often recognize the symptom and have a medicine, home remedy or suggestion to help relieve the problem. The ladies were always very grateful. And as time passed, Sara's reputation grew to the point where her back door became the local dispensary for minor medical problems for the surrounding villages. Sometimes Sara would have to tell them that the problem was beyond her scope and she'd send them to the government hospital, but most of the time she could help them. She kept a supply of medication sent to her from doctors in America; sometimes outdated, but when prayed over, they maintained their effectiveness.

Measles was one of the most devastating diseases they saw there, often wiping out all the children in a village in one epidemic. This was made more unfortunate because the remedy to prevent death was so simple. When the children would get a fever from the disease, the mother proceeded to wrap the child up tight in a blanket to protect him in 100 and 110 degree heat. As a result, the baby's temperature would continue to escalate, and soon the baby would die. When Sara learned this, they taught them that instead of wrapping up the baby submerge him in a pan of tepid water to bring the temperature down, and give him orange juice or something to replace the electrolytes loss in diarrhea. They would also treat them for malaria. There were times when the Pitts spent nearly all night in a village showing mothers how to save their babies.

And it wasn't just the local population that Sara cared for. Often whenever other missionaries got sick, Sara would care for them, especially the single ladies. As was mentioned earlier, the Whaley family lived in Freetown while they were there (after they returned from furlough), and once when Leola Whaley gave birth, Sara was the only one to go down and be with her while she recovered. The Keiths lived three hours away in Bo, and once, word reached Sara that Dorothy Keith had burned herself with a pot of scalding water that she was boiling for drinking water. As soon as Sara got the word, she raced to their home and stayed with Dorothy and her children for several weeks until she was able to function again.

Masanga and Bo and Freetown were three points on an equilateral triangle and with the Keiths in Bo, and the Whaleys and, following them, the Cartwrights in Freetown and the Pitts in Masanga, they regularly, at least several times a year, when possible, congregated at one another's home to have a really fun weekend, laughing and joking and reminiscing, way past bedtime, finding fun and pleasure in the simple things of life (there was certainly no place to go.) They all had kids about the same age, and the four families were very compatible, so they always enjoyed being together. Their friendships have stood the test of time and they still see one another as often as possible.

In conclusion, there are many, many other incidents and experiences the Pitts could relate in connection with their years in Sierra Leone, but these few give you some idea of what their time was like there. When they left the

John & Sara Pitts 1971-1977

U.S, their idea was to stay in the mission service until the Lord would come. However, they never anticipated the needs that would arise as their little girls became young ladies. The first four years were very pleasant ones while their girls were young and satisfied to be with their parents in a far-off land. But then, after the fourth year, the girls went home on furlough for three months, and discovered America, cousins, friends, and teenage life. John and Sara realized that it was not fair to ask them to spend their developing years in the Sierra Leonean "bush." They could have sent them home to stay with relatives while they remained in the field, but they did not feel that this was a viable option. At that time, they had an obligation to return to Masanga for two more years, but they promised the girls that they would return to the U.S. to stay, after that. And they did.

By the way, remember the nineteen bags of books they sent to Aba, East Nigeria? Well, months later they heard that the books had arrived and someone was storing them for the Pitts. It took more than two years before they saw those bags in Sierra Leone, and then only sixteen bags arrived. (I guess that that is not such a bad average, considering all that they went through.)

The Lord blessed their time in the mission field and they feel that they made a difference while they were there. They made many close friends and saw some important baptisms. They saw seventeen new buildings constructed at the hospital and changed the face of the hospital, and affected many individual lives in their six short years. Unfortunately, they have learned that much of that work was destroyed in the recent civil war in the country. But the Pitts know that they are living in the closing days of earth's history, and the Lord is soon to come. They believe that they are to do what they can to advance His kingdom while they are here, and leave the rest to His providence. They will never forget their time in Africa and the many friends they left behind and have never seen since. Their constant prayer is that they will all meet again, and be with Jesus and all of their loved ones around the great white throne in the earth made new, and enjoy the pleasures forevermore, throughout eternity. Amen.

Precious Memories of Missionaries of Color

John and Sara Pitts

John & Sara Pitts 1971–1977

Precious Memories of Missionaries of Color

Angela & Johanna Pitts and their dog "Wawa"

Angela & Johanna with the 'Kings Heralds'

The Cartwright Family

John & Sara Pitts 1971–1977

Walking through the "Bush"

Crossing A precarious Bridge

Precious Memories of Missionaries of Color

Our Houseboy, Amadu and his wife and Son

Bai our gardener, and Pineapple

31

CLARENCE LEMUEL THOMAS, III & CAROL BARRON 1971–1983

Clarence and Carol were the first Black missionaries to Brazil. Between the years of 1971 and 1980 they served the people of South America in three capacities. Their first call was to serve in the region of Campo Grande, Mato Grosso, as their Sabbath School Director. Later they were called to be the treasurer of the Belem do Para region. Finally Clarence was asked to be the Stewardship Secretary in Recife, Permambuco where he trained and equipped pastors to be soul winners, good financiers, and church builders. Many of these pastors have now become presidents, treasurers, Sabbath School directors of conferences and divisions in South America.

In 1980, Clarence and Carol received a call to be the Administrator of the Universite Adventiste d'Haiti (Haitian Adventist University in Port-au-Prince, Haiti). There, Thomas coordinated the construction of the auditorium on campus which was at that time the biggest auditorium in Port-au-Prince. He built the radio station that aired all over Haiti and into other countries. These rich experiences had afforded them the opportunity to learn two languages—Portuguese and French. This experience was also shared by their three children: Clarence Lemuel Thomas IV, Donna-Maria Thomas, and Torrence Edward Thomas.

The Thomases returned to the states in 1983 after a long and fruitful stay in South America. To God be the glory for the footprints that they left on the shores of this great continent!

32

ELDER ROBERT & ROSE CARTER
1971-1972

One autumn day in 1971, as Elder Carter was going about his duties as secretary of the Northeastern Conference, he received a long distance telephone call from Elder Roy Williams at the General Conference. As they greeted each other and continued to chat, Elder Williams informed Robert that the General Conference Committee had voted to ask if he would be willing to consider a mission to Uganda for over a year. During that time, the morale of the workers in Uganda had begun to slip, the tithes and offerings had declined, and baptisms also were at a stand still.

It was hoped that Elder Carter would provide the leadership needed at that time. The request was that he would go there to inspire them, help train the pastors and workers, and prepare some of them to be able to assume positions of leadership roles in their own country. Actually, by accomplishing this, he would work himself out of a job.

What a challenge! His initial reaction was to turn down the invitation. He was happy where he was, and really enjoying his work. Going to Uganda meant leaving family and homeland for three years to go live in an unknown country. However, he promised to discuss it with his wife, and together they would give it prayerful consideration.

Their friends and family members did not encourage them at all. So, as promised, they prayed earnestly, and looked to God for the decision in this matter. As the weeks passed, God impressed them that this was where He wanted them to be. Elder Dunbar Henri, who was serving as the president of the East

Elder Robert & Rose Carter 1971–1972

African Union, was very anxious to have them come. He assured them that he and his wife would be very happy to help them make the transition.

They read all they could about the country. One thing that impressed them was the fact that Uganda allowed its inhabitants considerable freedom. Twenty-eight different denominations had established churches there. The Adventist Church had approximately 11,000 members throughout the country, with many churches, primary schools, a boarding academy, and the Bugema College with mostly expatriate teachers. Also, there was the Ishaka Hospital owned and operated by the church. It was under the direction of a very capable Adventist national doctor. However, all the nurses and other medical staff were foreigners.

With all of this information, plus the description of the natural beauty of the country with its lush vegetation, adequate rainfall, mild temperatures, mountainous regions, etc., they were getting a bit excited about the prospect of a new assignment. They knew it would present lots of challenges and new experiences.

Their doctor gave them all of the appropriate shots before leaving. They sold their home, stored much of their furniture, sold, gave away, or threw out the rest of their belongings that they didn't need to take with them. They said their good-byes, and they were on their way half way around the world to be missionaries in Uganda, East Africa.

Their first stop was in London, England, where the bold headlines of the newspaper was being shouted out by the vendors—"President Idi Amin of Uganda expels all Asian citizens." Of course, this caught their attention, and they purchased a paper, and eagerly read every word of the article. The article explained that the president felt that the Asians (who were the main business persons and shopkeepers in the country) should leave because they controlled and owned the wealth of Uganda. His plan was to put the shops and businesses into the hands of the Ugandans. They wondered what was ahead for them. But, "Hon" reminded him that they felt God had called them, and they had answered, so they were in His care.

They flew on to Kenya, where Elder Henri met them and he expressed concerns not only for the new order issued by President Amin, but also let them know that there was a drought in Uganda which caused the water supply at the Kireka Mission Compound to be low. He suggested maybe they would like to wait in Kenya for a few days until it rained, and the water supply could be replenished. Elder Carter replied, "That if their believers in Uganda could manage, then they would adjust to the conditions also." Elder Henri smiled and used one of his favorite sayings, "Blessings on you, brother." And so, they journeyed on to Entebbe.

Precious Memories of Missionaries of Color

Upon arriving at the Entebbe Airport, they began to walk toward the building. They looked up and saw several people up on the balcony looking at them. They began smiling, clapping and waving at them. What a wonderful greeting! They took the Carters in a caravan of cars, stopping at two churches en route to the headquarters at Kireka. At each of the churches, there were several people lined up outside to welcome them to Uganda. Finally they reached Kireka. There they noted a church, the office building, the Publishing Department building, a primary school, and a couple of homes to accommodate the president and the treasurer of the field.

They were taken to the church, which was filled with people singing and awaiting the arrival of their new leader from the U.S. Greetings were given, welcome speeches warmly conveyed, and prayers of thanksgiving were offered for their safe arrival. Then Elder Carter was called upon to make a response. About five minutes into his remarks, the skies opened up and a heavy downpour of rain took place. And, to their surprise, the entire congregation immediately broke out in laughter and started to clap their hands with great delight. The interpreters explained to them that they took that as a sign that their new living quarters was full to overflowing. And, the people received them with overflowing love and gratitude.

They had to acknowledge that the country was not only a beautiful place, but, the people were indeed beautiful, gracious, and loving. They opened their hearts to them for making them feel comfortable in their midst.

During the next few days, Elder Carter started to meet with the staff of workers there on the compound to pray together and also to become better acquainted with each other. In the process, information was gained as to the needs of the work in Uganda. As these needs came into focus, Elder Carter began to fill his calendar with appointments. It was his goal to visit every pastor in his own district to better understand their particular needs and any existing problems.

One thing became very clear. Most of the pastors lacked transportation, therefore they were greatly handicapped in getting around in their territory. Maybe three or four pastors had a car. A few more had bicycles. The others walked where they needed to go. This was a major handicap. Something had to change.

Unfortunately, Uganda Field had not been able to raise the salaries of their workers for quite a while due to a lack of funds. So, plans were immediately set in motion to challenge each pastor to encourage their members to return an honest and faithful tithe to the Lord, and prove whether or not He would pour out the blessings from heaven as promised in Mal. 3:10.

Elder Robert & Rose Carter 1971-1972

The pastors began to catch the spirit. They passed the enthusiasm along to the laymen. Within a few months, the increase in tithes was so great that it was now possible for the workers to purchase bicycles for transportation. Not only did the finances improve, but baptisms were on the increase also. God had surely kept His promise!

In addition to the good work done by the pastors, they were blessed to have several strong laymen who were impressed to hold "street meetings." Two or three would go together with only their Bibles and perhaps a box to stand on. They would proceed to preach or give Bible studies to whoever was curious enough to stop each afternoon and listen. As a result, there were interested persons who started attending church. The laymen were told baptisms resulted from their witness.

As the Carters endeavored to visit the pastors and workers throughout the various sections of Uganda, Rose was always welcomed and encouraged to come along to become better acquainted with the people and share the experiences. She never declined an opportunity. The treasurer of Uganda Field was Ugandan by birth, so he always accompanied them. He served as interpreter, guide, companion, and friend for all occasions.

They learned quickly that driving through Uganda was a totally different experience than traveling in the U.S. It was explained to them that since the ruling to expel the Asians, the atmosphere was changing significantly. Policemen and soldiers were highly visible. There were check-points every few miles. On one safari (trip) they were stopped more than twenty times. At one checkpoint, a couple of soldiers had been drinking and were sitting under a shade tree out of sight. When they realized that the Carters had driven through the check point without stopping, they ran out into the middle of the road with rifles drawn and pointing toward them. Their treasurer saw the soldiers in the rear view mirror and had the Carters to back up slowly while he got out and spoke as courteously as possible to them letting them know they did not see the spot.

The soldiers had them get out of the car, open the hood and the trunk, and empty all of their goods on to the dusty road. They looked through every bag and case. After questioning them about the purpose of their travels, and reprimanding them for not stopping, they said the group could continue their journey. They drove in silence for the next half an hour. They were so thankful for God's protecting care.

On another occasion as they traveled in the western area of Uganda, they were approaching the Ruwenzori Mountains; their treasurer informed them that in this area, the Pigmy people lived back in the bush country. No sooner

Precious Memories of Missionaries of Color

had he finished telling them that than three little men (Pigmies) jumped out into the road. One placed himself in front of their car, causing it to come to a stop. Then, another came to the passenger window, just barely able to look in through the window. He proceeded to try to sell Rose a bow and arrow for a few shillings. It looked like he might have made it himself. Rose told him, "No thanks, not today." But, he wasn't accepting her refusal.

At the same time, over at Robert's window was the third 'little person' making his sales pitch. He too, tried to refuse the sale. With all the check-points, they didn't want the soldiers to mistake these bows and arrows for weapons rather than souvenirs. With the man standing in front of their car making it impossible to go forward, Rose finally relented and gave him a few shillings, hoping to be able to proceed on their journey. When the man on the driver's side realized he had not made his sale, he started to jump up and down and cry. With that performance, Rose melted and paid him. Now they had two sets of bows and arrows, which they had to carefully tuck away out of sight. Further up the road, they saw yet another Pigmy walking with a transistor radio on his shoulder. And, they thought, "Ah, yes, what a wonderful way for the gospel story to reach the people in these remote areas.

According to the treasurer, some of the areas they were privileged to visit had not had a visit from any of the former leaders of the Uganda Field. The Carters were so glad that they were able to make the journey. In some of those remote areas, they had to have double translations. The translator needed a translator in order to communicate with the people.

A couple of times when they were miles away from home, the announcement came over the radio from the government office, that all expatriates must come to Kampala, the capitol, to register the following day. They had to cut their visits short and hasten back. You see, many changes were gradually taking place. Six months after they arrived in Uganda, religious freedom began to erode. The President of the country thought that there were too many religions. He said that only three religions were needed, the Catholic, Moslem, and the Protestants. All others could merge into one of these three.

So, first the president banned twelve denominations. Their hospitals, schools, and other institutions were closed. Their financial assets were frozen, and their members were forbidden to conduct worship services. The expatriate heads of these banned churches were arrested and deported. The Carters were concerned, but felt very grateful that their church was not involved in the original twelve denominations. In one of the outlying areas, however, some persons thought the Seventh-day Adventist denomination was affected, and some lawless persons came to those churches and broke in—even trying to remove the tin roofs.

Elder Robert & Rose Carter 1971–1972

Robert and Rose continued to try to go about their regular routines. At this time, Rose was becoming involved with the Dorcas Society. Her portable sewing machine made it possible for her to make dresses for several of the children.

They were able to purchase a lovely upright piano for their home from one of the departing Asian families. Not only did it keep Rose from feeling homesick, but she was able to give music lessons to the Head Master of the Primary School and also the treasurer of Uganda Field. She formed a sixty voice mass choir, and planned to give a joint concert along with the "New Believers Choir" from New York City to raise money for the work in Uganda.

One memorable experience they had one Sabbath at the Luzira Church, is still as vivid in Rose's memory as it was back in 1973. There was a church not too far from where they lived. The members of Luzira were overjoyed with their beautiful, newly built church which was just completed free of debt. Invitations were printed, and the members hand delivered them to the neighbors living close to the church. They also invited family members, friends, prominent citizens, and of course, the church leaders. A delicious lunch was served, thereby encouraging all to remain for the dedication service at 3 P.M.

What a delightful day! The crowd of people was so great that everyone could not fit inside the church building. Fortunately, they had placed seats on the outside, surrounding the church with tree branches placed overhead to provide shade. It proved to be quite comfortable. Things went along smoothly as planned. The people were fed both spiritually and physically. The appropriate words of commendation and encouragement were spoken. They had a beautiful day of fellowship!

As the last service was about to end, suddenly they heard the screams of a woman coming toward the church. Between her sobs, she was shouting and calling out the name of God. Of course, since she was speaking in her own language, they didn't understand all of what she was saying. Rose wondered if she was perhaps under the influence of alcohol. Some of the church brethren quickly went to her to see if they could quiet her or assist her in any way. The story which later unfolded was this dear lady was one of the neighbors whose home was on the same street as the church. She and her family had watched as the church was being built, and when they received the invitations to attend the opening services, they decided to attend. However, the lady had a little five-year old daughter who was crippled from birth. She had never walked, and had to be carried wherever she went. When it came time to go to church, the mother told little Endidi that she would have to stay at home with her aunt because it would be too long a day for her. Also, no doubt, there would be a large crowd of people gathered there. She promised to come back and tell her all about the proceedings.

Poor Endidi! She was heartbroken. All day she stayed in her bed, and cried as she thought of being left at home. When her mother and siblings came home and told her all that took place, the singing, the stories, and the preaching, she thought about what she had missed. She exclaimed, "I told you I wanted to go. Now, see there. Nobody would take me, but God will help me!" She climbed down from her bed, and for the first time, began to walk. Her mother was so overcome with joy and excitement she came running to the church crying and praising God for the miracle that occurred that day.

They did not see the child that Sabbath. But, the pastor of the Luzira Church invited the mother to return with Endidi the following Sabbath, and relate this experience before the congregation. He also asked Elder Carter if they could possibly come back to meet with the mother, and to also witness this miracle. Of course, Elder Carter accepted the invitation. They saw Endidi, who still showed signs of some malformations in her legs, but we watched as she slowly walked from the back of the church to the front and stood. Prayers were offered thanking God for His miraculous blessings and asked for continued progress as the child grew and developed. From childhood, Rose heard many mission stories of miracles taking place in far away lands, but never dreamed that she would be in a far away land and actually see one for herself. God is good!

They were happily absorbed in the work of the church. However, they were also very aware of the changes that were taking place throughout the country. Religious freedoms were not only being withdrawn, but civil rights were also eroding. Many people were being accused of disloyalty to the government and to the president, and they were arrested or either disappeared never to be seen again. Some were executed. Gradually many of the educated people escaped to bordering countries for safety.

Rose recalled being on their way to church one Sabbath morning, and they noticed people running toward a public square. Some of the people climbed up nearby trees, others climbed on top of trucks so they could get a view of what was about to take place. They were hoping to witness the execution of thirteen persons accused of treason. The thirteen were dressed in white clothes to make it more visible as they were shot by the firing squad. The immediate family members were required to be present to witness the process. No doubt, this experience was to instill fear into the hearts of all present. The entire scene was captured on the television camera, and was played and replayed later on the news channel.

In a few more weeks, they would have been in Uganda for a year. There was a knock at the front door, and a well-dressed gentleman stood before Rose

Elder Robert & Rose Carter 1971-1972

and asked to speak with Mr. Carter. It was close to the noon hour, and she told him that Mr. Carter had gone to town to take care of some business. She asked if he wished to wait for him, or perhaps leave a message. He said he would come back at around 3:00 p.m. He then left.

When Elder Carter returned, they greeted each other, and she remembered to tell him of the gentleman who had come to see him. He wondered what it concerned, but soon dismissed it. They proceeded to have their mid-day meal and talked about other things such as their mail from their folks back home in the U.S.A. Shortly a knock came at the door. It was the gentleman who came earlier. He was invited in and an invitation was extended to join them for dinner. He graciously declined, and asked if he could speak with her husband outside. He identified himself properly as a government agent; they began walking away from the house. They talked about fifteen or twenty minutes. When they returned, the gentleman remained outside while Elder Carter came inside to tell his wife what was said. From the expression on his face, she knew it was not good. The gentleman was from the Central Intelligence Department and came to inform her husband that he was under arrest. He must accompany the man immediately to the central Kampala jail. She inquired what the charges were. The officer told him he was not at liberty to say.

Elder Carter asked for permission, and it was granted, to inform his staff at the office what was occurring. There had been so many people taken away from their homes quietly and never heard from again. So, while he was gone to talk with the staff of workers, his wife quickly gathered a few of his personal items along with his Bible. When he returned, she tried to encourage him to finish his meal. He told her he had lost his appetite. So, she followed him out to the car where he joined the gentleman. By this time, there was a growing crowd of concerned people gathering. One of the workers stepped forward and said, "How do we know where you are taking our president? I'd like to go along with you to see if indeed you are taking him to the Kampala jail. Whatever happens to him, will happen to me."

The gentleman answered, "You may come along, but you'll have to provide your own return trip." So, the worker got into the car. With that turn of events, his wife also requested to accompany her husband, and proceeded to get into the car. She had a key to their car, and quickly gave it to their Publishing Director, and asked him to follow. Off they drove down the hill and into town.

As promised, they were taken directly to the Kampala Central Jail, where Elder Carter was booked. The gentleman said to the prison keeper. "Take good care of this man, and do not lay a hand on him to harm him in any way." The guard replied, "Who said so?" The arresting officer said, "I said so!"

Precious Memories of Missionaries of Color

Elder Carter told his wife later that several times during the night, he heard what sounded like scuffling and rough handling, followed by screams from men being brought into the holding area. How grateful he was for the instructions of his arresting officer and for God's protective care!

Mrs. Carter will never forget the bravery of the young Ugandan pastor who insisted on accompanying her husband to jail. Although the authorities would not permit him to stay in the cell block with Robert, he slept in the main lobby of the jail on the hard floor, without mattress or blanket. Early each morning he rattled the padlocked gates that led down to the cell block and requested entrance. When the armed guards asked what he wanted, he insisted on coming to Elder Carter's cell to see if he was all right. Together they knelt in that drafty jail and thanked their heavenly Father for safekeeping. Elder Carter was concerned for this brave worker and urged him to return to his home and family. However, he replied, "Pastor Carter, as long as you are in jail, I will be in jail. When you are free to leave, I will leave. Wherever they take you, I will go, and whatever happens to you will happen to me."

For two days, Elder Carter was detained while the officials questioned him and worked on the documents to have him deported. Still, no charges were made against him. One other man had a similar experience—He was the religious leader of another denomination. He was being detained at this same time to be deported back to his homeland in England. There were no specified charges against him either. Neither of them was ill treated while in custody. Because they were expatriates, their meals were specially ordered from one of the hotels. They were allowed a visitor or two. In fact a representative of the U.S. Embassy visited Elder Carter and notified the State Department in Washington, D.C. of his plight. He also notified the General Conference headquarters in Silver Spring, MD. When the East African Union officers were made aware of the situation, they sought to get him released. All efforts were in vain. After the authorities checked his record and were convinced that he had said or done nothing subversive, Elder Carter was released. However, they insisted on deporting him immediately to New York.

It was late at night when about fifty or more church members accompanied Rose to the jail to bid him good-bye and escort him to the airport. The head master that Rose gave music lessons to, spoke on behalf of his fellow Ugandans. With tears streaming down his face, he said, "Pastor, our hearts are broken. Thank you for all you have done for us. We will follow you to the airport. We want to see you leave this country without harm. Don't worry about your wife. When you are gone, we will watch over her until she is able to leave. When she is safely on her way, then we will worry about ourselves." As the plane

Elder Robert & Rose Carter 1971-1972

took off at 1:30 A.M., the group of loyal members burst into singing "Under His Wings I am Safely Abiding."

True to their word, the members were very helpful and protective of Mrs. Carter for the following ten days while she made preparations to return to the States to join her husband. Each night, there were two persons who volunteered to spend the night in her home until her departure. The Publishing Director drove her everywhere she needed to go. She was able to sell all the furnishings and goods they didn't want to take back home.

Shortly after they returned home, the Seventh-day Adventist Church in Uganda was banned. They realized before leaving, that this was a strong possibility. Even before the official ban, many members faced some trying experiences. One member told Elder Carter, "My wife and I have already decided what to do. We are prepared to die if we have to."

During the time the ban was in effect, the Adventist Church had to go underground to survive. The church members would secretly meet in various homes before daylight on Sabbath mornings, and worship all day until dark. In spite of this, many persons were won to the Lord. In order to baptize the candidates, they would meet before sunrise at a secret location—often just a river under a bridge.

They went to Uganda, became involved with the people, and Elder Carter envisioned serving there for a three-year term. He felt it would take about that period of time to strengthen the finances, help train the workers to assume leadership roles as requested, and attend to a few other needs he was able to discern. However, their stay was cut short. Did they regret their decision to go to Uganda? "Not at all!"

It was a privilege to serve. They found many warm, loving, dedicated people who really loved the Lord. People who were willing to share their faith and willing to endanger their safety for the good of others. The Carters were the richer for all those experiences.

Revisiting the life of Elder Carter, he was born in Bridgeport, Connecticut, and the third of four children of William and Elizabeth Carter. He attended the Oakwood Academy and College receiving his degree in preparation for the gospel ministry. He was the first student chosen to receive a scholarship to the Seventh-day Adventist Theological Seminary where he received his M.A. Degree. Several years later, he received a DD from Faith College. In addition to his year in Uganda Field, he served as President of the Bermuda Mission for three and a quarter years. Elder Carter holds the distinction of being the first Black to become president of one of the church's ten Union conferences in North America. He was elected to become the President of the Lake Union Conference of Seventh-day Adventist with headquarters in Berrien Springs,

Precious Memories of Missionaries of Color

Michigan. He served as the chief executive officer for 448 churches and 145 elementary and secondary schools in the Great Lakes states.

Robert first met Rose in New York where she sang and played for the Bethel Church. Their relationship blossomed at Oakwood College where they both were students. They graduated from Oakwood College in 1950 and were married in 1951.

The Carters have a son, Kermit Leon Carter, who brings them a lot of joy. The joy multiplied when Francine joined the family through marriage. Then the joy turned into sheer delight as granddaughters, Kimberly and Kelli added the icing to the cake.

Elder Carter is now asleep in Jesus. His wife is looking forward to being reunited with him and many of the dear people of Uganda that they were able to serve briefly. It will be a wonderful day when all of us can be united with the Savior, Jesus Christ when He comes to take us all home to live in a perfect, sinless world where we can safely enjoy all that He has prepared for those who love Him.

—Maranatha!

Elder Robert & Rose Carter 1971–1972

Elder Robert & Rose Carter

The Carters in National Dress

Precious Memories of Missionaries of Color

The Carters in Uganda

Elder Robert & Rose Carter 1971–1972

Elder Robert Carter

Elder Robert & Rose Carter

33

SAMUEL & SARAH JACKSON
1973-1985

I t has often been said that "God works in mysterious ways." Never have the words been more accurate than in the sequence of events that led to the Samuel and Sarah saga of the couple's missionary journey. For unbeknownst to either spouse, each had a secret desire to serve as a missionary. This had been an unspoken dream, and the interesting thing is that each of them had a desire to go to the continent of Africa to serve. What follows is an account of how the Lord provided the desires of their heart in a round-about way—even though they were not initially sent to the continent of their choice.

Samuel was initially called to the mission field in 1972. At the time, he had signed a contract to teach in the Michigan Department of Education. Since he had already made an employment commitment, he turned the missionary request down. Within a couple of weeks, however, he received the same call again for the next school year and Samuel was jubilant. He accepted the call for serving as a missionary for the 1973 school year. They would be going to Jamaica to serve at the West Indies College (now known as Northern Caribbean University). Preparation to leave the States and begin a missionary adventure was set in motion. The Jacksons were finally physically, emotionally and spiritually ready to embark upon their first missionary journey. After many tearful good-byes to family and friends, they left Detroit, Michigan, for Miami, Florida—their port of departure to the beautiful and exotic island of Jamaica, West Indies. Arriving in Jamaica was exciting but somewhat frightening. Being so far away from home and, coming into an unfamiliar environment was difficult. However, Samuel and Sarah soon acclimated to their new surroundings and settled in to begin the work that God had chosen for them to perform.

Samuel & Sarah Jackson 1973-1985

Both Samuel and Sarah immediately became busy with critical activities on the campus. Sarah, a Registered Nurse, was designated as the school nurse. She also taught the Health Education Course which included the responsibilities of obtaining health cards for food handlers and other employees. She organized a club for the nursing students called Tender Loving Care (TLC for short). This group visited the shut-ins and the sick in the area of Eldoret. It was such a rewarding experience. Samuel, as head of the Music Department also had an interesting array of assignments. He began a singing group known as The Meister Singers that became well known in a matter of months for making beautiful, harmonious music. He also taught Music Education courses, played the organ for church services, and conducted the college choir. Under the leadership of President Fletcher, Samuel was permitted to develop, organize, and expand the Musical Department, as needed, and he'd got to perform as well. Another assignment was to assist students in their quest to master their music levels for English-based examinations.

Samuel and Sarah stayed in Jamaica just two years, as Samuel had to leave his mission post due to a medical crisis. The family returned to the homeland in May of 1975. Due to Samuel's illness, they never returned to Jamaica, but the Lord still had a job for them to do overseas. This became apparent two years later when they were then called to Beirut, Lebanon, to teach at Middle East College. Their mission stint in Lebanon began in August of 1977. As they made their departure from the plane in Beirut, they experienced their first "Homeland Security" experience—they were greeted by the peace-keeping Syrian troops! These troops were located all over Lebanon requiring the Jacksons to carry their national ID card wherever they traveled. They were frequently stopped many times during their travels throughout the country. Middle East College was set on a lovely hill, high above the city, with a spectacular view of the Mediterranean Sea. This country has great biblical significance and they were able to visit the Roman ruins, Bible ports, the fertility sites, and the route Abraham passed through known as Baca Valley. It was an exquisite country. The people were very kind, accepting, and hospitable. Samuel, as head of the Music Department, once again taught classes, directed the choir, and provided music for the church. The student body was very easy to teach and all were eager to learn. They showed Samuel great respect and his teaching methods appealed to them. They often commented about their love of the music he taught them. The students were very culturally diverse—not only were there Lebanese students, but also Egyptians, Syrians, Jordanians, Americans, and both East and West Africans. Sarah was asked to be the school's official hostess and to teach in the elementary school. Samuel and Sarah remained in the beautiful country of Lebanon until the Civil war broke out in fury in 1980. Gun battles occurred close to the school. On one occasion because this war was continuous, a bomb was actually tossed in a trash can in the Jacksons' back yard. Due to the constant fighting in the country, missionaries stayed close to the campus where the majority of most activities occurred for everyone's safety. There were many days during the school year that school was closed due to the war. Finally, the fighting became so intense, that all missionaries were required to leave the country. They were first sent to Cyprus and ultimately continued on to the United States. Middle East College was closed down and the Jackson couple returned to the States. It was their understanding they would remain home until the school reopened. In the meantime, however, negotiations began for the development of a new university on the continent of Africa.

The missionaries from Middle East College were all asked to transfer to Kenya, East Africa. The name of the new University would be, The University of East Africa in Barton. This place was gorgeous! It reminded the couple of the way the beauty of the Garden of Eden has been described. Since this was a new university, the homes were newly built, classrooms and other facilities including the library were renovated and with the rich soil all around, the quality of the agriculture made it very easy to grow a vast collection of vegetables and grains. Samuel was among the first missionaries in the new school with first students enrolled—there were 78 total students at the time. As head of the Music Department, Samuel established a choir almost immediately upon arriving at the University. At the 1985 General Conference Session, the University choir was selected to perform at the session but they could not attend due to lack of funds.

For the continent of Africa, The University of East Africa in Baraton, Kenya, East Africa, was a dream come true. It was also the culmination of a dream of both Samuel and Sarah as each of them initially wanted to be missionaries in Africa. They took the mantle of God's work as Samuel again served as Head of the Music Department. His responsibilities this time were multifaceted. In addition to teaching Music Education, conducting the choir, and providing private music lessons, Samuel developed a Men's Chorus of about 25 young men. This group was very special to him, and they performed regularly both on and off campus. Music became Samuel's passion. During the final two years of their tour of missionary duty at the University of East Africa, Samuel was asked by the Government's Ministry of Music to become an adjudicator at their annual two-week Music Festival. This provided excellent public exposure to the new Adventist-run university and was certainly a wonderful experience for both Samuel and the school. He entered the Men's Chorus in the music contest, thereby making it the first Adventist school ever to perform. In both of the years that the Mens' Chorus entered, they won first prize and they were actually

Samuel & Sarah Jackson 1973–1985

asked not to enter again! They were just that accomplished! In addition, all the first place winners were honored by being asked to perform privately for the President of Kenya, Kenyatta Arap Mai, and they were excited that they were also allowed to shake hands with the President. This same time that Samuel's group was selected to perform at the General Conference. However, due to the lack of funds for travel, the school declined to accept that invitation.

At the University of East Africa, Sarah taught Health Education and was in charge of An Adventist Disaster Relief Project (ADRA) which dealt with decreasing the incidence of malnutrition in children aged 0–5. The purpose of this project was to alleviate malnutrition by 1) providing food for families and 2) marketing the surplus harvest and recognizing good sources of protein for children. Students worked in the project by planning kitchen gardens, teaching the people about the nutritional benefits of the many vegetables available to them, and giving cooking demonstrations.

All in all, the missionary experience was the highlight of Samuel and Sarah's lives. Besides being part of God's army to help finish the work, God allowed them to travel in many beautiful, unique countries of the world. Isn't that just like a loving heavenly Father? He shows His favor by giving His children the desires of their heart. The special blessings are much too numerous to narrate, but the gratitude in their hearts was shown by their passion for service.

To be able to serve God in any capacity is a special privilege, but to be selected to serve abroad, and live among people of many cultures was a chance of a lifetime. Whatever the accomplishments made apparent in the work of Samuel and Sarah, they are confident that all the glory and honor goes to God. Recently, Sarah commented: "Many thanks to our dear Lord and Savior for this opportunity to go and serve." Sadly, Samuel became ill while serving in Africa and had to be sent home. He died in 1987, two years after his return from Africa. However, the legacy of the missionary spirit lived on in the Jackson family, for Samuel's only grandson, Craig Ridgley Jackson II, was a missionary teacher in Thailand during his junior year of college. Let us rejoice in knowing that Jesus is coming soon and we will see our missionary friends and loved ones once again. It brings to mind the comforting words of the song, "In that Great Getting up Morning Fare thee well! Fare thee well! In that Great Getting up Morning, Fare Thee Well!" It is Sarah's prayer that we will all be in heaven together and rejoice over those saved as a result of the many missionaries sent around this world.

Precious Memories of Missionaries of Color

Samuel and Sarah Jackson

Men's Choir

34

ELDER HARRY & BEVERLY CARTWRIGHT 1974-1979; 1981-1986

The Cartwrights arrived in the capital city of Freetown, Sierra Leone, West Africa, in November, 1974, as the Mission Evangelist and Pastor of the Freetown, Sierra Leone S. D. A. Church. It was decided by the Union that they needed to open the work and establish a church in Gambia. The country of Gambia in 1975 was 97% Muslim and had been officially declared a Muslim country. Gambia was under the territory of the Sierra Leone Mission while George Woodruff was president and Dennis Keith was treasurer.

The West African Union under the leadership of Th. Kristensen sent a literature evangelist by the name of Daniel Cudjoe and his family to Gambia. It was hoped that through the sale of books people would become interested in the biblical truth leading to the establishment of work in the future. He was sent more than a year prior to having someone come to hold an evangelistic meeting. After much planning, the Sierra Leone mission asked Evangelist Cartwright to assume the great responsibility of establishing work in that 97% declared Muslim country.

Evangelist Cartwright sent his team, S. D. Sandy and Tiawo Roberts to precede him on a ship sailing from Freetown, Sierre Leone to Banjul, Gambia in October of 1975. Accompanying them was a new '40 by 60' square-end tent that was especially purchased for that occasion. Pastor Cartwright arrived in Gambia on October 22, 1975. He and his staff teamed up with the literature evangelist and coordinated and organized the preparation and outreach work for this very historical meeting.

Precious Memories of Missionaries of Color

Dr. Karl Praestin, a missionary working at the Masanga Leprosy Hospital in Sierra Leone also accompanied Pastor Cartwright. He conducted a 5-day Stop Smoking Plan, which was very successful and served as an entering wedge into this 97% Muslim country. The government Department of Health was very cooperative and actually assisted Evangelist Cartwright by participating in the first anti-smoking program/clinic which was organized in the country in December, 1975. Of those persons who were able to attend at least four or more evenings, one hundred percent of them were able to stop smoking. Of those who attended at least three evenings, fifty percent threw away their cigarettes. Evangelist Cartwright followed this successful Stop Smoking Clinic with his six week meeting that ran from November 1-December 12, 1975. This meeting, however, was not without problems.

After about two weeks into the meeting, which were having a very good attendance, the Government officials sent out a mandate informing Evangelist Cartwright to take down the tent. The tent had been erected in the main park, King George the 5th Memorial Park, in the center of town. He was told to leave the country within 24 hours. The Chief immigration officer emphasized to him that they had no need for another church to be established in his country because this country was Muslim.

Elder Cartwright met with his workers immediately after receiving the ultimatum. They were waiting right outside the building and he told them everything the immigration officer had said. Their hearts were very heavy and they were very discouraged and felt defeated. Elder Cartwright, however, was determined and would not give up and told them that they were not leaving the country because the Lord would make a way for them to continue with the outreach meeting. So right there on the spot, they prayed fervently for God to intervene. After praying, Evangelist Cartwright and the workers were going back to their hotel when out of nowhere Evangelist Cartwright met the Gambian man who was responsible for printing their handbills and who was also over the government printing office. He had become Evangelist Cartwright's friend. The man sensed that something was wrong. Evangelist Cartwright then told him that the Chief Immigration Officer of Gambia told him to leave the country within 24 hours. He then said to Elder Cartwright, "Don't worry. I will go and see the Chief Immigration Officer myself, you just go home, I will take care of this problem for you."

After meeting with the Chief Immigration Officer the printer got in touch with Evangelist Cartwright and told him he should go see the Chief Immigration Office and take his passport. Knocking on the door of the Chief Immigration Officer, he heard a voice say, come in. Upon entering, he sat down and the

Elder Harry & Beverly Cartwright 1974-1986

Immigration Office said that he did not know that the Printing Official was a part of the evangelist's program which Evangelist Cartwright did not know either, but he responded by saying yes he is. The Chief Immigration Officer then asked to see the passports including those of his team. Without saying a word, the official stamped them for another six weeks. They thanked him and left. Their spirits were lifted and once again they had joy in their hearts because they had just experienced the Lord working for them.

Their meeting ended with seventy-five persons in this Muslim country accepting Christ as their personal Savior. Twenty-six persons were placed into a baptismal class and were baptized by Evangelist Cartwright. He found and leased a building and organized the first fruits of this meeting into a church. He also pastored them for a period of time by flying to and from the country of Sierra Leone. They thank the Lord for helping them successfully organize the first S.D.A. church established in the city of Banjul, Gambia.

The Union President invited Evangelist Cartwright to take his wife, Beverly, to visit that country extending him the invitation to become the first church leader. Evangelist Cartwright was asked to head up the work by the West African Union president, Th. Christensen. The West African Union president explained to Evangelist Cartwright that he wanted him to go there to help establish the work into a union station. Pastor Cartwright was very honored with this invitation, but due to other circumstances and his children's educational needs, he had to decline.

The Cartwright's mission service expands for more than the time spent in Gambia. They started their mission service in the Sierra Leone Mission, as Evangelist/Pastor; from there on to Liberia Mission as the Ministerial Secretary/Pastor in Monrovia, Liberia; the Ministerial Secretary in the Afro-Mid East Division in Nicosia, Cyprus; as Ministerial Secretary in the Eastern Africa Division in Nairobi, Kenya/Harare, Zimbabwe.

Pastor Cartwright was born in Dania, Florida, to Mike and Ellen Cartwright. He received his Associates Science Degree, from San Diego Junior College in San Diego, CA. He earned the B.A. Degree from Columbia Union College, Takoma Park, MD, and the Masters of Divinity Degree from Andrews Theological Seminary, in Berrien Springs, MI. His wife Beverly is also a graduate of Columbia Union College. They are the proud parents of Derrick Cartwright (deceased); Kimberly Cartwright, who has a B.A. from Loma Linda University and is a Deputy, Probation Officer in Riverside, California; Harry Cartwright, Jr. is also a graduate from Columbia Union College where he received his B.A. and is currently a Realtor/Songwriter in Marina Del Rey, California; Alvin S. Cardinal, their nephew, concludes this family and works as a Police Officer in the District of Columbia.

Precious Memories of Missionaries of Color

Dr. Carl-Aage Praestiin and Evangelist H. A Cartwright

Anti-Smoking Club organized by Elder Cartwright with Government support in 1975

Elder Harry & Beverly Cartwright 1974–1986

Some of the baptismal candidates Pastor Cartwright baptized in Gambia

35

ELDER JASON & CAROLYN MCCRACKEN 1975-1976; 1979-1986

In 1975, Jason McCracken, a theology student at Oakwood College was called by the Youth Department of the General Conference to serve as a student missionary in the Rio Grande Conference in the state of Rio Grande do Sul, in Brazil, South America. He was the assistant to Pastor Jose Maria Barbosa da Silva, the youth and Pathfinder director of that conference. He is considered the first African-American student missionary to serve in Brazil. His activities included preaching on youth and Pathfinder days, planning youth camps, designing and organizing the first Pathfinder camporee in Brazil in November 1975. The camporee was held at the youth campsite of the Rio Grande Conference.

When Jason returned to Oakwood College in 1976, it was several years later that the South Brazil Union youth director became president of the Central Brazil Mission, in the state of Goias. He called Jason, by way of the General Conference, to serve as the Youth, Pathfinder, Health and Temperance director for the Central Brazil Mission in 1979.

Jason married his wife, Carolyn Fitzgerald, of Philadelphia, Pennsylvania and together they began their missionary journey to Brazil after graduation from Oakwood College.

Elder and Mrs. McCracken began their ministry in December, 1979 in the city of Goiania, Goias, Brazil, as Youth, Pathfinder, Health and Temperance director. His duties included organizing Pathfinder and AY societies, developing youth camp models, and fostering the highest baptismal growth in the union. When he left, 95 percent of the organized churches had Pathfinder clubs and

Elder Jason & Carolyn McCracken 1975-1986

established youth camp ministries in every district in the state. He is the first American to be ordained in Brazil.

In 1982, President Neal Wilson inaugurated the Central Brazil Conference where Elder McCracken became its first youth director in their new facility in Goiania. The story is told that when Elder McCracken was promoting Pathfinder clubs in the Central church in Goiania, a young fellow named Lins Miranda was running from him. He chased Miranda around the church and cornered him in the men's room. He pointed his finger in his face and said, "You 'must' be a Pathfinder!" The young man took on the challenge and followed Elder McCracken's ministry. The young man became a talented Pathfinder and was invested as a Master Guide. Later the young man was inspired by Elder McCracken to enter the ministry. He completed his degree in theology and returned to Goias as a pastor. He followed in the footsteps of Elder McCracken's profile and later became a Youth and Pathfinder director of the Central Brazil Conference. It was Pastor McCracken's dream that the Pathfinders of Goias would have their own campground. Several years later it became a reality. Elder McCracken was invited back to his first love in 2004 in Goias where he was the speaker at the Pathfinder Camporee after 20 years of organizing the first camporee of Goias in 1984.

He was excited when they showed him a site that was donated by the Central Brazil Academy. There Elder McCracken was given an award as the ambassador of the first SDA international campsite of Brazil.

In 1986, Elder McCracken became the first American (African-American) to serve as Brazil's first Junior/Youth Specialist of the Central Brazil Union headquartered in Sao Paulo, Brazil. He organized the largest and first computerized Pathfinder Camporee of any union during that time in Brazil. He managed 450 Pathfinder clubs with a membership of 18,000. He was also the marketing director of the Pathfinder materials emblems for the union. The materials that were developed by Elder McCracken reached every conference in Brazil. The Pathfinder clubs in Brazil were baptizing at an annual rate of 15 percent of the total union baptisms. Today Brazil has the largest per capita of organized church Pathfinder clubs in the world.

Presently, Elder McCracken works at the Review and Herald Publishing Association as senior marketing representative for *Message* magazine and FHES products.

Information regarding camporees can be found in the book *We Are the Pathfinders Strong,* by Willie Oliver and Pat Humphrey; Review and Herald Publishing Association, 2000.

Precious Memories of Missionaries of Color

Elder Jason McCracken

36

Dr. Ruth Naomi Rhone
1976–1986

Ruth was called to the mission field in 1976 while she was studying in France. In August of the same year, she went to Rwanda where she taught French and English for six years at Gitwe High School. Her experiences in Rwanda were invaluable and she will never forget the kindness and gracious spirit of all the people she met in "the country of a thousand hills."

From there she went to Burundi, where she worked as a bilingual secretary at the Union office. Her stay in Burundi was much shorter (about two years), but the memories are indelible. After work in the afternoons, she used to give English lessons to some of the local residents.

The last mission field where she worked was the Ivory Coast. She was secretary to the Publishing Director of the AID. She left Abidjan in December 1986, and has been living in the Washington, DC, area since that time.

About three months after Ruth arrived in Burundi, she decided to go back to Rwanda to pick up items that she had left there. One of the workers was going to attend a meeting in Kigali, the capital of Rwanda, so she accompanied him. When they arrived at the border (Rwanda/Burundi) she was told that she did not have the proper papers so she had to return to Bujumbura, where she lived. The person she accompanied said that he could not miss his meeting, so he went ahead and left her in the hands of two strange men who had also been denied entry into Rwanda. The border guards told her that she could not stay at the border, because they were going to leave in a few minutes; she really had no choice but to leave. She had to hop into the Toyota truck with these two men. Can you imagine what was going through her mind? She was going to be with them for at least three hours.

Precious Memories of Missionaries of Color

Both men were drunk! You could smell them a mile away. Moreover, if you knew the terrain of Burundi, you would understand her fears. For the most part, the roads were not paved. They were so narrow that two cars could not drive side by side. In some areas, you could look down from your car and see very steep precipices on one side of the road and extremely high boulder rocks on the other side. If the car slipped……. she envisioned her mother crying as they broke the news to her that she had died in a car accident.

So there she was with two tipsy men who spoke a language she did not understand. She sat in the front of the truck between both of them. They asked her in French several times "Ça va, Madame?" and she reassured them that she was doing fine. They wanted to know what she was doing in Burundi, and she told them that she was working for the Adventist church. They made some comments about that (she can't remember exactly what was said) and continued to talk in Kirundi, their native language. Usually she is an extrovert, but that day she was too busy praying for her life to be very explicit about a job description. She prayed as she never prayed before. After driving for about an hour and a half, they stopped the car. The sky was pitch black, sprinkled with a few stars. There were no lights around. She heard voices and then suddenly she saw a glimmer of light coming from somewhere. She started to think: "Now where am I going to run? Lord, let them not kill me here. Nobody is going to find my body in this place." She has a vivid imagination, but dear readers, do not be too quick to judge. What would you have thought? In a few minutes, she realized that this light came from a lantern at the front of a little store. Several people were there. Her gracious drivers invited her in to have a drink, but she told them that she would be all right sitting in the car. How long did they stay there? She doesn't know! It seemed an eternity. She is sure that they had a little bit more to drink before they resumed the driving. On the second leg of the journey she began to feel somewhat more relaxed with them; moreover, the terrain had become more level so the risk of falling over a cliff was virtually non-existent.

Gradually they approached Bujumbura, and as she saw the lights of the city, she felt relieved. The two men drove her to her house and made sure that she got in safely. She thanked them profusely and thanked God that they had arrived safely. This incident occurred over twenty years ago. Some of you readers might say, "Well, you should have witnessed." Well, probably she did witness in a quiet way. She is still praying for those men.

"In as much as ye have done it unto the least of these my children, ye have done it unto me." She hopes to meet these men again in the kingdom.

It was time for Ruth to renew her Burundi visa. She went to the immigration office to do so. To her great surprise they refused to renew it. Curious,

Dr. Ruth Naomi Rhone 1976–1986

she requested an explanation. She was told that there was no explanation. She had to pack up and leave within a week.

This would not have been a problem if she had not brought furniture with her to Burundi. During her previous six years in Rwanda the mission had supplied the furniture. However, before she left for Burundi, she was told that policies had been changed and that she had to ship her own furniture from the States. How was she going to get rid of all the furniture she had brought over, within a week? Some of her Burundese friends bought several items (living room and dining room sets and the washing machine, household items) at a give-away price, but she was having tremendous difficulties selling the piano and all the electrical appliances she had. Nobody wanted to buy the latter because one had to use a transformer with them. On the eve of her departure she decided to go to her former boss's house. He had been asked to leave a week before. She really didn't know why she went there. However, she met a Baptist missionary from Zaire (Congo) who was just passing through Bujumbura and had seen the sign of a piano for sale. She had come to see the piano at her boss's house. Unfortunately, she did not like it. It was too big. As she was walking back to her car, Ruth said to her: "I have a piano you might be interested in. Do you want to see it? She said "Yes" and they made arrangements for her to come to the house that night. When she saw the piano she immediately fell in love with it. This was what she was looking for. She bought it and to Ruth's great surprise also bought all the electrical appliances and the transformer she could not sell. She wrote out a check in American dollars and paid her even more than what the items originally cost. The morning of Ruth's departure, an hour before she left for the airport, the woman came with a truck and picked up everything.

Whenever Ruth is in a seemingly unsolvable situation, she remembers this experience. Jesus never fails!

"Trust in the Lord with all your heart, and lean not on your own understanding. In all your ways acknowledge Him and He shall direct your paths."

Outstanding Achievements

1. In the Ivory Coast, two other missionaries and Ruth gave Bible studies with local residents. Every Sabbath afternoon they knocked on doors and invited people to study with them. Up to the date of her departure, no one requested baptism. At the last GC Session, she met a young man who told her that one of those with whom they were studying accepted the message, after her departure, was baptized and is now an Adventist pastor.

2. Ruth learned to fast in Rwanda. She was very sick and was told that it was malaria. She does not like to take any kind of medication, so unknown to the school nurse she threw away the medication he gave her. Of course, this got her into serious trouble, because she could not get out of bed and her principal wanted to know why she was not back at school. For about two weeks, she ate nothing and drank very little. One day, she finally got out of bed. Two people saw her and told her that she had never looked healthier. Her skin was "alive," and her eyes were bright and shining. She had lost a lot of weight, so her neighbors all thought it would be a good idea to give her some good food to fatten her. She started eating again, and she immediately became sick. It took her several years afterwards to understand what had happened: after such a lengthy fast, one should not eat "regular" food. On the contrary, one's diet should consist of food that would continue the elimination process.

She considers this an outstanding personal achievement. She has been able to get rid of some minor health problems, thanks to fasting. She has also suggested this method of cleansing to friends who have been pleased with the results. This was, for her, the beginning of a cure that has helped her tremendously over the years. Whenever she is sick, she stops eating and starts drinking a lot of water! Try it! You would be surprised at the results.

"Beloved, I wish above all things that you would prosper and be in good health."

Dr. Ruth Naomi Rhone 1976–1986

Precious Memories of Missionaries of Color

Dr. Ruth Rhone

ELDER KENNETH & ELIZABETH BUSHNELL 1977-1987

The Bushnells began their ministry in West Virginia in 1966 where Elder Bushnell had a district of four churches. Their first child, Stephanie, was born in 1970, the year they accepted a call from the Central California Conference to pastor a church in San Jose. Two years later they accepted a call to the East Allegheny Conference to pastor a church in Richmond, Virginia. Three years later they accepted a call to Pottstown, PA, to serve as the Youth and Temperance Director for the Allegheny East Conference. Their second child, Stephen, was born in 1976.

Their adventure in missionary work began in the fall of 1977 with an interview in the General Conference office of Elder Maurice Battle, who at that time was a General Conference Secretary. When they arrived at Elder Battle's office, they were introduced to Pastor Dennis Bazarra who was the president of the East African Union, located in the territory of Kenya and Uganda. After a long discussion of the pros and cons of working for the church in Africa, they decided this was the calling of the Lord, and they agreed to join with Pastor Bazarra to help spread the advent message in that part of the world field. Pastor Bazarra informed Elder Bushnell that he would be the Youth and Communication Director for the East African Union.

Their first move toward the mission project, once the call was confirmed by the General Conference, was to spend three months on the campus of Andrews University where they went through an extensive missionary orientation program. Here they were, in the middle of winter in the State of Michigan with sub zero temperature preparing to go to Africa, the land of sunshine. By the

Precious Memories of Missionaries of Color

time they reached Nairobi in March of 1978, they found themselves taking off their winter overcoats, scarves, and gloves. Needless to say, they received a "warm" reception at the Nairobi airport.

The East African Union office was located in the city of Nairobi on a large compound where the housing for the missionaries was also located. They were directed to their living quarters which were what they call today a condominium. It took several months for their household goods to arrive. During that time they lived out of their suitcases along with the few provisions supplied by the Union. When their belongings did arrive it was like Christmas time as they opened all of their boxes. Their children were at the ages where they could adapt fairly well. Their daughter was seven years old, and their son was one year old. They attended the Adventist school located in the city of Nairobi. Mrs. Bushnell also adjusted very well to their new home. She learned very quickly how to bargain at the open markets. She also learned to prepare many of their meals using several of the indigenous recipes. They soon became "spoiled" with the numerous and sometimes different sources of fruits and vegetables. By all standards, they found Nairobi to be a very modern city. The downtown area of Nairobi was always busy with both the local people and many tourists.

Nairobi is the "Washington, DC" of Kenya. There are many legislative halls for the nation, as well as, many government buildings for the local city. The Seventh-day Adventist Church is well known among the nation's government. One of Elder Bushnells' high moments of being a Seventh-day Adventist in Kenya was when the Union office administration and departmental leaders were invited to meet with the Kenya president, Daniel Arp Moi. They were ushered into a large room in the capital building which was located near the president's "White House." When the president entered the room they stood until the president was seated. Their group brought several gifts to give to the president. Among the gifts were several Spirit of Prophecy books. They had the opportunity to share with the president the work the church was doing throughout the nation. President Moi of course knew about Seventh-day Adventists, but he appeared to be impressed when they told him about their education system, as well as the medical work in Kenya.

Toward the last year of Elder Bushnell's work in the East African Union, Nairobi was chosen as the venue for the African Youth Congress (the first of its kind). An invitation was extended to President Moi, and they were happy to hear that he had accepted and would attend. When the President arrived he spoke to the youth and encouraged them to make plans for the day when they will be leaders in their respective nations. He was very expressive, and his speech encouraged many of the youth to become leaders.

Elder Kenneth & Elizabeth Bushnell 1977–1987

Elder Bushnell was determined to help the Adventist youth in the East African Union to become the kind of leaders that would bring other youth to Christ. He worked very closely with the youth directors in the various Conferences which, at that time were called Fields. Before the Bushnells left the East African Union to move to the Eastern Africa Division, they were happy to see the first Conference established. Since that time many other Fields have become Conferences. They enjoyed working with the Youth Directors throughout the Union territory. They would schedule regular meetings with these Youth Directors to help them build a strong youth program in their Field. The Union had a Youth Camp located on a beautiful site on the shores of the Indian Ocean. They conducted two annual youth programs at that location. One of the programs was for non-Adventist youth. The Youth Directors would bring youth from their respective Fields to this program. This program would last for one week, and when it was time to go back home, many of the youth wanted to stay longer. The second program was for their own young people. The program for these youth focused on being involved in the worldwide SDA youth program that would ultimately make Master Guides of their youth. They found that the Youth Directors enjoyed this program as much as the youth. On one occasion, the Youth Directors and Elder Bushnell took the young people to the shores of Lake Victoria. They pitched their campsite on the shores of an ideal location and had the time of their life. They all enjoyed being at this beautiful lake, and decided to have the following year's camp at Lake Victoria again, but at a different site.

One of the experiences Elder Bushnell had working with the Youth Directors was when they were at one of the training programs. Elder Bushnell got into a conversation with these men about the lifestyle he grew up in and now experiencing their lifestyle. He stated to them that he felt he was learning more from them than they from him. They would often share their experiences, and one of the requests they would often ask of him was to tell them what it was like to live in America. He would often share the good and the bad of what it was like to live in America. One of the things he would often share with them was how he admired their ability to live a very simple lifestyle as compared to his lifestyle of living in America. This is what he meant when he said earlier that he felt he was learning more from them than they were learning from him.

Part of his responsibilities was also to be the Communication Director for the Union. This department presented the challenge to prepare news reports for the Union newspaper of events that have taken place around the Union. They were able to get news reports from Kenya and Uganda. Most of the time, he had to be present at the event. He had the privilege to go to Uganda to cover

Precious Memories of Missionaries of Color

the event of a Ugandan Adventist Medical doctor, Dr. Kaseka, to become the Prime Minister of his nation. It was like experiencing what the prophet Daniel had when he was in Babylon.

Another experience they had in Uganda happened on the Bugema Academy campus which was also the campus for the Uganda Seminary. The school was not very far from the capital city of Kampala. Kenneth was invited along with Craig Newborn, another missionary, to teach at the Seminary while two of the Philippine missionaries went on furlough. They were to teach for about four weeks. Accommodations were provided for them to live in the homes of the missionaries that were on furlough. Craig brought his wife and family with him. Kenneth was without his family. They each brought along the necessary provisions needed for their stay. They had started a friendship with one of the teachers, Reuben Mugerwa, when the Uganda Seminary had to move to the Kenya youth camp site located north of Mombassa during the reign of Idi Amin. During his stay on the Bugema campus, Kenneth was invited to come over to Reuben's home, which was also on campus. He and his wife and family treated him as though he was one of the families. When he would visit their home he would bring some item of food to share with them. Usually the item was the kind of food that was not available in Kampala at that time, or if it was available, it was very expensive.

One evening after Kenneth left Reuben's house, he walked the short distance across campus to the house where he stayed. During the afternoon of that same day all of the electricity had been shut down. So it was very dark at night on the campus. He had brought with him a kerosene lamp which he lit up once he reached his house. He had borrowed one of Reuben's books, and he stayed up several hours that night reading. He noticed while he was reading that many of the dogs were continually barking. He tried not to pay any attention to it. He finally decided to turn out his light and go to sleep for the night.

It was not until the next morning that he was told by Craig Newborn, who knocked on his door early that morning, what happened during that night. As he said earlier, Uganda had experienced the leadership of their nation under Idi Amin's rule. By the time Craig and Kenneth reached Bugema, Idi Amin had been run out of the country, and there was very little law and order throughout the nation. Bandits roamed not only the streets of Kampala, but all over the countryside as well. Kenneth found out that it was a gang of bandits that shut down the electricity in the area of the campus with every intention to steal anything they could from the school that night. Reuben also told his side of the story. He said that not long after Kenneth left his house, there was a bang at Reuben's door. When he opened the door there stood several men with guns.

Elder Kenneth & Elizabeth Bushnell 1977-1987

They ordered Reuben to give them all of his valuables or they would kill him and his family. He gave them what little money he had and his watch which he bought while studying at Andrews University. Then the bandits told Reuben to take them to the Americans that are on campus. News travels very fast in the countryside. As much as Reuben did not want to follow their demands, he left his family, and with the bandits headed for the house where Kenneth was staying. About this time he was still awake in the bedroom in the backside of the house reading his book. As the bandits approached the house where Kenneth was, Reuben didn't tell them that Kenneth was staying in this house. The house looked as though no one was in it. As they were passing the house they noticed a light in the back window. Reuben managed, by the grace of God, to tell them that Kenneth didn't have anything. He told them that Kenneth had to come over to his house to eat—that's how poor he was. The bandits believed him and proceeded toward the house where Craig and his family stayed. Craig told me what happened when they reached his house.

God was in this experience. One of the persons living on the campus was able to reach the house where Craig and family stayed to warn them of the bandits approaching. Craig brought his two children into the bedroom where he and his wife were sleeping. Then he gathered all his valuables and put them under the mattress, and had his wife and children to sit on the mattress. When the bandits banged on the door Craig opened the door to let them in. Reuben told Craig why they were there, and the bandits began searching the house. They did not find any of Craig's things, but they took a few items left by the missionaries on furlough. All this was going on while Kenneth was listening to the barking dogs and reading his book. Finally, he decided to turn out his light for the night and go to sleep. When the bandits, with Reuben, passed by the house where Kenneth was, they noticed that the light was out, and they didn't bother to ask about him anymore. Craig told him that morning that he and his family were praying as they had never prayed before. Of course, God answered their prayers. Needless to say, the Lord blessed Craig's family and Kenneth to arrive back to Nairobi safely. But that's not the end.

Kenneth met Reuben sometime later in Nairobi, and he told him what happened when Kenneth, Craig and his family left the campus that morning to head back to Nairobi. Reuben said that a few days later the same bandits came back again. They probably thought that they were still on campus. Reuben said that they approached his home again, and ordered him to take them to the American teachers. When he told them they had left the campus, it made the bandits very mad. On the day they left the school Kenneth gave Reuben the rest of his food supply along with a fist full of Uganda money. Their money at

Precious Memories of Missionaries of Color

that time was worthless outside of Uganda. Reuben told me that he decided to give these items to the bandits for fear that they would do harm to him and his family. He said the bandits took the goods and left them unharmed. Praise the Lord!

In 1985, Kenneth was invited to be the Communication Director for the Eastern Africa Division. The Division office was located in Harare, Zimbabwe. They accepted the position and found themselves again packing up and moving. Including this move to Zimbabwe, this was the fifth time their family packed up to move counting their move from their home land to Africa. Now Kenneth's work involved traveling to more countries in East Africa. His travels included Ethiopia, Kenya, Tanzania, Malawi, and Zimbabwe, with visits to South Africa, and Botswana. On this move, they decided to leave their daughter, Stephanie, in Nairobi where she would continue her schooling at the Nairobi Academy.

Kenneth will never forget one story he wrote for the Division newsletter. In the country of Malawi he was introduced to an elderly couple that owned a small farm on the outskirts of the capital city. When he arrived at their farm with the Union Communication Director, the elderly man told him his life long desire. He and his wife took him and the Union Communication Director a short distance from their house to an open patch on the edge of a field. He pointed to a small building and said that it has been his dream to build a church. The structure that he pointed to only had four walls which were made of part mud and part cement. There were window openings but no frames and no glass. There was no roof, and a dirt floor on the inside, there were wood planks placed on stones for pews. The pulpit was a fifty-five gallon container. In his country it was very difficult to purchase the materials needed for his building project, and what materials were available were very expensive. As the old farmer pointed to his church he proudly said that one day his dream will come true. Kenneth was not able to stay in touch with the old farmer, but he is sure somehow God answered his request.

When their daughter, who they left in Nairobi, finished her junior year at the academy, they made the decision to return home. They made this decision realizing that when she finished her senior year they would have to decide whether they would send her home to start her college education or return with her. They decided to keep their family together as long as they could. When they returned home the Lord opened a place for them to continue their ministry for the church. They accepted a call to the Mid America Union in Lincoln, Nebraska. About three years later, they accepted a call to pastor the Kansas Avenue Church in the Southeastern California Conference. About two years later, they moved to Thousand Oaks, California, to serve as

Elder Kenneth & Elizabeth Bushnell 1977-1987

an associate director in Church Ministries at the Pacific Union Conference. About seven years later they moved to the Northern California Conference to pastor a church in Vallejo, California. At the present time they are still in the Northern California Conference, the pastor of a district of two churches in the San Francisco East Bay area.

The Lord has been good to them over the years. They often reflect back over their experiences in Africa, and how God guided them through numerous events during their stay in that part of the world. As an African American, Kenneth will always treasure the blessings of living in Africa and experiencing the life that was only possible through the will and blessings of the Lord, Savior and Friend, Jesus Christ, living in what Kenneth calls our "motherland."

38

ELDER EDWARD & DOROTHY DORSEY 1979-1981

The call came in the middle of April, 1979, when Elder Dunbar Henri, Sr., requested that Elder Dorsey consider going to West Africa as President of the Liberian Mission. After prayerful consideration, the Dorseys placed their lives in the hands of God for His leading as they accepted the call to go to Liberia.

The ball started to roll! They received communication from the General Conference Transportation Office concerning the shots, shipping and time of departure. They were asked to attend the mission institute at Andrews University to receive preparation for the task ahead. They arrived sometime in June at Andrews University and completed the training on July 21. While there, it was a pleasure to meet many other appointees as well as instructors including Gottfried Oosterwald and Werner Vymeister.

They left the shores of the United States via Pam Am Airlines on October 2, 1979 at 1:00 P.M. from John F. Kennedy Airport in New York. They were scheduled to arrive in Monrovia on October 3.

They shall never forget the breathtaking sunrise as they arrived at Roberts Field. They were met by M.I. Harding, the secretary of the mission, Mrs. Wright, treasurer, Bruce Roberts, Principal of Konola Academy, Pastor and Mrs. Olson, and Ken Flemmer, pastor and instructors from Konola Academy. Pastor Harding, also interim pastor at the Monrovia Seventh-day Adventist church, held a large sign that said "WELCOME HOME, PASTOR & MRS. DORSEY."

The Dorseys started home to the place where they would spend the next four years of their lives. Upon their arrival, they were greeted with another

Elder Edward & Dorothy Dorsey 1979-1981

welcome sign that was tacked to the door. They entered their new home which was clean though sparsely furnished until they added their personal touch from their belonging which would arrive later. The Hardings and Mrs. Wright took them on a shopping trip to the supermarket for groceries. The prices were staggering to the imagination! They purchased what they absolutely needed and than returned home.

On Sabbath, they attended the Monrovia Church and were formally introduced to the members as their new mission president. The people embraced them warmly and they felt a sense of oneness as they joined in fellowship with their brothers in Liberia. In the evening, there was a social gathering to officially welcome them to the mission. Several groups sang with such singing that they have never heard before! The music was beautiful and full of feeling and enthusiasm.

Ed's first day in the office was a day to get acquainted with the staff and to get a general idea of what was happening in the mission. Dorothy got the wandering itch and walked along Camp Johnson Road where there were shops and stores where one could buy food, clothes, furniture, and hardware. She also observed that further along, there were a few schools.

As is expected of all expatriates of American extraction, they went to the American Embassy to register. It was good to meet people from home!

On Sabbath, they accompanied Pastor Harding and his wife to Konola Academy which was about an hour's drive from Monrovia. On the way, they stopped to greet the believers in Kokata. They did not stay long because their destination was Konola Academy. As they made their way, it was nice to see the countryside, stores, villages, people colorfully dressed selling baskets, food, and other items.

When they arrived at Konola, the Sabbath school was already in progress. Bruce Roberts and Pastor Olsen came out to greet them. They took their seats at the back of the large white auditorium where they listened to the lesson study. Ed faced the challenge of speaking for the first time to students of another culture, one about which he was still learning. He spoke about different types of nails and compared them to different types of Christians. His message, short and to the point, was well received by the students.

On Sabbath afternoon, around 50-60 Pathfinders with flags marched in from the outside to the tune of "Onward Christian Soldiers." It was thrilling, and at the moment, Dorothy wished that their good friends Davis, Timpson, and other MV men could have beheld this spectacle! It was worthy of note! Many received honors and were invested as Friends, Companions, and Explorers.

Edward and Dorothy went to bed at 7:30 (unheard of in the States) for you see they had no television or record player so the evenings were long.

Precious Memories of Missionaries of Color

This evening they had just turned in when the doorbell rang. They opened the door and four charming ladies entered. The first lady handed Edward a package and said welcome to West Africa and here is something from East Africa. She introduced herself as Sister Picks, wife of the Ambassador of Ghana from Paynesville and a member of the Monrovia Church. She introduced her three daughters, one of whom was adopted. Her son was attending Walla Walla College in California, and one of her daughters would be attending Andrews University in Michigan. She recalled her visits in the states with the Vanderburgs, Banks, Cantrells, and Henris.

Dorothy was thankful to be able to spend time in the office assisting Ed with the filing. There were many opportunities like this one to assist in other ways as well! When Mrs. Wright, the treasurer, went on furlough to Jamaica, Dorothy took on the responsibilities of the treasurer until she returned.

The Dorseys shall never forget the night that Monrovia was in total darkness! The only lights that could be seen were cars passing on the road casting light now and then. The lights were out for about ten minutes and were a welcome sight when they came back on. The Dorseys had one little candle lit so they wouldn't stumble in the dark. Thank God for small blessings!

They went to Buchanan to visit the church there. On their way, they passed through the Firestone Rubber Plantation with many buildings and processing plants. This area had been occupied by American troops during World War II. They saw the harbor in Buchanan where iron ore was loaded onto the boats. The church service at Buchanan was nice and Ed's message was well received. Half of the church speaks English and the other half speaks the Bassa dialect.

Seventy days had passed since their arrival in Africa. They had visited every Seventh-day Adventist Mission compound where churches and schools were located—except Palmberg in Grand Bassa County and the bush churches in the interior off the main roads. They were planning to visit those churches during the dry season which they were entering into presently.

Ed and Pastor M.I. Harding boarded an Air Liberia twin engine propeller plane with a seating capacity of about 40. Their destination was Greenville in Sinoe County. In 1978, from the middle of October until December, Pastor Johjannes Onjukka, along with the assistance of Pastor Harding, Pastor R. Bestman, and Brother Nyempan, conducted an effort in Greenville. Thirty-nine persons were baptized and a company was organized. A friend of Pastor Onjukka's was so impressed with the results of the meeting that she donated $20,000 with which to construct a church building. The neat, well constructed building continues to stand as a monument to the glory of God in Sinoe County.

Elder Edward & Dorothy Dorsey 1979-1981

The plane arrived at the Greenville airport about forty-five minutes after take off. The African pilots brought the plane to a smooth landing on the hard, red clay runway. Pastor Harding worked in the Liberian Educational Ministry several years prior to his call to Secretarial Department of the SDA Mission. Elder Dorsey and Pastor Harding met and talked with several of their acquaintances who were making the trip to Greenville. He talked with one of several lawyers who were on their way to talk to about fifteen prisoners who were being held as suspects in a bizarre murder committed several weeks before. A young man who worked in the Greenville hospital had been brutally murdered. His body was dismembered and stuffed in a freezer. One person called the names of fifteen local, prominent businessman and clergymen as suspects in the crime. These men, upon the word of this one man were arrested, put in jail, beaten by the popo, and stripped of their clothes and made to sleep on a cement floor in a dark one room cell. One of the reasons for going to Greenville, besides that of visiting the members, was to visit Pastor T. Bestman, the pastor of the church and also a suspect in this bizarre murder.

The Dorseys took a taxi from the airport to the church. In contrast to the surroundings, the church building was outstanding. A white "A" style structure situated on a nice level site, it glistened in the sun like a pearl of a great prince. Indeed! It was just that-a priceless gem beckoning sinners to the "Pearl of a Great Prince"—JESUS!

When they walked into the church, several men were preparing for worship. They were delighted to see them. They introduced their Mission President to those present. The people sang, without music (there was no piano) from a typewritten sheet with about five songs for there were no song books. As the service progressed, several women and children came into the service, including sister Bestman, the wife of T. Bestman. In spite of the ordeal she was undergoing during her husband's arrest, she and her children were pleasant and showed great strength and courage.

Pastor Harding was asked to teach the Sabbath School lesson to all assembled. The Mission President was introduced before the lesson was begun. The lesson was taught from an old Sabbath School quarterly because the new ones had not arrived. Although Sabbath school quarterlies were mailed from the U.S. in time to be used currently, they were often buried beneath piles of other packages on the floor of the shipping dock warehouses for as long as six or even twelve months before they were discovered and sent to the mission. Pastor Harding, in his zealous and practical manner, taught the lesson so that it was easy to comprehend. The members were thankful and encouraged by the lesson which seemed designed for the problems they were facing.

Precious Memories of Missionaries of Color

By the time Sabbath school ended, the church, with a seating capacity of about 100, was nearly filled. They immediately entered into the divine worship hour. The service was prefaced with a Voice of Prophecy (V.O.P.) graduation exercise. Fifty people had completed the course, many of whom were present to receive their certificate of graduation. At the conclusion of the service, when Elder Dorsey made his appeal, everyone came forward for rededication and several V.O.P students came forward for baptism.

Brother Nyenpan, one of the teachers in the elementary school of about 200 students, was also their V.O.P. director in Greenville. He informed the President that he had successfully enrolled about 1000 people in the V.O.P Bible Courses. Besides teaching and assisting with the administration of the church work, Brother Nyenpan had to visit the VOP interest on foot, as he had no other transportation. "If I had a motorbike," he told me," I would be able to enroll many more people in the V.O.P course."

They greeted the members and visitors as they left the church with a warm handshake, African style—snapping the fingers as the hands separated. This was a way of saying, "You are my friend—you are one of us."

They left the church and walked about a half mile with brother Nyenpan, Sister Bestman and her children, and several other members to Pastor Bestman's house. While waiting for the taxi to arrive to take us to the prison for a visit with Pastor Bestman, we were refreshed with coconut water and a few sandwiches prepared by his wife Dorothy, the first lady of the Mission. They had hardly finished eating when the taxi arrived.

The prison compound was near the airport and consisted of several mud and cement buildings with vine roofs and cement floors. There was no fence around the compound, but there were prison guards stationed at various locations around the compound for security. The first building we came to after entering the prison compound housed the fifteen accused men. Pastor Bestman came out to greet us. Most of the other prisoners were acquainted with Pastor Harding and were happy to see him. He introduced Elder Dorsey and one of the wives who came with us to visit her husband to the men. Pastor Harding led the group in singing hymns, offered prayer, and the Mission President was invited to give a brief message. When he finished speaking, Pastor Harding told a story which Elder Dorsey had given on a previous occasion. They concluded the service by joining hands in a circle and inviting several of the prisoners, including Pastor Bestman, to pray. As they were about to leave, the prisoners expressed their sincere gratitude for the concern for them, and they were greatly encouraged to face their trial with confidence and renewed faith in God.

Elder Edward & Dorothy Dorsey 1979–1981

The taxi took them back to the church where they had a meeting to discuss some of the problems which had arisen due to the imprisonment of Pastor Bestman. They heard the complaints and allowed time for adequate discussion. They suggested an order of program to be followed to which the members present willingly agreed to. They set a tentative date of February 2 to return and conduct communion service, baptismal services, and ordain their local leaders and deacons. They felt a spirit of unity among the members as they returned to Sister Bestman's house to wait the arrival of their taxi to take them to the airport. When the taxi arrived, it was full of passengers, so they had to walk out to the main road and hail another taxi. On their way to the airport, they were cautioned to slow down by men along the side of the road. Further down the road, they saw the reason. A taxi and a jeep had collided. The jeep was upside down and the front of the taxi was smashed. The occupants of the vehicles had been taken to the hospital—the extent of their injuries were unknown.

The plane, Air Liberia, arrived one hour and fifteen minutes late. It was about 7:30 P.M. when they touched down in Monrovia. They were due to arrive at 6:00 P.M. It was good to leave the taxi and climb the steps of their mission house. Elder Dorsey greeted his wife with a tender kiss and settled down for a meal and a period of relaxation after another busy Sabbath in Liberia, West Africa.

The Dorseys truly enjoyed the rich culture and people of Liberia. Because of turmoil in the country, they had to leave the country permanently in 1981.

The Dorseys are the proud parents of one daughter, Joyce Martin, a teacher of many years at Sligo Adventist School, and their son-in-law, Dr. Norman Martin, and two grandsons, Kyle and Neal Martin.

After many years of service, Elder Dorsey rested from his services to await the trumpet call when the dead in Christ shall rise first!

Precious Memories of Missionaries of Color

Elder Edward Dorsey

Welcome Sign for the Dorseys !

Elder Edward & Dorothy Dorsey 1979-1981

They were met by M. I. Harding along with other staff at Konola Academy

The Dorseys at Andrews University

Precious Memories of Missionaries of Color

Workers meeting at Konola Academy; Left: Elder Dorsey, Mission President

Elder Edward & Dorothy Dorsey 1979-1981

Elder B. B. Beach–Northern European Division; Elder Johansen–Union President

The woman from Bosa teaches Dorothy a song in their language

Precious Memories of Missionaries of Color

The Dorseys fellowship with Ghanaians

A young lady Mrs. Dorsey met in Ghana at the Union Meetings

ELDER LOUIS & DR. JANICE PRESTON 1979-1991

"Mission Service at God's Request!" God's first request for the Prestons was in 1979 to go to London, England, and the second request came in 1989 to go to Harare, Zimbabwe, East Africa. To God be the glory that there was a positive response to both.

"Hello, what's your name?" The pastor asked the young seminary student passing by on the way to class. He replied, "I am Matthew Bediako." His invitation to him was "We would like you to come to our apartment and visit with us; if you'd like, you can bring some friends along, too. My wife is a wonderful woman and a great cook." The relationships that developed from this encounter sparked an interest within us for mission service. Jan and Louis felt a compassion for these young men who were so far from their homes. It caused the Prestons to open their home to them on a regular basis for fellowship and good food. They enjoyed their company and the perspectives they shared.

"How can you bear to leave your wife and children in Africa for so many years to study here in America?" was the question frequently asked by Jan to these international seminary and graduate students at Andrews University in the late 60s. The more the Prestons talked with Emanuel Attologbe, Matthew Bediako, Seth Okra, and others about their families, churches, and countries, the more their hearts longed to go see for themselves and serve. The students often said to them, "You ought to apply for mission service." As their new friends encouraged them, the Prestons became increasingly eager to get involved, but their initial application for mission service was turned down. The letter of response from Pastor Kenneth Gammon, the English Church Administrator

Precious Memories of Missionaries of Color

in Ghana, West Africa, stated that they were too young, and they were seeking someone with more experience at that time. Although disappointed, they believed that it was God's will for them at that time.

About five years later, after having pastored several churches in the Allegheny East Conference, the Prestons accepted a call for Louis to teach Greek at Bugema College in Uganda. Again, God saw fit to close another door. Because of the political unrest occurring in that country, the call was rescinded before they could even finish packing. Then, one sunny day in August, 1978, they received a phone call from Elder Frank Jones at the General Conference. He asked, "Are you still interested in mission service?" Louis called out to his wife, "Jan, do you still want to be a missionary?" She responded, "Yeah, I guess so. Where?" When he said, "England," her immediate and astonished response was, "England!? For what?" Clearly, the "mission field" had very different connotations for them and England was not part of that picture.

When the call came, they were in the process of adopting a son and knew they could not leave the country without him. They felt that if the Lord wanted them to go, then three-year-old Erin would be allowed to go with them. With this in mind, they prayed earnestly and shared the possibility with only their families, in case the move did not materialize. One Friday in October, they received unprecedented permission from the District government to actually take a ward of the District Court to live outside of the United States. Clearly, here was their answer. The next day was a Sabbath. With mixed feelings, they announced to their church family at Campostella Heights, in Norfolk, Virginia, that they had accepted a call to mission service in London, England. What a stir; what a life-changing decision; what a joy!

On a cold, grey, rainy day, April 2, 1979, they exited the Heathrow Airport in London. The children (and their parents) were fascinated to see black taxis, red double-decker buses, and cars all driving on the "wrong" side of the street. It was then they anxiously asked themselves, "What are we doing here?" Pastor Kenneth Gammon, now President of the South England Conference, and Elder Stuart Ware, the Youth Director, met and greeted them warmly. Imagine if you will, a young couple (39 and 34) with *four* little ones, Lauri (10), Randy (6), Erin (4), and Joy (3,) amidst mounds of luggage and having never worked outside of the U.S., arriving to take on the leadership of Holloway Church, the largest Seventh-day Adventist church in Great Britain. Along with this 700-member congregation, they were responsible for four other churches in the North London district: Hackney, Shelbourne, Stoke Newington, and Tottenham—with no assistant pastor or Bible worker.

Elder Louis & Dr. Janice Preston 1979-1991

Their uncertainty and unfamiliarity with the customs, practices, and societal expectations of a foreign country did not diminish their commitment to the purpose for which they were sent. Just before they left the U.S., President Neal C. Wilson called them into his office at the General Conference. He reiterated that their goal was to foster reconciliation and unity between the indigenous (the English) and the immigrant (predominantly West Indian) members of the Adventist church in Britain. This was the purpose of "The Pierson Package," created by former General Conference President Elder Robert H. Pierson because the disparate cultures were experiencing difficulty in relating.

The Prestons were one of six families of color sent to England to serve as leadership role models and advocates for these people of color. At that time, they were, and still are, the majority membership in the British churches. The other five families were Dr. and Mrs. Silburn Reid, Elder and Mrs. Everett Howell and family, Elder and Mrs. David Hughes, Elder and Mrs. Cecil Perry and family in the South England Conference, and Elder and Mrs. Bruce Flynn and family, in the North British Conference. The reception by the members—regardless of ethnicity—was overwhelmingly gracious and warm as they were eager to support the workers that God had sent in answer to their prayers.

After making assessments, the first job the Prestons undertook was to demonstrate to the British membership that they were able to handle this large assignment in spite of their apparent youth and the responsibilities of caring for four young children. Sabbaths were an all-day affair; they arrived at Early-Morning Prayer Service at 8:30 A.M. laden with everything a family of six would need for a day: Sabbath dinner, supper, changes of clothes, Sabbath toys, books, and Bibles (and eventually, their dog). They often didn't leave until after Louis had prayed over the dominoes game in the Fellowship Hall Saturday night–usually after 11:00 P.M. Jan would return to London on Sunday mornings to lead out in the 8:00 A.M. Women's Prayer Service she initiated–which is still functioning to this day, praise God.

Elder Louis' parents and Brother Gilbert recognized the pressure he was under and sent him scores of taped sermons to spark his imagination and reduce the stress of producing a powerful sermon every week. They knew that successful evangelism would require an outpouring of the Holy Spirit, resulting in unity of the membership. "Sabbath Evangelism" at Holloway Church proved very productive: each quarter they distributed handbills listing the Sabbath sermon titles and special music for the coming months. The Prestons taught the members how to greet and keep visitors and new interests. The fruits of this labor were 65 baptisms without a public campaign—breaking the existing John Loughborough baptismal record. Concurrently, they were teaching

Precious Memories of Missionaries of Color

similar programs in the other four churches to which Louis was assigned and assisting them to implement the same methods immediately in weekend public campaigns called "Step Up to Health and Happiness." During these campaigns, Louis preached the sermons, his wife Jan, would provide the health lectures, and their daughter, Lauri, would often sing. The church Elders and members gave unparalleled support every night.

On Sabbaths, they alternated between Holloway and the other churches—sometimes preaching two or three times per Sabbath to cover all the needs. Eventually, they spent most Sabbath afternoons at Holloway, training three hundred "Volunteers for the Kingdom." Each week the Elders and Louis prepared 150 pairs of lay Bible workers with the Bible study lesson they were to give for the coming week. The results of this laymen's outreach were that each month for three consecutive years (36 months) they had a baptism—all without a campaign. The one month that they had no one to baptize, there was no water. Elder Preston could announce quite honestly that "for a number of reasons" they would not have a baptism that Sabbath!

As a result of all of this evangelistic outreach, the Lord blessed them to establish five new churches in London: Crouch End, Harringay, King's Cross (Shelbourne II), Muswell Hill, and Tottenham Holcombe Road. In 1982, they were assigned a Bible worker for a short time, and a couple of years later, a series of ministerial interns—all of whom gave valuable assistance. This addition of "assistance" to lighten his workload was enjoyed only briefly, for soon after that, Louis was asked by the South England Conference to become the Conference Evangelist for the Cities—*in addition* to his pastoral duties. He teamed up with Pastor Derek Marley, the Conference Evangelist, for the suburban areas. Their teamwork was a God-send and their friendship continues to be an absolute joy! As they worked nightly under the huge "marquee" (better known in the U.S. as a "tent") the attendance averaged 2000. Their wives, children, and other vocalists sang, and Jan and other health professionals gave health lectures. Derek and Louis wore matching suits, sported beards and eyeglasses, were about the same build, preached alternate nights, and were known in the community and to the media as the "Ebony and Ivory" preaching team.

In the midst of all this work, there were tender, precious memories that their family cherishes. Their children attended Stanborough Park Primary and Secondary Schools, located two miles from their home—a small miracle. Within a few months or so of living in England their children developed crisp, British accents; they gravitated to soccer and gymnastics, and West Indian delicacies such as roti, rice and peas, bakes, ginger beer, and even mauby. They can still break out into a Jamaican *patois* at will.

Elder Louis & Dr. Janice Preston 1979-1991

One of their favorite family activities after Board Meetings was to go skating, especially in London's Hyde Park—the seamless sidewalks made for truly smooth sailing. Their all-black dog, Ginger, would pull the children as they held onto her leash for an effortless ride. One Sunday as they were playing baseball on one of the soccer fields of Stanborough Park School, Jan noticed that Randy was squinting to see Erin throwing him the ball. Several questions later and after making an appointment with their optometrist, this scenario played out three more times during that year. As Randy grew, so did his inability to see from a distance. Fortunately it was time for their first furlough home, and he was fitted with contact lenses which saved his pride (no more thick glasses) and slowed the progression of his myopia.

Furloughs home were always a highlight of the Prestons' lives—three months of whirlwind travel to see family and friends in the east and on the West Coast, get physical and dental exams, check in with Elder Maurice Battle and his secretary, Mary Haloviak, at the General Conference for a variety of procedural responsibilities, and expose our American-born children to the beauty and lifestyle of their homeland. LaJoy was three-years-old when they left for England, and they didn't realize how little she knew about living in the States until, while watching an American film one day, she asked, "What's a nickel?" They were all taken aback by her question, and promptly made every effort to educate her about U.S. currency. While on furlough, her responsibility was to often pay for purchases and to count the change for accuracy—not exactly her favorite task, but it worked!

Furloughs were the highlights of their lives as they anticipated "going home." They soon began to wonder if they would be highlights for family and friends who would end up sharing the task of hosting them for the three months they were in the States. After all, they didn't *have* a home of their own in which to stay and there were six of them—each one had one huge suitcase and a carry-on bag, there were suit and dress bags, cameras, tripods, and jackets, and…you name it, they managed to have it. They certainly could not stay in one place for the three months, and they had to "see everybody" in a short time.

The children were wondering how they would measure up with the other American kids, and Jan and Louis were wondering if they would be truly accepted by the families, friends, and acquaintances, or if people would think that they thought they were "something" because they lived overseas. Well, Jan's mother lovingly summed it all up really well one time as they were leaving by stating, "It's good to see them come, and it's good to see them go!" They could agree with and understand the intent of that statement only after they had been treated royally by *all* with whom they visited during their furloughs home.

Precious Memories of Missionaries of Color

People borrowed beds so the family could have their own to sleep in; Jan's sisters, Joan Lyles and Joyce Shepperd, planned, printed, and distributed itineraries for them while they visited with them and their family in California; other hosts invited mutual friends to come visit with them in their homes, and everyone treated them as though they were truly special. They were not foreigners here. Such loving care and those open-armed welcomes were the fuel that buoyed them up to pack up all their bags again and head back to the cold, grey days in "jolly old England" without their natural families.

It also helped to know that they would be returning to their new "family" and friends in England—the people whom they had learned to love, and from whom they continue to receive abundant love and appreciation today. Still, it was difficult to leave home again and again. On one plane ride back to the UK, when the pilot announced, "Ladies and gentleman, we are now approaching London's Heathrow airport," Erin looked up at Jan and asked, "Mommy, why are you crying?"

Their furlough experiences helped them to realize how much pride and awe for them their assignment had generated, not only with their families, but also with friends and church members as well. Their first furlough visit to camp meeting at Alleghany East Conference was an unbelievable experience. They could move about the campground only a few feet at a time because people were eager to meet with and greet them, wanting to know how they were faring in the "Mother Land" of England, how long they were going to stay over there, and what their impressions were of life outside of the U.S.

What an eye-opening experience! They had by that time become accustomed to going to the stationery store for paper plates, to the market or green grocers for fresh vegetables, or to the baker's for bread or rolls, having the milk man deliver small bottles of milk to their door, or trying to get to the post office or electrical shop on their lunch break only to find that the shopkeepers were having their lunch break, and they'd have to come back later. Thanksgiving in England was a normal work/school day, so their children did not grow up celebrating it, or liking candied yams. They also enjoyed an additional day of Christmas celebrations. In England, the day after Christmas is called Boxing Day. During Queen Victoria's reign, the tradition of boxing up all the leftovers from Christmas dinner and delivering them to the poor was the tradition; today it is still recognized as a national holiday. While this day off and other cultural differences had soon become "normal" to the family, they often had a good laugh as they shared such stories with their American family, friends, and churches. They did the usual missionary talks at camp meetings, various churches, and Oakwood College, but the essence of the experience was difficult to communicate in those settings.

Elder Louis & Dr. Janice Preston 1979-1991

How could they explain what they felt when Jan's chronic back pain caused her to collapse at home, and she was misdiagnosed by an interim National Health Service doctor with colon cancer as soon she walked into the examining room—without an exam? When she was referred to a cancer hospital for treatment, they couldn't understand how this could happen so far from home, with *little* children, while doing God's will, and wondered how their family could survive if she didn't survive the illness. It was several weeks before they knew that the fault lay with the inept doctor, not with their God! Praise Him for good, praying family and friends. Praise Him for supportive, resourceful church members who wouldn't take a fatalistic diagnosis as gospel.

If they had failed to return after their first furlough, church leadership in Great Britain may have taken another turn at that time. Historically, the conference constituency meetings were held outside of London for four days or so at a time. This meant that delegates would have to take time off of work, cover their own transportation costs, and provide many of their own meals if they wanted to attend. For those whose families had known no other homeland, this presented little financial difficulty, but for immigrants who were at the mercy of partial employers, this presented a major hurdle.

When the dilemma was discussed by trusted church elders and officers, they devised a plan that was God-ordained to accommodate and empower the "ordinary" laymen who previously had little or no voice in the Conference elections. In Great Britain, the total church leadership was approximately 90-95% Caucasian and the constituent body was approximately 85-90% people of color. Their mandate was to help lessen the strife that had built up within the church, and to model a leadership style with which the minority-majority could relate.

At Holloway, they decided to make this constituency meeting a user-friendly experience for the members. Louis engaged the Elders to assist him in teaching the members parliamentary procedure every weekend for several months. He rewrote the South England Conference Constitution in lay terms, maintaining the original pagination and policy numbers, and provided it to each delegate, along with the original document, so that all could understand. They then discussed what direction they felt the Conference should take, and over time, the other London churches joined in their training sessions.

They booked and paid for an entire hotel for their delegates, paid for their transportation, and provided vegetarian meat substitutes to the hotel chef for their meals. In the past, delegates from the city churches had been assigned varied accommodations in the vicinity of the constituency locations. Now, being all together in one place, they could strategize a plan of action on a daily basis.

Precious Memories of Missionaries of Color

At the constituency meeting, Louis sat on both the Selection Committee and the Nominating Committee. Committee member Pastor Clem Cook and Louis dialogued continually and he finally alerted Pastor Eddie Foster, the Union President, that the names suggested for the Nominating Committee did not represent the composition of the current constituency. He agreed, erased the names suggested from the board and then re-constructed the committee, making sure that 4/7th of the Nominating Committee were people of color. It was this Committee who nominated Dr. Silburn Reid for President and later for the first West Indian President of the South England Conference—paving the way for fair representation for, and recognition of, liturgical practices to meet the needs of the overwhelmingly West Indian church membership of the British Union.

One of the unexpected things that happened to their family was that Drs. Bill (then president of Columbia Union College) and Edna Mae Loveless told Dr. Jan Paulsen (then president of Newbold College) that the Preston family sang together, and that he should ask them to give a Friday-night concert at the College. They had NEVER presented any kind of program as a family—their youngest child was only four years old! Well, their habit of continually playing children's musical albums in their home, and singing those songs and Sabbath school choruses at worships, paid off.

With Lauri (age 10) as their "star vocalist" and Randy (age 6) as their "budding preacher," they accepted the challenge. At the time, they knew little about Newbold, especially about its professional musicians, or they would definitely have turned down the invitation. But on that Friday night in the late fall of 1979, there they were—two grown ups and four little kids singing in front of the student body at a college! Jan and Louis sang duets and Lauri her solos, Randy literally lisped the 91st Psalm which at that point seemed to have more "s" sounds than any other sound, and Joy and Erin sang heartily their melody and abstract tone respectively. The grand finale was when Dr. Paulsen's rich baritone blended with theirs in a glorious rendition of "Amazing Grace."

Later that year, Jan and Louis were asked by their seminary friend, Matthew Bediako, to come to Ghana for the month of April to do evangelism. As the Ghanaian Union President at that time, he had that authority to do so. God blessed Pastor Preston to baptize a record 202 souls in the city of Bekwai. Pastor Preston's Singing Band, the evangelistic choir, formed for the campaign, still functions today. It was there that they finally met Jan's namesake—Matthew and Elizabeth's third daughter whom they named Janice, and they shared lots of joy and happiness.

Elder Louis & Dr. Janice Preston 1979-1991

Jan's parents had come to England to stay with the grandchildren in their absence. Upon their return from Ghana, they were asked to give a live concert in Hornsey Town Hall in Central London. While they were still considering the request, an announcement was made about the pending event in front of a very large audience, generating a thunderous applause of approval. How could they say no? In September of 1980, they gave a full two-hour concert with band accompaniment, changing clothes and backdrops twice. They included a section of music in the Ghanaian language which they had learned and tape recorded while there. The Bediakos were in London at the time, and Elizabeth taught them how to wrap the Kente cloth on Louis and on the boys and made lovely dresses with Ghanaian cloth for Jan and the girls. After the concert, they learned that many people assumed the children had gone with them to Ghana, and had learned the songs there that they helped them sing that night.

After seven years in the South England Conference, Louis was elected as Secretary of the North British Conference in Nottingham, England. Their sons, Randy and Erin, were particularly happy with this move as it meant that on breaks from school, Louis would drive them and their friends into Sherwood Forest in the morning, and return for them in the evening. They would spend the day with their catapults, bows and arrows, walkie-talkies, and lunches, re-enacting the activities of Robin Hood and his men without fear of danger from predators or other potential evils. It was in England that Randy further developed his passion for reading and in Nottingham, his love of foreign languages. As part of the requirements for his German class he traveled to Germany as an exchange student.

At this time, Lauri had finished the English secondary school, an event marked by the school Speech Night several months after State exam results were released; there were no graduations. Lauri was given the opportunity to study at Monterey Bay Academy in California, so that she could graduate from an American high school—much more her parents' desire than hers. Her absence created a huge loss for the family, so much so that Jan's brother Raymond, and sister-in-law, Norma surprised them by sending Lauri home to England for Christmas. With British salaries being equivalent to $1000.00 a month for a family of six, they could not have afforded such an extravagance.

It is important to note that when they accepted the call to England, because of pet quarantine regulations, they could not take Lauri's seven-year old Siamese cat with them—a loss she still feels as an adult. After being in England a few weeks, she wept, saying, "This is not my home, and it never will be." However, six years later, when leaving for America, over 120 youth were at her farewell party, and many tears were shed as she was leaving "home" to go to America!

Precious Memories of Missionaries of Color

While in Watford (South England Conference), Jan had taught nursing. She later received her Midwifery certification and taught Childbirth Education classes, as well. When they moved to the North, she had the distinct privilege of becoming Louis' personal secretary! They thoroughly enjoyed working together and living close enough to the Conference Office that they could have lunch at home with their children on most days. Eventually, she resumed her professional role of nurse educator and midwife part-time at the Queen's Medical Centre in Nottingham.

As Conference Secretary and Stewardship Director, Louis traveled around the Conference to different churches most weekends. It was the role of Conference Evangelist, however, that took him over the moors to Manchester, England, where he held a School of Evangelism for all the pastors in the Manchester District. As a part of their course, they observed him conduct a public campaign and provided professional assistance. He then sent for evangelists from the United States to lead-out in two subsequent campaigns. This same practice of bringing speakers from the U.S. was implemented for their camp meetings which were his responsibility to plan and coordinate. He arranged for approximately 20+ American ministers to preach and give seminars during these holy convocations. What a high spiritual time they had.

His responsibilities in the North included being the conference Stewardship Director. This proved to be a stepping stone when, on a furlough in 1988, Elder Battle told him that the General Conference had voted them an assignment in Harare, Zimbabwe, East Africa (formerly Rhodesia). He was to serve as the Stewardship Director for the Eastern Africa Division there—educating conference administrators and pastors on the implementation of principles of stewardship. Joy, their youngest, was thirteen by then, and enjoying her friends from the Nottingham Central Church—there was no way she wanted to leave them. One afternoon Joy gave her mom a letter addressed to both of her parents. She stated that if they went to Africa, her life would be ruined; she had no friends there; who wanted to live in Africa? They tried reasoning with her point of view, and despite her protestations, they accepted the call to move to Harare, Zimbabwe—at God's request.

When they arrived in Johannesburg, South Africa, on their way to Harare for the first time, they were in awe of the tight airport security: armed soldiers, police dogs-"apartheid" was still in full authority. They later felt that this discomfort was a small price to pay for the beauty of not only the country, but also the people in it who were so very gracious to their family. When they arrived in South Africa to receive their shipped goods from England, they found that there was a dock strike in London, so the arrival of all of their household

Elder Louis & Dr. Janice Preston 1979-1991

goods was delayed. Since no duty would be charged on any item brought into Zimbabwe on their initial entry, they needed to take all of their goods in with them at one time. They had no choice but to wait for the full month for the container with their shipment to arrive in Johannesburg before they could proceed into Zimbabwe.

As they shopped for supplies to take into Harare, their children were at first pleased to be welcomed so kindly by the young sales clerks in "Macro," a store comparable to Costco. The clerks stroked Joy's hair, and told their sons that seeing them was like seeing Michael Jackson. These South African youth shared with the Preston children their futility born out of apartheid atrocities. The children were soon saddened and muted by the stark reality of the deprivation expressed by people so young, and who could have had so much potential. When they visited with the Adventist churches in Soweto, Bosmont, and Orange Grove, however, the joy and hope their youth expressed were absolutely refreshing.

Some pastoral families in Johannesburg took special pains to care for their family. They prepared a lunch, maps, and directions to travel with, as well as strict instructions on how to conduct themselves when actually negotiating the border-crossing into Zimbabwe. It was a daunting experience to think about driving the 900+ miles from Johannesburg, South Africa, to Harare, Zimbabwe. They did not speak the language, and Jan and Louis were both driving. They had their 12-seater mini-van and trailer, plus a second vehicle for a Division employee. It was not long after they began their journey that they greatly benefited from the sterling counsel of their new friends.

About 3:00 A.M. when they stopped for petrol in South Africa, a tall young man approached them for a ride to his home in Harare. Louis knew better than to pick up a stranger, so graciously refused. Several hours later, they crossed the border check points and stopped for petrol in the Zimbabwe border town of Beitbridge. Much to his amazement, this same young man appeared, seemingly out of nowhere, and repeated his request. Louis was taken aback that they were meeting again, and his resolve weakened. He decided to test his sincerity, by telling him he was a Christian. He answered that he was a Christian as well. When Louis asked him his church affiliation, he stood tall and said, "I am a Seventh-day Adventist!" Showing no emotion, Louis challenged, "You Seventh-day Adventists only believe in the law. If this is not true, prove to me that the Seventh-day Sabbath can be found in the New Testament. He gave him so many accurate texts that he nearly shouted, "Get in the car; I, too, am an Adventist!" As they were riding along, Louis asked him if he had any of Ellen White's books, and began naming them, seemingly to reassure him that he was authentic.

Precious Memories of Missionaries of Color

Some distance later they were about to stop along the roadside to rest, but their hitch-hiker passenger advised against it, warning that in that particular area, they could be in danger of harm from Mozambique rebels. When they needed rest room facilities in a village store that night, he negotiated for them in the appropriate language, and stood on guard while they were inside. Then, approximately an hour's drive from Harare, horror of horrors! The vehicle they were transporting failed to start–it was pitch black with baboons playing across the road, and they had no mechanics tools or weapons. Their only recourse was to leave one car and take the other into Harare for help. Who would go with Daddy, and who would stay with Mommy on the road? As they were preparing to send one car and leave one to wait, Joy said, "Why don't we pray once more?" They did, and the car started. When they arrived in Harare around midnight, the young man directed them to the police station where they were to be met by the Division Treasurer, Ron Lindsay. Even though they searched for the young man often, they never saw their passenger/angel again.

In 1990, they decided to take permanent return to the U.S. so that Joy could attend college. By then, Joy and Erin (Randy and Lauri were in the States at Columbia Union College) had become well-acquainted with several of the young people in Harare, and Joy tearfully protested their return to the U.S. Just the day prior, Jan had found Joy's letter of protestation against leaving England, and as she and Joy were riding in the car, Joy began to present reasons why they should stay in Harare. Jan reached in her purse and recovering the old, original letter, gave it to Joy to read. While she was not totally convinced about the move, she could see that they had "been there" before, dried her eyes, and never again mentioned the topic. She realized they had all learned that starting over is possible and eventually brings comfort and pleasures of its own.

The sequel to this missionary story will have to come at another time and place. It will include: their arrival in Zimbabwe, their children being in the American boarding school 3000 miles away in Kenya, Jan's nightmare facilitating the transfer of their credits from England, while Louis took his first official two-week trip to one of the eleven countries for which he was responsible, among other things.

Their return to the U.S. did not prove to be the joy that they had anticipated; it was actually more difficult to return home than it was to leave. Everything had changed, and so had they. However, all of them grew during and from the experiences they shared, becoming very close as a family: the six of them were the only blood family that they lived with for thirteen years while out of the country. They learned to know and love people in other countries who still are, and will forever be, a part of their lives and memories. Also, they praise

Elder Louis & Dr. Janice Preston 1979-1991

God for the opportunities He provided, and for their praying parents: Pastor Louis and Louise Preston, Sr., and Elder Raymond and Louise Montgomery, as well as all of their family and friends. Without their support, they could not have gone or come as easily as they did. Would they do it all over again? By all means, because they did it at God's request and they know without a doubt, that they were safely sheltered under the shadow of His wings through it all. Praise Him!

Precious Memories of Missionaries of Color

The Preston Family
LaJoy, Erin, Lauri, Dr. Janice, Randy and Elder Louis Preston

40

ELDER LLOYD & ETTA ANTONIO- 1979-1984

Lloyd was born in Jamaica, West Indies on June 19, 1936 in Gutarez, St. John's, and St. Catherine. He was baptized and brought up in the Church of England where his parents and many members of his family attended. His education began in the preparatory school beside the church. He studied there for about eleven years until he was sixteen. When he attended the Church of England grammar school in Spanish Town, St. Catherine (1952-54). After completing his education, he joined his father in England to study physics, chemistry, and biology with the ambition of pursuing a career in medicine. During his last years at the Church of England Preparatory, he was introduced to the Voice of Prophecy Bible course. A great change took place in his life. He was confirmed in the Church of England but was a Seventh-day Adventist at heart. His best friend was a Seventh-day Adventist young man by the name of Ernest Whitter. He invited his brothers and him to the Seventh-day Adventist Church many times; finally, at his sister's baptism in Spanish Town where he was living, he responded to the appeal by Pastor Walton and joined the Seventh-day Adventist Church on May 12, 1954.

Lloyd arrived in England on November, 1954, and began to look for work and the nearest Seventh-day Adventist Church. After the Christmas holidays, he began worshipping with the Adventist Church which met in the Court Room of the Brixton Town Hall. At that period of England's history the working week was from Monday to Saturday twelve noon. This created a problem for many, many Seventh-day Adventists. Many lost their faith as they began to work on Saturdays.

Precious Memories of Missionaries of Color

Lloyd found a job very near the New Gallery Centre where there was a lending library of Seventh-day Adventist books. While reading "Crowns and Crosses by Marjorie Lewis Lloyd, he came under the conviction that the Lord was calling him to the ministry to be a pastor. He fought this for many days at home, at work, and on the buses. He had no peace. Finally, one day while riding a London bus, he said, to the Lord, "I'll do anything you want me to do, if you will only give me peace in my heart." Immediately peace came and he had to begin to redirect his life. His friends, parents, and relatives had to be told since he was expected to begin Evening Classes at the Regent Street College, Westminster University.

Application was made to Newbold College, but their policy in 1957 was to accept no member of the Black race from the West Indies. Protests were made in writing and by a delegation. After much discussion and prayer, he began his studies at Newbold College in September, 1960. He graduated in May, 1964 and was asked to serve in Birmingham in the Camp Hill Church—the largest in the North England Conference.

Under the leadership of Pastor G.D.D. Bryan, the church began to grow at a very fast rate as they all responded to the love and care of this godly man and his wife and four children. They worked as a team.

In 1965, Lloyd met an Adventist nurse, Etta Flynn, on a trip to Youth Congress in Helsinki. They were married in the Camp Hill Church on December 4, 1966. The following year he was called to serve in Huddersfield, West Yorkshire. They began fundraising and searching for a larger building which was purchased with God's help.

In 1970, he was ordained and in 1971, after the birth of their son, they were asked to relocate to Birmingham, to take care of three daughter churches of the Camp Hill Church. The second largest church in the North England Conference, Handsworth, lost their pastor through ill health. Lloyd was asked to take charge of this church and Ward End Churches while the Yardley and the Chelmsley Wood Churches were given to others.

After his daughter was born in 1977, he was asked to pastor the Smethwick and the West Bromwich Churches—and also Walsall for a short time. It was while pastoring those churches that Lloyd felt the need for further education and began to make preparation. While he was researching and making plans for this, the call came in 1979 for mission service in Africa. This lasted until July, 1984. Before leaving Africa, Lloyd applied for service in the North England Conference and was offered service in the Manchester South Church, then the third largest in the Conference. This was indeed a challenge. The churches in Manchester asked for Tent Crusade in one of the local parks. All of the ministers

Elder Lloyd & Etta Antonio-1979-1984

and the members worked as a team and "Come Alive!" Crusades took off with Pastor Louis Preston as their first speaker. This became a yearly event with different guest speakers until he left in 1990.

He remained in the Manchester area serving Preston, Blackpool, and Lancaster district and the Oldham and Manchester North until he retired in 2003. In 2004, he joined his wife in her ministry of prayer doing the work which Jesus commanded them to do.

Recapturing their lives as missionaries, which began in 1979, Lloyd and Etta were trying to finalize plans to attend Andrews University. One day Dr. B. B. Beach of the Northern Europe West Africa Division asked them if they would be interested in serving Africa as the President of the North Ghana Mission. After discussion and earnest prayer, they gave a positive reply to Dr. Beach. They were invited to visit him and discuss the matter.

The Mission was without a president, so there was need for them to be there as quickly as possible. The Division made application for the necessary papers to enter Ghana. In November the Antonios left Heathrow Airport on KLM bound for Amsterdam and then on to West African Union Mission in Accra with all the food they could take. From there they were transported to the North Ghana Mission in Tamale. Pastor Sven Johansen, the Union President, had tried to prepare them for life in Ghana, the culture, the shortages because of the difficulties the country was facing, but they were totally unprepared for what they saw. Pastor A. Wahu, the church pastor and Mission officer, Mr. Addo Kwakye, the bookkeeper and Mr. T. Opoku, a member of the Mission Executive Committee did their best to welcome them. They made them feel at home and found a helper to help run the Mission house and to prepare their meals.

One of the first challenges Lloyd faced in 1979 when he arrived in Ghana was the emergency of salary for the Mission workers. At the end of each month they came to the Mission Office with their reports to collect their wages. Mr. Addo reported there was no cash in the bank to pay the salaries for the workers. The solution was to go the Central Ghana Conference in Kumasi and borrow cash from them.

They found some petrol late in the day, started on their journey hoping to arrive before everyone went to sleep. The journey was not without adventure. Kumasi was situated in the tropical rain forest area of central Ghana. It had rained just before they got to a steep unpaved hill. It was slippery, and the pickup could not climb it. Mr. Addo and Elder Antonio did their best to push and skid the vehicle up the hill. Eventually they got to the Mission by bedtime and got some accommodation for the night. The next day they explained their visit to the Treasurer of the Conference. With the knowledge that the West

Precious Memories of Missionaries of Color

African Union Mission would reimburse them; they were soon on their way home.

They were puzzled and prayed about what the Mission should do to reach the people of northern Ghana who were followers of Islam. They talked to the workers and the members and soon the answer came from an unexpected visitor. One Sunday morning a Mercedes Benz car pulled up at the Mission door. An official from the Regional Department of Education paid them a visit. He was Mr. Adjei Mensah, a member of the Mission Church. He welcomed them to the great challenge of the North Ghana Mission. He shared with them his burden to reach the people of that town with the message of the Seventh-day Adventist Church. He stated that education was the approach the Mission should follow. All the efforts of the past had resulted in only one Dagumba member who was hardly attending church whereas in the south where education was provided the church was very strong. He declared that he was a product of the Seventh-day Adventist education system.

Lloyd was very glad for the idea, but along with the dry season, the water scarcity, and the demands for visits to the far flung corners of the Mission, Lloyd only pondered the idea. The territory of the Ghana Mission covered approximately one half of Ghana with only a small membership of about one thousand. Most of them were southerners who were working in the north and returned south on transfer ever so often. The church building was very small for the membership and building a church seemed to be their biggest challenge. They had tried to build a much larger church beside the one Pastor Onjuka of Finland had built but it had collapsed recently.

Fuel was scarce, but they obtained some and began traveling to visit the members in Bolgantanga who were mainly southerners among the Fra Fra tribe. They were worshipping in a rented accommodation and needed to have their own building. They had acquired land and were busy working on their building project. They took them to the site and pointed out a building which was their greatest priority.

They soon arranged a visit to the Zangum Company. It was raised up by a southerner who walked the five miles journey several times each week to conduct Bible studies in the Moslem village with the Mamprusi people. They were cousins of the Dagumba people among whom they lived in Tamale. The southerners had a burden to reach the northerners with the good news of salvation. They arrived there on a Sabbath in 1980 and had a very warm reception. The interpreter for his message was a young boy who was twelve years old who was very good in translating from English into Mampurli, the language of the Mamprusi tribe. They saw the challenge to win the whole village for Christ.

Elder Lloyd & Etta Antonio-1979-1984

After the service the bookkeeper, Mr. Addo, asked if it were possible to take the young boy to the Mission and educate him because if he remained in the village with that talent he would end up herding cows. They went to his parents and asked if they would consent for them to take their son to educate him. After a short family consultation, they gave their consent. He packed his belongings and accompanied them back to the Mission. God was preparing them for the challenge that they would face. Mr. Addo had the task of arranging for his sleeping and entrance into one of the primary schools in Tamale, during which time Elder Antonio returned to England to fetch his family.

When his wife arrived she saw the potential that young Seidu Salifu had to make an impact for Christ. She gave him a copy of *Training the Light Bearer* and during the holidays and most weekends she sent him the 140 miles to his village to teach his people about Christ. He faithfully returned on Sunday for school on Monday. This was seed sowing, but soon the harvest would come in a baptism of over 40 persons. This baptism not only increased the membership of the company, but revealed the need for a school in the village.

Elder Antonio returned to England in January, 1980, but because of the many things they needed to take with them, they were not ready to leave until March–the very month of the year he was warned not to take his wife to northern Ghana because of the severe heat. He was told that the children would acclimatize but it could be dangerous for his wife.

On their trip to Ghana, Providence arranged that for the journey to Accra, they traveled in the company of Pastor Pokka Peltonen, They learned that Dr. Bjorkman and his family from Norway were working in Techiman, central Ghana. This knowledge would be valuable indeed. The food they brought with them lasted a long time as they supplemented it with what was available in the market. The container from England with their food, medicine and other belongings had not arrived and food and medicines were running low. They went to Techiman and borrowed some food from the Bjorkmans who did all they could to help the Antonios. On one occasion there were some expatriates on their way north to Burkina Faso (then Upper Volta). They offered them some food and provisions they had, but the Bjorkmans asked them to take them and give them to Elder Lloyd and family.

In September, 1980 the first preparatory school on the Mission compound was opened. It began with nursery and kindergarten classes which met in the church building and primary one met on the temporary extension erected at the side of the church. Although the school was not yet fully established, it was given the status of its own SDA Education Unit. The school was operated by the Church but was under the authority of the Ghana Education Service which supplied the teachers, paid their salaries, as well as the salaries of other workers in the school.

A few months after the first preparatory school began on the Mission compound; there was the need for a new manager. The Church decided to ask Etta Antonio to take over that position. Being a trained nurse with no experience in the field of education, she was hesitant. Eventually she agreed after some persuasion. For the rest of their stay in the North Ghana Mission, she worked diligently to build up and establish the schools. She worked closely with the Assistant Director of Education, Mr. F. Quansah, rendering her services free of charge although the Education Service wanted to pay her a salary. In the short period of four years, four schools were established. From those schools came the establishment of the Seventh-day Adventist Education Unit in North Ghana which has made a great contribution to the education of many Ghanaians over the past 25 years.

Work was done by a committee made up of leading men in the church, senior teaching staff, and Etta as chair person. They discussed the future of the schools, the guidelines for the teaching staff, and the logo of the school. On the logo was a hand holding a Bible and under the Bible was written the motto: "Knowledge is Knowing God." In addition was the School's own pledge—"I pledge allegiance to the Bible, God's Holy Word and will take it as a lamp unto my feet and a light to my path." That pledge is now said in the Seventh-day Adventist schools each day alongside the Ghana pledge.

Materials for making school uniforms were acquired with difficulty after speaking to the business men and managers in the town. Etta took care of everything that was needed, such as building materials and food to feed the children because of the coup and severe famine through which the country was passing. God's favor was upon her and she was able to get the materials for the uniforms. Soon the children were in their uniforms. The girls were in green dresses piped with white and boys were in kaki shorts and green shirts piped with white. They were easily recognized in Tamale.

The construction of the main school on the Mission compound began in 1981. It was supervised by Brother R. O. Opoka and assisted by Brother S. Addo who was also experienced in the building trade. The church members gave their time many Sundays to carry water, make the concrete blocks, and do whatever they could to help build the school. When the temporary building for the second preparatory school at the Kolpohin Estate was erected, the members also helped. Many parents gave furniture and did what they could to help. Ignatius Amedior, a faithful church member, assisted at times by another church member, Nr. A. Aych, made the furniture for the schools. Among the

Elder Lloyd & Etta Antonio - 1979-1984

first head teachers at the Mission school were Mrs. Euth Opoku and Mrs. Esther Asah. They did an excellent work in giving the school a good start.

Many of the children came from the homes of influential and leading men in Tamale. Due to the high biblical standards of the school, there were times when Elder Antonio'a wife had to defend those standards at the parent/teachers meetings. At such times she had to contend with some of those who were lawyers, but it was done in good faith and served as a witness and the Lord gave her wisdom to handle those cases. Toward the end of 1981, the school put on a Christmas program with the birth of Jesus as the main theme. Moslem, Christian, and secular teachers told the story of Jesus' birth. The concert brought the parents and other members of the various families and their friends to the Mission school to see the performance of their children. With the cooperation and support of the teachers and some brilliant students, Etta staged a concert each year, and the concerts improved each year. The new schools joined in the production and it became so popular that the authorities at the Teacher's Training College and the Tamale Secondary School located at the Education Ridge, as well as the Cultural Centre in the town, requested that schools stage the plays for them. One play included the legend of the "Fourth Wise Man." The success of these productions brought more pressure for places at the schools.

Due to the great demand for places more sites for schools were acquired in villages around Tamale. The Northern Region Town Planning Department gave three official sites in Tamale. Those sites were at Kolpohin Residential Area, Watherston Road Residential Area, and Kpano Residential Area. The authorities had seen the potential of the schools and willingly helped in every way they could. All of these sites were donated free of cost.

Some other challenging moments in the Antonios' lives occurred soon after arriving in Tamale from England. Elder Antonio went on safari visiting some of the churches. When he arrived home his wife was suffering from severe dehydration and was seriously ill and had to be admitted to the Tamale Hospital by a German doctor. His faith was soon to be tested even more when their three year old daughter came down with a stomach infection and severe diarrhea. They were at their wits end because all of their medicines had not arrived. They took her to the hospital to see the pediatrician, Dr. Amil Lall of India. There still was a shortage of the medicines that she needed. Only two were found in the Regional Deport, so the doctor gave her one.

On another occasion soon after their arrival in Ghana, their nine year old son became ill and was not eating. The Lord spoke through their three year old daughter who said to her mother, "Mommy, Anders is dying." Elder Antonio was out at the time trying to get water for their needs and his wife prayed earnestly to God for Anders' healing. Immediately after the prayer the Lord healed him. He asked for something to eat and went out to play. After that he frequently suffered from bouts of malaria and very painful boils on various parts of his body. This kept him out of school each time he had to sit for exams.

Water was always a problem. On one occasion there was absolutely no water to be had. Etta called the family together on that Sabbath morning and prayed earnestly. God heard their prayers and sent rain immediately at a time when the rains were not due.

The Tamale Church was burdened to reach the Dagimba people who were mostly Moslems. The education approach had taken root in the hearts of the members. A Seventh-day Adventist Preparatory School seemed to be the ideal entering wedge to get their attention for nothing else had succeeded since the time the Mission was established. The elder and the bookkeeper for the mission began to sell the idea to the members. Being southerners, they knew the great impact that the schools of Bekwai and Agona had made on the people of central Ghana. They did not need a great deal of persuasion.

Mr. Adjei-Mensah, the Regional Accountant for the Ghana Education Service, Mr. R. O. Opoku, a builder and contractor, and Brother Stephan Addo, then Mission bookkeeper and brick layer conveyed their burden of a school for the North Ghana Mission to Elder Antonio. This they wanted to see before they returned to central Ghana where they originated. They desired schools to be established in the villages along with a mobile clinic that would go into the villages and help treat the people with their various ailments such as malaria and worms, especially guinea worms. These ideas were taken to the Executive Committee and passed. The greatest obstacle to this development would be the Union. If they built a school without their knowledge they would dress them down but they would not demolish it. They set to work immediately to build the first school. Brother Adjei Mensah who was senior personnel in the Education Department began to implement the setting up of the school and got the necessary furniture for the classes. Mr. Opoku, the builder and contractor, assisted by Mr. Stephen Addo and some of the church members began to put a temporary extension at the side of the church building to house Primary One. It was an open extension aided by the large mango tree and surrounded by Zana mats and tarpaulins to shield the children and staff from the Hamatan winds and rain until building work on the school could begin the following year.

The fame of the schools spread and there were applications from other church groups in North Ghana who also wanted to begin schools, as well as to take over other existing schools. Unfortunately they were unable to help them at that time.

Elder Lloyd & Etta Antonio-1979-1984

Before returning on furlough in 1982, the school had a visit from the Catholic priest in the town. The fame of their school at the Mission had gained such a good reputation that the priest wanted to know what was their secret. Etta told the priest that its success depended upon God because each morning before school began there was worship for teachers followed by worship for the children. He wanted to see how it was done and came to both teachers' worship and children's worship and made careful observations. After that he took some of the SDA publications from the Mission's Book and Bible House for use in his schools also. The Catholic Church had established schools in the country and had their own Education Unit, but there was something lacking which they found at our newly established school. That missing link was putting Jesus first and at the heart of the school. By God's grace he discovered it and promised that he would do the same in his schools. It also brought a good relationship between the priest and them, whose compound bordered the Mission compound.

During the time the Antonios were in Ghana, building materials—including cement, nails, and other building materials—were very difficult to come by, as well as water. God blessed them and they were able to build the Preparatory school on the Mission compound which was almost completed before they left the Mission in March of 1984. They were also able to erect a temporary building for another Preparatory school in the Kolpohin village. That school took the overflow from the main school at the Mission. Another school began in Jackeyerilli, a Moslem village not far from the Mission. They restarted the Zangum village school 70 miles away to the north. The schools have broken down much prejudice.

As of March, 2005, there are 54 SDA schools in North Ghana. One of these schools is a senior secondary school; 10 are junior secondary; 23 are primary schools; and 20 are kindergarten. The total number of students in kindergarten is 2,060; in primary 5,845; in junior secondary a total of 2,982, and 238 are in the senior secondary school—making a grand total of the number of student in SDA schools in North Ghana 11,135. To God be the glory!

Those who dreamed of schools in various parts of the North Ghana Region had their dreams fulfilled and are numbered among the schools in operation in the North Ghana Mission. The schools brought many blessings wherever they have been established, including employment for some of the church members and other natives.

They give thanks to God for the work He has done through the schools. By His grace many souls will be saved in His kingdom because of those schools which were raised up to bring honour and glory to His name.

Precious Memories of Missionaries of Color

This area of God's vineyard produced other challenges such visiting the churches and companies. With his wife giving her energies fulltime to the school, running the home, and the Children's Sabbath School, this left Elder Antonio free to concentrate on administration and visiting the churches and companies of the mission. They made trips to Wa, Bawku, Yendi, Bamboi, Chinderi, and Kpanda. Traveling to the most distant ones was like taking a safari. They had to be sure they had acquired enough petrol for the return journey along with sufficient drinking water, a good amount of food, and other necessities. They also found it essential to travel with extra clothes for all ages and medicine—particularly guinea worm tablets. There was always someone whom they could help in one way or the other. Some trips were more memorable than others. Lloyd's visit to Nkwanta in the Volta region, the home village of Pasco Eyanch, the French teacher, was one of those memorable visits. He had taken the Adventist message back to the people of Nkwanta and he arranged accommodations for them with the Catholic priest, a special place for our Sabbath worship, and a trip on Sunday to visit the members, especially the yam farmers.

The memorable part of this trip was not the driving down the steep embankment with fear and trepidation onto the pontoon, but the joy of giving garden hoes and matches to the people who then showered them with gifts of yams and a chicken. The return journey had two occasions of anxiety: the climbing of the steep embankment after leaving the pontoon and driving through burning fields with fire on either side. When they went to check the chicken, they found fire in the pickup near the petrol cans. It is uncomfortable to think what could have happened had they not found that fire on time.

Camp meetings were not only a challenge but also very happy times for the church in Ghana. The venue, usually chosen about a year in advance, was circulated around Tamale, Bolgatanga, and Chinderi. Their first camp meeting was in Chinderi—a distance of nearly 150 miles. The Mission had to carry everything it could take including the tent and pegs and benches. The preaching and the singing were excellent. The joy of the members and the choirs as they sang and danced in the village was something Elder Antonio wished he could transport to Europe. Chinderi had its own block build church and the camp meeting strengthened the church there. It was a church that he was to visit more than once. In Tamale, camp meeting was held on the Mission compound. This made life easier for all concerned. The attendance was greater than that of Bolgatanga and Chinderi. The most memorable one in Tamale will always be remembered because one of their pastor's little daughters was discovered missing on the Sabbath evening. They searched everywhere, but

Elder Lloyd & Etta Antonio-1979-1984

without success. The following Sunday morning, they were advised to go to the Dagumba Chief and report it. They did and he promised that he would send a message by the talking drums. He kept his promise and soon little Elizabeth was brought to her father safe and sound. Someone had seen her wandering, discovered she was a stranger, provided her with food and a warm bed, and waited for some message. When it came from the chief's palace, they knew where to take her. The impact that was made on the Dagbani people is not known to them, however, the people certainly made an impact on them.

The camp meeting in Bolgatanga was remembered very well because of the amount of driving he had to do and the near fatal accident. On their last trip as they were nearing a bridge on the outskirts of the town, they experienced a sharp skid towards the railings of the bridge which could have meant a fatal or very serious accident. Pastor Azule's wife who was riding in the front with them prayed out aloud for God to have mercy on them. Immediately the pickup righted itself. God intervened and they were safe.

The experience of those multiple trips for camp meeting made all of them realize the pickup was too small and they needed a small truck for the Mission. Where was the money to come from? Help came in an unexpected area. Brother Lindsay Thomas was always raising funds for the Missions. When he heard their plight, he asked for a letter explaining their need and a lesson of thanks from the ministers who had received the Christmas gifts. It took time, but by 1984 there was a new truck that could transport the new tent, the new mobile generator and other equipment needed for campaigns, and camp meetings and to relocate the ministers when necessary.

Evangelism was another challenge—it is said that evangelism is the life blood of the church. There was one campaign run by Yaw Asubonteng on the Mission grounds which resulted in a very large baptism. Another was planned by the Tamale church in which they invited a prominent non-member from Accra then residing in Tamale to be the chairman of the meetings. He accepted the invitation and it resulted in his accepting Christ and being baptized. His wife, a Seventh-day Adventist for many years, was overjoyed and he was amply rewarded for taking the chair.

Yendi in the east had a campaign in which many were baptized including a witch doctor that burnt all his artifacts of his crafts before his baptism.

The town centre of Tamale always presented a challenge to the Mission. But, finally, they were able to schedule a crusade there. They engaged Pastor Wright who was ministering in Liberia—he and his wife and two children joined in the big effort. The meetings were well attended and a grand baptism was planned for the last Sabbath of the meetings. The candidates were transported by bus to the Mission grounds where they were immersed in the pool there. Over one hundred persons were baptized. One brother was so overjoyed that he held a banquet for all the new members. There also were baptisms which were the result of the pastor's personal work and the witness of the members. When the call came for baptism, Elder Antonio had to go since he was the only ordained minister in that vast territory. These were times of great joy and he would never have missed them for anything. There were calls from Zangum village to baptize about 49 people—the fruit of the work of Seidu Salifu, the young boy whom they were educating at the Mission. Bolgatanga had her converts from Pastor Hagan's diligent work. There were calls for baptism from Chinderi and a town where he baptized the candidates in the Volta Lake.

The growing Mission needed more workers and was always looking for young men who were committed to Christ and His church. They found one in Wa in the person of Brother Andrew Boateng, another in Thomas Didiyani of Chinderi, and Zac Asuboni of Bolgatanga. The Executive Committee sent him to pastor the Yendi Company. As employer, the Mission had to do its best to look after the health of its pastors. While Elder Antonio traveled around his wife made sure he carried basic medicines including worm tablets for the dreaded guinea worm. One of his pastors was infected by this dangerous worm by drinking water on one of his journeys to the Mission. He was unable to walk as it affected his thighs. They were able to visit him and leave him six guinea worm tablets. One tablet in the morning and one in the evening for three days was sufficient to affect a cure. Many found relief and whereas before they were not interested in what the Adventists were preaching, after ridding them of the guinea worms, they began to show an interest. Pastor Sumani had such an experience at Kpamdai. When the lives of the workers were threatened in any way as chief driver of the Mission, he had to hasten to move them out of the situation.

Pastor Sumani, a Mamprusi and cousin of the Nanumbas, was in this situation in the summer of 1982. However, on a Sunday morning the Nanumbas found they were surrounded by the Cumcumbas—who killed men, boys, and pregnant mothers wherever they found them. Pastor Sumani at Kpandai was in danger and sent an urgent message to get him moved out. Adventist policemen in Yendi accompanied them because they supervised matters in Wullency and Kpandai. The smell of death was in the air as they drove by.

Further Education of Ministers: Pastor Wahu, Addo Kwakye, Zac Asuboni, and Stephen Afari went for further studies. The Valley View College in Accra was started by Pastor Walton Whaley for the purpose of coping with the educational needs of the ministry. North Ghana Mission released Mr. Addo their bookkeeper and many others for further studies.

Elder Lloyd & Etta Antonio-1979-1984

Transport for the Workers: Another area that challenged the Mission was transport for the workers. Bicycles were greatly needed, but these were difficult to find. With the help of the brethren in England they were able to import a few. If all the ministers had had cycles, they could have done twice the amount of work they did.

Equipment for the Mission: The need of a small truck for the transportation of the tent has been mentioned. A new tent was needed because the one they met there had seen better days; so a tent was added to the shopping list—as well as a mobile generator. With the help of Mrs. Lindsay Thomas they were able to acquire a truck and a tent. The members of the North England Conference raised the cash for a mobile generator which was sent out in 1982.

Building and Agricultural Projects: Roofing sheets were needed for the Mission school and the Lord provided them. The Zangum Company building of mud brick walls was destroyed by wind and rain and needed rebuilding. Mr. Kwame Osafo helped them with the driving to the ferry to transport concrete blocks which took several trips from Bolgatanga while Mr. Addo and the villagers did the building. The Mission was also instrumental in getting a dam for the village.

Food Relief: Food was always a problem while they were there. The nationals did their best to help them. One brother in Accra, Brother Garney, was able to get flour for them to make bread. They were always grateful to him for his kindness and hospitality. Their home Division had made provision for them to travel to Ouagadougou in Burkina Faso then Upper Volta and purchase food every six weeks. They were able to fellowship with pastor and Mrs. Joachim and family, as well as, visit Mr. and Mrs. Wright from England who ran the Horticultural Project in Bazega. These trips were very interesting but long and dangerous. The angels of the Lord protected them from death by a stampeding herd of buffalo-like animals while driving through the huge game reserve. With their feet in the air as if divided by an unseen hand they went around their car in the form of a "V."

Traveling to Ouagadougou for food helped them, but it did not help the Ghanaians whose harvests were ruined because of late rains—especially in 1983-1984. During this time they were all hungry—natives and expatriates alike. In spite of this, they fed many from the little they had. Though the Mission tried to keep some high protein biscuits for helping out at that time, it was not adequate. There was need of massive food relief, but who was to initiate this?

God provided such a man in the person of Pastor Glen Howell from the U.S.A. He came to work as a departmental officer in the Union office in Accra.

Precious Memories of Missionaries of Color

When he saw the plight of expatriates and natives, he went to the American Embassy in Accra to find out what could be done. This was the start of a huge program of food relief for the people of Ghana. It also created employment for many because drivers were needed for the trucks that were brought to the ferry to get the food to different parts of the country. This was very hard work indeed, but this kind fatherly man was given wisdom and strength and the protection of humans and holy angels. So many people were blessed through his efforts!

The Antonios loved and admired the people of Ghana and just wanted to help in whatever way they could. They invested heavily and worked as if there were no tomorrow because they needed to return to England for their children's education—and did so in 1984. They count it a privilege to have served the people from whom their forefathers came.

Elder Lloyd & Etta Antonio-1979-1984

The Antonio Family

Precious Memories of Missionaries of Color

Elder Lloyd & Etta Antonio-1979-1984

Precious Memories of Missionaries of Color

The Antonio Family today

41

ELDER ROBERT & BARBARA PATTERSON 1980–1984

"THEY WANT YOU TO GO WHERE? WHEN? WHY?" These were the words that Robert received when he returned to the hotel room after attending a meeting at the General Conference session held in Dallas, Texas, in May of 1980. Barbara and the boys were watching the evening news just as they heard the news about their going to Africa. The TV headline for that hour was about war in Nairobi between tribes. They saw so much shooting and killing that it made Barbara sick. She looked at Robert and said "you are not taking our boys over there." She was scared to death. He just looked at her and said, "Let's pray about it."

The prayer came a long time later. First, Africa was something that you read about in the mission quarterly or thought of wild animals running through the jungle. It was not a place to take your family for six years. Plus, who did they know over there? The Pattersons were very comfortable living in the good old U.S.A.—and lovely Atlanta at that. But then Barbara came to herself. "You have a husband who is working for the Lord, loves the Lord, enjoys his work and wants to do all he can to hasten the soon coming of Christ. So what is your problem?" After Robert had left for his next meeting, she called their boys together. Because they were ages 10 and 12, Barbara tried to explain to them as best she could just what working for the church meant. This could and would be a new adventure for them. The fact that they would have to leave family, friends, school and churches, jobs and all that was familiar to them, they had a call to do work in the mission field. They looked at her as if she had fallen out of a tree, and this conversation lasted for the balance of the General Con-

Precious Memories of Missionaries of Color

ference session in Texas. She was praying very hard to believe what she was telling them. It was going to be a new life, in a third world country, in a place where they could not even say or spell the name properly. They were headed for Bujumbura Burundi, Central Africa.

After lots of paper work was completed, shots taken, short visits to family and friends, October, 1980 found them, the Patterson family, flying 18 hours to a new world. Lord have mercy, and He did. They arrived in Burundi and it was like stepping back in time. After going through customs, not knowing the language (French), the President of the Union, Elder Dewitt Williams was there to meet them. They traveled by jeep to their new home, and the view was beautiful. The people were watching the Pattersons just as hard as they were watching them. The colors they were wearing, some with lots of clothes and some with very little clothes on, especially the children. Now there were a few things that she had asked the Lord for concerning this move to a new country. One, please let the bathroom be on the inside of the house, and please Lord don't let her see any snakes. She was not too concerned about a car because she had heard that the Union Office was just down the road from their home. She had asked that they have a bath inside; however, she forgot to ask for running water all the time. That's another story. Needless to say the home was very nice—room for the boys and a guest room, a large porch, and lots of yard, front and back, and a place to put the car if they ever got one.

The boys were enrolled in home study. What a change from the classroom. But they had a student missionary teacher, Margie Smith, to get them through for the first year. Their second and third year of schooling was spent at the Maxwell Academy in Nairobi, Kenya. Yes, they were again sent away from home. Maxwell is an English speaking academy and a blessing for missionary children. That took some adjusting for them because the boys were away from their parents again and at such a young age.

Robert settled into his new office as Treasurer of the Union. His work day started early and ended late at night. There was so much "new" to get used too. For example, how to type again on a manual typewriter and use paper over again. Early hours at the office, meetings late at night, getting the workers used to him and he to them. In addition, he was assigned a church to pastor. He had to visit other parts of Africa: The Ivory Coast, Rwanda, Kenya, Paris, and places like that. He often stayed away from home when travel was rough because of the very bad roads—and flying was another story. Everywhere you went took official paper work, and things did not move as fast as they do in the USA.

Elder Robert & Barbara Patterson 1980-1984

Barbara will never forget their first Sabbath at the new church. She forgot where she was and put on heels, stockings, and a suit. It was hot, but she wanted to be dressed right. They rode for a long time and then they climbed up a steep hill. They had not seen anyone walking or driving as they traveled in the direction of the church, but when they arrived (without a translator) the little church was packed inside and out. They were waiting for the new pastor and his family to arrive and it was only 9:15 A.M. They entered the one room building with two openings on each side for windows, one small door at the back, and the seats were center blocks with a slab of wood to sit on. No backs, no soft seats, and the floor was dirt. It was dark inside; they had to let their eyes adjust to the light before they could enter. They did not act shocked at all, rather they acted like this was the type of church they always attended each Sabbath, but the boys did not do so well. They just held Barbara's hand really tight, and would not leave her side. After pulling them inside and asking the Lord to help them not to show how they really felt, they made it through that service. The music was beautiful! Harmony like they had never heard! Barbara understood the sermon because Robert preached and the people heard it through a translator.

The members were so friendly and kind to them. The service was short, because at noon it was very hot and they had to walk home. Services were held at the church only once on Sabbath and at times they would have a short afternoon program. When this was done, they did not serve lunch for the church, only for the pastor and his family. Barbara felt badly about this; however, this was a new culture she had to learn.

The one thing that she noticed when she attended the church the first week was that they had so many children and there was no place for them to have Sabbath school. Consequently, the children ran in and out of the service. This job was given to her. The children must have their own Sabbath school class. But where? The answer to this question was outside, at the back of the church. There were no Little Friends, etc. for them to use, no song books, no nothing. All she could think of was the waste they had of materials in their Sabbath school in Atlanta. So everything had to be hand made until she would receive materials from the States. She was sent old Picture Rolls, Little Friends, etc. from the South Atlantic Conference Sabbath School Department. It was like receiving new money from a long lost uncle. She was given a translator and away they went getting their class together. Remember now that this class was outside, and it was hot and there were about 50-60 children attending, and when it rains they had no place to go. The church was already crowded with adults. Barbara's dream was to have a Lambs Shelter built on the side of the

349

church—just four poles with a tin roof and they'd use straw mats on the dirt floor. The children were so excited for their new room that they brought stones from the lake to help build the sides of the shelter. After completing this task, Barbara felt so much better having the children under a roof. The attendance grew and God blessed. When they dedicated that room, they gave each child his/her own Bible. What joy came over their faces! A book of their own!

Several revivals were held in the low country. Barbara had attended many camp meetings in her life but never saw one held on the side of the hill. As far as could be seen, there were people sitting under trees and in the sun waiting to hear the word of God preached. They stayed all day until just before sunset. They seemed as if they could not get enough of hearing the Word. When they got tired, they wanted more, and more was given. Barbara would sit awhile, stand some, and then sit again. What a hunger and thirst for the Word! Hundreds gave their hearts and life to Christ. She had never seen anything like this before or since her stay in Africa. Baptisms were held down at the river. You could hear the singing for miles around. What a beautiful sight!

After the boys left for school in Nairobi, Barbara started working in the Union Office as secretary in the Education department. The first thing they wanted her to do was translate an English textbook into the Kurundi language. Now that was funny! She could only speak broken English, no French and could not spell Kurundi. However, it was her job, and she had to do it. Her boss, Pierre Ramseier, and Caleb Bru were a great help to her—they had her thinking that she could do anything. It was hard for awhile, but after a short time she could type those letters and spell the words correctly. God is good you know!

There were several other missionaries there from different parts of the U.S. They would meet on Sunday evening as a social outlet and to just remember the good old USA. After all, they were from a different world. They showed her how to shop at the "on the ground" mall, and how to check and see if the eggs that she bought at the market or off the street were OK. They always got stuck when buying the oil. Most of the time it was a five gallon can of water. How they did that she will never know. They wanted to celebrate one of the boy's birthday. When she went to buy the ice cream it was $23.00 a half gallon. They decided to have an "everybody's" birthday party twice a year. All food products were very expensive. And, don't ask her to make a cake! By the time you sifted the flour through your panty hose and then baked the flour in the oven for several hours, you were just too tired to add the rest of the ingredients to make a cake. As a result, the family ate cookies.

Elder Robert & Barbara Patterson 1980-1984

Their social life consisted of visiting the other missionaries, writing letters, taking a ride down to the lake, and watching the hippos cross the road. They held up traffic, but who was going to honk at them? Then they would stop at the roadside stand and have French fries with mayo and an orange soda. What a treat! They did a lot of walking up in the mountains. Africa was such a beautiful country. So many children, cows in the road, women in the fields with babies on their backs, men of all sizes pushing carts and trying to make a living, and no one was ever in a hurry. It was a much laid back way of life. If you don't get it done today, there is always tomorrow. So don't worry! This was a major lesson that she learned.

Remember Barbara asked the Lord for a bathroom inside, but she didn't ask for running water all of the time. Well, the water was there, but it ran when it wanted to. Many days they had to fill tubs and buckets to store water. This would go on for days. During the rainy season, they would be sure to catch water for those days that they had none, and those were often.

Barbara prayed that she would not see any snakes. God is good! She saw three and they were lying dead on a rock. The children saw plenty, but never told her about them. Ask and it shall be given to you, says the Word.

The Pattersons lived in Burundi for 3 1/2 years. It was a blessing for the family to learn about another way of life and to meet friends whom they still have today. Their faith in God grew. They were willing to share their faith at any and all times. There is very little that they take for granted. How could they have learned so much patience, and how to accept people where they are? They realized that they are a people blessed with many things when others have so little and do not complain. Their faith and trust was totally in the Lord. They took so much for granted. They wasted so much. They wanted what they did not need, and tried so hard keeping up with the Joneses. Many times they trusted in themselves only for what they wanted and asked God for their needs. They learned to study more, read more, (there was no TV), appreciate nature more, and a little could become a lot when used for the purpose of sharing with others. God did not send them to Burundi, thousands of miles from family and friends, to an unknown continent to go on vacation. They worked hard! His reason was to let them know that He is an all loving God, who will take care of His children, no matter where they are. He protected them from danger, by land and sea. He provided for all of their needs. Even when Elder Patterson was involved in a terrible car accident and the car was totaled, he only received a cut on his leg. Hospitals in Africa need so much! Most materials were washed and used again. They would leave them in the sun to dry and this was done time and time again. Believe me what you see on TV is real. But God takes care of His people.

Precious Memories of Missionaries of Color

What did they give to the people of Burundi? Barbara is not sure, but she knows what they gave to her; a better appreciation of the love of God, more faith in Him, and to trust Him with all of one's heart. They are His children and they wanted, along with their families and friends and the many people that they served in Burundi to meet Him when He comes. Never in her life did she ever think that the opportunity to live in a third world country would be hers. For the things she learned and experienced, may she always share with others. This is her prayer. She will always be thankful for the prayers of her mother and others while they were away.

At the time the Pattersons received the call to serve in the mission field, Elder Robert Patterson, Sr. was the treasurer of the South Atlantic Conference, and Barbara was employed with the General Services Administration, in the federal government. Their son Robert was twelve years old and son Roderick was ten, and they both were attending the Berean Jr. Academy in Atlanta, Georgia. At that time, the family was a member of the Maranatha S.D.A. Church.

Presently, Barbara is retired and living in Summerville, South Carolina. She is the proud grandmother of three—Robert III, Reyna and Miles Jordan Patterson. Elder Robert Patterson is deceased as of March, 2001. Their son, Robert Patterson, Jr., is an Assistant Treasurer of the Allegheny East Conference and Roderick Patterson, the second son is a student at Florida Metro University.

Elder Robert & Barbara Patterson 1980-1984

Visit from the G.C. President in the Union Office

Precious Memories of Missionaries of Color

Land of Beauty

Camp Meeting

Elder Robert & Barbara Patterson 1980–1984

Market

Church inside and outside

42

ELDER JEROME & YVONNE PONDEXTER 1981-1988

Jerome and Yvonne served as missionaries from December 1981 to July 1988. Initially, they were sent to Brussels, Belgium, to study in the language school.

The official language in Zaire, Africa (currently Republic of Congo) was French. It was extremely necessary for Jerome to have a good handle on the language because he was to serve as a history teacher. Shortly after the history position he served as Mission Director at Lukanga for three years.

The Lukanga mission was spread over 36 acres, approximately 7,000 feet above sea level. That particular area of Zaire was often referred to as the "Swiss of Africa," because of its fertile soil, luscious mountains, slopes and valleys. It consisted of technical, pedagogy, seminary, and elementary schools. Lukanga also had a boarding academy with a student body of about 200 students.

Some of the outstanding achievements that occurred during the Pondexter's service were:

- Extending the seminary school from 1 to 2 years
- Having evangelistic meetings in Goma with the Seminary students
- Baptizing more than 100 new converts.

Here are some of the exciting stories connected with our service:

The Pondexters took life for granted until they went to the mission field. The moment they arrived in Kinshasa, Africa, they had their first culture shock.

Elder Jerome & Yvonne Pondexter 1981–1988

They had to run to the airplane in order to get a seat to go to Lubumbashi. They had never had to do this in the USA because each passenger was assigned a seat. They believe they overbooked. There were more people running to the plane than there were seats available. Picture this with them. Jerome and Yvonne were running to the plane. Yvonne held their four month old baby Melissa tightly in her hands while Jerome ran ahead to try to save them some seats. In the meantime, his wife was pushed and trampled by people holding chickens and babies until she was almost on the ground. Suddenly, for some strange reason, the flight attendant noticed his wife and quickly motioned for the people to move aside so that his wife could move through the crowd. The Lord was truly with them, even through the busy crowd!

After arriving in Lumbombashi, Jerome ended up getting sick from the different kinds of food they ate. He ate some eggs that were white that were supposed to be yellow. He was sick for 3-4 days and lost a lot of weight that first week. He prayed and asked God to help him. His whole body definitely went through a culture shock!

The very first thing they had to do was to adjust to the traveling conditions. They boarded a mission plane wherein the pilot had to see the ground in order to safely land. Jerome felt like the co-pilot on their plane ride because he sat right beside the pilot. He never did that in the USA! What a different experience!

The food in Lukanga was very different, and they cooked most of it from scratch on a wooden stove. Almost all of their food was purchased at an open market. They stayed very healthy in Lukanga!

While in Lukanga, Jerome also taught the pastors to be more effective in their teaching methods. Most of the pastors had to leave their families to go to school for one or two years in Lukanga. While at school they studied and lived on campus. It was a major culture shock to see their smiling faces and hear their inward motivation to learn about Jesus and witness to others about His second coming.

Jerome remembers when they were on a trip headed to Goma. He was driving his Ford International Scout truck during the rainy season with his wife and daughter Melissa in the front cab. They had to cross a bridge to get to the other side. The bridge was made of long tree logs from the bark of a tree and laid flat beside four or five other tree logs. It was raining and the tree logs were slippery. He had to drive over them to get to the other side. He got halfway across the bridge and the truck tires got caught in the space between the logs. The driver's tire slipped over the edge and the truck tilted. With help from the Africans he was able to open his door and help his family out to the other side of the bridge. It took over a dozen Africans to move the truck. However, they still lifted it up then moved it, all along singing and humming. When working in unity as a family a lot can be accomplished. Heaven will be simply glorious because the family on earth and the family in heaven will be working together in unity.

There are two seasons each year in Africa. One was hot and dry, and the other was humid and wet—during the "moist" climate, travel was very slow —about 5 to 10 miles per hour. Travel was extremely slow because of the deep potholes in the dirt road. Sometimes people drove into the potholes not knowing whether they would be able to get their trucks out of the muddy water, or not!

Jerome remembers being elected to serve as the community service director for the campus church. He was immediately told that every female member of the church was automatically a member of this community service department. Instead of making an effort to enlist some men, he decided to work with the great force God had given him. This consisted of 20-30 women ready and willing to go out in the community and witness.

They would gather together singing, praising God, and marching towards the local village. What an awesome army for the Lord! As they walked up steep hills and down others, they would stop where they knew a family was struggling, offer words of encouragement, and have prayer with the families. Most of all, they tried to inquire about the immediate needs of families. Some needed food, clothes, prayer, but most needed medication. You did not need a prescription to purchase medication—you simply had to have the funds.

With the challenge at hand to purchase medications, they realized they needed to launch a project to replenish their long depleted treasury. They called a meeting and did some brainstorming. It did not take long for the ladies to decide the best method would be to plant and harvest a garden and sell the produce.

The teachers at Lukanga received a very meager salary; however, housing and a plot of land was provided for each teacher. After making some inquires, the administrator of the technical school, who was single and not using his plot, volunteered to loan them his plot for harvesting. God blessed because his plot was very moist and fertile.

They praised God for His gift to them and immediately set out clearing the land. This was done mainly with a hoe and a lot of strong physical labor. The hoes used in Zaire have handles about half the length as the ones in America. So this was some seriously, backbreaking work. Or rather, it was difficult for Elder Pondexter. They were amazed that he even had the courage to go out

Elder Jerome & Yvonne Pondexter 1981-1988

and work side-by-side with them in preparing the soil. The children could work faster than he; they laughed and teased him. However, they admired his courage. He was told they had only seen one other missionary wife with the motivation to work in the fields with them. They had a grand time planting and harvesting together for the Lord.

They decided cabbage would be the best vegetable to plant. They did all they could do in preparing soil, planting plugs and God did the rest. A drought came through leaving vegetable vendors totally stripped of supplying vegetables for the local community and their school cafeteria. As the drought was taking its toll on the local community, the cabbages were simply flourishing. When the cafeteria director could not find vegetable vendors to purchase from, guess who had them available and ready to sell? That's right, the community service department! God smiled on their garden and they reaped a great harvest. Their community service treasury had plenty of funds and their students continued to eat a good balanced diet! Praise God!

They purchased medications, blankets, and other items to help relieve suffering families. They designated a day to collect clothes from the dormitories and gathered more clothes than they thought possible. The Pondexters had a great year in service to God.

Pondexter Family: Jerome, Yvonne, Melissa, Tammy

Precious Memories of Missionaries of Color

Pastor at the Seminary school

Camp Meeting

Pastor Baptizing

43

ELDER PIERRE & JOCELYNE DESHOMMES 1982-1986; 1994-1998

Pierre was born in Limbe, Haiti, West Indies, and has dual citizenship in the United States and Canada. He received his early education in Haiti and a Bachelor's of Science in Business Administration with minors in Religion and Church History from Northern Caribbean University in Mandeville, Jamaica. He is presently enrolled in Century University where he is a candidate for the Ph.D.

In July of 1976, Pierre was invited to go to Canada to canvas or engage in colporteuring (Literature Evangelist who sell Christian books and magazine). to pay part of his college tuition at Northern Caribbean University, then West Indies College. He was assigned to the Ottawa Valley and by God's grace he was able to sell more than $6,045.75 worth of books. He was among the Champions of the Summer. While knocking at the doors of "Vanier," then a suburb of Ottawa, a lady from Jamaica came to the door. She invited Pierre in, and he was able to sell to her more than $500.00 worth of books that day. When he went back to collect the installment money, he offered her Bible study lessons. She graciously accepted his offer. As a result of this study, Pierre formed a group of three including her and her two children. Since he was leaving to go back to school, he invited them to keep in touch with him and let him know how the group was progressing.

In 1982 Ottawa Valley had only one English speaking church in the West end on Benjamin Street. While there, he was invited to preach in that particular church. At the end of the sermon, he saw a lady and her two children coming to greet him at the door. This was the same family he had formed into a group in September, 1976. Glory be to God!

At the end of 1982, the Deshommes received an official call to serve in the mission field—their first missionary journey in Ethiopia. Initially, the call was for Madagascar, but this was changed while they were at Andrews for the Mission Institute. When they came back, the Ontario Conference asked them to work with the Union evangelist, Gerard Dis, in conducting the first French Crusade in the Valley of Ottawa. As a result, they were able to baptize more than 29 souls and immediately organize a church. They found a very experienced bilingual pastor who was working at Swan River, Manitoba and who came and developed the field. Today, not only are there French speaking churches, but also more than seven to ten organized French and English churches in the Valley of Ottawa.

Pierre has the distinction of becoming the first National Director for ADRA/SAWS in Port-Au-Prince, Haiti. While in Ethiopia, Pierre was the Financial Officer, Development Director and Public Relations where he worked with the government in establishing the first official ADRA in Ethiopia from (1982-1987). Another first for Pierre was the signing of an official agreement in Cameroon with the propensity to cover the other six countries in the Central Africa with a special Franchise for the church.

Pierre's main mission in Ethiopia was to establish ADRA and sign an agreement between the church and the government of Ethiopia. This was done in less than six months, which was the first time that any such thing had occurred. The government listened and granted visas for his white colleague who was not even in the country but still in the USA, and one for himself—in less than three months. They were able to cover Entrea, Somalia, and Djibouti with food and medicines that came from the U.S., Canada, and Britain through a military Russian plane. Pierre was the first SDA and first missionary to visit this country. He remembered when Elder Bekele Heye authorized him to go to explore this part of the world and bring back a report so that a church could be started. Today, there is a firm presence in Djibouti.

Pierre will never forget the request made by officials from the government of Ethiopia after listening to some of his sermons on Sabbath to organize a crusade not only for young people in Addis Ababa but also for those of the government officials who were working on Saturdays so that they could benefit from his messages. He was obliged to use his "lunch-time" for two weeks to hold this crusade. The result was amazing how God can use a little time like lunch to bring people to his church. At the end of the two weeks, they were able to baptize over 35 persons with more than 150 to 200 waiting in a baptismal class. Later on, Pastor Pierre of the church of Filowa, in Canada, let

Elder Pierre & Jocelyne Deshommes 1982-1998

him know that the majority of the people were baptized. Unfortunately, some of his missionary colleagues were jealous of him for which he paid dearly, but God repaid him generously.

In 1994–1998, the Deshommes were called to serve in the African-Indian Ocean Division as one of the Sub-Regional Vice Presidents of ADRA International. Pierre has the distinction of becoming the first National Director for ADRA/SAWS in Port-Au-Prince, Haiti. He also served as the Union Health and Temperance Director. Once again he was able within less than six months to sign another Convention with the Cameroonian government with the propensity to extend Franchise to six other countries in Central Africa. Again this was one of the first of its kind within the church. Reflecting back, Pierre remembers that he was one of the instruments to translate into French ADRA (Le Secours Mondial Adventiste) for the French speaking countries while he was in Haiti in 1978-79.

Along with his responsibilities with ADRA, the Union called him to be the pastor of Nkoindongo—one of the most progressive churches in the Cameroon at Yaounde. After four years, the membership more than quadrupled, tithes and offerings increased, more than 72 people were baptized making it possible to build one of the most attractive churches in Yaounde. (Today in Yaounde, there are more than 40 churches as opposed to four churches when the Deshommes arrived in 1994.)

Under ADRA, water, electricity, and roads were organized for a community of more than 15,000 inhabitants at Dogba in the extreme north of Cameroun. The church had been in this community for seventy years. Since 90% of the population were Muslims, there was no contact between the two groups. Pierre remembers when he told the pastor and the Director of the College that he was going to visit the Muslims on the other side of the river that there was a lot of opposition. When he visited the Muslim people, they didn't want to believe that he was a missionary of the SDA church. They asked him what brought him to their place after 70 years of being distant. Usually, SDA churches came first with their Bible, and if you didn't agree with their doctrines, they simply ignored you.

Pierre asked them what they wanted to see in their community. They told him, water, electricity, and roads. He managed to arrange a grant between Canada and Europe with some money and the project was materialized. As a result, he was named the "Chiroma" of the Extreme North of Cameroon. The people and the government recognize this title as a "Dignitary Title". Some of his missionary friends were not too happy for all of these.

Precious Memories of Missionaries of Color

They were able to organize with the help of ADRA 12 schools for the children in Tchad, one of the poorest areas of our Union. Because these schools were self-supporting, they had an average of 160 children per school.

When the Deshommes went to the mission field, their children were 5 and 9 years old. Today, their firstborn, Sandra, is married and has one son, named Ayinel. Their other daughter, Patricia, attended PUC and graduated with a degree in Chemistry. She is now preparing for the MCAT while assisting in the Department of Research in the Science Department at Andrews University in Berrien Springs.

Jocelyne, Pierre's wife, writes that being in the mission field has been a very rewarding experience for her. More than any other place that she has been, the mission field was a place where she felt closer to Jesus, fulfilling his mandate to "Go into all nations and making them disciples." The mission field was the place where many creeds could be seen openly, and there was hunger, extreme poverty, lack of hygiene, etc. Usually, people in these places have no salary; they lived from day to day with no hope for a better future—without welfare where people can find help until they can get back on their feet, people rely on charity. Most of the people from the mission field have never heard about Jesus, or God; anything could be their god, even a stone. It was really a place where your help could be appreciated both physically and spiritually.

Jocelyne recounts that she did not work while they were missionaries in Ethiopia, but she had the privilege of helping an existing center where they made crafts which were sold to benefit the poorest in the church. During their stay in the Cameroon, she worked as an administrative assistant in the office—and most of her salary was used to help other people. She also had the privilege of helping these people physically and spiritually both within and out of the church. With the help of God, she had the privilege of forming a group of women who were willing to invest money each month to create a project where the less privileged in the church could find employment and earn some money to supply their needs. The church members were thrilled with this initiative, to the glory of God.

When they returned to America , the GC made arrangements with Atlantic Union College for Elder Deshommes to serve in various capacities as Assistant to the President to Grant Writing and Enrollment Associate Director before accepting a call with the Michigan Conference at N2N Ministry/ACS as the first Black Executive Director. The Deshommes are presently retired in Florida.

Elder Pierre & Jocelyne Deshommes 1982-1998

Pastor Deshommes

The Deshommes Family

Precious Memories of Missionaries of Color

Jocelyne, Sandra & Patricia

Farewell party just before leaving for Ethiopia

Child leading Father to baptism

Elder Pierre & Jocelyne Deshommes 1982-1998

Baptism in Cameroon

Pastor Deshommes conducting a fundraiser for Djongolo S.D.A. Church

Precious Memories of Missionaries of Color

Minister of Health in Cameroon

Foreign Minister of Affairs

Children of the orphanage in line for food

Elder Pierre & Jocelyne Deshommes 1982-1998

Deshommes in official outfit in Cameroon

Dorcas Society

Precious Memories of Missionaries of Color

Visiting project in the field

Nkolndongo S.D.A. Church

Deshommes with UNICEF in the Cameroon

44

Dr. Carmelita Troy 1989–1992; 1992–1994; 1994–1996

She was asked to be the dean of the three young women who were staying in the dorm over the summer at Middle East College in Lebanon, in Beirut, Lebanon, where she was teaching. So she moved herself down into the dean's apartment in the residence hall. This bedroom faced west and allowed her to sleep in a little longer than in her own bedroom.

Because Carmelita was up and about by 5.00 A.M., she was usually asleep by 9:30 P.M., but the dorm didn't close until 10:00 or 10:30 P.M. So she advised the girls that she would lock the doors to the main entrance of the dorm at 9 P.M. and if they were out after 9 P.M. they should enter through the dean's apartment which would be unlocked.

The first night they tried this, she woke up at 2 A.M. wondering if everyone was in. Unable to sleep further until she knew that her charges were accounted for, she checked the girls' rooms and found all three sleeping soundly. The following day the plan was modified. When the girls entered the dorm after 9 P.M. they would still enter through the dean's apartment, but they would tap her on the shoulder to let her know that they were back. Somehow she figured that she would be able to, in a semi-conscious or sleeping state, register three taps to the shoulder and continue in her slumber, knowing that all were accounted for. This system worked well.

In the middle of one night she woke up to the sounds of rockets being fired and slicing through the night air overhead. It was about 3 A.M. or perhaps a little earlier and she was concerned about the danger. She was confident that the girls were in the dorm—three taps had been registered, but the dorm was not the place for them to be while the fighting was going on.

That year the civil war was still raging in Lebanon, especially in the summer. It was not uncommon to hear rockets flying over head in one direction or the other anytime, but mostly at night. There was no bomb shelter in the girl's dorm, so every night she placed clothing and a pair of shoes by her bed, so that in case the situation became more serious, she could dress quickly and run up the hill to the bomb shelter.

One night she got up and dressed in the clothes that she had beside the bed, and then went to wake up the girls to go to the bomb shelter. No one was interested in going. The bombing wasn't very frequent, according to them—it was "some distance" away. The girls went back to sleep. She couldn't. The rockets continued to be fired sporadically, and she made her way, alone, to the bomb shelter. Mrs. England, one of the English teachers at the college, was the only other person in the shelter—but she had the reputation of being the first one to the bomb shelter.

The following morning Dr. Troy discovered that the bombing had started around midnight and that she had slept through about 2 to 3 hours of it. This was a little disconcerting. If she was starting to sleep through the racket of the rockets, then who knows what sort of danger she was putting herself and the girls in. She resolved that whenever she woke up to the sound of rocket-fire, that she would wake up the girls and despite any protestation, they would do something.

Just a few nights later she woke again to the sound of shelling. Immediately, she got up and woke up the girls. Again, none of them seemed concerned, but she begged the girls to come and sleep in the dean's apartment. In case things flared up again they could quickly move to the bomb shelter. They agreed and brought sheets and pillows down to her place. The night was warm and all were wearing thin short pajamas and Carmelita suggested that they bring some clothing. "No, no, not necessary," was the reply.

They had all barely settled down in the apartment when the shelling became the worst she had ever heard. It seemed that some sort of new rocket which exploded a second time after it was fired, but before it hit its target, intended or not was being used. The noise was deafening. It sounded as if the rockets were being fired from nearby on one side and landing very nearby on the other.

There was no need to encourage the girls to get to the bomb shelter. They were out the door before she was. After all, she was dressing and they were just grabbing sheets and running. They were squealing with fear as they ran up the hill to the bomb shelter. It was quite a show. The night sky was lit up with the

Dr. Carmelita Troy 1989-1996

lights of war and in front of them and the girls running for dear life with their sheets clutched around their shoulders and flapping in the air behind them, like angels on an urgent mission.

This time the bomb shelter was fully occupied, and more people, like them, were hurriedly arriving. The lights in the shelter were bright and everyone was noisily chattering about what was going on. The girls, being Egyptian, were very self conscious about their lack of attire in the presence of the men. They wrapped their sheets around them and whisked themselves off to a far corner of the bomb shelter to wait out the shelling. No one slept very much for the remainder of the evening, even though the talking did eventually quiet down.

In the morning everyone got to assess the damages. One rocket had landed on the campus, damaging a walkway near one of the school houses, but thankfully, no one was hurt. After that night there was no trouble getting the girls to the bomb shelter when there was shelling in the middle of the night.

Dr. Camelita Troy presently is a professor at Andrews University in Berrien Springs, Michigan.

45

Ronald & Marilyn Lindsey
1985-1990

Ronald's uncle, Elder Richard Simons, went to Liberia in West Africa in 1952, and returned for the 1954 General Conference Session in San Francisco. Ronald remembers well his visit to their home when he was 10 years old, because Elder Simons was a "missionary hero" to him. Ronald determined then that he wanted to become a missionary and go to Africa, but he didn't tell anyone.

As the years went by, Ronald heard stories about deadly snakes, and realized that he would have to learn other languages, and the missionary zeal wandered away from him. He never shared it with his parents, sisters, or wife until a call came in 1985. Ronald's story begins with his preparation for denominational service.

As a sophomore at Golden Gate Academy in Oakland, California, he took bookkeeping and determined then that he wanted to become an accountant. Furthermore, he observed that the church used ministers to do the work of treasury and decided that to change that he would need to become an accountant and then work for the church in the capacity of treasurer. It was his desire to work for the church throughout his career as an accountant.

The Vietnam War was in full swing when he finished college with a B.S. degree in Accounting. The possibility of being drafted into the Armed Forces was imminent, so starting a career with the church was certain to be interrupted with military service. Ronald was interviewed by the U.S. Army Audit Agency (Army Audit) and they told him that when drafted into the U.S. Army he could be assigned as an auditor to Army Audit during his military service,

Ronald & Marilyn Lindsey 1985-1990

an alternative that pleased him a lot since being a medic did not fit his interests—he fainted at the sight of blood. After serving with the Army Audit for six months after graduation from college, he was drafted, sent to boot camp at Fort Sam Houston, and returned to his home office of Army Audit in San Francisco immediately after completion of the six weeks of boot camp. However, the military slots for draftees were in Korea and Okinawa. So off to Okinawa he went as an auditor with the Army Audit for two years. It was now time to realize his dream and plans for denominational service for his church.

Ronald shared his desire to be a missionary with his wife and parents, but not for Africa. He offered his services to the Far Eastern Division, where he was located, with the interest of staying in that region of the world. During the eight years with Army Audit, he had also obtained the M.B.A. degree from the University of Hawaii through an extension program on Okinawa and became certified as an internal auditor (CIA), so he felt that he was qualified for denominational service. However, the Far Eastern Division stated that he needed denominational experience in the North American Division. As he was leaving Okinawa in 1973, for his first denominational assignment at Loma Linda University School of Health, someone from Loma Linda University was headed to the Japan Union Conference as a missionary to the Far Eastern Division.

In July, 1985 Ronald was at the General Conference Session being held in New Orleans, Louisiana. By this time he had been on the staff of the School of Health, Loma Linda University, the church/school auditor for the Southern California Conference, trust auditor and subsequently treasurer of the Pacific Union Association, and was presently treasurer of the Atlantic Union Conference, a position he had held for only eight months. The session was to end on Sabbath. Most of the business had been completed and positions filled, as he sat in the Atlantic Union Conference delegates' section. Lo and behold Roland McKenzie, chairperson of the Eastern Africa Division Nominating Committee Caucus, came to his section stating that he needed to talk to Ronald right away, even during the meeting. They went to a corner on the delegates' floor where he revealed that he was being invited to be the treasurer of the Eastern Africa Division (EAD). He was shocked! The thought of going to Africa had long ago left him. He immediately asked about snakes in Eastern Africa. Roland's answer was that there weren't any more snakes in Eastern Africa than in the state of California, a statistic that he later found to be somewhat "exaggerated." Then Ronald asked about the need to learn foreign languages. He told him that all countries within the EAD had English as their official language, so no non-English languages were required for his position. Suddenly the hidden desire to serve as a missionary in Africa resurfaced at the eleventh hour. They needed

375

Precious Memories of Missionaries of Color

his decision by 3:00 p.m. the next day, Friday, which would be the last business session of the General Conference Session.

Ronald's family had already returned to the hotel room for the evening, so they were not with him at the time he was notified concerning the call. He went to the hotel room, woke up his wife, and informed her of the pending call. Furthermore, the president of the EAD and his wife were downstairs in the lobby waiting to meet with them. They slipped out of the room without telling their two children. At their meeting in the hotel restaurant Elder Bekele Heye told them that they wanted an African American to be their treasurer and that he had been recommended by a number of his counselors for consideration of this position. This was the first time in his denomination career that his ethnicity was the basis for the call. Elder Bekele made the appeal that he was being called home to the "Motherland."

When they returned to their hotel room, Ronald shared for the first time his early ambition to be a missionary to Africa etched upon his mind with his uncle's visit from the mission field in 1954. This revelation was a shock to his wife. Ronald is not sure that she would have married him if she had known about his "secret ambition." He also shared the call with their children, waking them up for that announcement. They were not thrilled!

His parents (Elder and Mrs. Harold A. Lindsey, retired minister and nurse) and all of his siblings were in attendance at the General Conference Session. His brother-in-law, Elder Henry M. Wright was speaking for the Friday morning devotion, and his sister, Elaine Arthur, was singing the appeal for his message, so they were all there. After the devotion, they all went to a local restaurant where he shared the call with them. Surprisingly, his entire family was very supportive of the call. The rest of the morning and early afternoon was spent praying and counseling with friends, General Conference and EAD leaders, and the delegates of the Atlantic Union Conference. He was feeling that he hadn't been at the Atlantic Union Conference long enough to accomplish any of his goals. Yet, General Conference leaders (all but one) were telling them that mission service calls preclude all other calls and the short stay at his present post was not a valid reason for declining a mission call. He had absolutely no support for acceptance of the call from the delegates of the Atlantic Union Conference, especially from the president. What a tough decision in such a short period of time!

After sitting through all of the counsel and advice, they felt that the Lord was speaking to them urging them to accept the Macedonian call to Africa. They gave their response to Roland McKenzie about 2:55 p.m. just minutes before the last business session was to begin. As Ronald met the EAD delegation that Friday night and participated in the Mission Pageant that last Sabbath afternoon

Ronald & Marilyn Lindsey 1985-1990

of the Session, he felt a peace and excitement for this new call—responding to a seed sown in his heart some 31 years previously, by the Holy Spirit, as part of God's plan for his life. This belief in the basis of their call to Africa was going to be needed to help them with a crisis that was coming during their mission service.

Another confirmation of their "call" was to be so uncanny. They had not consulted with Marilyn's parents during the deliberations for acceptance. Her father had just undergone cancer surgery and they were returning from his bedside when going to New Orleans for the General Conference Session. None of her family was present in New Orleans. They did not contact them until Saturday night, after the Session was completed, and the acceptance of the call was finalized and approved. Her father, a retired minister and very supportive of Ron's denominational service, reacted with the response "How can you do this to me!" Here he was recuperating from his second cancer surgery. His daughter was the nurse in the family and his oldest child. He felt that they were abandoning him at a time of critical need. If they had consulted him before making their decision, they never would have accepted the call. Yet, because of their acceptance and the wait for a work permit, they were able to spend dedicated time with him during the last months of his life. He died on Christmas Eve while they were still waiting for the work permit, but after being relieved of their responsibilities at the Atlantic Union Conference. In other words, they were just waiting without any responsibilities other than looking after their ailing father.

The General Conference and EAD officers decided that Ronald should visit the EAD headquarters before the outgoing treasurer departed, so he traveled to Zimbabwe in August, 1985. He had owned a van during most of his children's life. They found that type of vehicle to be most convenient for the child-raising years, but realized that such a vehicle would not be in the plans for Africa. When he arrived in Zimbabwe for this visit, his ride home from the airport was with the publishing director of the Division in a diesel-powered mini-van! Ronald discovered Harare to be a clean, modern city with comfortable homes and the conveniences of the United States. Well, almost! What a far cry from what he had expected. The weather was much like that of San Diego, California—warm, but not too warm during the day and crisp cool evenings and nights for good sleeping. Humidity was low, and the bug population was tolerable—just like California. African cities were modern!

During this short trip to Zimbabwe, he discovered that the Division maintained local currency and U.S. dollar bank accounts in nine countries. The associate treasurer was accepting a call to another Division, and the previous Eastern Africa and Trans-Africa Divisions were completing their mergers with staff moving from Nairobi, Kenya, to Harare, Zimbabwe. Additional houses and furnishings would need to be purchased to accommodate the combined staffs. Also, over 60 percent of the Division's budget was for the funding of expatriate workers from other world divisions. He was introduced to his treasury staff and started the search for a replacement associate treasurer. Realizing that work permits were difficult to obtain within a short time, the associate treasurer needed to be chosen from those already in the Division territory. A decision was made based on recommendations from current staff and officers to invite a treasurer from one of the Division's unions. Although his heritage was from a European country, he was the son of missionary parents who served most of their lives in South Africa.

Ronald also returned to the EAD in November for Year-End meetings. Since this was the year of a General Conference Session, it was also the year that Union leadership was selected for all unions. This was done at the Year-end meeting of the Division Executive Committee. This would be his first administrative experience with the people of East Africa. The membership of the Year-End meetings was enlarged due to the election process. He first met with the nominating committee caucus from one of the unions and found that they wanted to change the union treasurer. He asked why they wanted to make a change and was told "He's not spiritual." When asked why they thought he wasn't spiritual, the reply was "He doesn't preach." He smiled and informed them that "their Division treasurer was not a preacher either. Does that mean that he's not spiritual?" Remember that Ronald became an accountant to work for the church as a non-minister. Needless to say, the union treasurer was re-elected.

Another one of the unions needed to replace a treasurer who was returning home on permanent return. Their nominating committee caucus decided that now was the time to elect national leadership for their treasurer. However, the person that they were recommending was working at the Division office as an accountant. He had been told that his expertise was not up to the union treasurer level even though he had his M.B.A. But he was considered a hero in his country. What do you do? Ronald felt obligated to share the opinions of his staff that his performance did not support expertise at the administrative level as a union treasurer. They politely listened to him, but later voted in favor of this office accountant.

Application had been made for a work permit allowing Ronald to work in Zimbabwe. Although they had assurances that the application would be approved, he did not realize that the process would take five months. They moved out of their house in Massachusetts, the family attended Mission Institute in California while he attended the Division's Year-End meetings, and then they

Ronald & Marilyn Lindsey 1985-1990

waited in California for the anticipated approval. As mentioned earlier, they spent this time caring for a father during his last illness. With assurances that the approval would be forthcoming within weeks, the General Conference cleared them for travel to South Africa to await approval there. They had ordered a used van from Japan to be shipped to South Africa plus ordered a new car in South Africa. They had a one-time opportunity to bring into Zimbabwe two vehicles duty free when first entering the country as a temporary resident. So they traveled to Johannesburg, South Africa, near the end of January, 1986.

They boarded a KLM jumbo jet at the Los Angeles International Airport for a 10-hour overnight trip to Amsterdam. They were at the Amsterdam airport all day and departed for Johannesburg that evening for another 11-hour overnight trip. When they were landing in Johannesburg, Ronald awakened all the family so they could see their new continent. They were so sleepy that they didn't fully awaken until after they had landed. To make matters worse, it took them so long to gather all of their carry-on luggage and disembark from the plane that the shuttle to the airport had already left. This meant their walking about a quarter mile to the airport with countless carry-on luggage in the middle of the summer (Southern Hemisphere). That was their family's introduction to Africa.

Ronald's new associate treasurer and his wife met them at the airport. They were also waiting for approval of their work permit. Ronald and family found Johannesburg to be as modern as Los Angeles with huge hyper-markets with over 100 checkout cash registers. They ended up spending 1 1/2 weeks shopping and relaxing before receiving word that their work permits had been approved. Their car and van were loaded with their purchases of food and supplies that they were told were not available in Zimbabwe. Again, they were mindful that they only had this one-time opportunity to enter duty-free. The associate treasurer and their family caravanned with the four vehicles across the 600 miles to Harare, Zimbabwe.

They did not have a house waiting for them when they arrived. The Division's two-bedroom guest apartment behind the office became their home for five months. A suitable house was finally purchased and clearance was given for shipment of their household goods. They arrived almost 10 months after being packed in Massachusetts. It was like Christmas when their shipment arrived.

Within three weeks of their arrival at the Division headquarters in February, Ronald was off on his first itinerary—a three-week trip to Botswana, Tanzania, and Kenya. It was to Botswana for a hospital board meeting (Kanye Hospital); Tanzania for treasurers' seminars at three different locations throughout the country, and on to Kenya for college and union meetings. At their last treasurers' seminar in Tanzania, they had treasurers present for all of the organizational levels of the church–General Conference, Division, Union, and local church.

In April, a continent-wide youth meeting was held in Nairobi. Afterwards, an education summit was held at their college. Although relatively new to the Division, Ronald had to roll up his sleeves and tackle the challenge of fairly distributing scholarship funds (called bursaries) to workers needing advanced education. Since so many did not have the basic undergraduate degrees, obtaining any degree meant almost guaranteed promotions to higher positions. Many were also clamoring to obtain degrees offered in the United States. However, the statistics showed that a number of those sent to the United States didn't return to their home countries. Ron led out on the discussions of bursaries, and out of that meeting they developed far sweeping guidelines that focused bursaries toward degrees most needed. For example, undergraduate degrees were the priority for ministers, graduate degrees were the priority for academy teachers, and terminal degrees were the priority only for college professors. Undergraduate and graduate degrees were available both in Africa and India. Terminal degrees were available in the Philippines. They began to use the United States only as a last resort for degrees not available elsewhere. Furthermore, bursaries were given according to the needs of the organization, not according to wants. Guidelines became the basis for committee actions. This was a major improvement to the process of granting bursaries.

Ron was not one to stay in the office and was determined to get out into the field to become acquainted with operations and needs at all levels of the Division. That meant travel to institutions (hospitals, publishing houses, and clinics), schools (colleges, and secondary schools), unions, and local conferences/missions. This meant a significant amount of travel, particularly to the northern regions of the Division territory, was expensive, so their itineraries were extended, most of the time for two to three weeks. Ron discovered through these travels that the remuneration structure was not uniform throughout the Division. While a three-tier system was accepted based on education levels of the workers, he found that workers were not assigned the proper wage percentages for their position. For example, a large number of pastors were not assigned the 100 percent level although they were ordained and had been working for many years. They were penalized twice for not achieving undergraduate degrees–first by being assigned to the third tier wage factor (which was correct), and secondly by being assigned a much lower percentage rate such as 50 percent (not correct). He also found that pastors had little input on administrative executive committees that made the remuneration applications and policies. It was Ron's determination that these practices be corrected, so he started the process during his first year in the Division.

Ronald & Marilyn Lindsey 1985–1990

Near the end of 1986, he visited the various unions of the Division during their Year-End meetings for the first time. While visiting one of the unions, the newly elected national secretary of the union showed Ron his house where he was living. He quickly concluded that the house was unfit for habitation. Meanwhile, the house of the outgoing expatriate Union secretary was vacant. He determined that housing segregation could no longer be tolerated. The Union treasurer agreed with him, and the new secretary was immediately moved into the vacant house.

In January, Ron was off for another long itinerary–to a publishing meeting in Abidjan, a visit to Ethiopia, and an exploratory trip to Djibouti to establish a dental clinic as the beginning work in that country. The trip to Abidjan was his first to West Africa. He found it to be a very modern city that was a vacationland for Europeans. On that same trip he also visited Ghana and Nigeria. He had communicated to his friend, the Africa-Ocean Division treasurer, that he wanted to visit the various countries en route back to East Africa. Particularly he wanted to visit the college in Nigeria. Somehow a telex had been sent to Nigeria announcing that he was a Black American coming for a visit, wanted to visit the college, and wanted to preach! Remember, Ron does not consider himself as a preacher. Fortunately, it took so long for him to clear customs that his arranged transportation thought that he wasn't on the flight that Friday night, and left the airport. He guessed at which hotel to stay at, went walking Sabbath morning after not being able to find the location of the church or union headquarters, and stumbled onto the union headquarters and church while on his walk about the time that church was letting out. He then found the treasurer that was to pick him up and found out about the mixed communication. He did get to the college for vespers and a baptism that evening before catching his plane.

When Ron arrived in Ethiopia en route to Djibouti, the Division president met him with a letter from his family, including a letter from his son. With tears he read his letter asking that he come home. He missed his Dad at home. His travels had been too extended. That touched his heart! Knowing that others wanted to be the Division treasurer, he penned a letter of resignation to the Division president that night stating that He would rather be the associate treasurer and stay at home rather than being a traveling Division treasurer. He meant it too! However, the Division president ignored his letter. He asked the Lord for guidance, and came to the realization that he was called there to be the Division treasurer, and that he would have to be more balanced in his time at home. Their trip to Djibouti began the process of the government donating land for construction of a dental clinic in that hot, one-city country at the neck of the Red Sea.

Precious Memories of Missionaries of Color

Peace had finally come to Uganda as government leadership changed hands. It became apparent that the East African Union which served both Kenya and Uganda needed to be split between the two countries. A commission was established to evaluate the ability for a new union to exist in Uganda. They ultimately recommended it and it was approved at the Annual Council. Ron was assigned the duty of determining the distribution of assets between the two unions. His recommendations were accepted by both unions.

Planning for and establishing the framework for a new expatriate remuneration plan was started by the General Conference during 1987. It was designed to connect the expatriate allowance, or home base deposit, to the wage scale and wage factor in the home division. With expatriate allowances being the same for all expatriate workers, some workers received a much higher percentage of their home division wages in the mission field than others. The EAD was chosen as a major test base for the study. Ron had to confine his work on this project to himself and the senor accountant for payroll, also an expatriate from the North American Division. He learned all about the "spreadsheet programs" during this project.

Ron attended the Annual Council at General Conference headquarters in October. Much time was spent working with the General Conference treasury staff during this trip on the new remuneration plan. Since his first meeting was on a Thursday morning in Washington, D.C. and he had to leave Zimbabwe on the preceding Sunday due to flight schedules, he flew directly to Los Angeles to visit family in lieu of waiting at a hotel in Washington, D.C. during that time. He had figured that the extra cost of flying to Los Angeles was equivalent to the additional hotel cost and per diem that would have been incurred by staying in Washington. However, the office person who processed all travel reports reported to the Division president that Ron had presented a dishonest travel report claiming reimbursement for costs that he had not incurred, although Ron had clearly identified the costs as reconstructive travel—a practice that they always did in government travel.

While in the U.S. for Annual Council, he was asked to travel to Andrews University for an African Students Emphasis Weekend to also meet with the students attending Andrews from EAD. During a question and answer period, one outspoken student grilled him on their new bursary guidelines and practices. He explained them as they had been voted. However, the student reported back to friends within the EAD that Ron was not a friend of the Africans.

With all of the expertise Ron gained from working on spreadsheets for the new expatriate remuneration plan he expanded the detail for the Division's operating budgeting by developing detail by worker for salaries, travel expenses for new appointees, furloughed and permanent returnees. Remember that over

Ronald & Marilyn Lindsey 1985–1990

60 percent of the Division's budget was for these expenses. This detail allowed them to develop more accurate budgets for the Division operations. The 1988 operating budget, presented at the 1987 Year-End meeting, was the first budget prepared with adequate detail to back it up.

After our Division's Year-End meetings, it was customary that all of the Division officers traveled to various union Year-End meetings within the Division territory. A number of local missions were now planning to become conferences. One principle that he advocated was that their pay scales had to be corrected for all workers before they would consider their financial strength to be satisfactory for conference status. He began to see the results of his labors. Some pastors' salaries were doubled as the percentages were corrected. Since they had very little representation on the executive committees, they didn't know why that was happening. Ron stayed very much in the background.

A new policy for furlough leave was voted at the 1987 Annual Council which allowed their family to return at the end of 1987 for furlough. With the 1988 Annual Council being planned for Nairobi in October, he knew that his only opportunity for furlough would be during the months of December, 1987 through the first part of February, 1988, so they made plans without much advance notice. Their daughter had just finished the top grade of the church school in Harare. With his heavy travel throughout the year, their furlough was needed then. They traveled to California and Hawaii during that time. While in California, their children pleaded with them to allow them to return to their old school in Newbury Park to finish out the school year there. They were sure that the Southern California Conference would not allow that since they would be starting a new grade in the middle of the school year, but alas they approved the request. Therefore, Mother and children stayed behind while Dad returned to Africa alone.

After much needed rest and relaxation, he was headed back to Africa via General Conference headquarters in Washington, D.C. They were still working on the expatriate remuneration plan so he planned to spend some days there with treasury personnel. When he arrived, he was told that Elder Neal C. Wilson, General Conference president, wanted to see him. Ron had no idea why. When he met with him, Elder Wilson shared about 20 complaints that the EAD president had brought to him about Ron. Furthermore, he learned a meeting of the EAD Executive Committee, which included all Union presidents, was held during his absence to discuss these issues with them. Obviously, he was not present and didn't even know that the meeting had taken place. He methodically answered each one of the accusations. When finished, Elder Wilson asked Ron what he could do for him. Realizing that a "secret tribunal" had already been held, Ron responded, "I request that you come to Africa and chair a meeting with the EAD Executive Committee regarding these charges as soon as possible. That's the only way I can receive a fair hearing." Elder Wilson called his secretary and cleared a 1-week time block for both him and the General Conference treasurer, Elder Don Gilbert, to travel to Zimbabwe in just two weeks from then. Elder Wilson spent 2 ½ hours with Ron that day for which he will always be grateful for that time that he gave him. Following the visit by Elders Wilson and Gilbert, they all survived the event with new appreciation for the other, and Ron truly learned to "lean" upon the Lord when the going gets tough. He realized that the Lord had sent him to Eastern Africa and that he would not return home until the task that He sent him to do was finished.

Having prepared a detailed operating budget for the Division, Ron set out to develop uniform budgets with details that would see the fruits of his labor as all unions ended up with uniform budgets that he considered to be complete and fully supported.

Many trips were made to Nairobi as they planned for the Annual Council meeting to be held there in October. In addition, Ron was tasked with the responsibility to develop an EAD multimedia report for viewing at the Annual Council. It would have been too expensive to have a video production done by either of the Media Centers in the U.S. or Australia, so they opted to take slide pictures of the progress throughout the Division and incorporate them into a video presentation with narrative. Shirley Burton, Communication Director of the North American Division, agreed to take their slides, write the script, and produce the video for them. Bob Sundin, one of their senior accountants, traveled throughout the Division territory taking pictures for the report. They then met in Johannesburg (where the slides were developed) to decide which ones they would send to Ms. Burton. They were isolated in a hotel room for two days for this process. They were all happy with the resulting report that was shown at the Annual Council.

Ron's family returned to Africa in August, 1988 after the children had completed another grade at their "home" school, Conejo Adventist Elementary School in Newbury Park, California. Their daughter was now ready for the 9th grade, and their son was to enter the 8th grade. However, their Division school in Harare did not go beyond the 7th grade, so they considered having the children attend a non-Adventist Christian school in Harare. However, the school year didn't start until January, so the children were free to travel to Annual Council with them in September and October. Ron's parents also planned to meet them in Nairobi and travel back to Zimbabwe with them. Since his wife did not enjoy flying, they decided to drive to Nairobi, Kenya, and also to all of

Ronald & Marilyn Lindsey 1985-1990

the unions (except for Ethiopia) for year-end meetings after Annual Council were completed. That meant travel to Tanzania, Uganda, Malawi, and Zambia in addition to Kenya, Nairobi, was about 1,500 miles north of Harare.

The great adventure started out from Harare in mid-September with a van and cargo trailer loaded with suitcases, a porta-potty, four spare tires and fan belts, extra engine oil and diesel fuel, tool kit, and bedding. They were going to cross country borders six times during the trip. Border crossings could take as long as three hours each. Their first day (Wednesday) took them to Lusaka, Zambia, where they spent the night at the Union compound.

They left early the next morning planning to arrive at the Tanzania border before it closed that evening. Representatives from the West Tanzania Field were to meet them at the border with the necessary papers for that border crossing. However, they had a tire blow-out within an hour's travel to the border. No problem, they had spare tires. To their dismay, the mounted spare tire went flat immediately, and they didn't have the tools to mount a new tire on the rim. Ron had to hitch a ride with two tires in hand back to the nearest service (about 50 miles) leaving his family on the side of the road near dusk on a lonely highway. The same person that took Ron to the service station was kind enough to bring him back to the van with the new mounted tire. What a good Samaritan! The delay caused them to reach the border after it had closed. They had no way of communicating with the Field representatives who were meeting them there. They ended up sleeping in the van at the border gate. They found that the Field representatives had taken a bus to the border the day before, then returned to their homes when the Lindseys didn't show, but returned to the border the next day even without their ability to communicate with them. The Lord was their communicator.

After crossing the border, another of their tires was getting low. They found out that it was going bad, so they had another one of their new spare tires mounted. They now had their two representatives in the van with them as they traveled to the West Tanzania Field headquarters in Mbeya, about 40 miles from the border. They toured the office, spent some time with the officers, but had to continue their trip. It had been their plan to spend Sabbath at their East Tanzania Publishing House compound in Morogoro, Tanzania. However, the tire delays made it clear that they would have to stop somewhere en route for the Sabbath. Just within sight of the city lights of Iringa, and after dark, another tire went flat. It was in fact the same tire that was mounted at the border. They found out later that it wasn't mounted correctly. Since they now had a good mounted spare, Ron was able to change the tire, and continue to Iringa arriving about 11:00 P.M. As they traveled north, the roads became increasingly bumpy. Their luggage trailer was bouncing unmercifully. When

Precious Memories of Missionaries of Color

Ron parked at the motel that night, he noticed something dripping from the back of the trailer. Further inspection revealed that it was oil. His spare 5-gallon oil can had been punctured during the bouncing roads, and oil was covering the entire bottom of the trailer. Their soft-sided luggage that was on the bottom of the trailer was soaked in oil. They had to completely unload the trailer that night and search for solutions to clean-up the next morning. He got up early the next morning and found a supplier of sawdust that he could put in the trailer to soak up the oil. After sweeping out the soaked sawdust, he put new sawdust on the bottom to rest the soaked suitcases on for the rest of the trip. They made it to the local church in Iringa for the 11:00 service and then continued on to Morogoro after that service.

    They arrived in Morogoro about midnight, long after everyone had gone to bed, but he knew where the treasurer's home was. They graciously ushered them to the guest house for their stay of one short night. They knew next day would be a long one–the roads were full of potholes. What used to be a 6-hour trip was now a 14-hour trip without mechanical problems. They were up early the next morning, treated to a good breakfast, and were off and on their way to keep their schedule. They were to meet the Division president and his wife at the Tanzania Union headquarters in Arusha, near the Kenyan border on Sunday evening, and they were to ride with them to Nairobi on Monday. They were driving along the beautiful mountain range that contained Mount Kilimanjaro, Africa's highest mountain. It was a beautiful day, but the roads were murderous. It was a previously paved road with numerous potholes. The whole day was spent dodging the potholes staying in second gear for most of the time. By mid-afternoon, the luggage trailer's springs had had enough. One of the springs broke. Fortunately, they were near a small village that had a bus repair facility. A repairman was able to weld the spring together so that they could continue on their trip. As he pulled into the Tanzania Union president's driveway 18 hours after leaving Morogoro, he noticed again something dripping from the trailer. This time it was the spare diesel fuel can that was punctured. The sawdust that he had spread on the bottom of the trailer had kept it from spreading, but the bouncing had shaken up the sawdust so that dust was on everything in the trailer, like it had been shaken upside down. What a mess!

    The next morning they were ready to continue their trip for the remaining 60 miles to Nairobi with the Division president and his wife. Ron had previously secured the proper insurance papers through the Automobile Association for entry into Kenya, but when they arrived at the border, they were informed that his insurance papers were not adequate. He would have to obtain a bond for clearance of the van and trailer into the country. They had to call for help

Ronald & Marilyn Lindsey 1985–1990

from Nairobi. Elder Craig Newborn of the East African Union drove down in his station wagon to get them and as much of their luggage that wasn't saturated in oil and diesel fuel as they could take. They left the van and trailer parked right in front of the customs office for safekeeping. It took two days for them to secure the required bond and return to pick up the van.

Annual Council meetings were held in an amphitheater that was well suited for the meetings. Visibility was excellent without any delegate feeling distant from the head table. There was one surprise that the EAD officers faced. A special item meeting was shown on the daily schedule for Sunday specifying the EAD and Far Eastern Division (FED) officers to meet with Elder Wilson. They did not know what the agenda was, but they came to the meeting as scheduled. To their surprise, the FED officers were suggesting that they close their continent-wide academy for expatriate worker children (Maxwell Adventist Academy in Nairobi) and send their children to Far Eastern Academy in Singapore, which served the FED. Apparently the Far Eastern Academy was suffering from low enrollment, and in order to keep it going it was important to boost the enrollment by expanding to the African Divisions' expatriate workers. They had not even visited Maxwell Academy until the preceding Friday. They had just relocated Maxwell Adventist Academy from the center of Nairobi to a beautiful countryside location outside of Nairobi. The dormitories were newly constructed, and temporary buildings were in place for classrooms and administrative offices. Plans were in place for completion of a classroom complex and chapel building. The FED officers admitted embarrassment at having called the meeting because they noted facilities and location were much different than they had anticipated. They had thought that anything in Africa must have been inferior to what they had to offer in Singapore. That premise was not true.

Their EAD Year-End meetings were held in Nairobi right after completion of the Annual Council. That meant that Ron had to have completed the proposed budget prior to arrival for the Annual Council with final adjustments after verification of General Conference appropriations to the EAD. Since he had the complete budget on computer spreadsheets, he was able to complete the budget on schedule. During the Year-End meetings, his parents arrived from Huntsville, Alabama. Ron was able to introduce them to the Division's Executive Committee. Meanwhile, their children had endured a long and arduous trip to Nairobi by van. They visited Maxwell Adventist Academy and decided that they would rather stay and attend school there than return home in the van with their parents and grandparents. With their son in the 8th grade, and daughter in the 9th grade, and Nairobi being 1,500 miles from home, this decision preceeded their timetable, but they agreed to it and enrolled their children at the Academy, leaving them behind.

With Ron's parents with them, they traveled to the University of Eastern Africa in Baraton, Kenya for board meetings. They proceeded on to Uganda for year-end meetings at Bugema College for the Uganda Union. Upon returning to Kenya for East African Union year-end meetings, they had crossed the border out of Uganda and approached the Kenya border for crossing. They told them that the border was closed to vehicle travel. Travel out of the country could only be made via airplane.

There had been some political tensions between Uganda and Kenya that led to the border closing. Their visas to Uganda had already been cancelled, so they couldn't return into Uganda. They were in no man's land between the two countries. Ron pointed out that his vehicle was from Zimbabwe and there was no other way to return it to Zimbabwe. They were told that even if Ron were an ambassador, he was not going to pass through that border. Ron and his father then walked through the gate to the Kenya side to call their office in Nairobi, while his mother and wife stayed behind in the van. This was done without the knowledge of the border officials. They knew that they had to stay on the Kenya side until contact was made. The local bank was kind enough to let them use their phone to call Nairobi. The communications director for the Division was not in the office at the time, so they had to wait for his return call. As soon as contact was made, he promised to go to the government offices immediately, and asked that they wait for his report. That they did! Meanwhile, Ron's wife and mother went to the border office to check on them. When the border officer found out that they had gone to the Kenya side, he ordered his wife and mother to have them returned immediately stating that they were in Kenya illegally.

They finally received a call from Nairobi telling them that the border officials had been notified to let them through the border. With that knowledge in hand, they gladly returned to the Uganda side of the border. Their wives told them that the border officials were very upset with them and that they should respond very apologetically. They approached the office, received a tongue lashing, and then were told that they could enter Kenya. The official never told them that he had received orders to let them through, but they knew that God had intervened in their behalf. They had spent five hours at the border. Now they were destined to drive late into the night through a mountainous area to reach Nairobi in time for meetings the next day.

After the East African Union year-end meeting, they traveled on to the Southeast Union Mission in Malawi while the other officers flew to Ethiopia for their year-end meetings. They drove back across the border into Tanzania to

Ronald & Marilyn Lindsey 1985–1990

Arusha, where the union headquarters were located. From there they planned to travel to the Ngorongoro Crater where many of the African wildlife is found, then on to Morogoro for the Sabbath traveling through central Tanzania on a much improved highway. Their travel to and through the Ngorongoro Crater was outstanding. They left the Crater en route to Morogoro. Suddenly, Ron noticed the temperature gauge rising. The engine was hot. They discovered that the fan belt that they had was too small–it was the wrong size. They tried the old panty hose trick, but that didn't work either. A truck came along and was willing to pull them back to a location where a phone was available for them to call the Union office. However, it was now Friday night, and the Union office was closed. They spent the night at the entrance to a power plant in the van—Ron, his wife, and parents. Sabbath morning they were able to reach the Union's publishing director who drove in his pick-up truck to where they were. They had a large rope with them, which they used to tie the two vehicles together. The ladies rode in the tow pick-up in air conditioned comfort while Ron and his Dad rode in the towed van. They had the choice to keep the windows up and suffocate in the heat, or leave the windows down and be covered with dust. They chose the latter. When they hit potholes, the rope would break. It became shorter and shorter. When they finally arrived back in Arusha, their vehicles were only three feet apart, and his Dad and he were black with dirt from head to toe, but so grateful that they were close enough to the Union office to be towed there. Throughout all of this, they noticed that the same trailer spring that had previously been repaired was broken again. So they found a welder in Arusha on Monday morning to make a new spring for the trailer, and they took the broken spring with them. Therefore, they weren't able to leave Arusha until 4:00 A.M. on Tuesday morning. They had that dreadfully long 14-plus hour trip over bad roads to Morogoro ahead of them. They knew that the trailer springs were taking a beating, so they tried to miss as many potholes as possible. They finally reached the good road from Dar es Salaam to Morogoro at about 1:30 A.M. They had been traveling since 4:00 A.M. and were exhausted. As they were traveling on this good but dark two-land highway, Ron noticed some branches on the road. Suddenly, he realized that they were the "emergency" markers for a disabled truck ahead. Just at that time, a bus was approaching from the opposite direction, so passing on the other lane was not an option available for them. Ron jammed on the brakes. They stopped just an inch from the back of a large dump truck parked on the highway. Their van was one with a flat front and the engine between the front and back seats. In other words, there was no hood to absorb an impact. Their protecting angels had again intervened and saved their lives. They arrived in Morogoro at 3:00 A.M., 23 hours after leaving

Precious Memories of Missionaries of Color

Arusha. The next morning they were told that on the Friday night that they were supposed to be traveling through central Tanzania to Morogoro, some foreigners traveling that same highway were stopped, robbed, and murdered. The Lord used a broken fan belt and a wrong-sized spare to turn them around and send them a different way. The Lord is good!

With all of the delays that they had endured, they were beyond the time period of their visa for Tanzania. They thought that all they had to do was explain the reasons for their delays. They traveled on to Mbeya on Monday spending the night with some missionaries from the Nazarene Church. From there, they traveled to a different border that took them into Malawi. They had planned to cross into Malawi in time to change their currency into Malawi Keacha at a bank at the border town. But when they arrived at the border, the Tanzania authorities stated that they were in the country illegally (they'd heard that before) with an expired visa. The only place that they could get the visa extended was in Dar es Salaam, a full day's journey from there. They explained the reason for their delays, even showing him the broken spring from the trailer. All to no avail! After being there for two and a half hours, Ron's father went into the border office and told the officer that he was praying that he would let them get through. The officer realized that he wasn't going to get any money from them, and was intimidated by his Dad's pronouncement, so finally stamped their passports and waved them on. Really, it was the angel's intervention again that got them on their way.

The bank was closed. They had no Malawi kwacha, and their fuel supply was barely enough to get them to the secondary school in northern Malawi where they were to spend the night with missionary friends whom they had gone to school with. They had detailed instructions to get to the school, but it was now quite dark and they were in a mountainous area. They went through valleys and over hills, but not reaching the landmarks that were noted. Finally they reached a landmark, but coming from a different direction. They realized that they had taken a wrong turn that had taken them out of the way before getting to the landmark. They knew that their calculations of remaining fuel told them that they didn't have enough to reach the school. It was late at night, raining, and the dirt road was muddy. Suddenly, he felt this dragging from the luggage trailer. They found that the repaired spring had completely broken again and that the axle was pushed up against the wheel well. They spent the night in the van waiting for sunlight to do what they could with the trailer. At sunrise, Ron crawled under the trailer in the mud and decided that he would have to put on the previously replaced broken spring just to keep the axle in place until they could get to the school. What a muddy dirty job, but it got

Ronald & Marilyn Lindsey 1985–1990

done. They continued on now with low fuel looking for any gas station even though they didn't have local currency. They didn't even pass a station. They were in a remote region. They kept asking passing motorists how far it was to Lunjika Secondary School. The first told them it was 15 kilometers, and the second told them it was 20 kilometers (after they had already driven the first 15 kilometers). They hailed down a third vehicle and asked if they knew where the Lunjika Secondary School was located. The ensuing big smile on the driver's face told them that they knew because they were from the school and were taking an injured student to the hospital. They ordinarily would have gone over the mountain pass on a different road, but because of the rain they were on the road where they met the Lindseys who turned around and followed them to the next village where the driver found the person that had keys to the diesel storage tank for their local mill press engine, awakened him, and brought him to the storage facility. Furthermore, a chief's wife was in the vehicle with the injured student. She paid for the few liters of fuel needed to get them to the school. They found an outdoor shower with hot water heated by wood logs. It was the best shower that Ron had ever had. And the meal they all enjoyed was the most anticipated meal that he had eaten! They thanked the Lord for sending the "ambulance" on the road along with a chief's wife and village diesel storage tank that provided the needed fuel for them to reach their destination.

By now, the delays caused them to miss the year-end meetings for the South East Africa Union Mission, serving the country of Malawi. So they traveled directly to Lusaka, Zambia, for the year-end meetings of the Zambia Union Mission. After those meetings, they headed due west for eight hours to the "port" city of Mongo, on the banks of the Zambezi River. From there, they boarded a speed boat for a 2 1/2 hour trip up the river to their hospital near the border of Angola, Yuka Adventist Hospital, one of the remote hospitals. While driving to Mongo, they noticed that their van was losing power, and blue smoke was billowing out of the back. There were signs that the engine rings were worn down–a bad and expensive sign of repair. They told Andy Herold, the hospital's maintenance director, of their plight. He offered to drive behind them back to Lusaka just in case they needed the help. Not only did he drive with them to Lusaka, but continued all the way to their home in Harare, pulling the trailer for them since they barely had enough power to climb the ridge after crossing the Zambezi River. Their van made it to the driveway gate, and then died. They had to push it into the driveway after opening the gate. The Lord had seen to it that they got all the way home, but no further. Ron ultimately had the engine rebuilt with parts obtained from a parts store during a shopping trip to South Africa. His parents opted to stay in Zimbabwe rather than risking anymore mishaps in Africa.

His assistant treasurer for Transportation, Ken Osborn, returned to the United States the first part of 1989 after spending 12 years in the mission field (Taiwan, Hong Kong, and Africa). As he considered names for a replacement, he decided to appoint Haile Zerai, an Ethiopian Division auditor. He became the first national worker to be responsible for expatriate affairs since that office handled all new appointee, furlough, and permanent return travel for their expatriate and national workers. That was a major step forward in the nationalization of Division positions.

Since the budget detail had been expanded to include transportation costs for anticipated new appointees, furloughed, and permanent returnees by name, Ron was able to adjust timing for new appointees to allow budget flexibility and deferments to generate expense savings for the current year's budget. Land was granted to them by the government of Djibouti for the establishment of a dental clinic—the entering wedge to a previously unentered country.

A number of local missions were requesting consideration to be organized as conferences. Missions received appropriations from their higher organization while conferences did not receive appropriations for operations. Ron continued his determination that a local mission must be using the appropriate remuneration rates for each of their employees before conference status would be considered. Some of the missions met the challenge and were organized into conferences.

Meanwhile, back at Ron's office at the Division headquarters, his administrative assistant resigned due to the heavy workload. Since he was traveling frequently, an administrative assistant was necessary to keep the paperwork going. Ron's office received more mail than any other office in the Division headquarters. He called a prior administrative assistant in California, Pat Masters, who had retired at the age of 65 the middle of June. He gave her the urgent Macedonian call on July 3. She accepted for a period of one year, obtained a passport, and arrived in Harare July 22! What a miracle! She knew Ron and his work habits well, so they were able to continue without missing a beat!

They had decided as a family that one term would be their limit in East Africa since the children were soon to enter college. They did not want to be in another part of the world while the children were attending college. Therefore, while at the 1989 Annual Council, Ron made contacts with the officers of the Pacific Union Conference (they still owned their home in that region), asking if there were any possibilities of returning to the Pacific Union Conference. Ron knew that it was important to keep ties with the home region, so that you weren't forgotten when returning from the mission field. An opening was coming available due to a retirement, and that he would be considered for it. He was also approached by General Conference personnel stating that they would like for him to come to Treasury, and by Atlantic Union College personnel indicating a desire for him to return to the college. So he had three options to consider.

Ron's family had let him know that they thought that the decision to go to Africa was his decision, and they didn't have much input, so he promised them that they would all be consulted before a decision was made upon their return to the United States. Ron and his wife stopped in Nairobi while en route home from the Annual Council. Their children were at Maxwell Adventist Academy there in Nairobi, so they had arranged for the principal to bring them to the airport so that they could have a family council regarding their permanent return in 1990. Both children voted to return to Thousand Oaks, California, where they had a home and where they could continue at the school where they knew the students. Ron didn't vote, but his wife indicated an interest to return to California, where her mother and a brother were living. He too had two sisters living in California. When he received an official call in February, 1990, from the Pacific Union Conference to be the Director of their Home Health, Education Service, he accepted. Although the position was open then, they were willing to hold it open until their return during the summer.

Returning to the Division headquarters for year-end meetings presented his last opportunity to present a budget for the following year. Each year he had added more details to the supporting documentation for the budget. This year was no exception. With foreign exchange (FOREX) being so important (foreign currency was needed to purchase anything that wasn't available in the Division territory such as new automobiles and trucks, equipment, computers, appliances, etc.) and the temptation to abuse its use for personal gain, Ron developed a detailed budget just for the use of FOREX. There was more interest in that budget than the operating budget. Great effort was made to make the distribution of FOREX on an equitable basis to all unions within the EAD. He was feeling like he had accomplished his goal of providing a framework for a detailed and documented budget—a budget that would also preserve working capital.

The big event for 1990 would be the General Conference Session to be held in Indianapolis, Indiana. Although Secretariat took care of the delegates and determining how many delegates they could afford to send, Ron realized early on that they could not finance all of the delegates that were entitled to go. With the membership growing rapidly, the resulting number of delegates also grew rapidly. After determining how many they could finance, the remaining open slots were offered to lay persons who were willing to pay for their own expenses. Since such expenses required the use of FOREX—only available by policies of each respective country—the cost of attending the Session was expensive. Yet, they filled almost all of their slots with self-funded delegates. It was Treasury's responsibility to coordinate the travel plans and arrange for hotel accommodations for all delegates, both EAD-financed and the self-funded delegates. Indianapolis was the first session where accommodations were scattered around the city with bus shuttle service provided for the outlying areas. This was done so that more inexpensive motels could be used than the big hotels close to the arena where the Session was being held. What a challenge! The delegates were scattered among several outlying motels.

They realized that they were entering their last six months in Africa, and began focusing on all the things that they hadn't done during the previous four years. Ron took final itineraries to the various countries within their territory—visiting publishing houses, schools, hospitals, and union offices. He helped each union to fine-tune their budgets and to plan for maintenance needs that were so needed throughout the territories.

But he also realized that a lot of personal desires had been put on the back-burner while all energies were directed to the work. They started by spending a weekend at Victoria Falls—not just driving there to spend a few hours. Ron and his wife took a raft trip down the Zambezi River just below the falls. That trip etched a memory that will be with them always. Then they traveled to South Africa to pick up a new van that had been ordered from Japan for the Division office. They flew to Cape Town then rented a car and traveled to Heidelberg College and Bethel College. It was a beautiful drive and trip. They returned to their favorite Zimbabwean hideaway in the Nyanga Mountains for a stay in Cabin 5 (discovered for them by the Sundin family.) These activities were all part of their "goodbyes" to Eastern and Southern Africa.

Their children had returned home from school in Kenya, and they started the packing process for their permanent return to California. They decided to return through Europe via a 10 day trip to Germany, Austria, Switzerland, Italy, France, Belgium, and Luxembourg via motor home and a 2-day trip to England. They left Zimbabwe en route to Ethiopia for their final official visit to that country. They proceed on to Germany where they picked up their motor home. Since 1990 was a year of the Passion Play in Oberammergau, they were able to attend this event that is only produced every 10 years.

When they arrived in New York on their way to Indianapolis, Ron discovered the two items that he missed most from the United States. The first

Ronald & Marilyn Lindsey 1985–1990

purchases that he made were for a bag of Frito corn chips and a can of root beer, neither of which were available in Africa.

Attending the General Conference Session as a treasurer of an overseas division was certainly different from that of a North American Division union treasurer. He spent most of his time during that Session attending to the needs of their delegates. That was his business of the Session. After the session was over, they bade their delegates last goodbyes as they departed for the airport, and their family embarked on a month-long trip throughout the United States visiting family and friends they had left behind five years earlier. They gorged themselves with American food, visited amusement parks, and totally relaxed before arriving in California. Once in Thousand Oaks, the task of preparing their house for renewed occupancy kept them busy right up to Ron's first day of work and the children's first day of school.

Ron had always felt that their children would best appreciate their African experience after returning home. Their daughter, Michelle, blended well with her former classmates, and ultimately was chosen as Senior Class president just a year after returning home. However, she missed the diversity of the student body that she had become accustomed to at Maxwell Adventist Academy. Their son, Ronald II, began bragging about the number of countries and states that he had visited and found that most of his classmates had very limited travel, if any, outside of California. He enjoyed world history and geography, a first for him.

Upon their return to the United States, Ron felt that he had fulfilled the commission that God had given him. Probably the greatest gift he was allowed to give to the Eastern Africa Division was a detailed and documented budget system for the Division and its unions. The Division was financially sound, and the wages for many of the pastors in the field were corrected. Denominationally-owned housing was no longer segregated between national and expatriate workers. But most of all, he gained an appreciation for the dedication and fervor of the members in Eastern Africa for the sharing of the Gospel to that entire region in spite of limited resources and personnel. The Lord was blessing them tremendously with baptisms and church growth.

"Thank you, Lord, for allowing this humble servant to be a part of the membership growth explosions that he saw himself as evidence of the Gospel reaching throughout the world in Eastern Africa."

Raymond & Carol Cantu
1987–1994

Their desire to live and serve the people of Africa began many years before it was actualized. When Raymond and Carol Cantu married in the summer of 1969, one of their dreams was to be of help to the people of Africa. This longing stirred in them before Afrocentrism was a word. Many African Americans were beginning to awaken to the beauty of being black. Bill Cosby's documentary on *Black History; Lost, Borrowed, or Stolen* was yet to be released. Their dream was born out of something deeper than the civil rights movement of the day. The Peace Corp seemed to them to be a viable route to accomplish this aspiration. As most young couples, they became busy with the challenges of life before them, and they put the dream on the back burner for some convenient time. Seventeen years and one child later, they found that they had become trapped in the American dream of pursuing houses and land, degrees and jobs, and the illusion of happiness at home.

One summer a brother spent a part of his vacation from Saudi Arabia with them. He was in the Middle East with the Army Corp of Engineers. He spoke of the richness of the experience of living and working in another culture. He spoke of how his family values changed when seeing life from a totally different perspective. His children had different standards for their lives because of their experiences. As Winston and his wife, Anne, spoke, Raymond and Carol remembered their almost forgotten ambition to live and serve in Africa. Their dream became alive again, and they began to actively pursue a way to bring it to fruition. It was too late for the Peace Corp because they did not allow children, so they applied to their church to be missionaries. On their application

Raymond & Carol Cantu 1987–1994

they listed every job either of them had ever done. They indicated that only one of them needed to work as they had made themselves financially solvent and would only need to take care of the expenses of life there; no bills at home would need to be paid.

It took a year from the beginning of their application to the actual appointment. They had begun to believe that they would never be considered; but with the help of a friend, already serving as a union officer in Zimbabwe, their call came through. They began the most rewarding, adventurous, and memorable experience of their lives. They would both be assigned work at Maxwell Adventist Academy. Ray would be dean of young men, assistant treasurer, and teacher of history, government, and business. Carol would be dean of young women and teacher of math and Bible. As the years went by, responsibilities would include for Ray: work coordinator, driver, and maintenance. For Carol the responsibilities would include: a brief time as school nurse, one summer as cook, elementary school teacher, Spanish teacher, driver, and maintenance.

The Adventure started with Mission Institute—a six week training period to get them ready. It was excellent. They learned the history and culture of Kenya. They were prepared for the cultural difference. They had insight into what their work would be like at the school and in the community. They did not experience the culture shock they had expected because of the preparation during the Mission Institute.

They arrived at the Nairobi airport on a very cool September day and waited for nearly six hours before being picked up (in Kenya they say collected). They had to go into their luggage for warm sweaters and jackets. Their daughter Mia and their niece Marilyn, for whom they were legal guardians, made up their family. The girls had also attended Mission Institute and were therefore prepared for anything that might happen including the long wait for their ride to Maxwell Academy. The campus was under construction and their home was a temporary metal building. They quickly became acclimated to their new home and environment and began their work.

The campus had a small elementary school for the children of the staff of the Academy. Mia enrolled and loved her teacher and the other students. Marilyn, too, loved being an Academy student. The Academy had been established for the children of missionaries all over the continent. Therefore, they had students from all over the world whose parents were working all over Africa. They were in awe of the contributions the families were making to the church and to Africa. There were medical missionaries, clerical, engineering, disaster relief, publishing, and many more whom they saw as on the front line of the work. They saw themselves as support staff and felt privileged to have a part

Precious Memories of Missionaries of Color

of the vast work that missionaries were doing all over Africa. Many countries in Africa were at war; many suffered devastating malaria and other diseases; yet the parents of the students were there in harms way dutifully carrying out their responsibilities.

The most memorable time there (and there are so many that they cannot all be told) was the impact of the Rwanda massacre. Kenya was considered one of the most politically stable countries of the world. Many other nationals flocked to Kenya to escape turmoil in their homes. Therefore, the academy had many nationals from all over Africa, but a large population from Rwanda. War and unrest had been going on years before it came to a head in 1994. They received word that the Massacre was taking place during the Easter vacation. Missionary students had left but most of the Rwanda students had not gone home. The Rwanda students on the campus were the first to report news of their family members being either dead or missing. They then heard that missionaries' families were missing and some were presumed dead. This was a time of trouble as never had been seen by any of them. They could not imagine what the Bible prophecy of a time of trouble could be like if this were not it.

The Cantus held prayer vigils on the campus and the staff in their homes. They had individual prayer sessions. They were proud of the Adventist Church and the United States government. As they listened to the BBC and the Voice of America they heard of the heroic measures the US government was taking to save Americans and others caught in the violence. They heard also and could see first-hand the work of the Adventist church in also rescuing many Adventists and others who would have perished but for the work of the Church. The newspaper in Kenya ran stories of the work of Adventists. They were excited and bursting with pride to be members of the Adventist Church and to be Americans.

Weeks after the start of the massacre, two Maxwell students had not been accounted for. So while they were happy to see many return and to hear of rescues, they continued to pray and felt burdened about the two missing students. One was an American and the other was Rwandan. There was excitement when they heard that the American was found in another country and would soon return, but there was no word about the Rwandan. Some students suggested that they stop their prayer vigils and get back to life as usual. No one wanted to admit that they believed he must have been killed, but they all knew this was a real possibility. In their own home, they kept a prayer journal. They recorded their prayers and the answers to them. For some reason, that they hate to admit, they had not placed the request for this student's return in the journal. Perhaps it was because all of the prayers in the journal had been

Raymond & Carol Cantu 1987–1994

answered and in their human reasoning, they didn't want the payer journal to have any unanswered prayers. Now, with the hope of this student's return seeming impossible, they decided to put his name in the journal and to kneel in heartfelt prayer. They knew that God was able to see this boy, dead or alive. They wanted so desperately for the boy to be alive, but they needed closure so that each of them individually could deal with life as it needed to be and the campus could get back to whatever the new normal would be. Before they could get up from their knees in prayer, there was a knock on the door. The academy principal was personally going to each home on the campus with the news that the boy had been found alive. He would be returning back to campus in a few days. The joy in their hearts and on the campus was indescribable! "Before they could call, God had answered."

Most Missionary tours of service are six years, but theirs was seven. Had they returned home after the sixth year, their daughter Mia would have completed one year of high school in the U.S. She loved Maxwell Academy, and all of her friends were there. They extended one year to give her the opportunity to graduate from Maxwell.

The seven years gave them the opportunity to understand the Bible more. The two rainy seasons a year taught them what it really means to experience the former and latter rains. Wearing sandals all year and having the dust and mud on their feet every day, gave a new understanding of the ordinance of humility. Living with thorn trees that have thorns the size of daggers gave a new view of the crown of thorns. Having cobras found in their home and bandits on the campus helped them personalize Psalm 91. Knowing that family and friends back home were praying for them made the hymns, especially hymn 505, very dear. They learned to garden, to cook healthfully from scratch, and to make all kinds of natural teas and natural remedies. Most of all, they learned to rest secure and peacefully in the arms of their Lord.

The lessons are too many to tell, the friends are too numerous to name, the experience was too wonderful to reveal. They are forever grateful to God and to their church for allowing them this life changing time that has made each of them more patient, less materialistic, and more loving of all God's children. The Cantus are who they are today because of being missionaries from September, 1987 until June 1994. Their home looks like a museum with all of the artifacts they brought home with them to remind them of this precious period in their lives.

Precious Memories of Missionaries of Color

The Cantu's house

Mrs. Cantu

The Cantu family

Raymond & Carol Cantu 1987–1994

Aunt Letty, Marilyn and Mia and their neighbors

Precious Memories of Missionaries of Color

Ray and Carol Cantu

Ray teaching Sabbath School

Raymond & Carol Cantu 1987–1994

Mia's graduating class–1994

Precious Memories of Missionaries of Color

Mia's graduating class—1994

Mia's graduating class—1994

Raymond & Carol Cantu 1987–1994

Mia's graduating class–1994

Neighbors visiting the Cantu's home

Mia with missionary boy from Rwanda

Precious Memories of Missionaries of Color

Raymond & Carol Cantu 1987–1994

Dr. Westney visiting with neighbors

Precious Memories of Missionaries of Color

After church at the Maxwell Academy

47

ANITA S. (MORELAND) JAMES
1992–1997

It all began in the summer of 1992 when Anita received a letter from the principal in Ebeye, Marshall Island. Anita had served as a student missionary from 1986 to 1987, and the principal indicated that he needed missionaries for the upcoming year. Anita went around to family and friends trying to convince them to go. As people gave her one excuse after another, she would get upset and ask, "What kind of Christian are you?" Then it finally dawned on her, "This letter came to you Anita." The Lord is not calling them, but you." She then called the Adventist Volunteer Service department at the G.C. to inform them of her interest in returning to Ebeye; however, upon learning that accounting was her major in college, they suggested that she go to Palau Mission Academy (PMA) in Koror, Palau, because they needed an accounting teacher. Although she enjoyed her experience in Ebeye and looked forward to returning, she decided to accept the call to Palau where the Lord was leading.

In light of the fact that it was only two months before she had to leave, she had to work hard and fast to raise $1,400 to pay for her airfare. She began soliciting funds from family, friends, and Adventist churches in the metro Atlanta area. Her cousin played the piano for some churches on Sunday, so he encouraged her to go there to solicit donations and there were generous contributors. She still didn't have quite enough money, so she went to the Conference office and requested a meeting with the president to see if they would also contribute. Talk about faith, while waiting, she offered a word of prayer then called the G.C. and informed them that she would be sending them the money for her ticket. God acted on her faith by leading the conference to give her the balance of what she needed.

Precious Memories of Missionaries of Color

At the orientation in Hawaii, the missionaries were being introduced in groups by the island to which they were going. They called out the twelve individuals who were going to the SDA elementary school. Then they went on to say, "There is one brave soul who is going to PMA." In her mind she was asking herself, "What are they talking about, 'One brave soul?'" What in the world had she gotten herself into? It turns out that some students had beaten up the dean in the previous year. As a matter of fact, there were a number of violent acts committed at the school. She did begin to worry a little, but it all passed away because she knew God called her; therefore, He would take care of her.

It was AWESOME! Had she not gotten married, she would still be there today. As expected, she had nothing to fear because God had everything under control so that she might perform the mission to which He called her. She was called to teach accounting and computers, but she ended up teaching those two classes along with vocal choir, bell choir, band, physical education, and biology. She also served as vice-principal her last three years which meant running the academy while the principal ran the elementary school in the city. So, please note, if you're ever interested in mission work, be FLEXIBLE and ready for anything. Her call to PMA was for two years, but each year she found herself adding another year until it became a total of five years. What caused her to extend her stay each year? Well, it was a combination of things. Her students, their families that had become her family, the church members, the beauty of the island, and the pressing need to spend her life making a difference. It was truly her home away from home. Whenever she would leave Palau for a visit home, she would cry because she feared the devil would not allow her to return safely to share her experience. When she would return to Palau from the states she would cry because she would fear the devil would not allow her to return safely to continue the work that God had already begun.

The academy was located out in the country, sitting on top of a hill overlooking the Pacific Ocean where there is always a cool breeze. The residents there watched a number of beautiful sunsets almost daily. It was initially a boarding school for grades 9 to 12, but due to various circumstances, it became a day academy for grades 7 to 12. The students were not only from Palau, but from Yap, Korea, the Philippines, Japan, Taiwan, Guam, Hawaii, and the mainland USA. Anita has more stories than time allows, so she'll share one with you now.

Bettlenut chewing is a part of the Palauan culture. It's a green nut that is stuffed with lime and wrapped in pepper leaf. All this together gives the chewer a buzz (high); therefore, it's considered a form of a drug. For this reason, students were not permitted to chew bettlenut or have it in their possession. Because

Anita S. (Moreland) James 1992-1997

this is a part of their culture some of the students started chewing when they were young. They informed Anita that they would chew the nut until it got soft enough for their older family members to chew.

One student got caught with this bettlenut and the faculty was to hold a board meeting to decide what to do with him for breaking the school rule. On the day prior to the meeting, the student approached Anita after supper with a concern of what would happen to him. Anita expressed how this saddened her and she asked him if he believed in prayer. After saying, " yes," she told him that was what he should do when he returned to the dorm and get the guys there to do the same. He shouted out, "Thank you Ms." as he ran to the dorm for evening worship. During worship in the girl's dorm that night, the girls talked with her about the situation. They expressed how much the school means to them and the vital role it plays in protecting them and making them better people. They asked, "If the school gives up on us Ms., who do we have?" They ended worship with a season of prayer.

At the faculty meeting the next day, Anita let everyone express their position concerning the matter first. It was difficult for her to be quiet with some of the things she heard because of her personal view of their purpose there. When her turn came around, she stated, "This is not an Adventist school—but a mission school. We are here to teach these young people what God desires of them. They were not raised in Adventist homes. Where as we are here to enforce what is being taught at home. If we are honest with ourselves, we are all struggling with something in our own lives that we know that we should not be doing. It is some form of addiction for us just as this bettlenut is for the student. Who are we to act as God/Judge? Who benefits by our putting him out of school?" She then went on to share with them the letters that the girls wrote that night after worship. Thanks to the working of the Holy Spirits on their hearts, it was voted that the student would not be put out of school. Upon hearing the results, the entire campus was elated and expressed their joy in seeing how God answered their prayers. This student got into no more trouble, as a matter of fact, he became a model student and went on to graduate from PMA in 1995. He is living currently in Denver, Colorado.

The phrase "Positive Mental Attitude" is what the faculty and students fondly stated what P.M.A stood for. Anita shares with you the following article written in the school paper by one of the sophomores.

"Many people think that Palau Mission Academy or PMA is not a good school, but it really is. They think it's bad because it's far and there aren't that many students in attendance. What they don't know is that very characteristic makes PMA a unique school.

Precious Memories of Missionaries of Color

Students get individual attention from teachers and build great relationship with friends. We're like a family here! We go on field trips, hikes, participate in the various clubs, and other fun activities with each other. We even sing and play sports together. We all hang with each other because we know we can trust and support one another in times of need.

Since PMA is a Christian school and its purpose is to provide students with a well rounded education that meets their spiritual, academic, physical, and social needs, it is easier to learn here. Here students can concentrate on school and are not distracted.

PMA's aim is to introduce all students to Jesus Christ, to invite them to accept Him as Lord and Savior, and to provide opportunities for Christian service in the immediate and wider community. Also to provide a solid college preparatory curriculum and to train the student to do their best in every activity they undertake. PMA students develop an appreciation of the rewards of physical labor and exercise. They are encouraged to treat everyone with consistent kindness."

By Regan Belechel

This student maintained high honors, was always a model student and went on to graduate from PMA in 1998. He attended Pacific Union College in California.

The call to Palau may have ended, but the connection, the love, the relationships, the memories and the mission are forever. Anita and the students fondly reminisce about their first Disney musical production at the community college, the years they won the spelling bee and the science fair competitions, the outreach programs, the overnight campouts under the full moon, and much more. But as she stated earlier, time will not allow her to share all the wonderful moments of serving as a missionary. You've got to take that leap of faith for yourself. To this day, she still keeps in touch with former students and church members. They solicit prayers for one another and send words of encouragement. It's been a thrill being able to visit with a number of them in the cities in which they now live:

Vence Beches class of '93 with the U.S. army in **Hawaii**; *Glenda Ngiramolau-Techur* class of '97 wife and mother of two with the U.S. navy in **Jacksonville, FL** who is currently stationed in Guam; *Joey Anson* a computer engineer in Miami FL; *Jennifer Anson* class of '94 a psychology grad student in **Miami FL**. (She came to Atlanta for my wedding which was way cool); **Phadra Ueki** a college student whose music program was cancelled at the Adventist college in the Philippines and who is now residing in **Virginia**; *Clyde Napoleon* class of '95 a hardworking father in **Denver Colorado**.

Anita S. (Moreland) James 1992-1997

Thanks to cell phones and email, she has been able to keep in contact with many others in Texas, Hawaii, and Palau. Just this summer, one church member from Palau living in North Carolina met her mother and aunts at camp meeting and surprised her with a phone call. It was great hearing her voice again. Anita remembers the year she got baptized and she remembers meeting her brother the year when he came out to do a week of prayer and speak for graduation. It is a small world after all. And when it comes to this Adventist family, it's even smaller. It's an indescribable feeling when you see the people you once told, "See you in heaven if I don't get to see you again here on earth."

Anita never thought she would do church work. As a matter of fact, she went so far as to state, "I will never work for the church." And yet, she served one year as a student missionary in Ebeye Marshall Island, then five years as a missionary in Koror, Palau, and now she is on her seventh year with the General Conference Auditing Service (GCAS). Her life adds a whole new meaning to the phrase, "Never say Never." We may have our plans, but God may have another plan. Whose plan are you living out today?

Presently, Anita S. (Moreland) James is the District Director of the Southeast Office in Orlando, Florida.

Precious Memories of Missionaries of Color

PALAU

Palau Mission Academy

Anita S. (Moreland) James 1992-1997

At orientation in Hawaii

Graduate of PMA

Precious Memories of Missionaries of Color

Yearbook Staff–1993-1994

Vocal Choir–1995-1996

Anita S. (Moreland) James 1992–1997

The Best of the Choir

The Bell Choir

Precious Memories of Missionaries of Color

Bell Choir Rehearsal at the dorm—1994-1995

SCHOOL OUTING—Nothing like fresh coconut milk

Anita S. (Moreland) James 1992-1997

Letting down my hair with a couple of the sophomores

Church and School group take an outing to one of the rock islands.
Anita with cap on backwards.

Precious Memories of Missionaries of Color

The Church Choir–1992-1993 Anita is in the center

Anita S. (Moreland) James 1992-1997

Anita and Giesher singing at a wedding reception held at the Academy

Anita with Felix

Precious Memories of Missionaries of Color

Felix Charfauros, Jr. and Anita. She says that he stole her heart.

Anita S. (Moreland) James 1992-1997

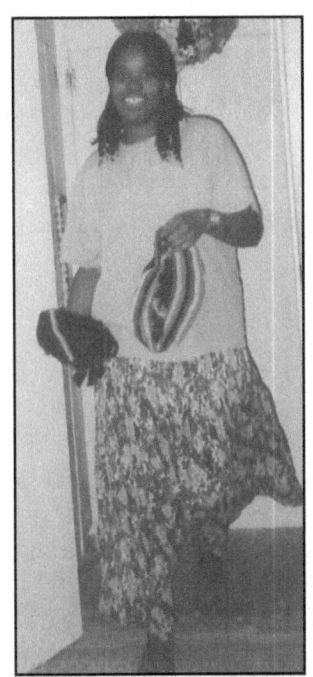

Anita before... And after
Her transformation into an island girl!

Students and teacher who said goodbye to Anita at the airport her first year

48

ELDER BENJAMIN & DR. JANICE BROWNE 2001–2005

On January 1, 2001 Ben was resting peacefully in his bed at his residence in Goodlettville, Tennessee. His wife, Janice, and her father had just returned from the family residence in Birmingham, Alabama and were relaxing in the den. The telephone rang at 10:45 P.M. The caller said, "This is Elder Ted Jones from the General Conference. Could I please speak with Elder Browne?" After exchanging greetings Elder Jones indicated that he was making an inquiry for the General Conference. He wanted to know if Ben would be interested in serving as the President of the Ethiopian Union Mission. Ben was at a loss for words. Elder Jones told Ben that if he was interested that he should send his CV as quickly as possible.

On January 17, 2001, the General Conference Appointees Committee voted their call to serve in the land of Ethiopia and Djibouti. Five days later they met Elder Jones at Washington-Dulles Airport and they were on their way to Addis Ababa, Ethiopia.

Long before they arrived in Ethiopia the Lord had been preparing them. Ben's wife's sister, Stephanie, reminded Janice of the time when she celebrated her sixteenth birthday and prayed that she would one day be a missionary. On January 23, 2001, the prayer was answered when Elder Ben and Janice arrived in Ethiopia.

The first thing that Ben was impressed to do after arriving was to pray and ask the Lord to be the President of the Ethiopian Union Mission. He realized that human administration is not capable of directing a divinely inspired church.

Elder Benjamin & Dr. Janice Browne 2001–2005

This is not my church to administer; it is the Lord's church to administer. Christ said, "Upon this rock I build my church…" Matthew 16:18.

Every morning when Ben arrived at the union office, he bowed down beside his desk and asked the Lord to be the President and he thanked Him for the opportunity to be His servant. When he prayed before meetings, in the churches and in public, he asked the Lord to be the President of the union. The members of the union knew that he wanted the Lord to be their President.

His wife, Janice, Dr. Kedede Daka—the Union Secretary, Elder Ted Jones and Ben arrived in Ethiopia on January 23, 2001 at 3:00pm. The next morning they went to the office of the Ethiopian Union Mission. The union staff was busy preparing for the Union Session that was to begin in two days. Members from around the union were at the office preparing for the session. It is impossible to express in words the sense of responsibility that was experienced. He knew that they needed the Lord to be their president.

Following the union session, the Union Executive Committee convened. Ben had chaired conference sessions in the South Central Conference, but he had to admit that he was very apprehensive about chairing this union committee. The night before the meeting, Ben prayed for hours. Early that morning the voice that comforted Abraham, Moses, and many others spoke to him and said, "It will be all right." And, it was all right! And, it has been all right for the four years that they have served in Ethiopia. The Lord has been the President and He has allowed them to witness His powerful presence.

From February, 2001, through February, 2002, Ben made four trips from the United States to Ethiopia. Finally on February 12, 2002 he was placed on the payroll of the Ethiopian Union Mission. Janice was working to complete her studies at Andrews University. She returned to Ethiopia with her mother, Dr. Mildred P. Johnson, on February, 2003. In April, they returned to the United States to see Janice Ann Johnson Browne receive the Doctor of Philosophy in Leadership from the School of Education at Andrews University.

Ben has experienced many evidences of the working of the Holy Spirit in Ethiopia. In March of 2002, the East African Division conducted meetings in all of the unions in the division. The purpose for the meetings was to promote the division's program. The meetings in the Ethiopian Union Mission were conducted at the Ethiopian Union College. At this meeting, they witnessed the power of the Holy Spirit as they have never experienced it before or after. All of the 230 plus ministers in the union were invited to the meeting. There had been a crisis in the union and the result was division between many workers. The Holy Spirit started moving and individuals started asking one another for forgiveness. Brother went to brother and asked for forgiveness and issues were settled. On Sabbath there was rejoicing, unity, fellowship, and rededication. The Lord, the true President of the Ethiopian Union Mission, had brought the union to the place where He could use it as He had never used it before. The persons that came from the East African Division and the workers in Ethiopia agreed that God had visited His servants. What happened at this meeting spread throughout the union and there was great rejoicing for what God had done. They all left knowing that they had been in His presence.

In August, 2002, Ben experienced what can happen when the ministry and the laity cooperate with the Holy Spirit. The lay members and the field (conference) administration organized a unique plan to witness. Fifty-one teams of two people each agreed to leave their farms and families for six weeks to witness and give Bible studies. Their friends and families agreed to care for their responsibilities and farms. At the end of the six weeks they agreed to bring the ones that wanted to be baptized to a central location for baptism. Elder Browne was asked to conduct a four-day reaping meeting [these were short meetings that were held after the seed was sow (members giving Bible Studies, etc.) This was like the harvest to bring members in the church]. More than seven thousand attended the meetings. On the third and fourth days of the meetings, 692 souls were baptized and 240 others made commitments and were later baptized. These laymen that left their homes and families ask for no salary or benefits from the field or the union. The sacrifice was made because or their love for the Lord. They were only able to carry with them the book *Desire of Ages*. They will forever be thankful to the Lord for allowing them to serve Him with His faithful servants in Tula, Ethiopia.

As a result of this experience an evangelist fire started in Ethiopia. The fires of evangelism are burning in many parts of the land. During the Year of Evangelism (2004), 12,437 souls were baptized in the Ethiopian Union Mission. They thank the Lord for allowing them to witness some of His mighty power and grace.

Many ministers and teachers in the Ethiopian Union Mission needed additional educational training. Ben would like to share with you how the Lord addressed this situation. His father-in law, Elder Washington Johnson, died in November 2002. Ben left Ethiopia to attend his funeral. Elder Ward Sumpter, the Secretary of the Southern Union Conference in the United States, visited their family. During his visit, Elder Sumpter asked him what he could do to help God's work in Ethiopia. Ben explained that they were trying to upgrade their ministers and teachers and asked him if he could assist ten workers. He said, "No, we will assist twenty-five." The Southern Union Conference has provided $50,000.00 for this project. This effort by the Southern Union has

Elder Benjamin & Dr. Janice Browne 2001–2005

provided two years of additional college training for twenty-five workers in the union.

Traveling in Ethiopia, Ben has seen many churches, schools, and institutions that God used missionaries from far away lands to open. Today, a new missionary has emerged in Ethiopia and in other parts of Africa. These new missionaries are the Global Mission Pioneers. They are Ethiopian laypersons that have left their homes and families and have moved to areas that the church has not entered. In the Ethiopian Union Mission twenty-three teams of two persons each went to work in areas that the Seventh-day Adventist Church had not reached. Future generations, if the Lord delays His coming, when they travel in Ethiopia, will ask how this church, school or institution got started at this location. The response will be "God used an Ethiopian."

During the four years that they have served in Ethiopia they have seen 30,740 persons baptized and 160 churches and companies started. The Ethiopian Adventist College enrollment has increased from 117 to 340. During these four years the tithe coming from the churches in Ethiopia has doubled. Praise the Lord!

During the four years that Ben has served in Ethiopia he has seen the Lord intervene in every challenge. He knows that God will direct this church if they allow Him. Ben has seen God work in this church. He has seen God correct situations that were impossible for human beings to change. During morning worship he has called the union staff together for special prayer and they have seen their prayers answered within hours. Committees have their place but committees can't replace prayer.

The Brownes thank the Lord for the unique opportunity that He extended to them to serve Him in the Ethiopian Union Mission.

ELDER VICTOR & CANDICE HAREWOOD 2002–PRESENT

How happy we were to get a Mission Report from the frontline! Elder Victor and Candice Harewood write to us from Emirates and Oman. The Harewoods left their four grown daughters and four grandchildren in the United Kingdom to serve the people in Emirates and Oman. Their story was written by Rema Latouche who is presently being blessed by their ministry. She writes:

What a privilege and honour it is to write about the two people who have transformed my life and made it richer with the presence of God Almighty. (It is God's blessings and the working of the Holy Spirit in Rema's life that has made a difference.)

Rema states that she has been associated with the SDA Church in Dubai since 2001 and apart from attending the Sabbath Service with her husband, whenever her work permitted, she did not have much to do with the Church at that point in time. The reasons were that she was not an Adventist, nor a Christian. Her husband suggested that she attend the Service since she was in search of answers in her life and there was this constant restlessness for peace–the peace which she had not yet found in her life. She belonged to a staunch Hindu Family where Christians, Christianity, and for that matter, any other religion were taboo.

Having studied in the Convent, she was familiar with Christianity and its tenets. She was able to further this knowledge while studying for her Masters in English Literature. She had often visited the Catholic churches and had always felt a strange kind of quietness.

Elder Victor & Candice Harewood 2002–Present

When visiting the SDA Church in Dubai, which then had a total membership of about 50-60 people, she felt a strange sense of peace—a feeling which was strange to her. The pastor at that time was taking study-leave in the States to further his education. She very desperately wanted religious guidance and on inquiry was told that the new pastor would be coming in soon.

She did not have to wait long. She was informed where the new pastor Victor O. Harewood was staying. She contacted him and was visiting with him an hour later.

When she met Pastor Harewood, she was impressed with his calm disposition. There was an aura of peace about him that she has yet to fathom. She has yet to come across a religious guide who is so very human but who is so distanced from worldliness. She spent about two hours with him and when she left the lobby, she was a changed person. She had a purpose in life and her only goal was to get baptized into the faith. She has finally found peace, and her Destiny.

The United Arab Emirates (U.A.E) is not an easy place to work in when it comes to caring for a religion other than Islam. U.A.E is an Islamic country in the Middle East. It consists of seven independent states—Abu Dhabi, Dubai, Sharjah, Ajman, Ras Al Khaimah, Fujairah, and Umm Al Qaiwain. Even though they are independent states governed by independent rulers who are called Sheikhs, these Emirates formed the United Arab Emirates and the capital city is Abu Dhabi. The ruler of Abu Dhabi is the President of the U.A.E. As an Islamic country, the rulers and the community are very tolerant towards other religions.

Pastor Harewood and his wife, Sister Candice Harewood, came to Dubai in July 2002. Since then they have relentlessly worked towards the development of the Church. Like Rema, many have found their haven under their guidance. The Harewoods originally come from the Caribbean, Victor comes from Barbados and Candice is from Jamaica. They started their ministry in England as laymen (not ordained in the ministry.) while he worked as an engineer. Because he felt he was called by God, he attended Newbold College in England to prepare for the Ministry. After graduation, he accepted a position from the New England Conference to be the Assistant Publisher Director, and after sometime he became the Church Ministries Director for the Conference. Victor and Candice have given a total of 28 years in ministry with Candice taking the supportive role with Children and Women ministries.

As Rema writes this she is not only expressing her views and opinions about Pastor and Sister Harewood as spiritual leaders, but reflecting the opinion of all those who have come in contact with them–irrespective of religion and nationality.

Precious Memories of Missionaries of Color

Having been associated with them for the past three years, both personally and professionally, Rema has always been awed by their dedication to the Lord. They are living examples of Advent believers, and the Seventh-day Adventist faith is richer because of people like them.

The Dubai Church as of today has more than 94 members (200 people meeting) and it is growing by the week. Rema attends the Sharjah Church due to work constraints, in spite of the fact that she lives and works in Dubai, and its membership has grown to 45. Likewise, our Abu Dhabi group, Al Ain group and the group in Ras Al Khaimah, too, is seeing good growth. Apart from the UAE, Pastor makes constant trips to Oman.

As an Indian, her outlook on life in general has always been different from the average Indian. She has always been amazed at the ease with which Pastor and Sister Harewood communicate and manage to build a strong bond with all of them.

The congregation consists of a good cross-section of many groups of people: Philippinos, Indians, West Indians, Africans, British nationals, Russians, and Indonesians to name a few—making it difficult to fulfill the demands of all and impacting all of their lives. Rema considers their ability to bring oneness to the group to be the greatest strength that Pastor and Candice bring to their community. They are Indians amongst Indians, Philippinos amongst Philippinos, Pakistanis amongst Pakistanis and English amongst British. The Sharjah church, consisting predominantly of Urdu speaking people, has quite a lot of singing in Urdu with the eastern musical instruments. It is a treat to the eye to see Pastor and Candice (Candice dressed in the traditional Salwar Kameez!!) taking part with them and enjoying themselves in the praise of God Almighty. This encourages others also to join in. Their enthusiasm has paved the way for many to take part in the services irrespective of language or nationality. They are constant reminders of the fact that there are no barriers when one is praising and worshiping God. It is the love of the Lord that matters and the rest is trivia.

While Pastor is busy in his pastoral work, Sister Candice is busy in her women's and children's ministries. They have the Pathfinders going at full swing and the numbers are increasing by leaps and bounds.

Their influence on the lives of all who come in contact with them is so evident that they have people willing to do anything for them. They are a part of each family. Any event in any home, be it a birthday party, a marriage anniversary or a simple gathering is incomplete without them. They are the model couple, the model parents, and the model workers.

Rema suggests that she has always had the impression that workers of this kind are those people who are chosen to propagate the faith of Christ.

Elder Victor & Candice Harewood 2002–present

Correcting herself she says that such workers are those people who teach us to see God in ourselves and in others and who teach us to lead our lives the way Christ wanted us to. They are people with love abounding—our parents, our guides, our friends, and above all they are Pastor Victor and Sister Candice Harewood.

May each Adventist Congregation be blessed with persons like the Harewoods because the Dubai Church is not planning to give them up so easily. There is much work to be done there and they need them around to complete it for them. They need the Harewoods to guide and instruct them—making it possible for them to achieve much and get a little closer to God.

May God Almighty help them in their work and may they touch millions of lives because the people whose lives they touch are richer for it. Rema is grateful for having them in her life and she considers herself fortunate that she has the opportunity to learn and experience life the Adventist way. She owes so much in her life to them. As she continues to serve God, she will praise the Lord for bringing Pastor and Candice into their lives because it has made all the difference.

The Harewoods are truly a blessed couple and the abundant blessing of the Lord is upon them always. This blessing is the reason why a Catholic friend of theirs called Pastor Harewood from miles across from Canada to request him to pray for her since she feared she had to go for a second session of radiotherapy. She feared her cancer had resurfaced. After the prayers, she went back to the hospital and it was revealed that every thing was clear! After one year she is hale and hearty—thank God and Pastor for his prayers. A possible cancer threat for her sister-in-law was cleared after Pastor prayed for her—again across the nations in Canada. Apart from these, Rema feels that she is the walking, living example of how a person's life can be changed with the presence and prayers of Pastor and Candice. Every day of Rema's life is a miracle, a miracle of the presence of the Holy Spirit—the presence she has achieved through the guidance of Pastor Harewood and Candice. Five pages will not suffice to tell the story of how many lives Pastor and Candice have touched during their ministry in the Middle East. Ms. Latouche hopes that one day the Harewoods will give their permission for her to write their biography. Their lives are truly an example of persons making a difference in this world and have led many misled souls to Christ.

Many thanks to Rema Latouche for her personal testimony of the affect the Harewoods have had on her life. To God be the glory!

—Rema Latouche

Black Seventh-day Adventist Mission Service Honor Roll

1. Abney, Benjamin and Celia
2. Alexander, Dolly
3. Aldridge, Sherman
4. Andrews, Robert and Cordelia
5. Antonio, Lloyd and Etta
6. Atkins, Edna
7. Banks, Nathaniel G.
8. Battle, Maurice and Esther
9. Bayne, Carlyle M. and Erma
10. Benson, George
11. Blake, Dr.
12. Boynton. Samuel
13. Branch, Thomas H,
14. Brantley, Paul Sr. and Alice
15. Browne, Benjamin and Janice
16. Browne, L. W.
17. Bryant, Paul Alonzo and Patricia
18. Bullard, Howard and Lois
19. Bullard, Naomi
20. Burke, Karen A.
21. Burns, Robert and Cynthia
22. Bushell, Art and Hope
23. Bushell, Ken

Precious Memories of Missionaries of Color

24. Cantrell, Theodore and Frankie
25. Cantu, Ray and Carole
26. Carter, Robert H. and Rose
27. Cartwright, Harry and Beverly
28. Cassimy, Clyde Peter and Barbara
29. Cherenfant, J. M.
30. Conner, Chauney L. and Bernadine
31. Crowder, Donald L.
32. Daniels, Lucius
33. Davis, Danny L. and Betty
34. Dent, Carl Dr.
35. DeShay, Samuel and Bernice
36. Deshommes, Pierre C. and Jocelyn
37. Dulans, Irwin
38. Edgecombe, James & Gerilean
39. Flyn, Bruce
40. Forde, Ronald and Dorothy
41. Francis, Danforth and Vera
42. Garbutt, Art
43. Gibbons, Sydney
44. Gibson, Boyd
45. Giddings, Phillips E. and Violet
46. Gooding, Samuel and Elita
47. Gordon, Caludine Ann
48. Gordon, Oswald and Thelma
49. Goulbourne, Alvin and Lucy
50. Graham, Greta
51. Green, Alfonso and Estele
52. Gunther, Eula
53. Hamilton, Leroy
54. Hammond, James and Carol
55. Harewood, Victor and Candice
56. Harris, Helene
57. Honore, Simon
58. Howell, Caddie
59. Howell, Glenn and Winnie
60. Hubert, Lucille
61. Hudgins, George and Jean
62. Hughes, David and Eunice

Black Seventh-day Adventist Mission Service Honor Roll

63. Hyatt, J. M.
64. Jackson, Caddie
65. Jackson, Samuel and Sarah
66. Jeanniton, Alcega and Veronica
67. Joachin, Roland and Marie Solange
68. Johnson, Johnny and Ida
69. Jones, Ruby
70. Jones, Ted and Esther
71. Jordan, Gertrude
72. Keith, Dennis and Dorothy
73. Knight, Anna
74. Laurence, J. P.
75. Lavender, John
76. Lawrence, E. A.
77. Lee, Harold and Barbara
78. Lewis, Celeste
79. Lindsay, Ronald A.
80. Mackson, Gloria
81. McDonald, Tim and Beverly
82. McKenzie, Monica
83. McKenzie, Roland
84. Miller, C.
85. Mitchell, Leland and Lottie
86. Mottley, Alvin
87. Mouse, Gerald
88. Mouzon, Hector
89. Muze, Mishael
90. Nelson, Ron
91. Newborn, Craig
92. Newton, Leonard and Ora
93. Parkinson, Lester
94. Patterson, James
95. Patterson, Robert and Barbara
96. Pieere, Max
97. Pitts, John C. and Sarah
98. Presley, Robert S.
99. Preston, Louis and Janice
100. Richards, Earl and Ann
101. Ricketts, Ray and Joan

Precious Memories of Missionaries of Color

102. Robinson, William R.
103. Rogers, John
104. Simons, Donald B.
105. Simons, Richard W. and Ruth
106. Smith, Marjorie
107. Smith, Ruth Faye (David)
108. Soulter, Henry T.
109. Stafford, Randy
110. Tate, Douglas
111. Thomas, Clarence III and Carol
112. Thomas, Edna Pearlie Atkins
113. Thomas, Lindsay and Evelyan
114. Troy, Carmelita
115. Troy, Owen A. and Ann
116. Vallery, Guy
117. Vanderburg, Herman and Philippa
118. Washington, James and Sarah
119. Whaley, Walton S. and Leola
120. Williams, DeWitt and Margaret
121. Witts, Gerald and Beverly
122. Word, Larry
123. Wright, Ronald J.
124. Yorke, Gosnel and Dorean
125. Young, Theus

Finally, mention must be made of the scores of Black student missionaries who have given a year and sometimes two years of service. A flow of pastors, evangelists, administrators, medical doctors, dentists, and teachers have also moved in and out of service abroad in short term assignments. They all have left behind valuable contributions to the progress of the work wherever they have gone and join our distinguished list of full time heroes and heroines as major contributors to the expansion of the Kingdom of God.

Letter from Elder Battle's Mom

7223 Parchall ave
Sept 6 - 56

Dearest son & daughter & ~~Baby~~ Carla
you dont know how we en-
joyed reading your nice (2)
letters it brought joy to our
heart to be able to read a letter
from you all. It was like reading a book not only did we enjoy reading it but friends
have been reading them. I am
putting them in a book form
maybe some day you might
write a book on your stay in
Africa.
As for news not much Anne
will began to teach next week
Turner will also both terms are
ending in June.

Letter from Elder Battle's Mom

2

coming elections – race question strike. Kidnaping a Baby boy was kidnap in N. y. a few weeks ago by a man that owe $2,000 found baby on a few yards from home in several weeks afterward Baby Staved to death

Last week in N. y. another baby was kidnap found today dead in Lake in Conn.

I am sending you a box of goodies next week Be on the out look for it

will send cloth later. Sol want be able to start to School until second semester He is looking for a job found 2 but 6 days a week

3

I hope by now you are getting use to the country.

We are praying for you all. There is hardly an hr. passing during the day that I am not thinking of you all and sending petitions in you all behalf.

We read in the Pittsburgh Courier that they are building (going to build roads) in go in the interior.

Dad has not heard from his papers as yet I hope it want be long.

We are trying to sell our store equipments to Tootsie (next Door) She talk like she would buy them. We hope to

Letter from Elder Battle's Mom

4

Bro Miller (that live in of Bro Britt) died from a heart attack last week.

Marian is getting ready for school also.

Everyone always asks about you all especially the Salesmans.

Am closing with lots of love & many kisses.

May God protect you and family and show Riche's blessing on you all in winning souls. These are my prayer continually.

Again lots of love & many kisses to my darlin Carla & tell her Grandma

Dolly Dot And Me
Our Call To Florida
By Elder Edward Dorsey

God called us to sunny Florida:
To the city of Delray,
Where we found a warm and friendly church;
People walking in God's way.

We worked in Delray for nine months:
Preached, and taught, and sang, and prayed.
Held evangelistic meetings;
A good foundation was laid.

With help of committed laymen
Fifty souls were won from 'night';
Now rejoicing in the faith;
In the glory of the gospel light.

One day our conference president:
Elder Woodfork is his name,
Urged us to accept a call
To a church with some 'daunted' fame.

We preferred to stay where we were.
We loved the people so much,
But how could we just spurn God's call
When we felt His holy touch!

Precious Memories of Missionaries of Color

The move was to Fort Lauderdale:
A large city further south.
The Delray folk did not consent
Without a passionate shout!

"You've only been with us nine months;
Serving us less than a year.
They can surely find someone else,
Please choose to stay with us here."

As time went by, the die was cast;
They saw that it was God's will,
And wished their blessings upon us:
Yet, they were so sorry still.

Our tenure in Fort Lauderdale
Lasted for three years and one.
In this district were three churches;
We ministered to all, bar none.

We were obedient to the call.
The Holy Spirit inspired us.
We did not feel 'against a wall.'
Instead, in God we did trust.

We called the G.C. the next day;
Talked to the office of missions:
Listening to what we had to say,
They accepted our submission.

They sent to us information
So we could read about the call
And, thereby, make preparations
To be adequately installed.

One requirement, as we were told,
Before embarking to leave,
Was to attend mission classes
At our university.

Dolly Dot And Me
Our Call To Florida

We made arrangements to go north
To the state of Michigan
So we could be trained for the task
Of serving a foreign land.

For six weeks, at this mission school,
We studied and prayed and caught
A vision of Liberia
Their culture to us was taught.

Other appointees, just like us,
Who were called by God also,
We met and fellowshipped with them
As we all prepared to go.

To an uncharted destiny,
Our teachers inspired us all
With experiences of their own
While fulfilling their mission call.

When orientation was complete
We packed our things and said good-bye;
And traveled back to our house
To prepare for flight through the sky.

Preparations had to be made;
Mission forms to be filled out.
Some furniture had to be stored;
This kept us running about.

The time did come, it seemed too soon,
To board that big jumbo-jet.
With excitement our hearts did pound;
It was too late now to fret!

Our seven-forty-seven flight
Was ready to leave on time;
We boarded and took our seats
And the plane begins to climb.

Precious Memories of Missionaries of Color

Up, Up, up and away we went
From this land of liberty
To our native land of Africa
Far away across the sea.

For eighteen hours the aircraft droned
Above fleecy clouds and earth.
We made new friends and slept awhile,
And enjoyed food that was served.

We saw the night burst into day!
The sun shone in its glory
Reflecting the ocean
Like an artist's picture story!

As time went by we thought of home,
Of loved ones we left behind;
Of good old days and many friends
Who to us had been most kind.

Our little schnauzer dog was missed:
Who was somewhere on the flight.
We prayed that he was safe on board
And was being treated right.

The stewardesses who walked the aisles
Were to us a pleasant sight,
And made our flight enjoyable
Through the day and darkest night.

After long hours in the sky,
And Africa's coast was near,
We heard the captain speak to us
His voice was both kind and clear.

"We are approaching Robert's Field.
Liberia is in sight.
We will be landing there real soon.
I hope you have enjoyed your flight."

Dolly Dot And Me
Our Call To Florida

The engines of the plane were slowed;
We saw right below–the land;
We soon touched down at Robert's Field,
And thanked God for his guiding hand.

As Dot and I stepped off the plane,
We did not expect to see
A sign that read, to our surprise:
"Welcome Home"–to the Dorseys!

M.I. Harding and Sister Wright,
Along with several others.
Were there to greet us at the port–
Our sisters and our brothers!

They took us to get our luggage
And to pick up our dog Jed.
We were so glad to see him;
He drank water and was fed.

Then M. Harding and Sister Wright
Took us to our mission house.
It was not too far away
By a straight and narrow route.

We soon arrived at the compound.
Two identical houses were there:
One for the mission president.
They both were kept clean and fair.

They toured us through the house to see
The five rooms that it contained.
The furniture there was quite sparse
Of which we were not ashamed.

We had to make a bed from crates;
The bathroom needed some work.
Lizards did make their home there too;
Throughout the house they lurked!

Precious Memories of Missionaries of Color

The water was good for washing;
'Twas not good for us to drink
But we had brought a distiller
Which we kept upon the sink.

We went outside to see the yard.
There were fruit-trees and nut palms.
A good fence around the compound
Made us feel secure and calm.

This was now our home for four years.
Our mission school had trained us
To accept things as they were;
We were now ready to adjust.

Our new friends took us out to eat.
The meal there was very good;
For this quaint Chinese restaurant
Was quite famous for their food.

Thus, we were initiated
Into a new home and land.
We looked up to God for guidance
As we held tightly to His hand.

That week, after our arrival,
We were busy as could be,
Adjusting to our environment
And seeing what we could see.

We visited Monrovia
About eighteen miles away,
We saw the mission office
And the Bible house that day.

The SDA Church and its school
Were together in this town;
And there were many things to see
As we were taken all around.

Dolly Dot And Me
Our Call To Florida

Shops and stores with African wares;
Ladies dressed in dashikis
Some with babies on their back;
All seemed happy as could be.

We saw a girl go down the street
With a basket on her head;
Stacked high with fruit and other things;
With her hands she carried bread!

Some men did wear their native dress;
Some of them dressed just like me.
The customs of America
Were all around for us to see.

The air was pregnant with odors
Of fish, and fruit and wine;
And there was the sound of music
Quite relevant with our time.

Some streets were narrow–some were wide.
The buildings were not too bad:
Much better than we expected;
The progress there made us glad,

We beheld the stately buildings:
The seat of the government
Of this land of Liberia
On this African continent.

We traveled back to our compound–
To the house where we would live,
Our mission life was beginning;
'Twas now time for us to give.

To give of our time and talents;
To practice what we had learned.
To help in this mission field
Was our heartfelt, deepest concern.

Precious Memories of Missionaries of Color

As time passed, we got adjusted
To the climate both wet and dry;
To giant spiders that spun their webs
Like palaces up in the sky.

Some snakes were there but very rare.
We encountered just a few
Crawling along side the house
And out in the back yard too!

But we had a good house boy named Bernard
Who was as fearless as could be;
Whenever some creatures lurked about,
Bernard would make these creatures flee.

He helped us around the house to clean
All of the floors and windows too,
He mowed the lawn and trimmed hedges;
There was nothing he would not do.

When the blessed Sabbath rolled around,
To Monrovia town we went
To worship at the mission there;
'Twas in this city our day was spent.

Hundreds attended the church that day;
All radiant with happy smiles.
We made lasting friends as time went by.
I was made happy as a child.

We felt their true, warm "agape" love
For each other and also for us.
Serving as their new president.
I would never betray their trust.

For the next six months I traveled much
To our churches both near and far;
Through those dusty, red and graveled roads
In our little blue Honda car.

Dolly Dot And Me
Our Call To Florida

It was our mission secretary,
M.I. Harding, a precious man,
Who took me throughout this mission field
And gave me a free helping hand.

We prayed and taught in homes and churches;
Held some meetings in our church schools.
We did fellowship with pastors,
And extolled heaven's golden rule,

With great joy we welcome precious souls
Who accepted the gospel prize;
They gave their hearts to Jesus Christ
And they came forth to be baptized.

The mission there was three thousand strong.
And it was growing every day.
Our evangelist was Ronald Wright
Who preached God's great, eternal way.

He and his good wife Acquilla Wright
And their sons Bon and Meloni
Were a blessing to this mission field
In setting precious people free!

We will always remember that day
When sixty souls were all baptized.
We traveled north to our youth camp.
The mileage was near sixty-five.

We traveled by buses and by cars
To take the candidates there.
The roads were good, the weather fine;
God's spirit was felt everywhere!

We soon arrived safely at the camp.
The water was clear and warm;
There was singing and rejoicing:
We felt the true Spirit's charm.

Precious Memories of Missionaries of Color

We sang. "Take me to the water,"
As into the lagoon we went;
We buried and resurrected
Those souls who were now heaven bent!

When Jesus comes to earth again:
We do hope that we shall see
These precious souls and many more
On heaven's great crystal sea.

There are church schools throughout the land:
Government buildings and airports.
Robert's Field is the largest one;
There are hotels and resorts.

There are modern housing projects;
Markets with some imported foods;
Vegetable markets in the towns,
And colorful cloth–rich and good!

African sculptors with their tools
Are seen on the streets day and night
Carving from their ebony wood
Depicting their African life.

Ghanaian tailors hard at work
Sewing leisure suits as you watch:
It does not take them very long,
As they work nearly round the clock.

The people are so colorful
They are there from around the world:
Germans and French, and Lebanese,
Chinese merchants and lovely girls.

The native African dance teams
Dressed in the most colorful clothes,
Are a real joy to hear and see
With paint on their face, drums and toes.

Dolly Dot And Me
Our Call To Florida

School children in their uniforms
So trim and so clear and so neat.
Walking to their schools on week days.
Make music with their little feet!

Their smiles and their chatter thrill you.
Their bright eyes are all filled with hope
For a still more prosperous land
Where there would be more room for growth.

The Moslem church is very strong;
They are seen in cities and towns
Dressed in their robes all gleaming white:
At the call for prayer, they bow down.

Religious freedom was upheld.
Our church was greatly respected.
The government did see their worth;
And hence, they were not neglected.

All things went well for quite awhile,
Until early one Sabbath morn:
There was disturbance round about;
A most evil day had been born!

Liberia's army rebelled,
Master-sergeant Doe took the reins
President Tolbert was dethroned
'Twas the beginning of much pain.

The President was sore accused
Of miss-appropriating funds
Which he applied to his account;
So this dark, alleged story runs.

It may have been true, and maybe not;
I guess no one will ever know;
But we do know he was building a house–
A mansion for himself to show.

Precious Memories of Missionaries of Color

A house that was almost completed
So he and his family could live in
But he was brutally slain that night
Without his side of the story given.

His staff was tried and convicted;
And to a strong post they were tied
Out near the Atlantic Ocean
That morning they were shot and died.

Liberia was in turmoil;
Many innocent people killed,
Soldiers who were in control there,
Were fulfilling the "sergeant's" will.

The country's airports were all closed,
There was a dusk to dawn curfew.
All of their borders were also closed
For citizens and foreigners too.

All missionaries were confined;
We dared not to leave the compound.
We were fortunate to have food
As we could not go into town.

When curfew was one day lifted,
And we were free to move about,
We set forth to get permission:
From this country! We wanted out!

The time was in April, nineteen eighty
G.C. session was to convene
In Dallas, Texas that same year;
'Twas our delegates cherished dream.

But, not permitted to leave,
They asked Dot and me to attend,
It was not easy, but it was done.
An unplanned furlough we did win!

Dolly Dot And Me
Our Call To Florida

The day arrived for us to leave:
We got packed and ready to go
VIA taxi to Roberts Field;
The taxi's coming was very slow.

The evening sun was going down;
And not wanting to miss our flight,
We to our heavenly Father prayed
That the taxi would come before night.

The taxi came to take us there;
When we arrived, to our dismay.
The seven-forty-seven jet
Was not there to take us away!

The new time for its arrival
Was now scheduled for two A.M.,
There was a small motel near-by,
But we chose not to stay with them.

We stayed, instead, in the lobby
Where others were waiting also.
Soldiers with guns were in and out
Seeking those with no right to go.

The big plane touched down–right on time!
People rejoiced when it arrived.
When it took off into the air
All were happy to be alive!

It was so joyous to arrive
In the good old states, UNITED!
Home again where there was sweet peace;
We were thankful and excited!

It was time for us to attend
The meeting in Dallas, Texas
Where the G.C. mission has asked us
To come and give a report

Precious Memories of Missionaries of Color

Of how the Liberian coup
Affected our missionaries,
And what our church there had to do.

We were just so very happy
In this mid-west metropolis
To greet so many of our friends:
'Twas for us a heavenly bliss!

Saints were there from around the world;
Many were clothed in their national dress.
Delegates with reports to give
Of how God, through their work, had blessed.

We talked with our mission leaders.
They encouraged us to return
When Liberia "cooled a bit."
For our safety, they were concerned.

From Dallas we went to Cleveland
And visited relatives there;
Then on to San Francisco
Once again we were in the air.

Our daughter, Joyce and her husband
Were stationed near the "Golden Gate,"
He is a medical doctor
In the army (United States).

With them we visited awhile,
Our grandson Kyle, was just a tot.
He was born while we were away;
To be thrilled by him was our lot.

While we were there, news came to us
That Dad Johnson was very ill.
Therefore, we returned to Cleveland
And found that he was not living still.

Dolly Dot And Me
Our Call To Florida

This was a shock for Dot and me!
Dot's father had fallen asleep
To awake when Jesus returns:
For God's commandments he did keep.

We thanked God that we were present
When our loved ones needed us most.
'Twas our God's loving providence;
We thanked Him for His Holy Ghost.

References

Seventh-Day Adventist Commentary Reference Series, (1966)
Encyclopedia, Review and Herald Publishing Association, vol. 10. Washington, D.C.

Dudley, C. E. (2000). *Thou Who Hast Brought Us Thus Far on Our Way*, 11. Dudley Publications, Nashville: TN 37207-4948.

TEACH Services, Inc.
P U B L I S H I N G

We invite you to view the complete
selection of titles we publish at:
www.TEACHServices.com

We encourage you to write us
with your thoughts about this,
or any other book we publish at:
info@TEACHServices.com

TEACH Services' titles may be purchased in
bulk quantities for educational, fund-raising,
business, or promotional use.
bulksales@TEACHServices.com

Finally, if you are interested in seeing
your own book in print, please contact us at:
publishing@TEACHServices.com
We are happy to review your manuscript at no charge.

www.ingramcontent.com/pod-product-compliance
Lightning Source LLC
Chambersburg PA
CBHW021133230426
43667CB00005B/94